Adrienne

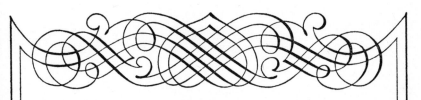

Adrienne

THE LIFE OF THE MARQUISE
DE LA FAYETTE

ANDRÉ MAUROIS

TRANSLATED BY GERARD HOPKINS

McGRAW-HILL BOOK COMPANY, INC.
NEW YORK TORONTO LONDON

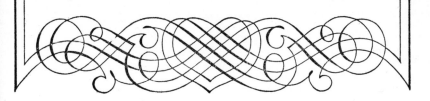

ADRIENNE

921
LAFAY

40984

152884

CONTENTS

INTRODUCTION

BY RENÉ DE CHAMBRUN

When Napoleon's victories over the Austrians caused the gates of the fortress of Olmütz to open in 1797, General de La Fayette knew freedom again after five years of imprisonment; but as the idealistic opponent of the French Revolution, he was *persona non grata* in his native land. It was his wife who returned alone to Paris to pave the way for his return.

All the La Fayette properties had been confiscated during the Revolution. Without a trace of self-pity, though suffering in health, Adrienne set about her salvage tasks. She took possession of the Château of La Grange-Bléneau-en-Brie, a fifteenth-century castle east of Paris. The building—it had belonged to her own family—had been neglected and was in wretched condition. Scraping money together, Adrienne began the work of restoration. At the same time, dealing tirelessly with Napoleon's ministers, she managed to have her husband's name struck from the official list of nobles in exile. By letter, she kept La Fayette, living in Holland, informed of her activities. "I am satisfied with what you do, with all you say, with all you are," he replied.

At last, in November, 1799, La Fayette was able to return to France. Now began the happy period that Adrienne had longed for in the prisons of the Terror and at Olmütz. The farm at La Grange helped to pay off the family debts. The children and grandchildren made the château their home. The family joy was crowned by the safe return of George-Washington de La Fayette, Adrienne's son, from the Napoleonic wars.

Then, in the autumn of 1807, undermined by the privations she had known in prison, Adrienne's health finally gave way. The family assembled at her bedside in Paris. La Fayette never left her except to fall asleep from exhaustion. One day he asked her, "Do you remember my first departure for America? How everybody else was furious with me, but you hid your tears? You did not want to appear unhappy for fear I would be blamed." She replied, "How sweet of you to remember things that happened so long ago." Another day she clasped La Fayette's hand and said, "If only God could let us have six little years at La Grange . . ."

On Christmas Eve, after a life of continuous self-sacrifice and achievement, Adrienne died. To Mme de Staël the grief-stricken husband wrote, "The soul has disappeared from La Grange." Only fifty when Adrienne left him, he felt that he had suddenly become an old man, a spectator on the scene of life. He seldom left La Grange after that, his second triumphal return to the United States (1824–25) being his only extended absence. At La Grange he followed a routine. At five in the morning Bastien, his valet, would wake him. For two hours, remaining in bed, he would carry on his tremendous correspondence. Then he would send Bastien away and, alone on his knees, holding in his hand a miniature of Adrienne and a lock of her hair, he would spend a quarter of an hour in meditative devotion. For the twenty-seven years that remained to him this was La Fayette's religion: the cause of liberty and the memory of Adrienne.

A practical part of this devotion involved the painstaking collection of every scrap of record pertaining to Adrienne, his family, and his friends. This work of preservation was begun, as it happens, not by La Fayette, but by Marie-Josèphe Beauchet, once Adrienne's maid. Passionately loyal to her former mistress and all her family, Marie Beauchet saved, during the Revolution, a considerable quantity of La Fayette material: papers, books, pictures. Add to this the family papers that Adrienne was able to save at Chavaniac, just before her arrest by the Terror, La Fayette's own life-long concern with his public image, and the children's dedication to the memory of their parents, and it becomes clear how the extraordinary collection that is today at La Grange first came into being.

Eight years after La Fayette's death, his grandson Jules de Lasteyrie (1810–1883) married Olivia de Rohan-Chabot (1813–1899), the daughter of the émigré Louis de Rohan, Vicomte de Chabot, and Lady Charlotte Fitzgerald, daughter of the second Duke of Leinster. Olivia, whose parents had condemned the French Revolution—and

La Fayette—lived at La Grange fifty-four years, a strong-willed British Tory who surrounded herself with British books, British newspapers, British engravings. She removed practically everything associated with the memory of her husband's grandfather and placed it out of sight in several unused rooms at the top of the northwest tower. The thickness of the old stone walls prevented excessive dryness or humidity, heat and light were absent, and in this stone fortress there were neither rats nor mice. Conditions could not have been better to preserve perfectly all that Olivia de Chabot Lasteyrie wished to forget.

One snowy night in 1870, with a determination worthy of Adrienne herself, Olivia saved part of the heritage of La Grange. German soldiers carried off two small cannons, given to La Fayette by the people of Paris as a tribute to his role during the revolution of 1830. Inasmuch as they were the general's, Olivia had removed the cannons from the castle hall to the dark corner of a carriage shed. Nevertheless, they were part of her property, and when her valet announced the theft, Olivia rose from her bed, put on her coat over her dressing gown, and in her nightcap caught up with the troopers in a village two miles off. She convinced the commander that she was an Englishwoman, not at war with the Germans—and she brought home her cannons. Today, cleaned and polished, their wooden wheels repaired, they stand once again in one of the halls of La Grange.

Olivia's son married his mother's goddaughter and near relation, Olivia Goodlake. Though neither husband nor wife was a partisan of La Fayette, they too fought the battle of their castle by remaining at La Grange during the battle of the Marne. The German cavalry by-passed the château the day before Joffre's victory, which took place, as it happens, on September 6, 1914, the anniversary of La Fayette's birth.

After Louis de Lasteyrie and his wife died, their only son, also named Louis, spent his long life looking after the property he loved more as his mother's and grandmother's home than because it had been La Fayette's. With one devoted servant he lived at La Grange throughout the German occupation of France in World War II. He and I had the same ancestor, La Fayette's daughter Virginie, and I was one of his nearest relatives. He asked me in 1935 if my wife and I would accept La Grange as a legacy. We offered to purchase the place from him on the understanding that he would remain there in peace as long as he lived. After he died, in the winter of 1955, I began with my wife the exploration of the fateful attics.

Our findings were at first unbelievable. In one drawer we came upon letters sent to La Fayette during the last few days of his life; they were still unopened. Other drawers contained his treasured mementos of George Washington and souvenirs of his visits to the United States. In locked cabinets were the three thousand volumes of his personal library, including the fine sets of books presented to him by the American states, their gold decorations gleaming as bright as when the books left the binders' hands. In trunks and boxes we discovered hundreds of Adrienne's letters to her husband, her children, her other relatives, her friends. The series began at the time of her marriage, when she was fourteen, and continued almost to her death. And amid the masses of other papers we found the thoughtful letters La Fayette wrote his young wife from England, just before he sailed in 1777 to join the cause of the American "insurgents." For years La Fayette scholars have wondered at the apparent nonexistence of such letters, and at the lack of documentary evidence at other key points of the general's career. The attics of La Grange have now given their answer to many such problems.

As my wife loves French history and old French homes, and as our admiration for Mme de La Fayette is unbounded, we decided that we would make the château into a private museum dedicated to La Fayette and to the admirable partner of his heart. We are doing this without removing the British relics from the walls, as we believe they now deserve to remain forever part of La Grange. We wish the rooms where La Fayette and Adrienne lived to be as they were during those "six little years" that were present in Adrienne's mind on her deathbed. We have been guided in our work by the detailed bills for the rehabilitation that was accomplished between 1799 and 1807—another discovery in the attics.

Today, we have restored La Fayette's bedroom and library, Adrienne's bedroom and boudoir, and the room James Fenimore Cooper used during his visits to La Grange. My wife is at present restoring the parlors, the entrance hall, and the main staircase. A great deal of work still lies before her, but we are both sustained by our vision of making La Grange substantially as it was in the lifetimes of the Hero of Two Worlds and his extraordinary wife.

PREFACE

BY ANDRÉ MAUROIS

The life of a writer, especially a biographer, is rich in unexpected opportunities and fortunate finds. Until René de Chambrun, my friend of thirty years, introduced me to the marvelous new material he discovered at La Grange, it had never occurred to me to make Adrienne de La Fayette the subject of a book. About the young French hero of the American Revolution I was reasonably well informed. What I did not know was that his wife is deserving of a place among the greatest and most appealing characters of history; nor did I dream that after the researches of so many other writers there could still exist two major collections of unpublished and unstudied documents relating to Adrienne, her husband, and most of the events of their dramatic lives.

In his introduction René de Chambrun tells how the Archives of La Grange, as they are now known, were assembled and then lost sight of for three quarters of a century or more. To me, there is something miraculous in the way this incomparable material survived intact through all the political storms and wars that have swept France since Adrienne's day. Miraculous, too, is the intimate understanding these records give us of a La Fayette whom some previous writers have perhaps underestimated, and of his inspiring wife whose own voice, so to say, has not been fully heard before. Studying the papers they resurrected at La Grange, René de Chambrun and his wife became devoted to the memory of Adrienne. I, too, was fascinated by her character, and I shared the Chambruns' opinion that she deserved a new biography. I admit that I was excited by the opportunity thus given me of reliving one of the most interesting periods of French and American history as seen through the eyes of two persons whose lives were so closely linked to the destinies of the two nations.

But in addition to the treasure-trove at La Grange, which was made available to me without reservation, there existed another revealing collection of hitherto unknown material. For a long time this was in the possession of George-Washington de La Fayette's descendants. Eventually it was sold to M. Dieudonné-Élie Fabius, and it is now the property of his heirs. They have generously allowed me to make such use of the material as I wished, and I am no less grateful to them than I am to my Chambrun friends. From both the Archives of La Grange and the Collection Fabius Frères I have in some cases drawn complete documents, in others only fragments, and in all cases only so much as I felt had a bearing, direct or indirect, upon my heroine. There is still a plentiful supply of unpublished matter in these two collections for French and American scholars to study.

I owe a great debt of gratitude to others who have helped me with Adrienne: to the Direction Générale des Archives de France; to the Bibliothèque Nationale; to Mr. Louis Gottschalk, whose fine books on La Fayette are regarded as authoritative on both sides of the Atlantic; to Mr. James Moffat, present owner of the Château of Chavaniac-La Fayette; to Mlle de Saint-Exupéry, departmental archivist of Haute-Loire; and to Dr. Pierre Balme. Finally, I give thanks to my wife. As always, she has been a partner in my researches and truly my other self. When I was absent in the United States, it was she alone whom I entrusted with the task of correcting the proofs of the French version of this book.

A *note on spellings*. The family name was written as two words, La Fayette, until the titles of the nobility were abolished in 1789. The general then made it Lafayette. Having to choose, I reverted to the earlier form, as I have also done with the family name Daguesseau, which later became d'Aguesseau. As for the place name Chavaniac, in the tenth century it was written so; in the twelfth it was Javaniac; in the fifteenth, Chavanhac. Later, it again became Chavaniac. Today it is Chavagnac, and both the château and the village have taken the name Chavagnac-Lafayette. As in the other cases, I chose the old form.

A *note on money values*. In Adrienne's day the livre or franc was not a coin but a measure of value. For our purpose we may assume that it was the French counterpart of the American dollar of today; in purchasing power they were approximately equal. The sovereign was twenty-four livres; the écu, three livres; the sou, one-twentieth of a livre.

PART ONE

THE GREAT FAMILIES

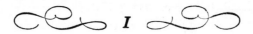

THE MARSHAL AND
THE CHANCELLOR

*The government of France was an absolute
monarchy tempered with songs.*

CHAMFORT

By affixing his name to the marriage contract, King Louis XV signified his approval of a union that linked two of the most powerful
families of his realm, and two of the most dissimilar. The year
was 1755; the bride was Henriette Daguesseau, granddaughter of
a famous chancellor. The groom was Jean-Paul-François de Noailles,
Comte d'Ayen, son of the Duc d'Ayen and grandson of Adrien-
Maurice, Maréchal-Duc de Noailles.

The Noailles family, courtiers and soldiers, whose ancestors had
taken part in the First Crusade, liked to be pre-eminent everywhere.
They wanted everything—and got everything. The Duc de Noailles,
the bridegroom's grandfather, had made a quasi-royal alliance by
marrying the niece and heiress of Mme de Maintenon at a time
when that favorite exercised a dominant influence over the king.
Louis XIV had himself drawn the curtains of the nuptial bed—a
signal honor—and had given the young couple jewels to the value
of 100,000 livres.

The courtier and memoirist Saint-Simon, who did not like
Noailles, acknowledged that he was gracious and affable when it
pleased him to be so, and called him "a fine figure of a man,

3

amusing, a good companion, skilled in music, knowledgeable in all matters, endlessly talkative, and a past master of women's tittle-tattle." Beneath the polished exterior, Saint-Simon perceived a "profound emptiness" and inordinate ambition.

Noailles' eldest son, Louis, Duc d'Ayen, became one of the most sparkling of the great nobles at the court of Louis XV, and made a name for himself with his sharp-edged sallies and facile verses. In the eighteenth century pert witticisms were common, but good manners saw to it that they were seldom taken seriously. The Noailles family members, laden with honors, gave one another mutual support, and the king was endlessly indulgent with them. By a unique act of royal favor, the Maréchal de Noailles had been granted the right to keep permanently in his family a cavalry regiment bearing his name. His son Louis commanded it, and when his grandson, the Comte d'Ayen (who a year later was to marry Henriette Daguesseau), reached the age of fifteen, Noailles was given permission by the king to make the boy a colonel. In short, the family lived on the steps of the throne. Not itself royal, it was irradiated by the setting sun of the monarchy, still high in the national heaven.

It must now be explained how it came about that the brilliant Noailles family sought for Jean d'Ayen, "the heir to their name and blazon," seemingly so modest an alliance, for the Daguesseaus had neither their length of lineage nor their status. The chancellor had won for his name prestige of a different kind. Born at Limoges in 1668, he had from boyhood made himself master of a multiplicity of learned subjects. As well as literature and the sciences, it was said that he knew Hebrew, Greek, Latin, and Portuguese. When, on one occasion, the critic and theorist Fontenelle was asked by an anxious mother to recommend a tutor who would be well informed, erudite, a metaphysician, and a theologian, "Madame," he replied, "the more I think of it, the more convinced I am that no one but Chancellor Daguesseau could adequately fill the position of tutor to your son."

In addition to being a man of unrivaled intelligence, Daguesseau was deeply religious and a champion of toleration. In an age of persecution, he always took a strong stand against violence and injustice, even at the risk of being persecuted himself.

So much perfection and so much wisdom got on Saint-Simon's nerves. He respected the chancellor, admitting that he had a good brain, was a hard worker and a storehouse of knowledge in many fields, that he was of a cheerful disposition, and that he led a blameless life. His chief complaint was that Daguesseau would never commit himself. The scales of justice, when Daguesseau held them, were forever evenly weighted. "The chancellor is possessed of a superior understanding," commented another critic, Cardinal Fleury, "but, for that very reason, he finds difficulties everywhere." We shall come upon this characteristic again in the chancellor's descendants. Daguesseau was a tender and indulgent father and loved nothing so much as to impart his learning to his children and grandchildren. Under his instruction they grew up to be exceptional, not only because of their accomplishments but also because of their piety, their nobility of outlook, and their happy relationships with one another. He neither scolded nor punished, maintaining that he recognized no authority other than that of feeling and reason.

His son, Daguesseau de Fresnes, married in 1736 the charming Anne-Louise-Françoise Dupré, Lady of the Manor of Bléneau-en-Brie, who died a year later in childbirth, leaving her husband a fine medieval castle (which will play an important part in our story) and a little girl—Henriette Daguesseau, future Duchesse d'Ayen and mother of our heroine. The widower lost no time in marrying again and boarded out his daughter at the Convent of the Visitation at Saint-Denis, where she was given into the charge of a Mme d'Héricourt, a woman of intelligence and character. Henriette quickly developed a passionate admiration for her, with the result —since Mme d'Héricourt was deeply religious—that she very early acquired a fixed point in her life: the love of God and the fear of disobeying His laws. This strong support was the more necessary to her, seeing that this precocious child had a marked lack of courage, both physical and moral.

When Henriette was fourteen she was taken out of the convent. Mme Daguesseau de Fresnes, her stepmother, had become much attached to her. They had the same virtues and the same scruples. In the eighteenth century the demands made on faith were the more exacting since it had to live in close proximity to an obdurate atheism. Henriette, like all the members of her family, combined a strict observance of her religious duties with a respect for the individual conscience. During the four years she spent in her father's house, where there was little enough in the way of distraction, she worked hard and completed her education. The natural gaiety of her nature led her to find pleasure in every new object she encountered. All the same, she had little liking for the customary pursuits of girls of her age: needlework, playing the harpsichord, and dancing the minuet. She preferred reading and gardening—into which latter skill she had been initiated, in the park at Fresnes, by her grandfather the chancellor. His death in 1750 came as a dreadful shock to her. She had adored the courteous and attentive old gentleman.

Shortly afterward her maternal grandfather, M. Dupré, died, leaving her, in addition to two châteaux in Brie, a considerable fortune. This wealth she regarded as a burden. The fact, however, that she had become a great heiress drew to her the attention of the court, and especially of the Noailles family. Shared memories and mutual services formed a bond between the two families. It was the Maréchal-Duc de Noailles who, during the regency of Philippe d'Orléans, had made Daguesseau chancellor.

A service always draws together the renderer and the recipient. Somewhat later the Duc de Noailles had done his friend the chancellor another favor, at the king's expense, by getting him the gift of a fine house in the Place Vendôme, which became (and still is) the Chancellery. The two men, different though they were in temperament, got on well together. The tradition of this Noailles-Daguesseau friendship became firmly established. In 1755 it occurred to the Maréchal-Duc that Henriette Daguesseau would be a highly desirable bride for his grandson, the Comte d'Ayen. She was his elder by two years, but what did that matter? Marriages in the eighteenth century were the concern only of the parents. They chose, they made the decision, and the young people obeyed. If the union turned out unhappily—and even if it did not—the husband took a succession of mistresses, and the wife, sometimes, a lover. This did not prevent them from keeping the family name alive by producing sons who were sent to school, and daughters who were sent to a convent.

Jean d'Ayen, born in 1739, had little in common with Henriette Daguesseau. Almost at once he showed as strong a liking for court life as she for privacy. The future captain of the Royal Bodyguard, at fifteen named colonel of the Régiment de Noailles, made it clear that he was a zealous soldier with an eye for detail, and a martinet at inspections. He was a philosopher, as that century understood the term, and a friend of literary men. He prided himself on his scientific attainments, and pulled every available string to get himself elected to the Academy of Sciences. At that time it was not good form to be religious. Like Voltaire, Diderot, and d'Alembert, the Comte d'Ayen held that man was a mold and the earth no more than a grain of sand. He believed in progress, not in Providence.

When Henriette Daguesseau became Henriette d'Ayen she remained faithful to the tradition of wide tolerance and charity in which she had been brought up. Herself an ardent believer, as we have seen, she was nonetheless indulgent in her attitude to her young husband's irreligion. Both of them had, though in different ways, generosity of character and an honest outlook. Unfortunately, the emotional responsiveness that Henriette brought to her marriage was not long reciprocated.

The young couple set up house in the Noailles mansion in the Rue Saint-Honoré, under the watchful eyes of Mme Daguesseau de Fresnes. The young countess' mother-in-law, who was deeply pious, lived very much in retirement, with the result that the bride saw no more of the great world than she had done before her marriage. She was taken to Versailles to be formally presented, after which she ceased to be seen there in the company of her husband.

A NEST OF DOVES

In all genuine feeling there is a
mingling of religion.   ALAIN

The Hôtel de Noailles, a Versailles cut to the measure of a private family, was situated in the Rue Saint-Honoré, with the Church of St-Roch and the house of the Jacobin friars immediately opposite, and the monastery of the Cistercian Feuillants next door. The main entrance was flanked by two fine Ionic columns carrying an attic storey and by two wings, each measuring 126 feet in length. Behind this façade lay an immense court of honor. The house itself was a veritable museum: buhl furniture, marble tables, porphyry consoles, vases from China and Japan, pictures by da Vinci, Raphael, van Dyck, Rubens, Rembrandt, and such contemporary masters as Watteau, Fragonard, and Boucher. Taste was happily combined with wealth.

Here in patriarchal splendor ruled the old Maréchal Adrien-Maurice, one of the pillars of the kingdom, and with him lived his granddaughter-in-law, whose life was soon to be dedicated to the single task of childbearing. She had first a son, who died at an early age; then, in 1758, a daughter, Louise, followed in 1759 on November 2 (All Souls' Day) by a second daughter, Adrienne, the subject of this book. At the time of her birth, her father was twenty, her grandfather forty-six, and her great-grandfather, the maréchal, eighty-one. The young Comte d'Ayen was seldom at home. He had

8

a high regard for his wife and asked her advice when important decisions had to be made, but he did not often seek her society. "It may be," wrote Adrienne at a later date, "that she made her own intellectual superiority appear more obvious than is wise when dealing with a younger man: or perhaps his neglect arose from the fact that she had neglected overmuch those things which serve to attach a husband. In the details of her life she did not sufficiently triumph over her natural indecision, and my father, thinking this to be the result of scruples, found less pleasure in her company than he should have done if our happiness, no less than his, was to be secured." [1] Expressed with filial delicacy though this is, it clearly indicates that the marriage was not a very happy one. Scruples, indecision, and an excess of reason were blemishes that Henriette d'Ayen had inherited from the chancellor.

Adrienne was brought up by her mother's old nurse, who, though her own education had been elementary, had the gift of winning the affection of her young charges and of making what she taught them pleasant. With her first foster child she had spent several years in a convent, where she had acquired a great store of Bible tales and a record of good deeds in general, and these she repeated in a manner so well suited to those of tender years that she enthralled the little girls, at the same time being careful to respect the intentions of their mother, "who," Adrienne said later, "wished not only that we should be instructed in only what was true, but that this should be done in a direct and simple manner far removed from the tricks and fancies usually employed in the teaching of the young." [2]

Three more daughters were born: Clotilde, Pauline, and Rosalie. The bond of affection among the five girls was unusually strong. It was particularly close between Louise and Adrienne, the two eldest. Louise was beautiful and gentle. Adrienne, though her good looks were cast in a less regular mold, drew attention by reason of her large, brooding eyes and her air of alert intelligence. Until they married the girls were known as Mlle de Noailles and Mlle d'Ayen. When the third sister Clotilde (Mlle d'Épernon) was born, her mother wished her to have as godparents two beggars of the parish of St-Roch. It was by such gestures that she sought to mark her contempt of worldly rank. It is possible that M. d'Ayen saw in this an affectation which in fact did not exist. In that same year, 1766, the old maréchal died. Louis, Adrienne's grandfather, became Duc de Noailles (soon, in his turn, to be a maréchal) and Henriette's husband Duc d'Ayen.

It is pleasant to picture the five little girls in that immense barrack of a building, brimful of marvels and thronged with servants, gathered for several hours each day around their mother, as in a convent cell. Mme d'Ayen, "a lady of the highest virtue, and wholly devoted to her home and her children," herself presided over their education, "though never with too heavy a hand, but in such a manner as to make them find the time spent with her too short. She began the morning with a kiss for each, and found them waiting for her when she set out to hear Mass at the Jacobin chapel or the church of St-Roch. At three she dined with them, and after the meal took them with her to her bedroom. This was very large, and hung with gold-fringed crimson damask. The bed was immense. The duchess sat down in an easy-chair, with her snuffbox, her books, and her sewing within easy reach, and her five daughters grouped about her in a circle, the elder ones on chairs, the younger on stools, quietly nudging and pushing in an attempt to get as close as possible to their mother. The talk was of the lessons of the previous day, then of the small events of the moment. Nothing could have been less like lesson-time, yet when it was over what they had learned stuck in their minds." [3]

In addition to visiting masters, the children had a resident governess, Mlle Marin, a woman of great learning. But the Duchesse d'Ayen was the moving spirit in everything, overseeing and regulating the tiniest detail. She strove to teach the girls how to combine their knowledge—moral, factual, and literary—into a coherent whole. She explained to them that they could not follow their own whims because God was watching. There was nothing despotic in her system. "She considered that she had done nothing unless she had convinced the child to whom she was talking. Though by nature lazy, temperamentally impatient, and perhaps too little accustomed to keeping her vivaciousness in check, she would listen to all the arguments of her daughters with a persevering kindliness." [4]

One of the natural results of such a method was to make the little girls less docile than other children. Their mother told them to think things out for themselves, and this they did, though their conclusions were not always identical with her own. Sometimes she complained of this. "That may well be, Mamma," said Adrienne, "since you permit us to use our brains and to formulate our objections, but you will see that at fifteen we shall be more docile than others of our age." [5]

What did they learn? Fleury's *Petit Catéchisme*; later on, his *Grand Catéchisme*; and later still the Gospels. They studied the Old Testament, the elements of geography, Rollin's *Histoire Ancienne*, and listened to a number of mythological tales. The Duchesse d'Ayen read aloud with them the best plays of Corneille, Racine, and Voltaire. She made the girls dictate letters even before they had learned to write, which is a sound method. This system of education, supervised by such a mother, produced a maturity of mind which today seems barely credible.

The family saw little of the Duc d'Ayen, who was frequently absent on military duty at Versailles, where, like his father and his uncle, the Maréchal-Duc de Mouchy, he lived in close contact with the king. Colonel since 1755 of the Régiment de Noailles, he took part in the campaigns of the Seven Years' War, after which he was promoted to the rank of lieutenant general. He was also governor of Roussillon and senior captain of the Royal Bodyguard. His biting tongue was reminiscent of his father's. He had an inquiring mind, which he applied to the study of science, literature, agriculture, court affairs, army administration, and philosophy. At the Academy of Sciences he read a number of papers which attracted attention. His life was entirely occupied by the activities of a brilliant world in which so many new ideas were circulating, and he had little time to give to a family in which his pious wife had established a somewhat Jansenist austerity. For her, all that mattered was eternal salvation; for him, worldly success and the royal favor.

Nevertheless, he admired his wife. When she came down with smallpox in 1768, just as she had been brought to bed, he made no attempt to conceal his anxiety. The attentions he lavished on her actually kept him away from the attractions of Versailles for several days. He tried to deceive her about the nature of her illness, and in his efforts to convince her went so far as to have the five young girls brought into her room, at the risk of contagion. Aware how ill she was, the Duchesse d'Ayen was profoundly troubled by the thought that, should she die, her daughters would be orphans. Her confessor or some other pious person asked her: "Do you really think that you are necessary to God, and that He will not find some other way of ensuring their salvation?" Deeply impressed by these words, she found new courage. Her convalescence was difficult, but everything she was told about the alarm and anxiety displayed by her husband was sweet to her. Misfortunes sometimes have a way of revealing sentiments which at other times tend to be hidden under a timidity bred of pride and an abruptness born of boredom. The children, for their part, were miserable when for the first time they saw their mother's face disfigured by pockmarks. They could not believe that they would never again see her as she had been before her illness. The boy to whom she had just given birth, and who would have been the Noailles son and heir, did not live.

The five sisters resumed their tranquil existence. In the summer they were taken to Saint-Germain-en-Laye to stay with their Noailles grandfather. He was a charming host who took them driving in the forest and much enjoyed wasting time and money over games of lotto with them. In the autumn they spent a week at Fresnes with M. Daguesseau, father of the Duchesse d'Ayen. He was very old, very deaf, and thrice married.

Among the other visitors to Fresnes was the sister of the Duc d'Ayen, the Comtesse de Tessé. She was an oddity, having "a mind so rarefied as to be almost fanciful, but also an imposing firmness of character. Her every action, when she could bring herself to act, was imbued with practical good sense. She had sound judgment and was completely devoid of prejudices, though her conversation seemed often far removed from the truth—sophistical, paradoxical, and obscure. All the same, she was a woman with a good brain and a warm heart." [6] While still young, she had lost her faith and been won over to the philosophical ideas of the age. She was a friend of Voltaire but, though flaunting her agnosticism, she invariably crossed herself within the privacy of her bed-curtains whenever she had to take medicine. She amused her nieces with her mannerisms, her pomposity of speech, and the glaring contrasts between her behavior and her talk.

The effect of their education on Adrienne and her four sisters was to produce young women with a more than usually high moral standard. They were for a long time complete strangers to those prejudices, then so powerful, connected with birth, vanity, and wealth. The idea that their lives could be regulated by any rule other than the will of God never occurred to them, and on the first occasion when they were brought in contact with instances of a contrary attitude among so-called decent people, their surprise was so great that it took several years of painful experience to dissipate it. Their mother concealed nothing from them, and the spiritual beauty which they saw in her was of so pure a nature that it left an indelible mark upon their characters. Not that the Duchesse d'Ayen never made mistakes, but she always spoke of them to her daughters so frankly that her faults no less than her virtues contributed to their upbringing. She taught them, too, to observe the people of the great world in which they would be called upon to live and to draw their own conclusions. Though exempt from anything that could be remotely thought of as malice, her judgment of others was not infrequently severe. On the other hand, when she came upon a fine character, her admiration was wholehearted. She had that supreme form of charity which grieves over the faults of others and delights in their victories.

She judged each of her children affectionately yet realistically. Having perhaps made a little too obvious her constant approval of Adrienne when she was a very little girl, she was careful to correct any excess of pride which this attitude might have produced, by "painting so true and vivid a picture of my shortcomings," Adrienne said in later life, "that I never forgot it." Fearing that this daughter had somewhat too lively an imagination, she took the greatest pains to direct her mind back to simplicity and truth.

Another effect of this training, based as it was on the girl's rights as an individual and on her freedom of choice in all that concerned herself, was to delay the date of her first communion. At the age of twelve Adrienne had admitted to having doubts. She did not consider that she was in a proper state of mind to receive the Eucharist. Her mother brought no pressure to bear. She thought it her duty to help her daughter through this uneasy period of her life, and to join with her in examining her difficulties rather than to push her into taking a premature decision. Never had her loving-kindness, her sympathy, and her understanding shown to better advantage than in providing just the help needed by this young mind intent on thinking out for itself the problems of faith. In 1771 Louise made her first communion. Adrienne's was left until later.

It was at about this time that the Duc d'Ayen began to receive from various quarters proposals of marriage for his two eldest daughters, young though they were. It is not difficult to imagine the distress felt by the duchesse at the idea of handing over to sons-in-law about whom she was imperfectly informed the wise virgins she had brought up with such care. But she never acted on first impressions. It was her custom to say that we are so little able to foresee the consequences of important decisions that all we can do is to keep the dictates of emotion well in the back-ground, to take such precautions as prudence dictates, and then, with a mind at peace, to trust in Providence, which knows better than we do what is best for us. Once she had put herself into the hands of God she took courage, with the result that setbacks and difficulties no longer put her out of temper, or even produced those outbursts of impatience to which she was subject. It was in this mood, therefore, that with an unbiased mind she heard from her husband that a proposal had been made on behalf of M. de La Fayette—who was fourteen—for the hand of Adrienne—who was only twelve.

Why did the Noailles family look with favor on the suggested engagement, and who was the young man in question?

III

AN OLD-STYLE MARRIAGE

*A man does not marry for himself, no
matter what he may say. He marries as
much, and even more, for his posterity
and his family. This manner of settling
the question in accordance with another's reason, rather than one's own,
pleases me.* MONTAIGNE

The La Fayette family was of ancient lineage, honorable and
honored. There is evidence that about the year 1000 it gave some
property, the Villa Faïe, to an abbey. Under Charles VII, a certain
Gilbert Motier de La Fayette won the battle of Beaugé, drove the
English from France, and killed the Duke of Clarence with his own
hand. His motto was *Cur non?* (Why not?) The elder branch of
the family settled in Auvergne as a result of the marriage of the
fourth Gilbert with a Polignac.

The La Fayettes never stirred from their province except to make
war; only a few of them, and that rarely, had put in an appearance
at court. So many of them, from father to son, had perished on the
battlefield that the family had become, in some degree, proverbial
in Auvergne. It numbered among its members two celebrated
women: Louise de La Fayette, who had resisted the solicitations
not only of Louis XIII but also those of the Cardinal de Richelieu

15

("which was much more difficult," *our* La Fayette commented);
and at a later period, the author of *La Princesse de Clèves*, whose
only granddaughter had married a La Trémoïlle. The Auvergne
properties on the distaff side, in the absence of a male heir in the
direct line, would have passed to that family "had it not been for
the fact that Madame de La Trémoïlle" (once again I quote La
Fayette) "had been worried by scruples and had made a deed of
gift on her deathbed by which she gave to my parents (who belonged to the younger branch) all the land which bore our
name."

In the course of time, the manor house belonging to the family
—Saint-Romain, Vissac—fell into ruins. In 1708 Edouard Motier
de La Fayette married Marie-Cathérine Suat de Chavaniac, who
brought him the château that became the permanent residence of
the La Fayettes. It was a rustic dwelling of the feudal type, surrounded by massive towers, standing in an exposed position. In
summertime the fertile volcanic soil around it was a spreading sea
of rye. In winter the pine trees were powdered with white.

Impoverished provincials though they were, the La Fayettes, as
the result of a series of marriages, had become linked with some
of the noblest blood of France—the Bourbon-Bussets, the La Tré-
moïlles, the Polignacs, the Bouillés—with the result that they
could exercise a certain amount of influence at court. Consequently
the future father of *our* La Fayette, Michel-Louis-Christophe-Roch-
Gilbert, born in 1732, was sent at the age of eleven with a single
servant to Paris, the fountainhead of all favors.

For a young lord setting out to make his fortune the first essential
was marriage. About 1754 a relation of the family, the Maréchal de
Maillebois, suggested as an admirable match for Gilbert a certain
Julie de La Rivière, a daughter of the Marquis de La Rivière, reputed to be a young woman of substance. Negotiations of a purely
financial nature were begun—the young people had never seen
each other. In those days a marriage was arranged like a treaty of
alliance: the lawyers of the two families took it upon themselves to
discuss the clauses, these having to do with such matters as the
dowry of the prospective bride, the amount of property to be held
in common, the pension to be settled on the husband, the value
of the presents. Each new proposal, as soon as it was made, was
referred by young Gilbert to his mother—his father, as was right
and proper in that family, having been killed on the battlefield.

FEBRUARY 22, 1754

*My dearest mother ... you may perhaps be astonished to learn that
the pension has been refused. I am not myself greatly surprised,
though much vexed. This, however, will not, I suppose, cause the
negotiations to be broken off, since we were agreed that the marriage
should take place without it.*

That "I suppose" is a charming touch. The issue was *his* marriage,
but the decision was left to his mother.

*Presumably the maréchale had better be informed that you would
wish the family to provide the trousseau rather than that they should
supply a sum of money for that purpose. It would doubtless be insufficient, and we should have to supplement it. ... I await your
instructions, my dearest mother, with impatience, and am greatly
desirous of carrying them out, whether you wish me to marry or not.[1]*

Gilbert was eager, should his mother agree, to marry Mlle de La
Rivière because her grandmother, a close friend of Mme Adelaïde,
the daughter of Louis XV, was doing all she could to get him a
commission in the grenadiers. A company was worth a nuptial mass.

Mme de La Fayette decided not to break off negotiations, and her
son declared himself to be

*enchanted at the idea of setting up an establishment in accordance
with your wishes, which, in addition, cannot fail to be a source of
happiness to me. ... It is unfortunate that we have failed to obtain
the pension, but it is to be hoped that this will be made up to me by
some other advantage. After all, a man of my name need not be rich,
though it is only decent that he should occupy a rank suited to his
condition, and a way to this will be opened by a commission in the
grenadiers.[2]*

Gilbert had not yet seen his future wife, who was still in the
convent in which she had been brought up, but the Maréchale de
Maillebois, who had arranged that he should do so (though rather
late in the day) informed him that she was "neither good nor bad,
with an excellent figure and a very white skin." The maréchale
had informed the girl that she would have to live in a château in
Auvergne. Gilbert reported to his mother:

*She replied that this prospect was in no way distasteful to her. She
is said to be intelligent. The maréchale is particularly desirous that*

the marriage should take place in a month's time. I objected that Lent would make this difficult, but she assured me that she could obtain the necessary indulgence.[3]

Gilbert now went to Versailles to consult with his relative, the Duchesse de La Trémoïlle, who was of the opinion that the marriage was suitable. True, the financial advantages were not great, but she agreed, according to Gilbert, that it was not possible to

find a young woman of good birth, and with a considerable fortune, who would be willing to live in the country. . . . I have made my bow to the king, and all the royal family. Tomorrow, I am to see Madame de Pompadour.[4]

The favorite had some say in the matter, at least where the grenadiers were concerned.

It was necessary, Gilbert wrote, to give thought to the presents:

I have told Madame la Maréchale that you wish to give a dress, but she said she thought it was for the family to do that. If such is the case, you can give the buttons. I have asked the maréchale to decide what presents I should give, because not only will she be able to get them more cheaply, but, should they prove to be unacceptable, the blame will not fall on me. . . . As soon as I receive your letter I shall arrange to be formally presented to Monsieur de La Rivière and ask to be introduced to Mademoiselle.[5]

At the very last moment, there was nearly another breakdown, because Gilbert's mother insisted that Julie's father should settle on her the sum of 100,000 francs. This M. de La Rivière refused to do. Gilbert pleaded that the marriage should go forward. The maréchale, he said, was furious. After all the trouble she had been put to in getting him his commission it was quite impossible to reverse the decision. Besides, M. de La Rivière was a great deal richer than he said he was. The lawyers had seen the declaration made by him of the twentieth part of his fortune, and he was not the man to exaggerate his actual revenue. His daughter would, in fact, have considerably more than 100,000 francs. Above all, there was the question of the grenadiers:

My dear mother [Gilbert wrote], we cannot break off now without my running the risk of setting the minister against me.[6]

The mother gave way. The son saw M. de La Rivière and told him that he had had no hand in the monetary arrangements and did not even wish to talk about them. La Rivière, now in a calmer frame of mind, went into all the details of his own fortune, his wife's, and his father-in-law's. Gilbert realized that sooner or later Julie would be very rich.

My impression is that Monsieur de La Rivière is a very great gentleman. He told me that his daughter is not pretty, but that, if she grows up to be like her mother, he feels sure that she will bring me happiness. Whenever he spoke of his wife, there were tears in his eyes.[7]

The lawyers, continuing to discuss the details of the contract, ran into difficulties at every turn. Threatening letters arrived from Chavaniac. At long last the suitor met his fiancée. The La Rivières had a suite of rooms in the Luxembourg Palace, and there Gilbert de La Fayette was taken:

I have never in my life been so much embarrassed. At first the conversation was general. Then it turned on ways of making oneself pleasing. I said that I should like to know all of them, never before having so much wanted to be thought so. Then the question of destiny was raised. Turning to Mademoiselle de La Rivière, I said: "Mademoiselle is the mistress of mine, and I await her decision with no less impatience than fear." I was given a most obliging answer.[8]

To his sisters, Gilbert wrote:

Do you not . . . think it quite shocking, quite ridiculous that I should not have seen this young woman? One must needs be as indifferent as I am, must one not, not to have taken even the necessary steps? Well, you can cease your scolding, for I have seen her at last. I have written to my mother a detailed account of our interview. Here is another, of her person. I studied her carefully so as to be able to give you an exact account. . . . Her demeanor is extremely pleasing and truly deserving of the limner's brush. Her skin is white, her hair light and of a good color. Her eyes are small, and her nose somewhat long, but turned up at the end (though that does not produce at all a bad effect). She has pretty teeth, pouting lips, and there is a cleft in her chin. Her bosom is very fine, though in general she is thin. Of her mind I know nothing, but there is character in her face. . . . All in all, she is no beauty, but neither is she ugly, and fortunately her appearance pleases me.[9]

There was another thing in her favor:

She has a very fine gold watch, given to her by the Queen of Spain, and two or three gold snuffboxes which belonged to her mother. So I shall be freed from the necessity of giving her any. But I shall give her the diamond buttons and some netting-needles in a case.[10]

The Comtesse de La Rivière (Julie's maternal grandmother and great aunt, her parents having been first cousins) was ill and now took a turn for the worse. "Her death," wrote Gilbert, "would be very vexatious for me: in the first place because the period of mourning would delay my marriage; in the second, because it was she who spoke to Madame Adelaïde in the matter of the grenadiers." By great good luck the minister, d'Argenson, took it upon himself to make the necessary representations to the king and obtained the royal consent to Gilbert's commission. At last the road lay straight ahead, and the superior of the convent authorized Gilbert to do his courting in the reception room, with a nun present to listen to what was said.

Gilbert wrote his sisters from Paris a few days later:

You may well say . . . that I must be much in love if I can find my wife intelligent after only three conversations! You would be even more convinced if you could hear what I say to her! I scarcely recognize myself, so gallant have I become, and you would laugh indeed could you listen to me. . . . I have bad news for you, other than that of the Comtesse de La Rivière's illness: Mademoiselle has but a small acquaintance with music, plays the harpsichord badly, and has no voice.[11]

On April 22, 1754, the Comtesse de La Rivière died in her husband's arms. La Fayette hastened to the house of mourning, where he found the entire family in tears. He was much afraid that the wedding ceremony would be postponed, but this was not the case.

The death is to cause no such great delay as I had feared, provided it be seemly to have the contract signed by the king in such melancholy circumstances. . . . Two days ago the Marquis de La Rivière

*revealed his plans to me, and I find them to have been dictated by
great good sense. He intends to appear at court, officially, as a
mourner one week from tomorrow, and to have the contract signed
seven days later. Two or three days after that the marriage will be
celebrated as quietly as possible, after which he suggests that I should
retire to the country as soon as it can be managed.*[12]

The young La Fayette thoroughly approved of this program, for
he was anxious to return to Auvergne without delay, the more so
"since I realize how devilishly expensive a thing marriage is, and
that a man would be well advised never to indulge in it, save
once." He had to put his domestics into mourning and there were
several additional outlays. He engaged a servant for his wife: "He
is monstrously ugly, but plays upon the violin and seems an honest
enough fellow. He has some proficiency in the dressing of hair, and
I am having him instructed in his other duties." He had found a
traveling-dress for his wife which was a "real bargain" and had
ordered a set of muslin underclothing to go with it, "lace being
too dear." He sent a man with six dogs, including a boarhound,
in advance to Chavaniac. "I am being as careful as I can be, but
it is impossible to get married in Paris without having to spend
a deal of money. There are a thousand and one little things that
never occur to one." [13]

At last all that remained was to obtain the signatures of the king
and the princesses, make his confession, and receive the nuptial
benediction. To his mother, he wrote:

*I am very happy to tell you that I make my confession tomorrow.
The expenses are so much less than I expected that I shall be involved in no sacrifices. It will be far easier for me to be prudent with
a wife at my side.*[14]

With her he was well contented. "She would be gay were she
not always in the company of such gloomy persons. She seems to
be a rational being."

She had to be if she was to live at Chavaniac. But perhaps she
did not find it so very difficult after all. She was fresh from her
convent and her future sisters-in-law, Charlotte (Mlle de La
Fayette) and Madeleine (Mlle de Motier), would be, so Gilbert
told her, very charming neighbors. She would have her coach, two

coachmen, her manservant, and her women. In spite of all the delays, in spite of the haggling over the contract and the presents,
the marriage turned out to be a very happy one. Youth and good
sense can get the better of most difficulties.

In April, 1757, France being at war with England, Gilbert de
La Fayette, now a colonel of grenadiers, had to go on active
service. He rejoiced at the chance of distinguishing himself. His
wife was pregnant and hoped to present him with an heir to the
family name. The only cloud on the horizon was lack of money.
The young couple was in debt, though not seriously. When his
son-in-law passed through Paris, the Marquis de La Rivière oblig-
ingly offered to stand surety. He was becoming quite human.

On September 6, 1757, was born at the Château of Chavaniac
the Most High and Powerful Seigneur Marie-Joseph-Paul-Yves-
Roch-Gilbert Motier de La Fayette (our La Fayette), lawful son
of the Colonel-Marquis and the Most High and Powerful Marie-
Louise-Julie de La Rivière. The colonel divided the year 1758 between his regiment, Paris, and Auvergne. He loved army life. He
could live well at little cost, and there was not much fighting.
Money was still his only trouble; money with which to buy horses
and pay his grooms, though from time to time he managed to get
a few louis from his father-in-law or his mother.

His mother sent him news of his son. The new Gilbert, aged
two, was cutting his teeth. The colonel seemed to think that he was
to blame, and apologized. There was no need to worry about *him*:

*The enemy is withdrawing all the time, and though we follow him
at a distance, it is with no very great eagerness.... Everybody is convinced that Monsieur le Maréchal has secret orders not to engage.*[15]

He had plenty of leisure, therefore, in which to worry about the
state of affairs at Chavaniac. His letters home are full of concern:

*It is indeed unfortunate that the price of wheat should have dropped
so suddenly. I suffer very much more, my dear mother, from your
embarrassments than from my own.*[16]

On July 19, 1759, while the young colonel was in camp at Minden, the Anglo-Prussian forces sent forward a strong detachment.

*There was not a shot fired [he wrote], and it was only through our
telescopes that we had sight of the enemy.*[17]

On August 1 he was killed by an English cannonball. He was twenty-seven years old. Much later, to a now unknown correspondent, his son wrote this account of his death:

When a colonel in the grenadier regiment, he was killed at Minden. This corps, made up of picked grenadiers from all sections of the army, was needlessly exposed by a brute of a lieutenant general in command, Monsieur de Saint-Pern. It had been sent to occupy a ravine, and, out of sheer bravado, he had had it drawn up on the top of the slope, where it was mowed down to no purpose by the enemy batteries. The Prince de Chimay, a close friend of my father's, was killed while leading the first battalion. It was my father's duty to take his place. This he did, and was at once carried off by a ball from an English battery, commanded by a certain General Phillips. By a strange coincidence, twenty-two years later two of our cannon opened fire on the English headquarters at Petersburg, on the Appomattox in Virginia, and one of the balls passed through the house in which General Phillips was lying sick. He was killed outright.[18]

An English artilleryman had killed his father: he himself had killed the artilleryman. Throughout his life La Fayette was fond of noting these curious freaks of fortune.

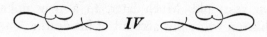

THE MAGIC CIRCLE

*Love is pleasanter than marriage for
the same reason that romances are more
amusing than history.* CHAMFORT

My family [wrote La Fayette] had as its center my grandmother, a woman of the highest merit, respected throughout the province. People used to come from as far as eighty miles away to ask her advice on domestic matters. Her sound good sense, her nobility of mind, and the way in which she identified herself with the life and fortunes of the countryside were indeed remarkable. She had two daughters, one of whom, having married Monsieur de Chavaniac (her cousin), settled permanently with her mother after her husband's death. . . . The other daughter (Mademoiselle du Motier), unable to resign herself to leaving the family circle, never expressed any wish to marry. It was she who assumed the responsibility for my education as a child, and she was in every respect a most excellent person. My Chavaniac aunt had an only daughter, one year older than myself.* Never was the bond of affection between a brother and sister stronger that that which existed between us.[1]

The picture we must conjure up for ourselves is that of the Château of Chavaniac, whose powerful mass of masonry dominated

---

* This much loved cousin, the daughter of Guérin de Chavaniac, Baron de Montio-loux, and of Charlotte de La Fayette, married the Marquis d'Abos. During La Fayette's first journey to America she died in childbed at Mende, at the age of twenty.

the village, and in it, of an eight-year-old boy with red hair and a long, aquiline, pointed nose, being brought up by three women of sterling worth and a tutor, Abbé Fayon. The Chavaniac aunt, Charlotte, had the same narrow face and long nose as her brother, La Fayette's father. She wore a frilled cap, and the only relieving touch in her widow's weeds was a linen fichu with a pleated border. She was forty-four, energetic and authoritative, and passionately devoted to her nephew, the sole heir to the family name. Her sister, Mlle du Motier de La Fayette, was also of a masterful disposition. With their mother, they did their best to administer the estate which one day would revert to Gilbert.

They had entrusted him at the age of five to a highly intelligent Jesuit, and then, when the Jesuits were expelled from France two years later, to Abbé Fayon, an excellent man, but—as his pupil recalled later—full of prejudices

and lacking in those qualities which a man who is destined to live in the great world should have. But a child's real education, I think, comes from the feelings and the attitude of the family in which he grows up, and in this respect no one was ever more happily placed than I. It was but natural that I should hear much talk of war and glory among close relatives whose minds were ever filled with memories and regrets and a profound veneration for my father's memory.[2]

His young mother, the Marquise de La Fayette, spent only the summers at Chavaniac. During the winter she lived at the Luxembourg Palace in Paris, with her father and grandfather. In 1762 she had herself presented at court, and made frequent appearances there in order to conserve some small amount of credit, which might one day be useful to her son. This was by no means merely a virtuous pretext for escaping from the three ladies at Chavaniac.

My mother [wrote La Fayette] was a woman of lively temperament who had once had a liking for the frivolous, but after her husband's death had plunged into religion with all the strength of her character. Though she loved me devotedly it would never have occurred to her to take me away from my La Fayette grandmother, for whom she had a deep reverence.[3]

It was only to be expected that the three priestesses of the family cult should take it upon themselves to watch over the only male hope of their line. Since the cannonball of Minden the boy had been Marquis de La Fayette, Seigneur de Saint-Romain, Vissac, and other places, head of his name and style—and well he knew it.

The family was not rich. His grandmother and aunts had obtained from the king a pension for the son of an officer killed in action. The yearly sum was 780 livres—a far from generous bounty. The Marquis de La Rivière was reputed to own immense tracts of land in Brittany, not far from Saint-Brieuc, as well as in Touraine, but he was far too closefisted to reveal the full extent of his worth. The young La Fayette led a rustic existence. He read Plutarch, never forgot that he was the son and nephew of heroes, and was profoundly conscious of the duties imposed upon him by his name. When he drove through the neighboring village of Saint-Georges-d'Aurat wearing his three-cornered hat, buckled shoes, knee breeches and stockings, the peasants saluted him as their young master.

The Marquis de Bouillé, a cousin who lived nearby, paid a visit to Chavaniac in 1768.

I spent some days there [he wrote] and found the young La Fayette much grown and singularly well-informed for his age, astonishingly advanced in reason and skilled in argument, remarkable for his thinking, his wisdom, his discretion, his self-control, and his powers of judgment. Yet I discovered in the boy the seed of self-esteem and even of ambition. His tutor asked me what I thought of him. I replied that the child had the qualities of mind that are proper to great men, namely the power to think and judge, and that if a vigorous character were added to these, he would some day do very great things.[4]

Until he was eleven La Fayette lived at Chavaniac. Then, toward the middle of 1768, his mother at last prevailed upon his guardians to let her take Gilbert to Paris.

It grieved me [he wrote later] to part from a grandmother, two aunts, and a cousin, all of whom I adored. I felt no curiosity to see the capital. I remember my astonishment on the road when I found that people did not raise their hats to me, as they did at Chavaniac when the young lord of the manor drove past.[5]

Sent to the Collège du Plessis, the boy made such progress with his Latin that, thirty years later when he was a prisoner in Austria, he was able to overcome the difficulties of communication by using that language.

I spent four years in the college [he recalled later].... During that time I experienced two years of the most ardent religious devotion. My confessor told me that all through that period I was an object of envy to him. All my energy of character was concentrated on that one concern, and if I cannot really say how I became so pious, I should find it still more difficult to explain how I ceased to be.

I was all on fire to have a uniform. When I was thirteen I was made to enter the company of musketeers that my grandfather had commanded. I enjoyed the honor of being reviewed by the king and of riding to Versailles on horseback in full dress.... I found it all very delightful, the more so since before I could take part in the review I had to learn the evolutions with my comrades. I will venture to say that I was much liked in the college. I even acquired such an ascendancy over my fellow pupils that when I appeared in the schoolyard I was immediately surrounded by my young friends, many of them bigger than I was, who were all eager to assume the appearance of disciples and would, had the occasion arisen, have fought fiercely in my defense. Once I tried to stir up a revolt to prevent one of my comrades from being unjustly punished. I was not so well supported as I had hoped to be. I was never myself threatened with any disciplinary action. I was determined not to deserve it, and should, I think, have put up a pretty good resistance with my sword, for in accordance with the good usage of those days, all the boys wore swords when they were invited out to dine, and this matched well with their embroidered coats, their hair-bags, and their powdered and pomaded curls.

One of the subjects I was given for an essay was to describe a perfectly trained horse, who, at the mere sight of the rider's whip, became immediately obedient. I drew a picture of this perfect animal throwing his rider when the whip was shown to him. My professor of rhetoric, Monsieur Binet, a man of intelligence, laughed instead of scolding me. He has, since then, often reminded me of the incident.[6]

In 1770 Gilbert's mother died at the age of thirty-three, and shortly afterward he lost his grandfather, the Marquis de La Rivière. It was then that the boy first learned of his enormous inheritance.

He found himself, at the age of thirteen, the possessor of an income amounting to 120,000 livres, a revenue worthy of a prince of the blood, all derived from good Breton and Touraine land. In a single day he passed from relative poverty to opulence. "Of the two of us, my tutor was the more impressed," he wrote. "I was conscious only of sorrow at the loss of my mother and had never been in need of money." As was natural, a guardian was appointed to administer the estate. This was his great-grandfather on his mother's side, the Comte de La Rivière.

The young marquis, like his father, wanted to serve in the king's armies. The Comte de La Rivière, a former captain in the Black Musketeers, saw to it that he should be admitted to that elite corps. He completed his military training at the Academy of Versailles. There he met the scions of all the most illustrious families in France and got to know the Comte d'Artois, Louis XV's grandson. In the riding school he had to yield pride of place to the brilliant Artois —but he had his income of 120,000 livres and a stable of fine horses which he lent to his friends; in spite of his provincial shyness, he came off pretty well. He had now grown tall and slim, with a long narrow head and face. His habitual expression was indicative of gentleness and frankness, though it was rather cold. His arched eyebrows gave him an air of ironic astonishment.

On two occasions I spent my holidays in Auvergne [he wrote in his autobiographical letter]. It was there I celebrated my fourteenth birthday and there that I received the news that my grandfather had arranged for me to marry Mademoiselle de Noailles, the second daughter of the Duc d'Ayen, at that time only twelve years of age.[7]

Ever since he had come into his splendid inheritance, all the court families had had their eyes fixed on this magnificently endowed orphan for their daughters. The Duc d'Ayen knew the Comte de La Rivière and suggested one of his five daughters—Adrienne—to him. Adrienne was only twelve and the Duchesse d'Ayen, as soon as she was more fully informed about the young man, was uneasy. The young La Fayette was well spoken of, to be sure, but his extreme youth, the isolation in which the loss of all his nearest relations had left him, and his great inherited fortune (Mme d'Ayen regarded this as an added danger) at first prompted her to oppose the match. Her attitude, which persisted for several months, made the Duc d'Ayen so angry that he stopped coming to Paris. Some members of the family pointed out that he was wrong to insist and that his wife had gone too far to withdraw. But in spite of the quarrel (for that is what it was), he paid high tribute to her native integrity. "You do not know Madame d'Ayen," he said. "No matter how far she may have gone, you my be sure she will prove as docile as a child once you have proved to her that she is wrong."

And so it was. When the duchess had been assured that the marriage would be deferred for two years, that her daughter should not leave her side during the first years of the union, that the couple should be housed in the Hôtel de Noailles, and that steps should be taken to complete the bridegroom's education—she agreed. On September 21, 1772, the nest of young girls witnessed a reconciliation between their parents, the reason for which was no more explained to them than had been the quarrel to which it put an end. All the same, the general feeling was one of inexpressible relief. The Vicomte de Noailles, second son of the Maréchal-Duc de Mouchy, had meanwhile been suggested as a suitable husband for Louise, the eldest of the five sisters, who was his cousin. Of him, too, nothing but good was spoken, and plans for the double marriage were approved. It was agreed, however, that nothing should be said to Louise about the matter until a year had gone by, nor to Adrienne before eighteen months. But it was decided that the two prospective suitors should be allowed to see their future brides, either at the Hôtel de Noailles or out driving, though nothing must be allowed to disturb their studies.

On April 7, 1773, the Duc d'Ayen had Gilbert de La Fayette transferred to the Régiment de Noailles with the rank of second lieutenant. He was already treating him as a member of the family. At some time in the later summer Mme d'Ayen spoke of the Vicomte de Noailles to her eldest daughter. "The extreme liking which Louise had ever entertained for her cousin made the idea excessively pleasing to her." During the two months of betrothal the duchess helped her daughter to prepare for the new state "in a manner worthy of the Patriarchs." The four sisters protested loudly. A man, and a man of the world at that, within the precincts of this pious house was like a hawk swooping upon a nest of doves and carrying one of them off. There were loud cries and torrents of tears all around.

Mme d'Ayen also spoke of the Marquis de La Fayette to her second daughter. For a whole year, keeping a careful eye on him, she had taken note of his good qualities. Adrienne's heart had also spoken, and she was delighted to learn that "her mother looked upon, and loved him, as a son." Mme d'Ayen depicted in glowing colors his generosity, his courage, his enthusiasm. But she was preaching to the converted; it was more necessary to calm the girl's "somewhat too lively and susceptible imagination." At fourteen and a half, Adrienne found the idea of marriage not a little frightening, but there was reassurance in the knowledge that she and her husband would be living in the Hôtel de Noailles.

The nuptial benediction was given in the family chapel on April 11, 1774. Mlle d'Ayen brought with her a dowry of 200,000 livres. This was a small amount compared with her husband's wealth, but the Noailles alliance was in itself the equivalent of a fortune. From the very first days of her married life, Adrienne felt for Gilbert the most tender devotion. Everything contributed to this: an education which had made of love within the limits of matrimony a bounden duty; the influence of Mme d'Ayen, who had the highest esteem for the character of her son-in-law; the infatuation of the young bride for her lord and master.

It might be said that her feeling for him was passionate in the extreme, were that expression in accordance with the bewitching delicacy which kept it a stranger to all jealousy, or at least to those evil impluses which are as a rule its consequence. Nor for a single moment did she ever show herself demanding.[8]

Not only was La Fayette never conscious of any desire that might be disagreeable to her, but Adrienne in her heart of hearts never felt any bitterness she need conceal. From the very first, her husband was to her a hero who could do no wrong. He had his faults, but it took her some time to discover them, and when she did her imagination at once transformed them into virtues.

Needless to say, she was no sooner married than she had to write to the revered Chavaniac aunt. The handwriting is that of a child:

I trust, Madame, that you will permit me to ask that you think kindly of the new little niece who dares to call you her aunt.[9]

Somewhat later she wrote again to this same Aunt Charlotte, congratulating her on the marriage of the cousin who was so dear to Gilbert. She was commissioned by the ladies of Chavaniac to buy the trousseau in Paris, which she did with the most scrupulous care, asking for measurements, models, and samples of hair. For all her extreme youth she was already a woman of sound sense.

In May, 1774, Louis XV died of the smallpox. He was not widely regretted. France was in a mood to expect marvels of the new king and his young queen, Marie-Antoinette. It was known that they were good-hearted and easygoing. They were on a footing of friendship with the whole Noailles set. The Vicomte de Noailles, Louise's husband, was one of their intimates, as was also the Comte de Ségur who, scarcely older than La Fayette, was to marry in 1777 the younger sister of Mme d'Ayen (née Daguesseau) and thus to become Adrienne's uncle-in-law. The Duchesse de Mouchy (her great aunt) was the queen's First Lady-in-Waiting and Controller of her Household. Her irreproachable life and the outstanding virtues of her husband, who was as austere as his Noailles brother was worldly, caused her to be generally respected, though her limited outlook made her not a little tiresome. Etiquette was the breath of life to her, and Paris soon learned that the queen had nicknamed her "Madame Etiquette," which made the young laugh and the old find fault.

The Duc d'Ayen, always quick to ask a favor, had obtained from Louis XVI, a bare week after his accession, a captaincy in the Régiment de Noailles for La Fayette. It had been agreed that he should not report for duty until he was eighteen, but his father-in-law insisted on his going to Metz, where the regiment was stationed, at least for a few months. For Adrienne, already pregnant, it was heartbreaking to have to part from a husband so recently acquired, but loving letters reached her constantly from Metz.

MARCH 26, 1774

You write me the most charming letters, my dear heart; in them you do justice to the feelings which I entertain for you and give me living evidence of something done for the purpose of giving me pleasure—two ways of making me happy, and it is a delight for me to receive my happiness from you. How can you ask whether your being with child pleases me? You yourself have given the answer to that question by adding, at the bottom of your letter, an account of your own feelings. Our happiness is something shared, my dear heart, and this sharing should be true not only of our feelings but of our thoughts. I swear to you that my joy is even livelier than I should have believed possible. . . .

*I have made an acquisition of inestimable value. You know the
vicomte's charming servant; he is a man well above the common
run. His master has given him to me because I have greater opportunities of being useful to him, and because I have long wanted him.
There were tears on both sides when they parted company, and now
that he is my own, no man of fashion could be better served. His former master has been today to Frascati, but I preferred to stay here,
chatting with you, rather than with the Marquise de Laval, as you
may well imagine. Tonight I sup with the Maréchal de Broglie and
some of the local beauties. I have no idea what they will turn out
to be like, but, judging from such samples as I have met now and
again, I should say but middling. Good-by, my dear heart.[10]*

The Maréchal de Broglie, in command at Metz, was a relative;
the vicomte was the Vicomte de Noailles, Gilbert's brother-in-law.
Another relative, the foppish and conceited but kindhearted Prince
de Poix, eldest son of the Maréchal de Mouchy, was Gilbert's
commanding officer. The world at large seemed to be a family
affair, and the government of the kingdom, no less than the command of the royal forces, to be the exclusive privilege of the Noailles
family. By marrying Adrienne, La Fayette had taken his place
smoothly and easily in a magic circle. His letters continued.

SUNDAY, JUNE 19, 1774

*You have not written, my dear heart, and I realize only too well how
I miss even one of those postal deliveries which are necessary to my
happiness. I have had news of you from Monsieur le Duc d'Ayen,
who tells me that you are to go to Saint-Germain. Though I truly
wish that you may enjoy yourself, it will give me pleasure to think
that you will sometimes say to yourself: "I was here three weeks ago
with Monsieur de La Fayette who loves me so well that I cannot
refuse him some small part of my love in return, though his sole
merit consists in his lively tenderness for me. But he does so love
me!" That, I hope, is your constant refrain. . . . My heart cannot give
it the lie. So you miss me, do you? How happy it makes me to be
loved by you! So far as refrains go, that is mine.*

AUGUST 23

*You no longer write to me, my dear heart. Is it that you wish to make
certain that I have a tender spot for you? Well then, I have, and
begin to find the ordeal overexacting. I flatter myself that your neg-*

lect of me is not without design, for lukewarmness of feeling would
be worse to me than nothing. Three posts have gone by without my
being told what is become of you. It is true that I receive the Gazette
with great regularity. You asked me for news of the vicomte. He is
very well and is at Chanteloup. I shall have to write to somebody
for news of you. Are you sick? Surely not, for I should have been informed. The most satisfactory explanation is that this silence is the
fault of the mail. I shall send someone to the office four hours after
midnight, which is when letters arrive. Meanwhile, I await your
news. That of my heart you know already: it loves you madly.

THURSDAY, SEPTEMBER 1

I have let two posts go by without writing to you, my dear heart.
You must know that this was not my fault. I was detained at Melet,
the house about which I wrote to you in my first letters. From being
dreadfully boring, it has become delightful. The presence there of
Madame de Voïer, Madame de La Porte (the younger), and
Madame de Melfort makes it excessively agreeable.[11]

It is clear that La Fayette had the pen of a ready writer and a
charming, tender style—though perhaps a little too ready. Coming
from a sixteen-year-old lover, the letters lack intimacy. But in those
days feelings paraded in court dress, and it may be that this pious
and serious young girl made her youthful husband feel shy. He
was beginning to find out that he had a distinct taste for women.
In the châteaux of Lorraine he found several who were somewhat
more lightweight than his wife, and his Noailles brother-in-law
furnished him an example of irresponsibility. Meanwhile, Adrienne
was happily reading and rereading his affectionate protestations.

After three months of army life, in which private theatricals,
local beauties, and neighboring châteaux bulked much larger than
military exercises, Gilbert returned to Paris, where his mother-in-
law, his wife, and her sisters surrounded him with attentions. The
Princesse de Poix was a frequent visitor at the Hôtel de Noailles,
as full of wit and vivacity as her "petit Poix," who ate his meals
sitting on a special high chair, was lacking in those qualities. She
had been born a Beauvau-Craon, the daughter of a Prince of Lorraine who was Voltaire's friend. She had made a ridiculous marriage, knew it, and consoled herself accordingly.

The somewhat eccentric Comtesse de Tessé, the Duc d'Ayen's
sister, conducted a brilliant *salon* and adopted a maternal attitude

toward her brother's children, since the sluggish Comte de Tessé, who loved hunting and would go considerable distances to get it, had failed to beget an heir in the conjugal bed. Each time one of her Noailles nieces got married and the house in the Rue Saint-Honoré was illuminated, Madame de Tessé, aggressive and generous, made a point of presenting the bride with a magnificent present and was furious if some other relative outdid her.

When La Fayette returned from his regiment, he expressed a wish to be inoculated against the smallpox. The procedure was still a novelty in France, and he loved novelties. Much was made of it. So that no one should see the sufferer, the Duchesse d'Ayen rented a house at Chaillot and shut herself away in it for the whole period of the treatment with her son-in-law and her daughter, acting as nurse to Gilbert and doing everything she could to keep him amused. Having had the smallpox herself, she knew what had to be done and was immune. For Adrienne, this enforced isolation in company with the two persons she most loved in the whole world was a godsend.

As soon as he had recovered, Gilbert paid a visit to his aunts at Chavaniac; he had not seen them since his marriage. Adrienne, being pregnant, could not contemplate making so long a journey. He therefore took with him as traveling companion his old tutor Abbé Fayon, who found the journey easy and quick, though not so the task of exercising any influence on a pupil who had married a Noailles!

In the course of our drive [Gilbert wrote] he discovered that I was lacking in prudence and devoid of principles. This furnished us with many excuses for argument. He is of the opinion that I am a ne'er-do-well, but that at least I have a good heart.[12]

Returning to Paris by way of Brioude, La Fayette at once plunged into the pleasures of Versailles. Mme d'Ayen thought it her duty that winter to accompany her daughter and son-in-law to the Queen's Ball each week and afterward to entertain their friends at supper. (There was an Hôtel de Noailles at Versailles, in addition to which a suite of rooms was at the Duc d'Ayen's disposal in the château itself.) It was not lightly that Adrienne decided to sample the diversions of the fashionable world with Gilbert. Before she could bring herself to do so there had to be some call of duty involved, superior to the voice of conscience which forbade such an indulgence: the need, for example, of keeping her young husband entertained. When she was finally convinced that she might enjoy herself with a clear conscience, she did so freely. We are justified in thinking that these deliberations à la Daguesseau may have seemed long drawn out to La Fayette, who prided himself on being, as Abbé Fayon had said, a "ne'er-do-well."

A very special set had come into being at Versailles. It contained Messrs. de Noailles, de Ségur, de Durfort, and de Coigny; the Prince de Ligne; the two Dillons; and a carefully chosen group of young women. Together they frequented a tavern called L'Epée de Bois in Les Porcherons (one of the Paris suburbs), where they were frequently joined by Monsieur (the Comte de Provence) and the Comte d'Artois, the king's brothers, and sometimes too by the Duc de Chartres, the son of the Duc d'Orléans. The queen herself occasionally ventured secretly to become one of the Epée de Bois clique. The same group was also to be seen at the Palais Royal and at the Opera Ball.

License was the order of the day. Many of the ladies regarded themselves as being either not married at all or "not much." The Princesse de Poix, for example, regarded her diminutive husband as a joke and felt for him no more than a condescending affection. He might be a favorite with the royal family; to others he might be a great personage—but all this meant nothing to his wife. The Prince d'Hénin gave all his time and attention to the actresses Mlle Arnould and Mlle Raucourt. The princesse, who was having an affair with the Marquis de Lally-Tollendal, treated the whole thing as a jest. The talk among the members of the set was highly unconventional (they read Diderot and Rousseau) and there was a general attempt to make a display of energy and enthusiasm. Anything approaching coldness of manner was indignantly repudiated. Morality was no longer based upon religion, except by the Duchesse d'Ayen's daughters, who watched the social scene with surprise, grief, and charity.

It was in this circle that La Fayette learned about the "new ideas." At Chavaniac and at school he had read little except Plutarch and the Latin authors. His mind had not been formed, as had the minds of Noailles and Ségur, by Montesquieu, Rousseau, and Voltaire. After the shameful Peace of Paris in 1763, which terminated the hostilities between France and Britain, La Fayette, like all the younger generation, had taken the humiliation of France much to heart, feeling a personal resentment against the English because of the cannonball that had killed his father at Minden. He bitterly criticized the government's weak foreign policy. His intimates, all beneficiaries of the old order, were working to undermine it. Why should they have feared the consequences? Nothing in France was changed. Everything was just as it had always been: Versailles, the throne, the peers of the realm. In the *salon* of the Oeil-de-Boeuf the same old ceremonies were still observed. Madame Etiquette saw to it that the queen, on rising, should receive her shift from the hands of the highest-ranking lady of the household. The heads of the great families, completely indifferent to the interests of the state, thought only of promotion, decorations, and the snubs and favors of royalty.

To us, the scoffers at old custom [said Ségur, one of La Fayette's *most intimate friends*], *feudal pride, the solemn manners of our fathers, and all that was ancient seemed cramping and ridiculous. The old doctrines weighed heavy on us. The laughing philosophy of Voltaire seduced our minds because we found it amusing. We made no attempt to study seriously the books of more weighty writers, and we admired our idol as the symbol of courage and of resistance to despotism.*[13]

By nature, as by education, La Fayette would have inclined to seriousness, but the lack of ease of a young man, and of a provincial young man in the bargain, "led him," said the Comte de La Marck, "to seek out with care everything that, so he thought, gave an air of distinction to persons and things.... His manners were awkward. He was very tall, and his hair was very red. He was a clumsy dancer and an indifferent horseman. Those with whom he spent his days were all more adept than he at the bodily exercises then considered modish." [14] The queen's only hope of escape from the rigors of Madame Etiquette was in the company of her personal friends. She invited the members of the Epée de Bois set to practice ballet dancing in her private apartments and much enjoyed taking part in the performances. La Fayette was included in one of the quadrilles but was so awkward that the queen could not help laughing at him. She loved all that was natural and graceful. This tall youth was stiff, solemn, and self-conscious. Ségur, who knew him well, said that his cold exterior and his reluctance to talk—in such glaring contrast with the glittering loquacity of his companions—concealed a quick wit, an ardent spirit, and a very strong character. But the queen had laughed, and that laughter had set up an echo. It caused an awkwardness between the Noailles son-in-law and his sovereign. Many years later he was still speaking, in his letters to Adrienne, of that indiscreet spurt of laughter.

In order to prove that, in spite of everything, he too could achieve an air of distinction, he made up his mind to embark upon the conquest of a mistress. Since he was so recently married to a girl who adored him this may seem not a little surprising. But at Versailles a faithful husband was an object of fun. Adrienne was very young, very pious, and—in addition—pregnant. Perhaps what chiefly decided him was the fact that he made it a point of honor to imitate in everything his brother-in-law Louis de Noailles, who was as graceful as Gilbert was clumsy, as witty as Gilbert was dull (or seemed to be), a good horseman, a redoubtable drinker, a beautiful dancer, and a brilliant conversationalist. "I remember," says La Marck, "how, at a dinner from which the Vicomte de Noailles was absent, Monsieur de La Fayette got himself so drunk that he had to be carried to his coach when the time came for him to go home. In the course of the drive he kept saying to his companions: 'Do not forget to tell Noailles how drunk I was.' " [15]

If he was to be on a footing of equality with Noailles and Ségur, it was essential that Gilbert should have an "adventure." For this purpose, his choice fell on the young and pretty Aglaé d'Hunolstein (née de Puget de Barbantane). Her husband, Comte Philippe-Antone d'Hunolstein, was colonel of the regiment of the Duc de Chartres. It was common knowledge that His Royal Highness the Duc de Chartres, son and heir-presumptive to the Duc d'Orléans, was in love with Aglaé and was viewed by her with favor. Aglaé was one of the small group which had the Duc de Chartres as its leader, and danced, supped, went stag-hunting, frequented the gaming tables, and indulged in mad frolics—such as driving through Paris with the Duc de Chartres riding postilion, the Duchesse de Chartres and the Princesse de Lanballe in the carriage, and her charming self perched on the back seat, arms folded, dressed as a groom.

To lay siege to the acknowledged mistress of a prince of the blood was foolhardy, but foolhardiness appealed to La Fayette. However, success was denied him. How could it have been otherwise? He was less charming than the Duc de Chartres. Nevertheless he was determined to be consumed with passion for Aglaé, and made a great display of jealousy though he had no right to do so. He concluded, heaven knows why, that Ségur was his fortunate rival.

In love with a lady as gracious as she was lovely [wrote Ségur], he believed, without any reason, that I was his rival, and, in spite of our friendship, spent one whole night in an access of jealousy trying to persuade me to fight a duel with him for the heart of a beauty on whom I had not the ghost of a claim. . . . Some time after our quarrel and our reconciliation I could not keep from laughing when the Duc de Noailles and other members of the family begged me to use my influence with him in an attempt to impart some warmth to his coldness, to rouse him from his indolence, and to strike some fire from his character.[16]

Did Adrienne get wind of this attempted infidelity? It seems likely. Few secrets could be kept at Versailles, and when she whispered into the ear of her sister Louise, confidences were no doubt unrestrained. But what of it? Adrienne knew the habits of her world and age. Her father had deceived her mother. Men were like that. They caused much suffering, no doubt; but faith brought consolation, and the knowledge that she was irreproachable. Besides, she loved her husband, no matter what he might do.

Like many timid souls, La Fayette was prepared to take great risks in order to prove to his own satisfaction that he was a man of daring. On one occasion when the Epée de Bois set staged a parody of the Parliament, Gilbert played the part of the Attorney General with great gusto. Members of the court lost no time in making it clear to M. de Maurepas, the first minister, that it was highly improper to allow princes of the blood to associate with young sparks who showed no respect for the law officers of the crown. There were rumblings of a storm. Ségur averted it by telling the whole story to the king, who was much amused. The storm passed over, but La Fayette remained in a state of repressed revolt against a society whose frivolity struck a blow at his submerged cravings for grandeur.

The Duc d'Ayen had managed to obtain for his son-in-law a position in the household of the king's brother, the Comte de Provence. La Fayette, who had no wish to be chained to the court, decided to make himself impossible. At a masked ball he recognized the Comte de Provence behind a green domino and tried to pick a quarrel with him. Monsieur had been boasting of his memory. La Fayette said rudely: "Everyone knows that memory is a fool's substitute for wit." It was a piece of unseemly insolence, and quite pointless except in the eyes of the timid La Fayette, for it put an end to the projects of the Duc d'Ayen, who furiously sent his son-in-law headlong back to Metz.

This the son-in-law did not mind in the least. At Versailles he had succeeded neither as a lover nor as a courtier. He was now glad to give all his attention to his profession as a soldier. Just at this time, the strategy and the system of discipline introduced by Frederick II of Prussia were the fashion. At Metz, the Comte de Broglie kept a firm hand on his group of brilliant and highborn young officers.

In her twelfth year, as we have seen, Adrienne began to have religious problems. Her perturbation had continued, and it was only now, a year after her marriage, on Low Sunday, that she made her first communion.

From Metz she again received letters as tender as though her husband had never had eyes for any other:

MAY 8, 1775
I have taken the opportunity of entrusting this to a man who is traveling post. I am jealous, and convinced that I should make better speed than he will: but a little is better than nothing, and since I am reduced to writing to you, I like to think that this letter will reach you sooner than if I sent it by ordinary mail. I have had two from you, which have given me a happiness which no words can express. . . .
This of mine will, I know, be well received by you, but it will be incapable of feeling the pleasure which the sight of you would give me and therefore I am no longer jealous of it. Give my respects to Madame d'Ayen, and a thousand compliments to the little sisters who have the happiness of spending their lives with you and Mademoiselle Marin.[17]

Adrienne's first pregnancy had ended in a miscarriage, but soon after her husband's departure for Metz she discovered with delight that she was once more with child. Her letter with the announcement brought this reply:

You may imagine how happy I am. It is on such occasions, my dear heart, that I realize how much I love you. Your news is the bringer of a joy on which I was not counting. This little creature is our creature, and that makes me happy. It gives me a feeling that we love each other more than ever. I am already the father of a wonderfully loving family. Everything is so easy when one loves as I love you. I could never have believed that any news from you would move me so deeply. Since yesterday I have known it, and I am in the first flush of joy. You too dear heart, must feel it. I share your feelings most tenderly. We have all things in common.

Let us then rejoice and turn our thoughts to the Coronation. It has been decided that you shall make the journey. I would go to hell to embrace you. Wherever you may be, I shall see you. I am writing to my grandfather at once to tell him your news. Monsieur le Duc d'Ayen has written to me. I read his letter with feelings of gratitude for all his good offices on my behalf, which can be compared only with the love I bear him.

Good-by, dear heart. Take care of yourself, and think of me. I love you madly. I ask your pardon for my reproaches, but nothing will ever cure me of loving you. It is an emotion which grows continually, but can no longer acquire any merit other than that of lasting eternally. That I swear to you, my dear heart. I only wish that you could read my feelings.

We live in a state of confusion and desolation here. The whole garrison is going into mourning, for Monsieur le Maréchal has made a clean sweep of women. They are driven away or shut up. He is their sworn enemy, and they in their turn call down curses on his head.... Reform is the order of the day. Only legitimate passions are permitted.

Legitimate or not, my dear heart, it would, I assure you, be a difficult matter to uproot what I have pledged to you for life.[18]

For life.... How could any woman not be reassured by such a letter, especially when she is fifteen, expecting a child, and putting her future in the hands of God?

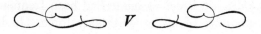

WHY NOT?

All princes are bored: that is why they go hunting.

MONTESQUIEU

In August, 1775, the Duke of Gloucester, brother of King George III of England, passed through Metz, traveling with his wife, their child, and a numerous entourage. The Comte de Broglie, commanding the troops in the area, gave a dinner in honor of the illustrious travelers to which he invited the two sons-in-law of the Duc d'Ayen: the Vicomte de Noailles and the Marquis de La Fayette. This was the time of the American colonies' revolt against England, and the Duke of Gloucester had a great deal to say about the matter. He was far from fond of his brother and was critical of his boneheaded obstinacy. The Americans had risen in the name of an old English principle: "No taxation without representation." Why, then, should they be blamed? They now wanted to be free men. The insurgents (or, as they were called in France, the Bostonians) had an army and a general—George Washington—and were putting up a brave fight.

More than one French officer at the table listened with interest to the bitter things said by the English prince. To the Comte de Broglie the subject was familiar. He had formerly dealt with foreign affairs, and it was his opinion that the policy of France should take the form of giving unstinted support to the insurgents. If France did so, England would be weakened and so make it possible for the French to stage a revenge for the deplorable peace of

1763. Ever since 1768 Choiseul had been reorganizing the French navy. The Comte de Broglie's name had been frequently put forward as commander of an expeditionary force. He had secretly hoped that he might become governor or viceroy of America in the name of the French king. He was careful not to communicate these thoughts to the Duke of Gloucester, but it occurred to him that the time had now come to revive the project. Vergennes, in order not to give England a pretext for declaring war, had limited French support for the Americans to supplying arms and technicians through a go-between, Beaumarchais, virtuously denying any basis for the complaints put forward by the English ambassador, Lord Stormont.

To young men like Louis de Noailles and Gilbert de La Fayette these first cannon shots in the defense of liberty sounded a summons and a signal. They had been brought up to admire the Greek and Roman heroes. It was in the works of the most celebrated republicans of the ancient world that they had learned to read and think. They had seen with their own eyes the scandalous inequality on which French society was built, and the spectacle had caused them distress. It was their dearest wish that political institutions should be made to conform with life as it was actually lived. The accession of Louis XVI and Marie-Antoinette had given rise to the hope that a Golden Age was about to begin. To a generation in love with ideas of renewal and reform the temerity of the Americans who had revolted against a reactionary monarch seemed wholly admirable.

Suddenly the same thought came to Noailles and to La Fayette: Let us go and fight shoulder to shoulder with the insurgents! La Fayette, in particular, burned with eagerness, reflecting that he would have the revenge he felt it his duty to take on the English for having killed his father. He spoke of his plan at once to his commanding officer, but the Comte de Broglie threw cold water on it. "No," he said. "I saw your uncle die in Italy; I was commander-in-chief when your father was killed at Minden. In my opinion your first duty is to your family. You have recently married; you are about to become a father. I will have nothing to do with jeopardizing your life unnecessarily."

On his return to Paris to await the birth of his child, Gilbert found his wife fully prepared to share his pro-American fervor. The American insurgents were all the rage. In this new France bursting with ideas, the talk was all of independence in the camps, of democracy among the nobles, of philosophy in the ballroom, of morality in ladies' boudoirs. In the eyes of a loving wife her husband is always right. La Fayette had only to side with the Bostonians for his "dear heart" to approve.

However, he carefully did not speak to her of his plan for going to America. Volunteers were besieging the house of Silas Deane, who—though he did not know a word of French—was temporarily acting as American envoy pending the arrival of Benjamin Franklin. Deane was signing on all and sundry, and was rather too ready with his offers of commissions. La Fayette was faced with a complicated problem. He could not act openly. His all-powerful in-laws would never countenance so fantastic a plan. In December, 1775, Adrienne bore a girl, who was baptized Henriette after her grandmother. Throughout the following year La Fayette, with his two best friends, Noailles and Ségur, was secretly engaged in taking the necessary steps for carrying out their plan for the great adventure. In June, at his own request, Gilbert was transferred from the active list to the reserve and so had greater freedom of movement. The three friends had sworn a mutual oath of secrecy.

Meanwhile the Comte de Broglie had submitted a master plan to Silas Deane. It was all a question, he thought, of "finding a man whose standing and reputation alone would serve to discourage the enemy.... Such a man," he said, "can be found, and I believe that I have found him.... It remains for you to bring sufficient pressure to bear on him, and this can be done by loading him with honors ... for instance, by appointing him field marshal–generalissimo." [1] The field marshal, needless to say, would be himself. A headquarters staff would go on ahead, consisting of a German professional soldier, the Baron Johann von Kalb, the Vicomte de Mauroy, and fourteen other officers. This plan, however, failed to obtain the royal sanction. Broglie thereupon fell back on an earlier plan, and authorized Kalb to introduce La Fayette to Silas Deane. The rather naïve Gilbert was overcome by this display of "paternal generosity." In point of fact, it was very much in Broglie's interest (or so he thought) to send Kalb and La Fayette to America and thus prepare the way for himself.

The ardor of the three musketeers (Ségur, Noailles, and La Fayette) was keyed too high to remain long within the limits of discretion. They revealed what was in the air to a number of friends whom they hoped to enlist in the enterprise. News of the "plot" reached the royal ears. The ministers were much concerned at the idea of such socially prominent volunteers embarking for America. The English would never believe that these young hotheads were acting without official support. They insisted that the plan be stopped. The parents took fright, and Ségur was much amused at the surprise shown by the La Fayette family. The Duc d'Ayen said to his son-in-law: "This sort of thing is all very well for the Vicomte de Noailles, who is strong, energetic, and sufficiently determined to undertake anything, but what on earth would *you* find to do over there?"

Nothing was better calculated to ruffle Gilbert's touchy sense of honor. He was determined to put his plan into action. His father-in-law, trusting wholly to appearances, was utterly wrong in his judgment of the young man who, though he might give an impression of shyness and timidity, was a daredevil at heart, all impulse and feeling. The *Why not?* of his ancestors was still his motto too. It was scarcely a year since the Maréchal de Noailles and the Duc d'Ayen had begged Ségur to rouse Gilbert from his apathy. "Consider their astonishment when they suddenly learned that this prudent young man of nineteen, so seemingly cold and easygoing, was on fire for glory and danger to such an extent that he proposed to cross the ocean and take up arms in the cause of American freedom!" [2]

The only persons who were not surprised were the Duchesse d'Ayen and her daughter Adrienne, who had plumbed more deeply the secret recesses of that well-protected heart. Their relief was great when it looked as though official disfavor would bring the great adventure to nothing. Adrienne was pregnant for the third time and needed the presence of her husband. But the opposition had an unexpected effect upon him. Noailles and Ségur, who had nothing to fall back upon but the allowances made them by their parents, were forced to comply. La Fayette, on the other hand, an orphan whose revenues, well administered by the Marquis de La Rivière and Mlle du Motier, were increasing all the time, felt independent. He continued his secret negotiations with Silas Deane and Kalb. On December 7, 1776, he put his signature to a deed enrolling him in the American army. Both he and Kalb were given the rank of major general. For an officer of nineteen without any serious military experience this was an almost indecent promotion, but Silas Deane had been dazzled by his success in landing a volunteer of such quality. Adrienne knew nothing of the transaction. Gilbert had kept it from her, no doubt because he feared that she might reveal it to her parents and so spoil everything—which shows how little he knew her. She was the type of woman who would always keep a secret, even if it endangered her happiness.

It is difficult to believe that the government was really opposed to this expedition, for it was the Comte de Broglie's secretary, Boismartin, who undertook to go to Bordeaux for the purpose of making arrangements for the purchase of a vessel to take Gilbert and the other officers to America. The owners promised delivery for March, 1777. The price they asked was 112,000 livres, a quarter to be paid immediately in cash. To lull suspicion and to make it appear that, like Noailles and Ségur, he had submitted to family pressure, La Fayette decided to spend the time of waiting in London with his relative and friend, the Prince de Poix. The Marquis de Noailles, the Duc d'Ayen's brother, was at that time French ambassador to the Court of St James's. It would never occur to anybody that he would make such a visit on the eve of taking up arms against England. Such a conclusion could have been reached only by persons who knew nothing about La Fayette, for in fact he felt the piquancy of the situation as an added temptation.

GILBERT TO ADRIENNE: CALAIS, FEBRUARY 20, 1777

We have reached Calais without mishap, my dear heart, and I am expecting to embark tomorrow on my journey to the famous city of London. I shall set sail with a pang. I am leaving behind me all those whom I love. I am leaving you, my dear heart, and truth to tell I know not why. But the die has been cast, and go I must. . . . I beg of you, dear heart, to send news of me to my aunts. I shall write to you from London as soon as I arrive, and hope soon to have a letter from you. Write to me punctually, for by so doing you will give me pleasure. Good-by, dear heart. In whatever country I may find myself, I shall always love you tenderly. I would you knew how sincere is this assurance, and how much your feelings for me contribute to my happiness.

FEBRUARY 25

I have reached London, my dear heart, though not without difficulty. The time we spent at Calais was tedious in the extreme. But it came to an end, and I arrived here yesterday. I write this from the house of the Marquis de Noailles, who received me most warmly. I have as yet seen only a few men. I have just dined with our ambassador, and am about to leave for the opera, after which I am bidden to supper and a ball, where I shall see all the ladies. I still think that Paris is a better place than London, for all our friendly welcome. I am very impatient to see all the ladies, and the famous Duchess of Devonshire. It is this evening that I make my entry [into society]. I very much hope that the prince will behave himself well. He declares that I am always frightened lest he say something stupid. Good-by, dear heart. I am so much in a hurry that I have time only to tell you that I love you with all my heart.

(UNDATED)

I have been much put about, dear heart, at having received no news of you for two posts. Fortunately, I know you are not sick but only lazy, because I have heard from the vicomtesse and other friends, who say nothing of you. The pleasures of London move at great speed, and even I, who am not used to leading a secluded life, am astonished at their briskness. But to leave the dining table at half past seven and to sup between two and three in the morning seems to me a very bad habit. I find much to amuse me here. There are many very charming women, and the men are agreeable and welcoming. When the former can be persuaded to leave their assemblies and the men their clubs, their society is very pleasing. The term of your exile at Versailles approaches, and I send you my felicitations on that score.

Good-by, my dear heart. I am obliged to write to you somewhat hurriedly. The probable shortness of my stay in London makes the time more precious than it would be were I to remain here for four months, like my predecessors. Had I need of fresh proof to convince me how dearly I love you, I should find it in the pain I feel at not receiving letters from you, though I have them from all my friends. Good day to you!

MARCH 7

At last, my dear heart, I have had news from you. I expect still more today, and no matter how great the bustle of London, am impatient for post days and happy when they come. I dance and sup and sit up very late into the night, and well-nigh all my occupations are of the social kind. Today, however, I went with Monsieur de La Rochette (whose side I can never leave) to see the Port of London and other remarkable places in this city. Tomorrow or the day following I am going to Portsmouth, armed with a plentiful supply of introductions, which will enable me to see everything. Consequently, I may not be able to write to you for one or two posts. Favors are still being showered upon me in this country, and nowhere could I be treated more amiably. Monsieur de Poix has become a great arbiter of fashion, and determines what hats all the ladies shall wear. . . .

Good-by, my dear heart. I send my respects to Madame d'Ayen, and a thousand tender compliments to the vicomtesse and to my sisters. It always grieves me to take leave of you, even in a letter, and it is my evil star that keeps me in continual movement, so that I have no one but myself to blame that I see you only for the sixth part of the time I could wish. But you know my heart, or at least its sincerity, and will, I hope, always believe me when I say that it is yours for life and loves you with a true tenderness.

Give our darling Henriette twenty kisses from me. Do not forget my compliments to your father. . . . I hope to write to you once again before my little expedition.[3]

"Before my little expedition. . . ." It is of the trip to Portsmouth that he is speaking, but that simple phrase certainly had another meaning for La Fayette. Two days later, on March 9, he wrote to the Duc d'Ayen, confessing the truth. He felt sure that he would be well on his way before his family-in-law could stop him.

You will be greatly astonished, my dear Papa, by what I am about to tell you. It pains me more than I can say not to have consulted you in this matter. My respect, my affection, and my confidence in you should be sufficient assurance of that. But I had given my promise, and you would have thought the worse of me had I broken it, whereas the step I am taking will, I hope, give you a good opinion of my good intentions at least. I have been presented with an unique opportunity of distinguishing myself and of learning my trade. I am now a general officer in the army of the United States of America. My zeal in their cause and my candor have won their trust. On my side, I have done all I can for them, and their interests will always be more dear to me than my own. At the present moment, my dear

Papa, I am in London, still awaiting news from my friends. But, as soon as I have it, I shall take my departure and, without stopping in Paris, shall embark upon a vessel which I have chartered and which is now my property. My traveling companions are Monsieur le Baron de Kalb, an officer of great distinction, a general of brigade in the king's armies who is now, as I am, a major general in the armed forces of the United States, and several excellent officers who wish to share in my adventures. I am overjoyed at having found so good an opportunity of doing something and of learning a great deal. I know that I am making tremendous sacrifices, and that no one will suffer more than I do at having to leave my family, my friends and you, my dear Papa, because I love them more tenderly than anyone has ever loved. But the voyage is not considerable, and many people every day make far longer ones solely for their pleasure. Besides, I hope when I return to be more worthy of those who may have been so kind as to regret my departure. Good-by, my dear Papa: I hope to see you again soon. Think of me with feelings of kindliness. I am much desirous of deserving them, and do already deserve them by reason of what I feel and of the respect which I shall ever entertain for you.

Your affectionate son,

LA FAYETTE

I am making a brief stay in Paris after all, but shall remain only long enough to bid you farewell. I wished to write to my uncle and to Madame de Lusignan, but am so much pressed for time that I must ask you to present my respects to them.[4]

On his way through Paris he stayed incognito for three days with M. de Kalb at Chaillot and went to see his friend Ségur, who wrote:

At seven one morning he suddenly entered my bedroom, locked the door, and, sitting close by my bedside, said: "I am setting off for America. No one knows of it, but I am too fond of you to leave without having you hear my secret." "By what means?" I asked him. "Have you taken steps to ensure your getting a passage?"

I learned from him that, having on some pretext or other made a journey outside France, he had bought a ship which was to await his arrival in one of the Spanish ports. He had armed her, collected a good crew, and put aboard not only weapons and munitions, but also a great number of officers who had consented to share in his fortunes.

There was no need for me to tell my friend at any great length how much it pained me not to be in a position to accompany him. He felt it as deeply as I did. But we both entertained the hope that war would soon break out between England and France and that this would remove any obstacle to our meeting again.

La Fayette, after confiding also in the Vicomte de Noailles, immediately left Paris. His departure was a cause of much affliction to his family, the members of which suffered greatly, not only at the thought of those many dangers he was about to encounter, but because he was sacrificing a great part of his fortune in the interests of a country very far removed from France. Only his wife, who suffered more than anybody else, loved him too well not to share his feelings and approve his generous resolution.[5]

Gilbert did not see Adrienne, nor did he inform her of his presence in Paris. She was living at the Hôtel de Noailles and he could not have met her without sounding the alarm to all the family. Nevertheless, he felt how unfair such a separation, without a word of farewell, would seem to her. He was deeply remorseful, and wondered whether she would ever forgive him.

He set off for Bordeaux with Kalb, and still further to conceal the purpose of his journey, visited in that city his powerful uncle-by-marriage, the Maréchal-Duc de Mouchy, while Kalb went to take a look at their ship, La Victoire. La Fayette appeared on the passenger list under the name of Gilbert du Motier, Chevalier de Chavaniac—a very transparent pseudonym, had the government really wanted to stop him.

Meanwhile, Versailles was resounding with the Duc d'Ayen's fury. The news of La Fayette's departure had quickly spread. The Marquis de Noailles complained from London that a trick had been played on him. To think that he, Ambassador of France, Envoy Extraordinary and Plenipotentiary to the King of England, should have presented to that sovereign a nephew who was already in the service of the insurgents! The Duc d'Ayen had a hurried interview with the minister, Maurepas, who laughed (he was always laughing) and promised to keep the ship from sailing. Just as La Fayette and Kalb were pushing off in the longboat to go aboard, a messenger arrived to warn them that the king was about to issue a restraining order. According to Kalb, La Fayette seemed inclined to obey.

However, they went aboard *La Victoire*, weighed anchor, and set
sail for Spain. In the small harbor of Los Pasajes they found the
order of which they had already been informed. The Marquis de
La Fayette was to proceed at once to Marseilles, where he would
find the Duc d'Ayen, with Mme de Tessé, his sister, about to start
on a trip to Italy and Sicily. He was to accompany them, and not
to return to France for six months. When La Fayette made up his
mind to return to Bordeaux and communicate with Paris, Kalb
was fully convinced that he would see no more of him, and suggested that he should hand the ship back to the owners, offering
them an indemnity of 20,000 livres. For that sum he could have
washed his hands of an abortive escapade, and it would have meant
very little to so rich a man.

Once back in Bordeaux, however, La Fayette failed to follow
Kalb's advice, which was to go back to Paris (for the idea of touring
Italy with an highly incensed father-in-law was little to his
taste). Kalb had already written to his wife: "So here he is,
back from his sea voyage and the American war." But at Bordeaux La Fayette learned that an arrest warrant had been taken out
against him. This threat of arbitrary imprisonment reawakened his
pride and his feelings of revolt. On a sudden impulse he chose rebellion. Our most serious decisions are often the result of a "small
majority."

To Bordeaux came the Vicomte de Mauroy, like La Fayette a
major general by the grace of Silas Deane. Mauroy told him not to
be alarmed. It was only the Duc d'Ayen who had prevailed upon
the king to issue that severe order and to grant his request for the
warrant. Everybody else at court thoroughly approved his conduct.
There was open criticism of his father-in-law for having tried to put
a stop to so fine a gesture. The die was cast. La Fayette, in disguise,
slipped through the fingers of the police, crossed the frontier, and
rejoined Kalb.

PART TWO

IN WHICH THE WIFE OF A REBEL

BECOMES THE WIFE OF A HERO

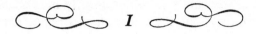

LETTERS FROM AMERICA

What, then, is to be done? I take refuge
in my heart, where I love him as I wish.

PAUL VALÉRY

The spring of 1777 was a sad season for the young Marquise de La Fayette. Near her time, she spent her days wandering alone in the beautiful Noailles garden. After so many letters from London, full of love and tenderness, without so much as a word to warn her of his decision, the boy-general had started on a long and perilous journey which might end in his death. Adrienne's enraged father had spoken ironically of the weakling who thought he could make fools of the strong. Fortunately, however, the Duc d'Ayen had set off for Italy and Adrienne was left alone with her sisters and her mother. In the room hung with red damask the nest of doves was once more as it had been, though now with the waiting cradle close at hand and the Vicomtesse de Noailles often absent at Versailles with her family-in-law.

The duchesse did her best to soften a situation which was more than usually painful for Adrienne by singing the praises of the absent husband and, what was even more important, proving that in spite of appearances and his furtive departure he loved her still.

Monsieur de La Fayette [wrote Adrienne in later life] carried out during the month of April the plan he had been meditating for six months of serving the cause of American independence. I was with

*child, and I loved him dearly. When the news reached us, my father
and the rest of the family were furious. My mother, however, was
concerned mainly about the effect all this might have upon me,
and about the safety of a son, now so far away, to whom she was
deeply attached. Though no one could be less interested than she
was in ambition, glory, and rash enterprises, she judged the conduct
of Monsieur de La Fayette as, two years later, it was judged by the
world at large. She refused even to consider that he might have been
wrong in making such a decision, and cared nothing about the cost.
She clung to her conviction that there was something a great deal
more important than the folly of a hotheaded young man involved
in it, and maintained that this was proved by the manner in which
the whole undertaking had been planned. In view of the elaborate
preparations he had made, and the sincere regrets he had felt at
leaving behind him his wife and everything that was dear to him,
she realized that she could not fear for my happiness without fearing
for her own. The depth of her feelings for him made it the more
possible for her to soften the pain of mine. It was she who informed
me of his departure, and she who sought to console me by trying
in every way to serve Monsieur de La Fayette with that generous
tenderness, that superiority of views and conduct, which she displayed in her every thought and action.[1]*

Her brother-in-law and her elder sister, Louis and Louise de
Noailles, also rallied to her support. The third of the musketeers,
Ségur, had married on April 30, 1777, Mlle Daguesseau, the half-
sister of the Duchesse d'Ayen, and was now the uncle-by-marriage
of his two best friends. The bonds that united this intelligent and
affectionate group were drawn still tighter. Through Ségur and
Noailles, Adrienne learned that all the people who mattered at
court were so strong in their support of La Fayette that many said:
"If the Duc d'Ayen does not withdraw his opposition, he will never
be able to find husbands for his daughters." The Maréchal de
Noailles, however, persisted in his churlish attitude, and the Marquis de Noailles, by reason of his position as ambassador in London, declared that he had more reason than anybody else for feeling outraged. He had written to the First Minister, Maurepas, as
follows:

*My surprise, Monsieur le Comte, was extreme on learning yesterday
in letters from Paris that Monsieur de La Fayette had left for Amer-*

*ica. His age, fortunately, may excuse so irresponsible an action. This
is the sole consolation left to me for the annoyance caused me by
such inconsiderate behavior.*[2]

Maurepas reassured him with the lightest of light touches:

*You will have heard, Monsieur le Marquis, that all our precautions
relating to Monsieur de La Fayette have proved to be unavailing.
Monsieur le Maréchal, whom I had the honor to see yesterday,
seemed as much afflicted as you, most certainly, will be. Neither you
nor your family have any reason for self-reproach, and the king in
no way holds you responsible for the behavior of a young man whose
head has been turned.*[3]

The scandalmongers of the news sheets put their own interpreta-
tion on the escapade. They asserted that La Fayette was in love with
the pretty Comtesse d'Hunolstein and was concerned only with
gaining favor in her eyes. Some months later Aglaé d'Hunolstein,
corresponding with a Russian friend, Ivan Ivanovich Shuvalov,
gave the lie to these rumors:

*Say what you will, he has had no thought in mind but personal
glory, and to suspect anything else is to tarnish his good name. To
think me the object of his endeavors would be to do me too much
honor. The highest reward of doing something fine is the pleasure
of knowing it well done.*[4]

Madame d'Ayen wisely kept these journalistic impertinences
from her daughter, who was successfully brought to bed of a second
daughter on July 1. She was baptized Anastasie-Louise-Pauline.

Not until August did Adrienne have news of her husband. The
crossing of the Atlantic, even under the most favorable conditions,
then took several weeks. Some of the English papers were announcing that he had made landfall at Boston on May 30, but on that
date he was still on the way.

At last, Adrienne received the first of his letters. He had started
it on board ship and finished it ashore. It was a good letter, written
with style and genuine affection:

MAY 30, 1777

*It is from very far away that I am writing to you, my dear heart, and
to this cruel separation must be added the still more horrible uncertainty of when I am likely to hear from you. I hope, however, to*

have news of you before long, and among my many reasons for wishing to arrive none causes me more impatience than that. What fears, what anxieties have I not reason to join with the pain, so sharp already, of having separated from all I hold most dear! How did you take my second departure? Did it make you love me the less? Have you forgiven me? Have you reflected that in any case I should have had to be absent from you, wandering about Italy, dragging out an inglorious existence with persons who were among those most hostile to my plans and to my way of thinking? But no such reflections could keep me from feeling a terrible pang during those hateful moments when I saw the land falling away behind me.

Your regrets and those of my friends, the thought of Henriette—these things were all present to my mind in the most heartrending fashion. It was then that I could no longer find excuses for my conduct. If only you could know how much I suffered, could picture those melancholy days I spent fleeing from all I most love! Must I have one misery the more in hearing that you have not pardoned me? . . .

Since my last letter, I have been living in the most tedious of all places: the sea is so sad, and I think she and I impart our own sadness to each other. I should have arrived by this time, but the winds have been cruelly up in arms against me. It will, I suppose, be another eight or ten days before I can hope to reach Charleston. It is there that I expect to disembark, and that will be a great happiness for me. . . .

But let us now talk of more important matters, of you, dearest, of darling Henriette, of her brother (or her sister). I find her so charming that she gives me a taste for girls. Of whichever sex the new child may be, I shall hear of its arrival with the liveliest joy. Do not lose a moment in hastening my happiness by telling me that it is born. Whether it is because I am twice a father I do not know, but it is certain that I feel myself to be more of a father than ever. . . .

There is no great difference between letters from America and letters from Sicily. I cannot but confess that I think passionately of Sicily. It would have made me feel so much nearer to seeing you again. . . .

Eight days later, still at sea, Gilbert continued his letter:

I am still upon this melancholy plain, and it is beyond comparison the most tedious place imaginable. To console myself a little, I think of you and of my friends. I brood upon the pleasure of being back with you. What a wonderful moment it will be when I arrive home again, when, though not expected, I shall embrace you! You will, I imagine, be with your children. Even to think of that happy time gives me a delicious pleasure. Do not think of it as of something far distant, though to me it seems a long way off. But in fact it will not be so long as you imagine. Though I cannot decide the day nor even the month until I have seen for myself the state of affairs, the period of exile until the month of January imposed upon me by the Duc d'Ayen seemed so immense when I heard of it that you may be sure I shall not take it upon myself to make this one really long. You must admit, dear heart, that the occupations and the existence to which I am going will be very different from those which would have been forced upon me in the course of this tiresome journey. Defender of the liberty I worship, myself more free than anybody in coming hither as a friend to offer my services to this exciting republic, I bring to it only my own integrity and good will, nothing of ambition, no self-interest. In working for my glory, I work for their happiness. I hope that just to please me, you will become a good American, for it is a feeling for virtuous hearts. The prosperity of America is linked with the prosperity of all mankind. She will become the sure and worthy asylum of virtue, honesty, tolerance, equality, and tranquil liberty.

Gilbert thought nostalgically of Ségur, Poix, and Noailles. The latter was inclined to repeat rather too often that "travel is the best of all schools for the young," and indeed La Fayette felt himself growing ever more reasonable as the endless sea unfurled before him. Finally the interminable crossing seemed about to end:

Today we have seen several species of bird from which we gather that land is not far off. The prospect of arriving is sweet, for this kind of living is very tedious. Fortunately my health has been good and made it possible for me to occupy my mind. I divide my reading between military works and English books. I have made some progress with the language which is to be so necessary to me. Good-by. Darkness makes it impossible to continue. For the last few days I have forbidden the showing of any lights. See how prudent I am! So good-by. Since my fingers are to some extent governed by my heart, I do not need to see clearly in order to tell you that I love you, and shall all my life.[5]

In Charleston, on June 19, he wrote a glowing description of America and the Americans:

They are as my enthusiasm had led me to expect. Simplicity of manners, a wish to be obliging, love of country and of liberty, and a delightful equality are to be seen in everybody. The richest and the poorest are on the same level, and though there are immense fortunes in this country, I defy you to find the least difference in men's manners toward one another.[6]

Gilbert had staked his honor on finding everything superlatively good in the country for whose sake he had left his own. The city of Charleston was the finest in the world; the American women were very pretty, unaffected, and delightfully clean. In short, everything was for the best in the best possible of new worlds. In order to understand the idyllic view he took of America, we should remember what he had been in France: the half-provincial son-in-law of a great and dictatorial nobleman, the friend of young men more brilliant than himself, a soldier hungering and thirsting for glory reduced to carrying out minor duties. Suddenly he found himself independent, welcomed and acclaimed. He blossomed in the warmth of popularity.

One can imagine the effect of such letters in Paris and Versailles: on Adrienne first of all, proud of her husband's protestations of love and happy because she could now show proofs of his affection; but also on Ségur, Noailles, and Poix, who made much of them at court and saw to it that they were read by the queen, and by their friends the philosophers. Benjamin Franklin, as American envoy, had joined forces with Silas Deane and Arthur Lee. From the very first he enjoyed a prodigious popularity with the French. These were the days of *La Nouvelle Héloïse* and the Trianon dairy, when a simple country life was all the rage. Actually, there was nothing of the countryman about Franklin, but he was a master at playing the part in which the French had cast him. The young nobles admired him, just as they glorified Voltaire and Rousseau, just as they praised Gilbert de La Fayette.

In rich families money never loses its importance, even when drama holds the stage. In August, 1777, when the first news of La Fayette was reaching France, his business manager, the old Parliament lawyer Gérard, received from Reculès, de Boismarein & Co., shipowners of Bordeaux who had sold *La Victoire* to the marquis, information to the effect that the ship had reached Charleston and would make the return journey to France with an important cargo which it would be wise to insure. They offered to advance the amount of the premium. The dangers of ocean travel and of war were considerable. Why risk losing 200,000 livres? The Duc d'Ayen was traveling in Sicily. The duchesse, a very capable woman, took the matter in hand.

We have received, Monsieur [she wrote her husband], fresh information which leaves not the least doubt the Monsieur de La Fayette's ship should be insured, and that with the least possible delay. I enclose detailed instructions which I have had drawn up by a reliable individual who is well versed in this type of business. These, I think, will save you a good deal of trouble. You will see from them that Monsieur le Maréchal de Noailles thinks, as I do, that it is of the first importance to write not later than Tuesday to Monsieur de Boismarein, and that no further discussion of the matter is necessary. You will see, too, that the principal difficulty, namely the finding of the money, has been entirely removed, since these gentlemen are prepared to advance it, which they could scarcely refuse to do. It is, however, essential that you should keep a copy of the letter containing a statement of the debt, which can be used in case of necessity.

Beneath her mother's signature, the wise Adrienne added, in her still-childish hand:

I have nothing further to add to my mother's letter, Monsieur. You will realize, as we all do, how important it is not to miss Tuesday's post, so as not to expose Monsieur de La Fayette to the danger of losing a capital sum of between a hundred fifty and two hundred thousand francs, against which we shall be insured.

I am well aware, Monsieur, of your zeal in all that concerns us. I need not therefore feel any anxiety, and trust that you will accept my thanks.

NOAILLES DE LA FAYETTE [7]

As it turned out, at the very moment these ladies were busying themselves about insurance *La Victoire* had already suffered shipwreck. Messrs. Cripps and May, shipowners of Bordeaux, were informed by their correspondents in Charleston that on August 14 Captain La Bourcier, leaving harbor under full sail, had been driven onto a rock. Before this news reached them, the Bordeaux shipowners had already taken out policies in Nantes, Bordeaux, and Cádiz. Consequently the loss to the family was very small. But a difficulty arose. It was learned that La Fayette had also insured the vessel in America. The insurers could not claim compensation on both sides of the Atlantic, and, as always happens in cases of doubt, payment was long delayed in both Bordeaux and Charleston.

Gilbert's brokers in Paris, the lawyer Gérard and his young assistant Morizot, were beginning to receive letters of exchange to a considerable amount. The signature of a minor was held to be not valid in law. But how could they let such a signature be questioned? The Duchesse d'Ayen, Adrienne, and the ladies at Chavaniac were in full agreement: they must pay.

On his arrival in Philadelphia, La Fayette had made serious miscalculations. Conscious of the sacrifice which he had made, in possession of letters couched in the warmest terms from the representatives of the American government, and holding a major general's commission, he was fully expecting the same delirious greeting with which he had been welcomed in Charleston. But unfortunately the first members of Congress he met took him for an adventurer who had come to America in the hope of making a fortune rather than to offer his services. He was treated without respect, without even common politeness. A major general, this boy? The American generals would never recognize him!

Gilbert did not mention this state of affairs in his letters—in the first place because it went against the grain with him to blacken the picture he had drawn of the best of all republics, in the second because the misunderstanding did not last long. He made one of those gestures in which he loved to indulge and which were not without nobility. He offered his services without pay. Such a disinterested action set people thinking. They began to realize that this gentleman, young though he was, represented those powerful French influences of which the Americans were going to stand in need. On second thought Congress decided to establish him in his military rank and to present him to the Commander-in-Chief.

Gilbert's meeting with George Washington marked him for life. Never had a king seemed to him so royal. The picture of that grave-faced man, who carried himself with incomparable dignity and wore a powdered wig no less well than the Maréchal de Noailles, never left him. In Washington he recognized a leader and—as he said later—a father, that ideal father of whom the cannonball at Minden had deprived him. All the same, when this twenty-year-old Frenchman asked to be entrusted with a command, Washington would not commit himself. He was prepared to give the Marquis de La Fayette the scarf of a major general, but a division was a very different matter. At that time the English were threatening Philadelphia. La Fayette was allowed to take part in the engagement known as the battle of Brandywine and had the good fortune to receive a not very serious wound. This was the baptism of fire for which he had longed so ardently. He hastened to send a modest account of his adventure to the Hôtel de Noailles.

SEPTEMBER 12, 1777

I will begin by telling you that I am in good health, because it is my intention to wind up by informing you that we had yesterday a full-dress engagement from which we did not emerge victorious. Our Americans, after standing firm for a reasonably long time, were finally routed. While trying to rally them, I was honored by my lords the English with a musket ball in the leg. But that, my dear heart, is a mere trifle, neither bone nor nerve being touched, so that I came off lightly, my only inconvenience being that I shall have to stay on my back for a while—which has put me in a mighty bad temper....

Two weeks later he sent a further communiqué.

Let me tell you about this wound of mine. The ball passed through the fleshy part of the leg without touching either bone or nerve. The surgeons are amazed at the speed with which it is healing. They fall into an ecstasy each time they renew the dressings and maintain that it is one of the wonders of the world. I, for my part, think it an infernal mess, extremely tiresome and not a little painful. It is all a matter of taste.... So there, my dear heart, is the whole story of what I somewhat pompously call my wound, just to give myself an air and to be an object of interest.

And now, seeing that you are the wife of a major general in the American army, I must give you some degree of instruction. People will say to you: "They have been beaten," to which you must reply: "That I cannot deny, but when you have two armies, equal in numbers and not entrenched, old soldiers always have the advantage over

young levies; moreover, they have had the pleasure of killing many
—yes, many—more of the enemy than they have lost of their own
men." To which the answer will come: "That is all very well, but
Philadelphia, the capital of America, the bastion of liberty, has been
taken!" This you counter politely with: "You are no more than fools.
Philadelphia is a dismal town, open on all sides, its harbor already
closed to shipping, and rendered famous only because it is (though
why I do not know) the seat of Congress. . . . It is full of a scurvy
kind of persons, doltish Quakers, who are good for nothing but to
go into a room with great hats on their heads, no matter what the
weather, and to wait there in silence for the Holy Spirit to descend
until one of them, grown tired of waiting, gets to his feet and talks
a deal of nonsense, with the tears pouring from his eyes. So much for
the people of Philadelphia. So much for this famous city which, let
me tell you, we shall sooner or later take back again." Should they
still plague you with questions, you must send them packing in terms
with which the Vicomte de Noailles will supply you, for I do not
wish to waste such time as I have for writing to you in talking
politics. . . .

Just think, my dear heart, I have received but one letter from you,
from the hands of the Comte Pulaski. . . . I am terribly out of luck's
way and feel cruelly miserable. Judge the horror of my position: I
am far from all whom I love, and in a state of uncertainty and despair beyond endurance. But I know that I deserve no pity. Why was
I ever so disordered in my wits as to want to come here? I have been
well punished for it. I am too sensitive, dear heart, for such violent
exercises. I trust, all the same, that you will pity me. If you only
knew how I am suffering, especially now when news of you means
so very much to me. I cannot think what it will be without trembling.[8]

Casimir Pulaski was a Polish soldier who had just arrived with
the intention of offering his sword to Washington. While passing
through Paris, he had seen the Marquise de La Fayette and her
family and was the bearer of letters from her. The Duchesse d'Ayen
was appalled by the news printed in the English papers to the
effect that La Fayette had been seriously wounded, some even said
killed. She managed to keep them from Adrienne first by taking her
into the country to the house of M. de Fresnes, and later by send-

ing her with her sister to stay with the Comtesse de La Marck at Raismes.

The news of Gilbert's wound, his courageous conduct, his now being a general, produced a tremendous effect in Paris, where it not only enhanced his own renown but also increased the general enthusiasm for the American cause. The setbacks of the last few months had led to a marked coolness in the attitude of the French government. It was all very well for Benjamin Franklin, the American envoy, to say "It is not General Howe who has taken Philadelphia, but Philadelphia which has taken General Howe," but Maurepas and Vergennes were showing considerable hesitation about forming an alliance with the defeated. La Fayette's explanations brought about a change of view. The French love glory. That La Fayette and his companions in arms should have given luster to the name of France across the ocean, and at the expense of the English too, enchanted them. La Fayette's friends Ségur and Noailles envied him. A movement in favor of declaring war began to take shape, in spite of the king's prudent advice. Who would have thought six months earlier that the tall, red-headed young man with the thick eyebrows and receding forehead would become a national hero?

The national hero, meanwhile, had gone into winter quarters at Valley Forge with the American army. It was in a pitiable state. The men were without boots and left a trail of blood upon the roads when they marched. Many deserted, and those who remained were half naked. La Fayette was now in command of the Virginia Division, but the eleven regiments mustered among them no more than three thousand men. He lived in a wooden hut, buried in snow and completely unheated. What a contrast to the Hôtel de Noailles, with its crystal lusters shining on gilded paneling, where he could see in imagination his charming sisters-in-law and the adoring Adrienne. He shivered in his hut and dreamed of the future.

GILBERT TO ADRIENNE: VALLEY FORGE, JANUARY 6, 1778

What a delight it will be to embrace my two poor little girls and ask them to crave my pardon from their mother! You cannot, surely, think me so insensitive or so absurd as to let the sex of our new child diminish in any way the joy I feel at its birth. We are not so far

gone in senility as to be unable to produce another without the aid
of a miracle! But when we do, I insist that it shall be a boy. If the
burden of my name shall seem distasteful to him, let me tell him
that I fully intend to carry it myself for several years to come. . . .

Do not you think that, after my return, we might be sufficiently
grown up to have a house of our own where we might live happily
together, receive our friends, establish a pleasing liberty, and read
the newspapers of foreign countries without having the curiosity
to go there and see for ourselves how they live? I like to build dream-
castles in France where all shall be happiness and pleasure. You
figure always, dear heart, as one half of myself. Once we have been
reunited no one shall separate us again or keep us from tasting, each
through the other, the sweetness of a mutual love and the most
delicious, the happiest tranquility.[9]

All things considered, he regretted nothing. He was a major
general; his hero, Washington, treated him as a friend and even
went so far as to consult him. On December 16, 1777, he had
plucked up courage to write to the Duc d'Ayen:

I am impatient for news of your expedition. I count chiefly on
Madame de La Fayette to supply me with a few details, for she must
be well aware of my eagerness to have them. Monsieur le Maréchal
de Noailles tells me that the letters which have reached him from
Italy assure him that all the travelers are in good health. It is through
him, too, that I have been informed of Madame de La Fayette's
being brought to bed. He does not speak of it as being the happiest
occurrence in the world, but my anxiety has been too great to let
me worry about the sex of the child, and his kindness in sending me
the news has given me a hundred times more pleasure than he could
possibly imagine in his informing me that I have but a daughter.
So now the Rue Saint-Honoré is discredited forever while the
other Hôtel de Noailles has acquired fresh luster by the birth of
Adrien.*
It is truly a shameful thing thus to bring dishonor on a house in
which I have had such happiness.[10]

The "other" Hôtel de Noailles was that belonging to the Duc de
Mouchy, in the Rue de l'Université, where the Vicomtesse de

---

* This short-lived Adrien died in babyhood, but Louise de Noailles had two other
sons: Alexis (1783–1835) and Alfred (1791–1851). Her daughter, Euphémie, married the Marquis de Vérac in 1810.

Noailles, Adrienne's elder sister, had given a male heir to the younger branch.

La Fayette sent the Duc d'Ayen high praise of "his" general:

He is a man truly made for this revolution which, but for him, could never have been brought about. I enjoy his intimacy to a greater extent than anybody else and see how worthy he is of the adoration of his countrymen. His friendship and his entire confidence in me, so far as all matters concerned with the war and with politics, both great and small, with which he is concerned, allow me to judge what tasks there are still for him to perform in the achievement of victory and conciliation. I admire more and more, with every day that passes, the beauty of his mind and character.

Gilbert then turned to propaganda:

America is waiting impatiently for us to declare in her favor, and I hope that one day France will resolve to humble the pride of England. This consideration and the approaches which, so it seems to me, America has decided to make, give me great hopes for the glorious establishment of independence. We are not, I think, so strong as I expected, but we can fight, and will fight successfully. With the help of France we shall, though at some cost, carry to victory the cause which I have at heart because it is a just one; because it does honor to mankind; because it is of importance to my country and because my friends and I are firmly committed to it.[11]

The Duc d'Ayen was perhaps somewhat irritated by his son-in-law's new tone of authority, but he was too astute a navigator not to bear in mind that La Fayette was sailing with a following wind. When a new American envoy, John Adams, arrived in Paris with letters from the marquis for his wife and father-in-law, the Hôtel de Noailles gave a dinner in his honor. Adams was an ardent Puritan, rough but honest. He had no objection to ceremony provided he was the star performer, and he seemed pleased at being received with great pomp in the Rue Saint-Honoré.

II

THE ALLIANCE

The House of Noailles not only forgave its rebel member: it now dressed itself in his robes of glory. The young marquise took the center of the stage, was sought after and complimented. In February, 1778, Voltaire left Ferney for Paris, into which he made a triumphal entry. He was to be seen in the streets, strangely accoutered in a great cloak, with a woolen periwig on his head surmounted by a scarlet fur-lined cap. He received visitors from court and city in a dressing gown and nightcap. Sickness and genius combined make all things permissible. And of course he was favorably disposed toward the Americans. Franklin went to see him and presented his grandson, for whom he requested a "blessing" from the author of *Candide*. The patriarch of Ferney laid his hands upon the young Franklin's head, uttering as he did so the three words *God, Liberty, Tolerance*. At the house of Mme de Choiseul he met Adrienne de La Fayette. He had frequently expressed his admiration of the marquis and now asked to be presented to his wife. He went down on one knee before her. "I wish," he said, "to make my obeisance to the wife of the hero of the New World. May I live long enough to salute in him the liberator of the Old."

Aglaé d'Hunolstein, who had once rejected Gilbert's advances, regretted her attitude of proud disdain now that he was the lion of the day. To her Russian friend Shuvalov she wrote:

It seems probable at the moment that we shall have a war, and we expect it from two sides [Prussia and England]. Everyone in Paris is convinced that we have signed a treaty with the insurgents and recognized their independence.... Milord Stormont maintains a calm and serious bearing. We receive very little news from America: it is three months since we had any of Monsieur de La Fayette. The last was to the effect that he had received a wound in the leg, serious but not dangerous. If we are engaged in a war at sea with the English, it will be very difficult for him to return to France without being captured. There is general anxiety about this long silence after his wound. One can only hope that the reports are without foundation. His return will be a most interesting event. I will write to you about it, for I know how much interest you take in him.[1]

It was not only Shuvalov who took an interest in him. Mme d'Hunolstein was beginning to crystallize (in the Stendhalian sense) on the absent hero rather more than was good for Adrienne —or herself.

It says a great deal for Lord Stormont that he was maintaining a "calm and serious bearing," for he was well aware that, though the French ministers continued to pay him a thousand polite compliments, they were all the time negotiating with the American commissioners. What would not have been said about the perfidious Court of St James's had it indulged in some such double game! In November it was learned that the General Burgoyne had surrendered to "*Mr.* Gates," as *The Times* put it—since a rebel, even a victorious rebel, could not be looked upon as a general. This success was decisive. In December, 1777, Louis XVI informed Franklin that France recognized the independence of the United States. In February, 1778, a treaty of trade and friendship was signed with a further promise of a military alliance should England, as a result of this recognition, declare war on France.

The news was taken to America by Silas Deane's son, Simon. Washington passed on the information to La Fayette, who, intoxicated by success, kissed him on both cheeks, embarrassing the reserved general. But the great man smiled kindly at La Fayette and complimented him. "You have done more than anybody," he said, "to bring about this great event." That was true. Gilbert rejoiced when he saw the note sent by the French to the British government, with its explanation: "The Americans having become independent as a result of their declaration of July 4, 1776. . . ." "That," he said, "is a principle of national sovereignty of which the French will some day be reminded."

The days that followed were days of celebration, of banquets and bonfires in the American camp. Gilbert added the white sash of the House of France to his American uniform. He fully realized the importance of the role he had played. Unluckily, the blazing glory of his happiness was obscured by a tragic piece of news which reached him by the same post: his elder daughter, Henriette, had died after a long illness, as had also little Adrien, the son of Louise de Noailles. He wrote to Adrienne, whose distress he could imagine only too well.

VALLEY FORGE, JUNE 16, 1778

How monstrous it is to be at such a distance from you! Never have I felt so cruelly how horrible this situation is. My heart is oppressed with misery, and with yours which I am not there to share. The immense stretch of time which it took to apprise me of what has occurred makes everything worse. Think, dear heart, how terrible it is that while weeping for what I have lost, I should have to tremble for what is still left to me!... The distance which separates Europe from America seems to me vaster than ever. The loss of our unhappy child is scarcely ever absent from my mind. . . .

Had the news reached me at once I should have left immediately to join you, but that relating to the treaty, which arrived on May 1, prevented me. The campaign then about to open made it impossible for me to leave, to say nothing of the fact that my heart has ever been convinced that in serving the cause of America I am fighting in the interest of France. Another reason, my heart, for my staying here a while longer, is that the English commissioners have arrived and I am conveniently placed to be within easy reach of the negotiations.[2]

It is easy to understand that he should not have wanted to return home at a time when circumstances were giving him so fine a part to play. Ever a dreamer, he was formulating plans far more extensive than he could carry through with the means at his disposal. Why should he not move northward at the head of an American army and reconquer Canada? Or, if he were given a few ships, attack the English in the West Indies? He suggested to the Prince de Poix that they should join together in equipping a vessel of war. Washington, both prudent and shrewd, was never churlish in his refusals. He was fond of La Fayette; indeed, without the dashing temerity of that young man the French alliance would never have materialized. So he gave him his head, feeling convinced that the pressure of events would serve to calm the colt who was proving so restive between the shafts.

Circumstances showed his wisdom. The expedition to the West Indies was soon forgotten, and the Canadian project turned out to be impossible for lack of an adequate army. La Fayette was dismayed. He had sent word to France that great matters were in preparation.

How I fear they will laugh at us [he wrote Washington]. . . . I confess my dear general, that I cannot control my feelings when my reputation and my glory are in question.[3]

Washington consoled him and declared that the blot upon his honor existed only in his imagination. Moreover, in July, 1778, a French fleet under the command of the Comte d'Estaing dropped anchor at the mouth of the Delaware. Charles d'Estaing was an Auvergnat and, like La Fayette, a liberal. Gilbert, filled with enthusiasm at seeing his compatriots disembark, was not a little uneasy at the prospect of the coming interview. He had left France in defiance of the king's orders. How would a French admiral receive him? He went on board, his heart pounding with happiness and anxiety. No sooner did he step on deck than d'Estaing took him in his arms. "You," he said, "will take command of the French infantry as soon as it is landed." The young marquis was intoxicated with joy. To command both Frenchmen and Americans—that would be the realization of his dream!

But alas! problems of prestige, and so forth, are never easy to solve when nations cooperate. If things went wrong Sullivan, the American general, blamed the French; d'Estaing, the Americans. La Fayette refused to listen to a single word of criticism where the squadron was concerned, and was prepared to risk his popularity in America rather than be lacking in his patriotism as a Frenchman. Washington, ever wise and paternal, saw the danger and suggested a temporary absence in France. He wrote to La Fayette: "This winter you should pay a visit to your Court, your wife and your friends." The young general was on fire with eagerness to see his own people again. He knew how happy his presence would make the gentle Adrienne. But would it not be said that he was abandoning the Americans? Washington advised him to apply for a short period of leave only, at the end of which he would return to fight shoulder to shoulder with his comrades. During his stay in France he could render great service to the cause of the United States. Congress not only granted his request for leave but also passed a vote of congratulation to the marquis and put at his disposal a fine vessel with the symbolic name *L'Alliance*.

The voyage home was bad, with tempestuous seas and mutiny on board. La Fayette, off Newfoundland and in the throes of sea-sickness, said one day to a French friend, Pontgibaud: "A pretty state of affairs, I must say, for me, at twenty, with my name, my rank, my fortune, and having married Mademoiselle de Noailles, to come all this way just to make a meal for fishes!" But the storm died down, the mutineers were disarmed, and Gilbert began to think of the great welcome he hoped was waiting for him in France.

He was not disappointed. Aglaé d'Hunolstein continued singing his praises to Count Shuvalov:

APRIL 12, 1778

You ask me to send you word of Monsieur de La Fayette. His situation is more brilliant than ever, now that France has made treaty with the insurgents, for the whole nation, by thus imitating him, has given justification and authority to what he did. . . . He has attacked an English detachment and conducted himself like a hero. He is an object of admiration to some, of envy to others. His return, if return he does, will be an intoxicating experience for him, dearly purchased and well deserved. But of that there is no immediate prospect.[4]

While La Fayette was still at sea his trusted agent, Gérard, died. Jacques-Philippe Morizot, his young assistant, wrote to Mlle du Motier, asking that he might be given the succession. He knew La Fayette's affairs inside out, and had found "in Madame la Marquise, and other members of the family, a disposition to grant a request which would be a matter of great happiness to him." But there was one objection: he was still three months short of his legal majority. He had, however, an honest and virtuous uncle Gratte-pain who was prepared to act as La Fayette's nominal agent while

leaving all the work to Morizot. In a letter to the ladies of Chavaniac, Adrienne expressed warm approval of this arrangement.

*I find, my dear aunts, that the year [1779] is already far advanced
without my having had an opportunity of presenting my duty to
you and expressing my sincere wishes, if not for your happiness, at
least for your consolation.*

As in so many families, there was a fiction at Chavaniac that after
a sad loss—the death of Gilbert's cousin—nobody could ever be
happy again.

*And now, having spoken of these concerns of the heart, I must
revert, my dear aunts, to other matters which, though touching us
less nearly, must nonetheless be discussed. You have been apprised
of the fact that the death of Monsieur Gérard has placed us in a
position of some embarrassment. . . . You are, I believe, aware that
the late Monsieur Gérard had an assistant of the name of Morizot,
who, as you will remember, is extremely intelligent. . . .*[5]

She went on to explain, with a clarity and sense of balance worthy
of Chancellor Daguesseau himself, the pros and cons of the suggested solution. It would be a great advantage to have at their disposal somebody who was already familiar with her husband's
affairs. On the other hand, it would be a matter of some inconvenience to have to deal with an agent who was without that
personal fortune which would have made it possible for him, when
borrowing in the name of his employer, to give a guarantee for
loans. Fortunately, however, he had an uncle who possessed property
to the extent of 100,000 livres and access to all the files relating
to Gilbert's business interests. Morizot would act in everything as
his uncle's junior and on that same uncle's surety. "The uncle would
pay frequent visits to our estates." The Duc d'Ayen had consented
to the arrangement, as had also the La Rivière side of the family.
All that remained was to get the consent of the dear aunts, without
which—needless to say—nothing could be finally concluded. The
ladies of Chavaniac, put in a thoroughly good mood by so defer-
ential an approach, agreed. Morizot, duly appointed to the wished-
for position, lost no time in embarking upon a long correspondence
with Madeleine du Motier. Adrienne had won the battle for her
protégé, and never afterward had reason to regret her decision.

On February 6, 1779, *L'Alliance* sailed into the port of Brest.

French cannon saluted the American flag. In the ears of the young marquis these salvos made an agreeable sound. Two years earlier he had left his native land as a fugitive. He was now returning to it as a major general and the hero of two worlds. His own family had forgiven him, and the Duc d'Ayen had written in person to welcome him home. He was impatient to enjoy his triumph.

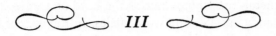

III

THE HERO'S RETURN

*The ardors of love are not so sweet as
the first glimpses of glory.*

VAUVENARGUES

At the Hôtel de Noailles nobody had a thought to spare for any-thing but the marriage of Mlle d'Épernon. She was Clotilde, third of the five sisters, now engaged to the Marquis du Roure.* The nest of doves was in a state of gentle flutter. No one was expecting La Fayette: there had been no announcement of his impending re-turn. Though he was in a hurry to see Adrienne again and to make the acquaintance of his daughter Anastasie, he considered it his duty to pay a formal call on the ministers at Versailles before doing anything else. He had dispatches for them from America and plans to lay before them. The statesman must precede the husband and the father. Gilbert took himself seriously, and it must be admitted that he had good reason to do so.

It was two years since that day in February, 1777, when, passing through Paris after a stay in London, he had announced to his Noailles brother-in-law that he was about to take ship for America. At that time Gilbert was generally regarded as a shy young man, and he felt, rightly or wrongly, that he was to some extent bullied by

---

* Françoise-Antoinette-Clotilde de Noailles, Mlle d'Épernon, married, on November 28, 1779, Scipion de Grimoard de Beauvoir, Marquis du Roure. The marriage was brief and childless. Widowed in 1782 at the age of nineteen, Clotilde married, in 1784, the Vicomte de Thésan, by whom she had two children.

his overpowerful family by marriage. Now here he was back again, a major general, the ambassador of the head of a state, a man who had commanded armies and won battles. In the eyes of his former companions Noailles, Ségur, and even Poix (who had once been his colonel), he was a great man and a hero. They felt no jealousy: they admired his daring, his success, and were on fire to follow in his footsteps.

Gilbert knew that his arrival would cause a sensation, and the idea of making a triumphal entry into a ballroom filled with the prettiest women in the kingdom was far from unpleasant. Accordingly, he sent his aide-de-camp on to Paris with orders to deliver the instructions of Congress to the American commissioners while he broke his journey at Versailles. Perhaps he thought it only good manners on his part to wait upon the king, whose orders he had flouted two years previously, and ask to be pardoned. That he would be, he did not doubt.

He spent that night in the house of the "petit Poix." Next morning the first minister, Maurepas, received him. What with the young man's stories of America, messages from Washington, and La Fayette's plans for an expedition against Canada, there was more than enough material for a long conversation, and even the frivolous-minded Maurepas was interested in listening to somebody who had seen so much. La Fayette asked for an audience with the king. But the dignity of the crown demanded that the rebellious subject should first be mildly castigated before the hero could receive the compliments of royalty. He was ordered to go at once to the Hôtel de Noailles and to consider himself under arrest. His own grandfather-in-law would be his jailer, and he would be allowed to see only members of his family—in other words, the whole court.

Mme d'Ayen, informed during the morning of Gilbert's arrival, used all that delicate tact of which she was a mistress to prepare the unsuspecting Adrienne for her impending happiness. This preliminary step was very necessary, since the young mother, abandoned without warning, had suffered in her dignity as a woman and in her feelings as a mother, having just brought a child into the world and witnessed the death of her first-born daughter at a time when Gilbert was not with her to share either the happiness or the grief. She felt no resentment but, on the contrary, a dangerous adoration which she could not keep from passionately exhibiting, though wisdom would have counseled some degree of reserve.

It must be admitted that her husband had given her every reason to be proud of him. Before his departure he had been ill at ease and taciturn. His dominant feeling had been a longing for the approval of others, and the consciousness of a pride that had no sufficient basis. So long as these two profound needs of his being remained unsatisfied they had merely had a depressing effect upon him. Washington had made an admirable diagnosis of the trouble: "Your lack of confidence," he had said, "is the result of an unusually acute sensitivity where your reputation is concerned." Now, in February, 1779, the young man's hopes had been fulfilled. Two worlds were at his feet, and he showed a new and easy self-confidence.

For Adrienne, the ten days of "house arrest" were ten days of happiness. She had her husband to herself. The family (it amounted to a whole tribe) crowded the Rue Saint-Honoré in the hope of seeing and hearing the "visibly concealed hero," as Mme du Deffand described him. It was necessary, too, to inform the other —the Chavaniac—family. On Adrienne fell the responsibility of writing to the aunts:

My joy is easy to credit, but impossible to describe. . . . Monsieur de La Fayette has come back to me as modest and as charming as when he went away. . . . Just for the moment he is in disgrace with the king and is forbidden to show himself in any public place. God has preserved, in the midst of tremendous dangers, the most lovable person in all the world. . . . When I reflect on my good fortune in being his wife, I am truly grateful to God. The knowledge that I am very far from being as good and gracious as he is makes me sad, and then I hope that my affection may make up for my shortcomings.[1]

A woman in love can find no better confidante than the aunt, who combines maternal feelings with a generous admiration for the man she adores. Adrienne was wrong in thinking herself less "good and gracious." This letter alone is enough to prove the contrary. Her intelligence, though less bubbling with projects than Gilbert's, was a great deal more reliable. Strong in her humble submission to God, she gave vanity no opportunity to establish a hold on her. It was true that La Fayette, reassured by success, could be very charming. He now had agreeable manners and the brilliance of talk of those who have plenty to say, as well as an aura of chivalry. All through his life even his enemies had to admit that he possessed, as Sainte-Beuve noted, "a sensitive and polished intelligence, and anecdotal and often racy gift of conversation, and, when he was in the company of his intimates, a lively and unaffected power of describing the famous persons he had met."

The Maréchal de Noailles and the Duc d'Ayen between them drafted the petition in which the marquis-general appealed for the royal pardon. This was no easy task, for care had to be taken not to offend His Majesty and to avoid ruffling the touchy suscepti- bilities of the offending subject. Their son-in-law gave them a good deal of trouble but also an increased sense of importance. With his collaboration they succeeded in producing a masterpiece of dignified submission:

Love of my country, a strong desire to see her enemies discomfited, a political instinct which the recent treaty would seem to justify, those, Sire, are the reasons which decided me to play a part in aiding the American cause. When I received the orders of Your Majesty, I attributed them more to the solicitations of my family than to the formal relations then existing between ourselves and England. . . . The nature of my misconduct leads me to hope that I may be able to efface it. It will be to the goodness of Your Majesty that I shall be indebted for the happiness of cleansing myself from the strain left upon me, by whatever means Your Majesty may graciously afford me of serving you in any country and in any manner.[2]

Some days later [La Fayette recounted] I wrote to the king ac- knowledging my fortunate fault. He allowed me to go to receive a gentle reprimand, and while restoring me my liberty, advised me to avoid those places where the public might acclaim my disobedience. On my arrival, I had the honor to be consulted by all the ministers, and, better still, was embraced by all the ladies. The kisses ceased on the next day, but for a long time I enjoyed the confidence of the Cabinet. I lived at Versailles in the royal favor, and in Paris I was regarded as a celebrity.[3]

Even the queen, who had not hitherto shown much apprecia- tion, received Gilbert affably and used her influence to obtain per- mission for him to purchase from the Marquis de Créquy the regiment of the King's Dragoons, which cost him 80,000 livres and gave him the rank of colonel. This rapid promotion in the French army caused much jealousy. Many wild stories went around. For instance, it was said that the queen in her eagerness had gone downstairs to meet him. This was entirely untrue. The queen praised his courage, recognized the value of his work, but had little personal liking for him.

The Comtesse d'Hunolstein, on the other hand, flaunted this squire of dames who had now become so flattering an appendage. To her Russian correspondent she wrote:

Here, for the past five weeks, we have had the honorable General-Marquis de La Fayette. He has conducted himself with such distinction and nobility, and has made himself so much beloved in America, that the temerity and courage betokened by his departure is now the thing least spoken of. He has won universal approval and his vanity must be greatly pleased. I see him frequently, and consider myself happy to have earned some part of his esteem. He has asked me to speak to you of him.[4]

Women have a taste for heroes: they are not only the weary warrior's repose, but also his reward.

Adrienne, his legitimate partner, had her share in the public tributes rendered to him, and, in spite of her modesty, could not but be happy at receiving as much praise as once there had been blame. On one occasion, when they went to the Comédie Française to see a play by Rochon de Chabannes, the author added a few lines in La Fayette's honor:

Behold this youthful courtier, your age, or thereabouts,
Abandoning while new the joys of wedded bliss,
Th' delights of life at court, Parisian gaiety and routs,
His mind and soul inflamed, burning for naught but fame,
Hastening to seek it in another hemisphere,
Then, seeing the war clouds o'er his homeland hovering,
His love of country, his honor without stain
Prevail, and thus restore a doughty vassal to his king.

The audience applauded loudly, and the marquis had his part in the ovation. This incident made the Duc de Chartres ridiculously angry. As the acknowledged lover of Aglaé d'Hunolstein, he resented the homage rendered to the rival about whom she had once laughed with him but whom she now seemed to regard with favor.

The Prince de Ligne, another of Mme d'Hunolstein's admirers, considered her the prettiest woman in Paris but had few illusions about her feelings. He told how once, when she took him shopping with her, she pretended to have forgotten her purse and made him pay for everything she bought. He added that La Fayette, "the same lady's lover, but in quite a different way" (meaning that he was successful), had confessed that the same thing had happened to him. The Prince de Ligne found it very difficult to understand that any woman could be in love with "so wishy-washy a creature as La Fayette, null in mind, body, face, and disposition." The only explanation he could find was that "an excessive amount of noise has been made over a few wretched little skirmishes in America." It is never easy to be fair to a rival.

The hero, now a statesman and a strategist, frequently absented himself from the charming wife with whom he had only just been reunited, to spend long hours closeted with the ministers of the crown. Young though he was, his two years in America had turned him into an expert, and Vergennes, no less than Maurepas, consulted him. His plan for an armed landing in Canada did not appeal to the French government. Why conquer new lands which would eventually link up with the Americans? La Fayette then suggested that two ships should be entrusted to the famous American privateer, John Paul Jones. These would carry a small force of soldiers with which he, La Fayette, would carry out a number of raids on English ports. "Why not?"

The navy was already busy assembling a flotilla at Lorient. Secrecy was essential, but the constant comings and goings of La Fayette between Paris and Versailles, and his interviews with Franklin and Vergennes, soon drew the attention of the gossip-writers. It was said that he was to command an expedition to the United States. In the salons which he frequented with Adrienne, efforts were made to pump him. The Duc de Croÿ was impressed by his modesty, discretion, and simplicity. Even the queen, who kept her ear to the ground where public affairs were concerned and passed on what she found out to her mother, the Empress Maria-Theresa, could get nothing out of Gilbert. He excused himself by saying that he had "promised Monsieur de Maurepas not to say anything." Marie-Antoinette was incensed, and felt her hidden antipathy for the young man increasing.

Suddenly he received orders to join his regiment, the King's Dragoons, at Saint-Jean-d'Angély. What a tedious business for a man who had commanded soldiers in the field to have to take part in summer maneuvers! But perhaps this moving from the capital of an officer who was too much in the public eye meant that an expedition was being prepared. That was what the court said— and what La Fayette hoped. He found consolation in writing to his general, his *only* general, about Adrienne:

I have a wife, my dear general, who dotes on you, and her feelings seem to me to be so well justified that I can raise no objection. She begs you to accept her compliments and to offer the same to Madame Washington.[5]

It was true that La Fayette had so lauded his "great man" at the Hôtel de Noailles that the Duchesse d'Ayen and her five daughters now worshiped at the same altar.

The homecoming of heroes is apt to be fruitful. Adrienne was once again with child, happy at the prospect of having another and hoping it would be a son. She had a few days with her husband when he passed through Paris and Versailles on his way to Le Havre, where he had been appointed assistant quartermaster-general to the army which was being secretly prepared for the invasion of England. He spent ten days in Paris, working with Franklin and Vergennes, who was no longer opposed to the idea of sending an expeditionary force to the United States. For the Fourth of July, the anniversary of the declaration of American independence, La Fayette, who had a flair for publicity, had arranged for a portrait of Washington to be exhibited at Franklin's house. Washington was shown holding in his hand the Franco-American treaty of alliance and trampling under foot the proclamations of George III. Unfortunately, by the time the Fourth of July came around, La Fayette had had to return to his duties at Le Havre. Adrienne deputized for him with her customary dignity and was treated by the small American colony with the honor due the wife of the hero. The following lines were written for the occasion:

I limned for you the hero, La Fayette;
Now let me sketch his better half, his wife:
Imagine Kindliness and Love and Virtue in one person met—
And there's the portrait finished, true to life.[6]

The preparations for an expedition, plans for which were constantly changing, kept La Fayette for a long time on the Normandy coast. Adrienne was far from well. The effect of the shocks she had already undergone, of her anxieties about the future, and of a difficult pregnancy had undermined her health. She felt too great an admiration of Gilbert not to approve his projects, and loved him too much not to tremble for his safety. Did she believe in the cause for which he was fighting? What precisely was the political doctrine in which he had instructed her? He could scarcely be called a wholehearted republican. Experience had taught him the drawbacks of democratic government: rifts, delays, indiscretions. But in his eyes Washington had become the ideal of what the head of a state should be. The American way of life had confirmed him in his love of freedom and equality—two ideas Adrienne found easy to accept, for she had been brought up by a mother who had imbued her with feelings of respect for her fellowmen, and had practiced what she preached.

Adrienne was now nineteen. She was growing into a woman. As she herself was to say later at a tragic and solemn moment of her life, she loved her husband not only because it was her duty to do so and because she admired him, but "voluptuously" as well. Whenever he returned to her unexpectedly, she came close to swooning. The self-denial with which she spared him all jealousy brought its own reward. A closer intimacy from now on made her a partner in all his plans for the future. He welcomed this complete agreement between them. He never wrote to Washington without talking of his wife, and Washington—always gallant—replied on one occasion:

WEST POINT, SEPTEMBER 30, 1779
Tell her (if you have not made a mistake and offered your own love instead of hers to me) that I have a heart susceptable of the tenderest passion, and that it is already so strongly impressed with the most favourable ideas of her, that she must be cautious of putting loves torch to it; as you must be in fanning the flame.[7]

Gallantry of a Southern gentleman, no doubt. But he assured La Fayette that if he returned to America, whether at the head of a force of courageous Frenchmen, whether as a major general in the American army, or—when peace had been signed—as a friend and old comrade-in-arms, he would always be made welcome in the modest cottage so different from his own sumptuous dwellings: ". . . and if the lovely partner of your happiness will consent to participate with *us* in such rural entertainment and amusements, I can undertake in behalf of Mrs. Washington that she will do everything in her power to make Virginia agreeable to the Marchioness." [8]

In August Gilbert went to Paris and had a further interview with Maurepas. He insisted on being given a detachment of two thousand men for the purpose of harassing the English. Had he sufficient experience of war? More, certainly, than most general officers! Chance and his own merits had brought him, at the age of twenty, to positions of command reserved as a rule for field marshals. It was not as the grandson of the Maréchal de Noailles that he was now asking to be employed:

I am not a man of the court party, still less a courtier. I beg the king's ministers to regard me as a product of the guardroom.[9]

His tenacity amused the skeptical Maurepas, who said with a laugh that this young man was perfectly capable of stripping Versailles bare if it would help him to go to the aid of the Americans. He was not far wrong.

On Christmas Eve, at Passy, Adrienne gave birth to a son. Gilbert was in Paris, deep in political discussion. She scribbled a short note to him:

Accept my congratulations, Monsieur le Marquis. They are very sincere, and very deeply felt. America will put up illuminations, and, in my opinion, Paris should too. The number of those who resemble you is so small that any addition to their ranks is a public service.[10]

Though it was two o'clock in the morning when Gilbert received the news, he wanted to give it at once to Franklin and to tell him that the boy would be christened George-Washington "as a tribute of respect and affection to my dear friend, General Washington."

Adrienne in her note had urged him to indulge for a time in the joys of fatherhood: "They are so sweet that nothing else is near so good." She had endured some months of suffering in order to give him this son, and had a right to his presence. Had he not written to her from America: "Once we are reunited nobody shall ever part us again"? He spent a week with her, then resumed the round of correspondence and visits.

He had obtained 15,000 muskets and the powder for them for the American army. He wanted something more: an expeditionary force and the honor of commanding it. This, he said, had nothing to do with personal ambition. He knew English, he was conversant with American ways, he was the only French leader for whom no problems of precedence would arise in America. At last a solution was agreed upon. He should go back to the United States, secretly announce the imminent arrival of an army, and resume his American command. The Comte de Rochambeau, an old soldier of great experience, would command the expeditionary force.

La Fayette accepted this disappointment without bitterness. The cause was carrying all before it, and that was what really mattered. The immediate necessity was to arrange for his departure and to raise money. That was up to young Morizot, who was a devoted colleague but not a little scared. He had found the Breton estates in a bad way. The absent master was being fleeced on every side. Morizot had restored order and got some of the rents in, but he wrote to Mlle du Motier: "I am in an acute state of embarrassment. The more I take these debts in hand, the more they grow! If only your nephew could be more economical in America." Economical in America! La Fayette was prepared to equip a whole division at his own expense. For this new trip he needed ready money and demanded 120,000 livres. Morizot would have to sell land. He was given full power of attorney by La Fayette. If he were in any doubt what to do he must consult the marquise, whose decision should be absolute. This was a great mark of confidence, fully justified by the young woman's intelligence and sense of responsibility. Morizot warned the marquis that he was purchasing glory at the expense of his fortune. Gilbert was of the opinion that glory was beyond price, and his wife agreed.

Early in 1780 he was ordered to proceed to America to make arrangements for the arrival of the French troops. The government put at his disposal the frigate *Hermione*, commanded by Captain La Touche-Tréville, who was instructed to carry the marquis to Boston and to treat him with the greatest consideration. The promised army was to consist of 6000 men, but as things turned out only 4000 sailed. However, La Fayette knew that the most brilliant young men about the court—Noailles, Ségur, Lauzun—would be with them. This convinced him that the force, though small in number, would be kept well supplied, and that when the

moment came a fleet would assure him the mastery of the sea—
which, in his eyes (and he was perfectly right) was the essential
point. The approaching departure of Noailles and Ségur and the
more immediate one of La Fayette plunged the Hôtel de Noailles
in gloom. The doves, struck to the heart by misgivings, fluttered
their wings.

On February 20 he put on the blue, white, and gold uniform of
an American major general and went to Versailles to take his leave
of the king and queen. The queen in particular showed a marked
affability and expressed her confidence in the influence La Fayette
would exercise on the furthering of the common cause. Gilbert
returned on March 4 and 5 to receive his orders from the ministers,
went back to Paris to embrace his wife and children, and finally,
on March 6, left for Rochefort. In the course of this short journey
he wrote to Adrienne from each stagehouse.

ÉTAMPES, TEN O'CLOCK

*I have stopped here for a moment, my dear heart, to say how sad I
am at leaving you, how much I love you, how much my happiness
depends on you, and how touched I am by your affliction. Ah, my
dear heart, well though I knew my feelings for you, I could never
have imagined that leaving you would cost me so dear or that this
parting would be so cruel a desolation! Love me, take care of yourself, and be assured that I love you to distraction.*

*My compliments to Mamma, to the vicomtesse, to my sisters, and
to the Comtesse Auguste.**

SAINTE-MAURE, WEDNESDAY MORNING

*I slept here last night, my dear heart, to get some rest for myself and
my people, and the few hours of sleep have much benefited us. I
hope to be at Rochefort tomorrow morning, from which place I will
write to you as soon as I arrive. Yesterday I met Monsieur Gérard* †

* The reference is to the Comtesse de La Marck, later Princesse Auguste d'Arenberg. Born Marie-Françoise-Augustine-Ursule le Danois de Cernay, daughter of Lieutenant General the Marquis de Cernay, she had married on November 23, 1774,
Auguste-Marie-Raymond d'Arenberg (1753–1833), to whom his maternal grandfather, the last Comte de La Marck, had left, together with his title, the regiment in
the French service which was his own personal property. An intimate friend of
Adrienne and a frequent visitor to the Hôtel de Noailles, she was always referred to
in La Fayette's letters as the Comtesse Auguste.

† Conrad-Alexandre Gérard, Louis XVI's first envoy to Philadelphia. This diplomat
had asked to be recalled for reasons of health. He was succeeded as French minister
to the United States by the Chevalier de La Luzerne.

with whom I had some talk about America. You will perhaps be pleased to see him, in which case I beg of you to show him much civility because he overwhelmed me with kindnesses at Philadelphia. From what he tells me, I am more than ever sure that I am regarded there with the friendliest feelings. . . . Good-by, my dear heart, I embrace you. It costs me much pain to think that each step carries me still further from her who is my happiness and my delight, whom I have made so unhappy in spite of the lively affection I have for her.

ROCHEFORT, MARCH 10

I have been here at Rochefort since yesterday, my dear heart, and this morning shall board the frigate. We shall not, however, sail immediately, and certain arrangements may occasion us a brief delay. I am extremely well satisfied with Monsieur de La Touche: he is a man of the most exquisite politeness and I shall pass the time agreeably with him. The wind is setting in the right quarter, and I am filled with hope that we shall have superb weather. . . . The moment when I set foot in the longboat will bring me a foretaste of the terrible pang which I shall feel when I look my last upon the land! My health is very good, dear heart. I beg you to have a care of your own in the name of all the love I bear you, and in that of the delight I find in knowing that to you I owe all the charm of the most delicious of homes, and that I am tied to you by the sweetest of bonds. Good-by, my dear heart. I am about to get into the longboat. Though this farewell is not the last, it is a terrible grief for me to speak it.

My compliments to my dear prince. I shall write to him tomorrow, as also to Madame de Tessé, to whom I ask you to give a thousand affectionate greetings.[11]

On March 12 La Fayette wrote to his cousin the Prince de Poix, announcing his approaching departure and asking him to deliver into the hands of Marie-Antoinette a letter from him. "I send you with this a letter for the queen. Give it to her yourself, and explain that I have yielded to the temptation of a wish to write to her, but that, not knowing how far I have the right to do so, shall not again take that liberty." Then he added:

I have a somewhat unusual favor to ask of you, and that is to buy for me a piece of blue material—the blue of summer skies—soft leather or vicuna, dyed, or French linen. But it must be of the finest stuff to be found anywhere. The price does not matter, because I want

to give the Americans a sample of our manufactures that will aston-
ish them.

Could you not find for me a tea set like the one Madame de
Boufflers has, with this difference, that the porcelain must be of the
finest white Sévres and the spoons silver-gilt. I wish to make a gift
of it to Madame Washington.[12]

Adrienne, sad and abandoned, had at least the satisfaction of
receiving many affectionate letters of farewell.

ON BOARD *Hermione,* MARCH 13, 9 O'CLOCK AT NIGHT

This, my dear heart, is in very truth a cruel, an agonizing, moment,
as I sit down to write to you. Our sails are spread, and now, about to
send to you my last farewells, I must confess that emotion forbids
me to write reasonably. I know that I shall soon lose sight of the land
which holds all that is most dear to me, and that by tomorrow it will
have become invisible. My heart, I would have you truly believe that
going from you is a cruel torment! You must not feel concern about
my crossing: our frigate flies over the waves; she is commanded by
a most charming man; I am as comfortably lodged as it is possible
to be, and there can be no doubt that I shall arrive. As soon as I
reach Boston I shall write to you, dear heart. Think only that my
absence will be no longer than it would have been had I set off upon
an ordinary campaign—a matter of a few months only—and that
I shall be home again in time to spend the winter with you. Be careful, if you love me, of your health. Write to me often: you will have
many opportunities.... Look often at my portrait, for it will tell
you a part at least of what I feel. My heart is deeply troubled, but
I do not wish to add to your affliction by painting a picture of my
own. Farewell, farewell, dear heart. Give a thousand thousand kisses
to our darling Anastasie, and kiss our other child for me. Oh, happy
they to have you there to see. Must it always be, dear heart, that I
to whom you give such happiness must always make you sad by absence? Forgive me: the pain I feel is punishment enough....

At this moment I feel I love you more than I could have believed
possible.

OFF THE ÎLE D'AIX, MARCH 18

Here we are back again, dear heart, having been forced to return to
Rochefort as a result of losing our mainyard. The accident occurred

when we had been at sea but one day and a night, and since fog con-
cealed the land we could not make the harbor immediately. . . .

ON BOARD *Hermione,* MARCH 20

You may rest assured that I shall have a pleasant journey—if the
word pleasant may be used of my present situation. . . . Our frigate
is astonishingly seaworthy, and capable of making good speed. Mon-
sieur de La Touche has again issued orders to give a clear berth to
any sails which may be sighted, and to stear straight for the nearest
American port. . . . The first spasms of seasickness are now over. . . .
Weather and sea are superb.[13]

It was not until March 20 that the *Hermione,* having completed
all her repairs, was able to steer a course for America. Adrienne,
in spite of her courage, was for some days in a state of almost complete collapse. Her husband had become dearer to her than ever,
and now once more she had to fear for his life. Then she did as
the Duchesse d'Ayen advised and placed herself entirely in the
hands of God. "Hope is a duty," said Mme d'Ayen. On March 25
Morizot wrote to Mlle du Motier at Chavaniac

that A. has become somewhat calmer. She hopes that Providence
will keep him from all harm. Everybody shares that hope. There is
probably not a single man in Paris who would not consider himself
happy to make some sacrifice for your nephew. It is much to his
credit that at so early an age he should have gained the confidence
of all.[14]

Rarely has so young a couple borne such a heavy weight of responsibility.

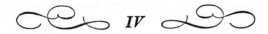

ALL'S WELL THAT ENDS WELL

> *Though women have not the same op-*
> *portunities of showing courage, they*
> *must have it none the less.* FÉNELON

Waiting for news of a husband exposed to the dangers of a sea
voyage and the accidents of war was a painful experience in an
age when letters could scarcely be expected to arrive from America
in less than three months. Adrienne had made a slow recovery from
childbirth and was still far from well. Her baby was put out to nurse
at Versailles, and since his mother could not face the necessary
journey, it was his grandmother who lavished on little George-
Washington the care and attention without which he would probably not have survived.

But at last news began to come from across the Atlantic. Gilbert
had landed at Boston on April 28, receiving an enthusiastic welcome
from the inhabitants. He had found time to write several letters,
including one to Washington announcing his return and one to
his wife to set her mind at rest about his journey.

WATERTOWN, MAY 2, 1780

I am so surrounded by friends, dear heart, so overwhelmed with at-
tentions and the evidences of good will, that I have scarce a moment
to myself. I shall take every opportunity to write, but, for the mo-
ment, will say no more than that I am in good health and that, after
thirty-eight days on the ocean, am safely come to Boston. It is im-

possible for me to describe the welcome with which the people here have honored me, and it would be still more difficult for me to express the gratitude I feel....

The English are attacking Charleston. General Washington is still in Jersey, and I am on my way to join him. In truth, dear heart, all that I have experienced here more than justifies my love for America.[1]

Four days later he wrote Adrienne at great length about his arrival:

... the marks of good will that have been showered upon me cannot be described without something of that pomposity for which I have little liking. Nevertheless, dear heart, since this opportunity seems reasonably safe, I will, under the seal of secrecy, be somewhat more of a chatterbox than usual....

My arrival was made known by the men who went in search of a pilot. It was afternoon before I landed. There was an immense crowd, and I was welcomed with a salute of guns, with the ringing of all the church bells, with a band marching ahead, and with cheering from the assembled multitude. It was in this way that I was conducted to the house which the Council and the Assembly of Representatives of Boston had had made ready for me. A deputation from these two bodies received me. I asked to be presented to the two chambers there assembled, and tried to remember my English during the hour I spent there. In the evening a great crowd gathered in front of my door, where a great bonfire had been built, and the acclamations lasted until after midnight. When I left Boston all the people of the place crowded in front of the house to await the moment of my departure, and there was no manifestation of kindliness and affection that this immense concourse did not lavish on me, accompanying me beyond the town. In every place through which I passed on my way here I was shown the greatest kindness, and my arrival and departure were hailed with gunfire. The leading personages rode with me on horseback: in short, the reception accorded me has been beyond anything I can describe. But do not, I beg of you, show this letter to anybody. If I have wished in some degree to justify the wrong of which I have been guilty in leaving you, I should be very vexed were it said that I wished to send my friends descriptions of my welcome....

Do not read to anyone that part of my letter in which I speak of my arrival. Should, however, my friends press you for details on this matter, you have my leave, after swearing them to secrecy, to read what I have said to the little family group which dines every day at the Hôtel de Noailles—Madame de Tessé, Monsieur le Duc d'Ayen, Monsieur de Mun, Madame de Boufflers, the widow, Monsieur de Poix, and Madame d'Hénin.[2]

There is something charmingly ingenuous about this modified modesty. He begins by breaking the seal of secrecy regarding his triumphs only in favor of his wife, then extends the privilege to include the family circle.

In July, 1780, the French expeditionary force under Rochambeau arrived at Newport, Rhode Island. Sent there by Washington, Gilbert met his brother-in-law Noailles and his friends Lauzun, Custine, Damas, and Montmorency. Ségur was with another section. Washington asked Rochambeau to make all necessary arrangements with the young major general. This was a role Gilbert found enchanting, though Rochambeau found it a great deal less so. He was fifty-five years old, had fought in more than one war, and had agreed to serve under Washington. To receive his orders through a mere boy went very much against the grain. He was fond of the "little marquis," but spoke to him more as a father to his son than as one general to another. "The warmth of your feelings," he told Gilbert with devastating frankness, "has to some extent affected the soundness of your judgment." La Fayette was all in favor of taking New York. To this suggestion Rochambeau replied: "We can do nothing unless we have command of the sea," and he insisted on a conference with Washington. The two generals were in complete agreement on the necessity of asking the French king for a fleet and for additional troops.

LA FAYETTE TO THE PRINCE DE POIX: IN THE CAMP OF THE LIGHT DIVISION, CLOSE TO THE ISLAND OF NEW YORK, SEPTEMBER 3, 1780
The fine appearance of the French troops, their honesty and admirable discipline have made a tremendous impression on the Americans. It would be impossible to behave better than do our compatriots. Their general will find it easy to work in harmony with the generalissimo, who for his part will, I assure you, issue no orders but such as are agreeable to the French and have been agreed upon in advance with Monsieur de Rochambeau. You will ask me what all this amounts to, and my reply will be that they are awaiting at

Newport the arrival of the second division and the establishment of our supremacy at sea.

My own command is all I could desire. It is composed of about two thousand men of the light infantry, drawn from different regiments, like the grenadiers and chasseurs in Europe, and led, under me, by two brigadiers; a hundred riflemen—a sort of half-wild trappers; and a legion of three hundred men, half infantry, half cavalry. These two thousand four hundred make up a mobile column, moving always in advance and independently of the main body.[3]

In Paris Louise and Adrienne were now waiting with the same impatience for the arrival of letters. The fact that their husbands were comrades-in-arms added a new bond to those which already united the two sisters. The third of the married trio, Clotilde du Roure, was not happy. Poor health and her husband's indifference were bringing to nothing the hopes the Duchesse d'Ayen had been building on the match. However, the duchesse had the satisfaction of knowing that the fourth fledgling in the nest, Pauline, had been completely cured, since the date of her first communion, of every trace of the violent nature that had been so frightening when she was a child. Mme d'Ayen remained deeply attached to her sister-in-law, Mme de Tessé. They were a well-matched pair. They appreciated each other's qualities and were linked by genuine affection. But Mme de Tessé moved in a very different world, composed mainly of "philosophers," and the consequent lack of harmony between the two women—one so devout, the other an unbeliever—made any real intimacy impossible. Mme d'Ayen's only close friends were her daughters.

La Fayette, for his part, was on the best of terms with Mme de Tessé, whom he called "cousin." He strove to mobilize her influence in support of the Americans:

Without ships [he wrote] we can do no more than wait for the enemy to strike . . . and that makes our business here as tedious as a war in Europe. . . . Moreover, while we wait, our condition is one of such frugality, poverty, and nakedness that I hope it may be taken into account in the next world and credited unto us as a substitute for Purgatory.[4]

Frugality, poverty, and nakedness were also part of the picture he painted for Adrienne: "We Americans are not, like French headquarters at Newport, faring sumptuously. It is from the people—our sole master—that we republicans must demand the means to continue the war."

IN CAMP, NEAR TATAWA, OCTOBER 13, 1780

To console me for the ships that do not come, there are many, my dear heart, ready to leave. The first of my pleasures in America is to receive your letters, the second to send you my news and to tell you again and again how much I love you. I am confident I need not fear being tedious, so I intend to scribble away as often as there are persons prepared to take charge of what I write.

I will begin with a duplicate of my news sheet. The French army is at Rhode Island, from which it has not moved. Monsieur de Ternay's squadron is there also, blockaded in the harbor. Admiral Rodney is lying off the coast with nineteen ships of the line, to say nothing of those of fifty [guns] and a multitude of frigates. Our army in Carolina under General Gates has been given a fine drubbing. That commanded by General Washington in person has spent the summer not far from New York and, thanks to the efforts made by the states, from June onward we have been in a position to offer battle to General Clinton, which offer he has not accepted.

On our way back from Hartford, where General Washington and I had had a conference with the French generals, we discovered, as the result of a lucky chance, the existence of a conspiracy which would have delivered West Point into the enemy's hands and might well have resulted in our being carried as prisoners to New York. The traitor, General Arnold, fled to the enemy, and the adjutant general of the English army has been hanged as a spy.... General Washington's main body is preceded by a mobile column, made up of the best men we have and commanded by me.

There exists a perfect understanding between the Americans and the French, who appear to be altogether contented with the generalissimo. I do not know when the troops of the two nations will be combined under his orders, but I am sure that they will work together in complete harmony. It seems likely that the English will send a force southward in the hope of pressing their advantage in those parts. Our naval situation being what it is, I need scarcely tell you that any offensive operations on our part would be difficult, and that it is enough for us to know where the English are, to see what must be done to seek them out with advantage. So you see, my dear *heart, that my part in this campaign has not been dangerous, but I have done a great deal of talking and scribbling, and have been engaged in a deal of journeying. If the Duc d'Ayen does not receive the letter which I have just dispatched to him by a first-rate frigate, I beg you to communicate to him the contents of my journal.*

I am writing to my charming sisters, and am sending the vicomtesse news of her husband, who is loved and esteemed by all at Rhode Island, though he is suffering terribly from boredom. His reputation stands very high with both the French and the Americans. . . .

It seems a thousand years, dear heart, since I had any news from you or heard anything about my children. Give them a thousand thousand kisses from me, and tell Anastasie not to forget me, because I love her with all my heart. As to our poor little George, I can scarcely expect him to know anything about me. Present my compliments to Monsieur le Maréchal de Noailles. I wrote to him two days ago, and spoke about his trees. A thousand compliments to all my friends of both sexes. Embrace the Comtesse Auguste from me, likewise Madame de Fronsac and my aunt Ségur. I have written to her husband and to many of my friends. My letters have been divided between two ships which are sailing at the same time. Give my news to my aunts.

Farewell, farewell, dear heart. When shall I be permitted never to use that word except with the certainty of seeing you the moment after? When shall I be able to give you a thousand thousand kisses, and to assure you of a love which no words of mine can sufficiently express, and which few hearts are capable of feeling so intensely? [5]

The American campaign was in the doldrums: in France the war of competing influences was at its height. Since an offensive against the English was impossible, an offensive against the ministers was being mounted instead. There was a flood of pamphlets, lampoons, and epigrams. Monsieur de Maurepas, a "philosopher" who wanted nothing but to be allowed to enjoy the good things of life in peace, did not read them. The only news from America was that brought by the Vicomte de Rochambeau, the general's eldest son. When war is at a standstill, there is nothing to be said about it. The impatient curiosity of the gossip columnists had produced nothing but such lines as:

> "What's the news, Rochambeau?"
> The king asked. "What news can you tell?"

"Sire," said he, speaking low,
"My father is doing quite well!"

Worn out by the interminable stagnation at Newport, the French officers asked to be allowed to go and see La Fayette at his headquarters. Many would gladly have served under his orders, though senior to him in the French army, but Rochambeau would not permit it. Nevertheless, Chastellux, Noailles, and Damas obtained an authorization to pay him a visit. He showed them his troops, whom they found to be better equipped than the rest of the American army—not very surprising, since La Fayette had footed the bill. Chastellux, a professional soldier, took note of the respect and affection which the marquis had inspired in his men. It was impossible not to admire the influence, both political and military, inspired by so young a man.

For Gilbert it was an intoxicating pleasure to let the friends of his youth see what real power he wielded. He seemed to feel far more satisfaction in offering them a tot of rum in a rain-soaked tent on a hill in New Jersey than he would have entertaining them in his Auvergne château. These expatriated Frenchmen, at the height of the War of Independence, talked together of Versailles, their families, their social sets. La Fayette and Noailles in particular had many confidences to exchange. In Philadelphia, where they were made much of, astonishment was expressed at their gaiety, their high spirits, and the faculty they seemed to possess of carrying France with them wherever they went.

In February, 1781, an American, Colonel Laurens, was sent by Congress to the French court on a special mission. Adrienne was asked by her husband to take him under her wing:

NEW WINDSOR, ON THE NORTH RIVER, FEBRUARY 2, 1781

He who will hand you this letter, my dear heart, is a man of whom I am very fond, and I should like you to get to know him well. . . . If I were in France, he should live for the whole of his visit under our roof. I would take him to the houses of my friends, both men and women, and do everything in my power to enable him to meet as many people as possible and to make his stay at Versailles agreeable. Introduce him to Madame d'Ayen, to the Maréchal de Mouchy, to Monsieur le Maréchal de Noailles, and treat him as a friend of the family. He will tell you all that has happened in the course of our campaign, about the situation in which we find our-

selves at present, and will give you such details as concern me....

I rely on Colonel Laurens to present you with a detailed account of the campaign.... America made great efforts last summer; she will renew them this winter, but in a more durable manner.... I trust that they will not be dissatisfied with us.[6]

When Noailles was not with him, Gilbert wrote him frequent letters. In several he discussed his attitude toward women:

CAMP WAGHAROUGH, OCTOBER 23, 1780

I hope, my dear vicomte, that our mistresses will never be so exacting as to keep us from giving female supper parties, nor we so stupid as to cancel one in the name of obedience. If I had a mistress, my feeling for her would be founded in part on the tact or the proper pride she would display in never showing herself jealous, and on the liberty I should enjoy in the matter of doing what I wished, even to the point of neglecting her without being pestered by her demands. A mistress so constituted could hold me forever—or so at least I think—if not in the bonds of a violent passion, then in those of tenderness. I have no liking for "professionals" because their stupidity is boring and their impudence productive of disgust. But provided they have my charming friends to be their lovers, their good taste can reconcile me to them.[7]

"If I had a mistress." The implication is that he did not, and we must take his word for it. All the same, among the messages he asked Colonel Laurens to deliver was one for Aglaé d'Hunolstein, nor can there be any doubt that she was the woman Gilbert referred to in another letter to his brother-in-law:

RICHMOND, MAY 22, 1781

If you are writing to France, my friend, give them my news, for there are no opportunities in this part of the world for doing so. Tell them that your poor brother is in process of taking a drubbing. I must inform you that somebody of whom I am very fond has been made the victim of a piece of spitefulness, the result of which will probably be to make her permanently unhappy, so that I shall be forced to cross swords with a certain man against whom I can only half-heartedly defend myself. But Paris society will find consolation in a song, and after all, private misfortunes do not deeply affect it. The cream of the joke is that I have to be hunted out at a distance of two thousand leagues to play the hero in the latest fashionable rumor, and a woman who is two thousand leagues removed in character from the intrigues and cabals of Paris has to act as the victim of somebody's malicious imagination. . . . Be sure to tell me, my dear brother, if you hear it spoken about jokingly or whether it is a piece of intentional malice.[8]

Apparently what had happened was that somebody had written a ballad on the subject of Gilbert's relations with Mme d'Hunolstein. Although he was full of concern for her, one cannot help thinking that, when writing to his brother-in-law, it might have occurred to him to say something about the pain caused to his own wife by the incident.

Given an important command in Virginia, La Fayette found himself facing an experienced English general, Lord Cornwallis, and the traitor Benedict Arnold. It amused Cornwallis to be opposed by such a youngster. "The *boy* cannot escape me," he said. La Fayette wrote discreetly to Noailles, saying that if he failed in this campaign he ought not to be judged too severely, since the disproportion in numbers on the two sides was immense.

But "the boy" had learned much about war. Instead of attacking Cornwallis, he retreated, feinting, until such time as he could be reinforced. When additional forces joined him, it was Cornwallis' turn to retire rapidly. Information reached La Fayette that the English had taken to their ships and were shut up in the harbor of Yorktown.

GILBERT TO ADRIENNE: AUGUST 24, 1781

The self-esteem which you do me the honor of laying to my charge has perhaps been gratified by the role I have been forced to play. You will have been hoping that no one could be equally inept in all the activities of life; but I should accuse you of a terrible access of vanity (for, since we have everything in common it would be foolish to esteem me too highly) had you not trembled at the thought of the dangers I was running. It is not of cannonballs that I am speaking, but of the far more dangerous blows of a master, which the presence of Lord Cornwallis led me to fear. It was not reasonable to entrust me with such a command, and had I incurred misfortune, public opinion would have said that it was given to me as the result of blind partiality.[9]

This letter must have delighted Adrienne. He had been called inept at court, but he was certainly no such thing on the battlefield. She had needed this reassuring message. The year had been a difficult one for her. Over and over again Morizot had sounded warnings:

You will see that instead of bills of exchange to the value of twelve thousand livres, the real figure will be nearer twenty, Monsieur le Marquis having said nothing about one for eight thousand francs which, fortunately, is in the hands of a friend.

But not only was the young agent a devoted servant: he was also a past master at saving himself:

The deficit is large. I shall manage to get over that difficulty. There is nothing about which I am more concerned than to prove how dear to me are the interests and the reputation of Monsieur le Marquis. I love no less than I honor and respect him, and for him, I feel, I would sacrifice much.[10]

This devotion he was to prove later in circumstances that were infinitely more dangerous.

In June, 1781, the Comte de La Rivière died. There was much work to be done in administering the estate, paying the legatees, and distributing alms. In this Adrienne and the agent collaborated. To Mlle du Motier Morizot wrote: "Madame la Marquise is, for me, an admirable guide and counselor. But then, all her actions bear the imprint of virtue and reason."

Adrienne had other troubles. Her sister Louise had once again lost a baby, a girl. George-Washington's teething was giving rise to considerable anxiety. And the fears for the boy's life yielded to those for his father's. The English gazettes, which were the only source of news, described his military position as desperate. Mother and daughter tried in vain to conceal from each other the dangers of the situation. But in spite of her anxieties, Adrienne had to play the role for which her husband had cast her, that of hostess to the visiting American. The wife of the hero had herself to be a heroine.

Then, suddenly, just when the queen had given France a dauphin, Lauzun brought the news for which they had not dared hope: Yorktown had capitulated.

LA FAYETTE TO M. DE MAUREPAS: OCTOBER 20, 1781

The play draws near its end, Monsieur le Comte, and the fifth act is about to finish. I had been not a little uneasy during the first four, but the last has filled me with delight, nor is my pleasure less in congratulating you upon the happy issue of our campaign.[11]

But, as was only right and proper, it was to Adrienne that a longer letter and the most heartfelt confidences were addressed:

ON BOARD THE *Ville de Paris*, IN CHESAPEAKE BAY, OCTOBER 22, 1781

This is the last moment, my dear heart, at which it will be possible for me to write to you. Monsieur Lauzun is about to join the frigate and sail for Europe. Business with the admiral has given me the pleasure of being able to send you news which is later by two days. Monsieur de Lauzun will bring the detailed description of the more public matters. The end of this campaign has been a brilliant achievement for the allied forces. There has been a rare unity in all our movements, and I should hold myself in contempt if I did not feel much satisfaction in the conclusion of my campaign in Virginia. . . . I count among the best moments of my life that when Monsieur de Saint-Simon's division joined hands with my army, and those occasions when I was by turns commanding the three field marshals and their troops. I am sorry for Lord Cornwallis, for whom I entertain feelings of the greatest respect and esteem, and these he is very willing to reciprocate. He has given me the pleasure of paying him back for the incivilities of Charleston, and I wish no further vengeance.[12]

Gilbert was long to retain a special liking for his unlucky adversary.

For Adrienne, acclaimed and complimented by all, the drama had ended in an apotheosis. With her mother and sisters, she rendered thanks to God.

PART THREE

IN WHICH THE WIFE OF A HERO

BECOMES THE WIFE OF A REBEL

REST FOR THE WARRIOR

I am free to love God and to serve him,
and I can very happily be shared be-
tween my Lord and my dear husband.

PAUL VALÉRY

On January 21, 1782, the king and queen went to receive the homage of the city of Paris on the occasion of the birth of the dauphin.
All the streets had been sanded, and window space had been rented
out at fantastic prices. Adrienne, with all the Noailles family, was
present at the festivities at the Hôtel de Ville. She did not know that
Gilbert had disembarked at Lorient four nights before.

With his brother-in-law and two other friends, he made straight
for Paris in a fast post-chaise. There he found the streets swarming,
with everybody shouting "Long live the queen!" The American
uniform was recognized. When the people realized that its wearer
was a general and no less a person than La Fayette, they gave him
a tremendous welcome. He hurried to the Hôtel de Noailles, but
found the house empty, the whole family being absent at the festivities. There was nothing for it but to wait, with all the impatience
of a man who has long been conjuring up the picture of the warrior's return, of delighted welcome and happy surprise, only to be
met with disappointment.

Crowds have a wonderful gift of spreading news. Very soon the
glittering company at the Hôtel de Ville learned that La Fayette
was back. For Adrienne it was agony to know he was so near and

yet so far. The king and queen were full of kindness. She was immediately sent for and told that she must not delay for a moment embracing a husband who had been so long away. Adrienne, a great respecter of the laws of etiquette, refused to go home immediately. The only favor she asked was that when the procession passed the Hôtel de Noailles on the return journey, the marquis should be allowed to pay his respects to the queen. Not only did Marie-Antoinette acquiesce; she insisted on the marquise riding in one of the royal coaches, so that she should not be held back by the passage of a far from short cortège. The queen, stopping her own coach in front of the Noailles mansion, greeted the young general and made him go at once in search of his wife. So deeply moved was Adrienne that she fainted dead away as she was getting out of the carriage. Gilbert caught her in his arms and carried her upstairs, according to a newspaper report, "in the midst of the applause of a vast multitude which could not keep from expressing its appreciation of so moving a scene of conjugal affection."

Throughout the following days Adrienne had much cause to rejoice. She had suffered when the court had shown its disapproval of Gilbert, but now, even more than at the time of his first return to France, he was unquestionably the hero of two worlds. King Louis XVI gave him an audience at Versailles, welcomed him warmly, and questioned him at great length about Washington. The old Maréchal de Richelieu gave a dinner to which all the marshals were invited to do honor to the general of twenty-four. When the couple attended a performance of *Iphigenia in Aulis* at the Opéra and the chorus sang the words "Achilles is crowned by the hands of Victory," the entire audience turned to face La Fayette. The actress who was holding the laurel wreath offered it to him amid the storm of applause. This was popularity indeed—unanimous and intoxicating. All the young scions of the aristocracy were loud in their demands to be permitted to join the army of Rochambeau. "They want," it was said, "to be little La Fayettes."

Though Gilbert called himself a republican and a democrat to mark his distaste and contempt for the men of the French court, he had come to realize the dangers and risks inherent in democracy. Washington himself had offered Gilbert this counsel: "In a free and republican Government, you cannot restrain the voice of the multitude; every Man will speak as he thinks, or more properly without thinking, consequently will judge of Effects without attending to Causes." [1] But the French monarchy seemed solid enough to be attacked without running the risk of being destroyed. La Fayette's ideal head of state would have been a liberal sovereign with all Washington's virtues, frugality, and natural nobility of character. In his moments of pride, he undoubtedly thought that he himself would have filled the position admirably, though when he considered the matter more coolly he realized how far removed he was from his idol. Talleyrand, at a later date, said of La Fayette: "What he does seems not to belong to his own nature. It is as though he were following somebody's advice." What Gilbert was really doing was imitating a model.

In June Adrienne, as previously after her husband's return following a long absence, found herself again with child and was happy to be so. Unfortunately she had good reason for being uneasy, not about the future of her marriage, which she knew was indestructible, but about the frankness of her relations with her husband. Though fervent in protestations and sincerely affectionate, Gilbert nonetheless lost no time in renewing his intimacy with Aglaé d'Hunolstein, who, now that he was famous, had become more accessible. It was common talk at court that she was his mistress. Her husband showed no open resentment, but the Barbantane relatives made their disapproval very plain.

Already, too, word was beginning to go around—not without good reason—of another attachment. In the house of Mme Necker, wife of the Controller-General of Finance, La Fayette had made the acquaintance of the dazzlingly beautiful Mme de Simiane. Before her marriage she had been Diane-Adélaïde de Damas d'Antigny, the sister of three supremely elegant brothers. Charles Damas had been one of La Fayette's comrades-in-arms during the American war, and this had created the first bond between the hero and a young woman who was generally considered to be the prettiest in all France and the most discreet, since no "adventures" had ever been attributed to her. In 1777 she had married Charles-François, Comte de Simiane, Marquis de Miremont, to whom she had borne no children. She was both beautiful and good, always anxious to please, and possessed of a delightful gaiety. Her mere presence produced a magical effect. A contemporary said of her:

She had a darling heart, a lofty spirit, and a fund of good sense. Conscious of her advantages, she had since girlhood ever felt a strong *desire to disarm the envy and jealousy of others. Perhaps this attractive disposition, combined with the then fashionable warmth which had affected her, as it had so many other women, gave to her approbation an excessive quality. There was always a tinge of enthusiasm about her satisfaction.*[2]

This enthusiasm had a great opportunity for display when Gilbert returned in triumph. No woman but was not ready and eager to throw herself into his arms; so generally was this recognized that when, a few days after his homecoming, he happened to be with Mme de Simiane in a box at the performance of an opera, and an aria was sung which contained the line "Love crowned with laurels finds few women cruel," the audience responded in a manner that left no doubt of their sympathy and approbation. What can a young woman do who wishes to please, when a whole people forces a lover on her? It seems probable that the Simiane–La Fayette liaison actually began at a later period, since at the time with which we are dealing the affair with Aglaé d'Hunolstein was still in its early and passionate phase.

Adrienne suffered from all these rumors but, far from indulging in self-pity, she was afraid of nothing so much as being a burden to Gilbert. So sincere was her humility that she considered herself unworthy of him and, having a naïve admiration of Adélaïde de Simiane's charm, thought it natural, though painful, that Gilbert should show a preference for her. She tried to moderate her own feelings, or at least the expression of them, and was so skillful in her determined self-effacement that for a long time the faithless husband did not so much as suspect the existence of that private drama of which he was the hero. He saw her subordinate her every action, quite without affectation, to his wishes and accustomed as he was to his wife's perfection, found it only natural that she should do so. She, however, was almost physically overcome whenever he left the room.

She was terrified [wrote her daughter Virginie] of the intensity of her passion, and by the thought that she might not always be able to conceal it from my father and thereby become an embarrassment to him.[3]

Meanwhile, Adrienne saw that more and more of the royal favor was being accorded Gilbert. The old minister, Maurepas, had died shortly after the American victory, but the king, in agreement with Vergennes, had decided that the young marquis should be given the rank of field marshal as soon as peace was signed, that being the equivalent of major general in the army of the United States—the rank he had held during the war. This promotion, which meant the bypassing of all the intermediate ranks, caused a great deal of jealousy among the older officers.

When, in June, 1782, the future Emperor Paul I of Russia came to Paris under the name of the Comte du Nord, a number of fêtes were given in his honor at Versailles. The court ball was particularly magnificent and the queen, in fancy dress, chose La Fayette to dance the quadrille with her. There had been a time when his clumsiness made him a laughingstock, but now the court was unanimous in praising the perfection of his dancing. So great is the power of fame to change the color of appearances. He had made for himself a unique position at court, independent of all the normal procedures of etiquette. "On one occasion, when his wife was received in audience on the same day as the Comte du Nord, the Counsel General of the Court of Peers complimented the Marquise de La Fayette and the son of the Empress Catherine in almost the same breath." [4] Both age and reason were powerless to resist a charm by which all were subdued. Adrienne's husband had gone to her head, and fame to his.

On September 17, 1782, Adrienne gave birth to a daughter, two months before her time. La Fayette named her Virginie, after the American state. Benjamin Franklin, told of this, said that he hoped the couple would have as many children as the Union had states, so that each might be honored in turn.

La Fayette had just attained his legal majority (twenty-five at that time), and was therefore entitled to exercise complete control over his fortune. Up till now, he had been living with his parents-in-law at the Hôtel de Noailles, but he had long been determined to have an independent establishment. The first instruction he gave to the excellent Morizot was to find him a house in Paris.

Meanwhile, since England appeared to be of two minds about coming to terms with the Americans, the French and Spanish governments set about preparing a new expedition, this time against the English possessions in the Antilles. Admiral d'Estaing was to command the fleet. He proposed that the army should be entrusted to La Fayette. Gilbert left at once for Brest whence he would sail to Spain, where the final plans for the operation were being made. "I am sad, very sad at leaving," he said, "and the thought of bidding farewell to my friends has never before been so painful." His friends were not confined to the male sex, and from Brest he wrote to Mme de Simiane:

When we said good-by I did not think that I should be writing to you again, but until now the winds have been contrary. . . . Perhaps there will be time for me to have an answer to this.[5]

The d'Hunolstein scandal had by this time become so public that Poix took the liberty of speaking openly about it in his letters to his cousin. Gilbert replied with a string of bitter complaints. The great public, he said, had honored him with its love, the fashionable world with its jealousy. Why should his "angelic friend" be tormented? Was it in order to punish her perfection, or to strike at him in the most painful manner possible by making her unhappy? Aglaé was suffering from all the tittle-tattle that was going the rounds, and had suggested more than once that Gilbert should give up seeing her. But this made him very angry, and each time she tried to persuade him, she ended by yielding to his entreaties.

Toward the end of December, joining Admiral d'Estaing at Cádiz, Gilbert assured Adrienne of his undying affection, with all his habitual effusiveness.

My dear heart, I reached Cádiz yesterday. . . . We are awaiting certain political decisions: I wish only that they might be the occasion of bringing me back to you. . . . I embrace my dear sisters and my sweet children. Farewell, farewell, dear heart. How I long to embrace you in person! [6]

This did not prevent him from reminding Mme d'Hunolstein of his devotion by the next post, or from sending Poix a letter filled with eulogies of Mme Simiane: "so pretty, charming, engaging, noble, and sincere," mentioning as well a "dear princess" (probably the Princesse d'Hénin) to whose kindness his heart responded "with the most tender devotion." Success has a way of changing men, and it must have been difficult to recognize in this flattering Don Juan the shy youth who only a few years previously had fled from the ladies of the court.

At Cádiz Gilbert was appointed Chief of the Combined General

Staffs, but, like all too many combined general staffs, this one seemed incapable of combining anything at all. Should an attempt be made to seize Jamaica? Should a revolution be fomented in Canada? La Fayette would have been best pleased if the two plans could have been acted upon simultaneously, but when d'Estaing advised the Spanish king to give the Jamaica command to the young general, the aged Charles III had answered sharply: "No, no! he would turn the place into a republic." The king was no fool.

Just when the Franco-Spanish plan had been agreed upon, news came that England had signed a peace treaty with America. There was nothing for La Fayette to do but return to Paris. From Cádiz he wrote to Washington, congratulating him on the final outcome of the War of Independence:

Were you nothing but another Caesar or King of Prussia, I could find it in my heart to regret for your sake the termination of this great drama in which you have played so outstanding a part. But as it is, I join with you in welcoming a peace which has realized all our hopes.[7]

He spoke of the joy with which his grandchildren would celebrate these great events, and he expressed a desire to go back to the United States. Then he wrote Washington of another plan:

Now that you are about to enjoy some measure of repose, my dear general, I hope you will allow me to suggest a plan which might be of the greatest benefit to the black portion of the human race. Why should we not, in partnership, purchase a small property where an experiment might be made to enfranchise the Negroes and employ them only as farm laborers? Such an example, given by you, might well be generally followed, and, were it successful, I would gladly devote part of my time to making this idea popular in the Antilles. If this idea seems fantastic, I would rather be thought a madman than sober and sensible in adopting its opposite.[8]

By March Gilbert was back in Paris. Vergennes was as good as his word and had him reinstated in the French army with the rank of field marshal, the appointment to date from the capitulation of Yorktown. But instead of giving himself a little time in which to enjoy his successes in the intimacy of his family, Gilbert decided to leave again at once for Chavaniac. The reason he gave to his d'Ayen relatives and to his wife was that Mlle de Motier had recently died and that Mme de Chavaniac, now left alone, needed his support and affection. Furthermore, the harvest had been poor in Auvergne, and the fear of famine was very real. The peasants on the estate had applied for help to the bailiff, who happened to be at Versailles. In the absence of their lord, then in Cádiz, Adrienne had intervened with him in person, and brought to bear the authority she derived from her husband's name and her own strength of character. Thanks to her, the danger of famine was averted.

She would have liked to go with Gilbert to Auvergne. She had not yet met his aunt, nor had she seen his ancestral home. But he wanted to be alone. He was passing through a sentimental crisis. Aglaé, who was being persecuted on account of their liaison, was asking him to break with her. She implored him to go away and to reflect at a safe distance on a situation that was becoming intolerable. As soon as he arrived at Chavaniac, he wrote to her:

MARCH 27, 1783
You are too cruel, my dear Aglaé. You know the torments of my heart: you know that it is wrenched in two by love and duty, and now you ask me to come to a decision in the matter of this wretched resolution! You have so often seen me coming to a decision and then finding myself incapable of abiding by it. A hundred times I have thought it all out and made myself a hundred promises . . . and a hundred times, as soon as I have seen you and touched you, I have realized how weak I am. . . .

When I came back from America, my charming friend, was it you or was it I who preached a solemn sermon about this way of our being together? Remember my insistence, your refusals, our disputes. I accused you of having an aversion to me: you accused me of showing a lack of delicacy. Our lovers' quarrels ended as such quarrels always do, but, thought carried away by passion, I was constantly recalling both the reproaches of your relatives and the efforts I was making to break down your resistance. Each day brought renewed resistance, and consequently a renewal of remorse. All the same, I was happy, that I must admit—but you were not, and it is you who run all the risks, while I have almost all the enjoyment. . . . At every moment you risk ruin for my sake, and, the better to make me realize it, you deliberately refuse to participate in my feelings. Can you still insist that it is I who must decide? You know only too well my passion, my transports, my complete surrender. . . .

For over a year now you have been trying to break the bonds that hold us. With every day that passes, your efforts are redoubled. . . . Now you are taking the last and cruelest step, but the only one that has a chance of success. All that remains now is to know whether I am an honorable man. You have placed your peace of mind and your safety in my hands, and, what is more, you know it. I say nothing of your family.

You are well aware of the extent of the sacrifice. You have often seen me grow pale merely at the idea of a reconciliation. But for the last year I have seen that it is now only a question of my happiness. I will silence my heart. As you in your wisdom have foreseen, I am more master of myself in a letter than in a conversation. It would have been kinder to spare me the misery of taking the decision, but since that is what you wish, you may set your mind at rest, my dear. . . . What must be, must be. . . . It took me a long time to make up my mind to write, but this is what you want, what your family wants, and for you everything depends upon it. Why should you stand in need of my opinion? Could a man of honor advise you to ruin yourself? No, my friend, whatever the cost to myself, I counsel you to follow what reason dictates and what honor imposes on me. . . . So be at rest, since duty forbids us to be happy together. . . . After a year of struggle, you are where you wished to be!

As to the stupid things you are being told, I would not deprive your family of those ineffectual weapons. . . . But at least my heart is my own, dear Aglaé: all that you are, all that I owe you, justifies my love, and nothing, not even you, can keep me from adoring you.[9]

So the sacrifice was made, the rupture completed. The presence in the background of Adélaïde de Simiane must have made the decision easier. Gilbert sought forgetfulness in work. At Chavaniac the bailiff explained with pride that in spite of the prevailing scarcity, his barns were filled with wheat and rye.

"Monsieur le Marquis," he said, "now is the time to sell your grain."

"No," replied La Fayette, "now is the time to give it."

True to his word, he made a free distribution to the poor. Love of fine gesture and true charity are closely related, and Gilbert was soon as popular in the countryside as he was in Paris. Wherever he went there were cries of "Long live La Fayette!"

He had found his Aunt Charlotte terribly changed, looking much older and consumed with grief. The loss of her sister, with whom she had always lived, was a shattering blow. Her only daughter had died some years previously, and she had no one left in the world to love but Gilbert.

Social duties are an effective remedy for mental pain, which is primarily a sort of obsession. La Fayette prescribed for his aunt a round of entertaining.

Ever since I came here the house has been full of guests [*he reported to Adrienne*], *and she finds much occupation in doing the honors. . . . I think only of my aunt. She discusses with me my own affairs and hers, and I talk to her of you, of my children, and of America. . . . And now, a word or two about our affairs, dear heart, and let me say first that I take steps without consulting your little memorandum.*[10]

For, distant though she was from him, Adrienne had foreseen the needs of Chavaniac. She had a more orderly mind than her husband, who was a man made wholly of feeling. The situation, as she saw it, was this: the peasants of Saint-Georges-d'Aurac had been ruined by the bad harvest, but they had their sheep. Why not spin and weave the wool? She had written to the controller-general, asking for a subsidy to open a weaving school, to pay two or three women to give instruction in spinning, to buy the necessary carding frames and spinning wheels, and to employ a winder and six craftsmen. In addition, they would get a weaver who should be exempt from tax. The supervision of the school must be entrusted to the curé, who would see to it that the "instructresses were treated with respect." Adrienne had foreseen every need. She shared the view of St Teresa of Ávila that the Lord pays less regard to the size and extent of our labors than to the love with which they are performed. She gave the whole of herself to even the smallest matters.

GILBERT TO ADRIENNE:

Thirty thousand francs is what we hope for in order to establish your weaving factory, which will be of great help. You are rendering an immense service to this countryside. On Monday I am meeting a committee of curés and will discuss with them what is best to be done. I expect to leave here on Thursday. It is essential for my aunt's sake that I should stay till then. . . . Do not forget to press on with the work in our house.[11]

Morizot had found a house for the young couple and their children at 183 Rue de Bourbon (now Rue de Lille). It had cost 200,000 livres, plus 100,000 to make it habitable and furnish it. To raise this sum La Fayette had had to sell some land. His expenses during the war, and now this house, had reduced his revenues by 28,000 livres, but he still had an income of 118,000 (in contrast to 146,000 livres in 1777). This was still great wealth.

During the rest of his stay at Chavaniac, Gilbert listened patiently to his old aunt prattling away about business matters and household details. She was in straitened circumstances. He offered to buy such property as she had in exchange for a life annuity. In this way he and Adrienne tried to augment the resources of this aged relative.

GILBERT TO ADRIENNE:

But so extreme is her delicacy that it is impossible to pull the wool over her eyes. . . . Before suggesting this transfer, I made it my business to make quite sure that it was her wish to give me everything, and I am doing my best to augment the portion of others who, not being rich, have a right to be remembered by her. . . . The curé of Aurac is in love with you, and I am beginning to think that his feelings are reciprocated. . . . Send him one of those letters which only you know how to write.[12]

In all these letters to Adrienne we find a profound respect for the most perfect of characters, affection, a wish to give her a part to play in all the most important concerns of his life, a barely perceptible condescension, and that form of badinage with which guilty husbands so often conceal their feelings of remorse.

On his return to Paris, Gilbert was decorated with the Cross of St Louis, an unheard-of distinction for so young a man. He was received into the order by his father-in-law. On May 12 his sister-in-law, Pauline (Mlle de Maintenon), was married to Joachim, Marquis de Montagu, a captain in the dragoons. He was a rather fat young man of nineteen, with a pock-marked face, and he combined a rare delicacy of feeling with a sound intelligence. In short, he was a son-in-law worthy of the Duchesse d'Ayen. All the Montagus were present in full battle dress at the ceremony, and so were all the Noailleses. The bride's four sisters wept and prayed. The bedroom of the duchesse served as the nuptial chamber. Before supper Madame d'Ayen contrived to have a talk with the young wife, and, in lieu of final instructions, made her read several chapters of the Book of Tobit.

ALARUMS AND EXCURSIONS

Who can find a virtuous woman? for her
price is far above rubies.

PROVERBS 31:10

As soon as the marriage festivities were over, the La Fayettes moved into their own house in the Rue de Bourbon. Adrienne proved a marvelous hostess and organizer. The Hôtel de La Fayette became the headquarters of Americans in Paris, who met each other there every Monday and dined in company with the Noailleses and all the liberal youngsters of the nobility who had been brought together by the War of Independence when they were all serving in America. Franklin (Gilbert called him "the Doctor") was a frequent guest, as were also the Jays and the Adamses. Mrs. Jay and Mrs. Adams went often to the house to talk of children and housekeeping with Adrienne.

Gilbert became a figure in society. He went to Chaville to see Mme de Tessé, his witty confidante, whose face was never still, being forever jerked this way and that by the oddest twitches and grimaces; to the house of Necker the financier (out of favor at court, very much in favor in Paris), where he met the "cabal of princesses"—the Princesse de Poix, the Princesse d'Hénin, and the Duchesse de Lauzun; and to the home of Mme de Boufflers, who had first introduced him to Aglaé d'Hunolstein.

Poor Aglaé was no longer received in these circles. A scandal was attached to her name. She was accused, without a scrap of evi-

dence, of living a life of the vilest depravity, and was credited with
having borne two children, both of them fruit of adultery—one by
La Fayette, the other by a lackey. There were those who declared
that they had seen her at night among the prostitutes of the Palais
Royal. Perhaps it was the Duc de Chartres to whom she had formerly been unfaithful who spread these tales. Perhaps La Fayette's
personal enemies (his rapid promotion had produced a crop of
them) were taking their revenge by attacking his mistress. Mme de
Genlis, who had once been jealous of Aglaé, speaks in her memoirs
of the "terrible adventures" of Mme d'Hunolstein. The Marquise
de Barbantane had gone so far as to express a wish that her daughter might be shut away and so "prevented from bringing more disgrace on the family name." This implacable mother had actually
written to the Duchesse de Chartres to say that Aglaé's reputation
was now so bad that she was unworthy to be one of her ladies-in-
waiting. In short, calumny and malice did their work so well that
the unfortunate young woman retired into a convent after selling
her jewels and distributing the proceeds to the poor. In her retirement from the world she lived an austere and exemplary life.
Her loyal husband gave her a pension of 6000 livres, the greater part
of which she distributed in alms. It takes sinners to make saints
and egoists to make sinners.

Adrienne was not unaware of her husband's new infatuation for
the dazzlingly beautiful Adélaïde de Simiane, but she remained
firmly determined not to be a burden to him. Like her mother and
her sister Louise, she gave most of her time to her house, her children, and her charities. She had set up her son in a small apartment close to the Rue de Bourbon with an excellent tutor, M.
Frestel, and went there every day to superintend his lessons. Every
day, too, when darkness fell, the doves alighted on the Hôtel
de Noailles. The Duchesse d'Ayen had now only two daughters at
home: Clotilde, the widow of a husband who had given her little
reason to mourn him, and Rosalie, the "Benjamin" of the family.
Adrienne confided her troubles to her mother. The Vicomtesse de
Noailles was skilled in smoothing away all unhappiness and calming all distress "by a combination of solid good sense and a deli-
cately sensitive heart." Another neglected wife, the vicomtesse was
a living example of indulgent tolerance, free from all resentment.

In the course of the year 1783 Gilbert took Adrienne to Chavaniac. This was an occasion of great happiness for her. Now, nine

years after her marriage, she saw for the first time the place where her husband had been born. Adrienne was at once drawn to the Chavaniac aunt, who solemnly addressed her as "Madame." In manner the outspoken Mme de Chavaniac reminded Adrienne of Mme de Tessé, though in her political opinions and religious feelings the lady of Auvergne was poles apart from the Parisienne. Adrienne found her chief occupations in the peasants, the churches, and the estate. Thanks to her, the weaving school had been established, and the indefatigable promoter of the enterprise got from Calonne, the controller-general, a further 6000 livres for its maintenance. She made an effortless conquest of all the local parish priests. It was a great comfort to her to find that the Auvergne peasants were deeply religious and scrupulous in their attendance at church services.

The visit lasted for only two weeks, and then great matters called La Fayette back to Paris. He was known all over France as a champion of the Americans and was active in his defense of their commercial and maritime interests. In October, 1783, the young English minister, Pitt, accompanied by two of his colleagues, Eliot and Wilberforce, came to France, and La Fayette invited all three of them to dine in the Rue de Bourbon. He wanted them to meet "Doctor" Franklin and his own rebel friends, and he saw to it that they did. This showed considerable courage on his part, so soon after the war, but the event turned out to be no less amusing than it was daring.

Adrienne with her charm and tact helped to smooth away uncomfortable memories, and the Englishmen were full of admiration for their host's wife. Wilberforce praised the simplicity of the young couple. He noted that their house was run on English lines and that the La Fayettes much preferred serious conversation to the frivolous amusements of the court. Nevertheless, both he and Pitt found the marquis rather too much of a republican and thought his views more advanced than befitted a French aristocrat. La Fayette, for his part, was delighted:

My dinner yesterday was a great success. Mr. Pitt was supported by five Englishmen, and there were also present a dozen rebels, including the ladies . . . Mr. Pitt declared that so long as England remained a monarchy, they could scarcely expect to see me in London. In spite of this banter, however, I very much want to go there one day.

... Now that we have won the game, I confess that I find the company of English people extremely pleasant.[1]

In September, 1783, Gilbert had made a hurried trip to Épinal to renew acquaintance with his old Régiment de Noailles. He was kept for several weeks at Nancy because of the illness of Roger de Damas, the brother of Adélaïde de Simiane, who had hurried to his bedside. If we read between the lines, Gilbert's letters to his wife are both touching and richly comic. Quite clearly, he was trying to conceal under a show of concern for the invalid the pleasure he found in sharing the duties of nurse with Mme de Simiane. Adrienne was far too sensitive not to catch the shades of meaning in what he wrote.

SEPTEMBER 10, 1783

Roger's condition is keeping me here, dear heart. It is still very alarming. Monsieur du Châtelet is in despair, and we are all of us greatly afflicted. He has had a recurrent putrid fever, with the addition of worms, inflammation, and a particularly disturbing complication. His complete inability to evacuate made us think yesterday that the end was near. Fortunately, however, he managed to do so in the evening and we thought him to be out of danger. But this morning he is as bad as ever. ...

It gives me much concern to know that you are fretting, dear heart, and I share your anxieties to the full. Keep them, I beg, within reason. Excess is injurious to your health, and would even make your work less effective should you multiply them.

SEPTEMBER 17

Now that our correspondence has been renewed, dear heart, it gives me great pleasure to receive your letters. ... Since you know where to find me, I hope that you will send me news of yourself. I am happy for your sake that you have enjoyed some degree of tranquility so far as your patients are concerned, and could wish that your troubles on their account were at an end. Our own are somewhat relieved, though they still exist. The doctors have been too ready to believe that Roger was well on the way to recovery. I can see that he is far from that, but at least he is out of danger. Having seen him twice at death's door, I am happy to realize that he is no more than seriously ill. ...

Madame de Simiane is as well as can be expected. She is deeply *touched by your concern for her. We have had successive visits from the ladies, the father, the three brothers, and the Comte de Roche-chouart.* The mutual affection and unity of this family is truly touching. . . . My departure will cause a deal of grieving, because they all believe that I am necessary to Roger, and I must confess to you that I feel somewhat embarrassed, in spite of my longing to see you again and to return to my friends and to the dear walls of Paris.*[2]

In February, 1784, La Fayette's "dear general" informed him that he had resigned the presidency of the United States and retired to Mount Vernon:

At length My dear Marquis I am become a private citizen on the banks of the Potomac. . . . I am not only retired from all public employments, but am retiring within myself; and shall be able to view the solitary walk, and tread the paths of private life with heartfelt satisfaction. Envious of none, I am determined to be pleased with all; and this my dear friend, being the order for my march, I will move slowly down the stream of life, until I sleep with my Fathers.[3]

The American hero was of the stature of the heroes in Plutarch. He invited Gilbert and his wife to visit him at his own fireside:

APRIL 4, 1784

Great as your claim is, as a French or American woman; or as the wife of my amiable friend, to my affectionate regards; you have others to which the palm must be yielded. The charms of your person, and the beauties of your mind, have a more powerful operation. These Madam, have endeared you to me, and every thing that partakes of your nature will have a claim to my affections. George and Virginia (the offspring of your love), whose names do honor to my Country, and to myself, have a double claim and will be the object of my vows.[4]

La Fayette was eager to make the journey. Not only did he long to see again his old comrades-in-arms, but Congress had as a mark of gratitude presented him an extensive tract of land, which he

---

* The father was Jacques-François de Damas, Marquis d'Antigny (1732–1811), to whom his wife, Zéphyrine-Félicité de Rochechouart (who died in 1776), bore six children. The brothers were Charles (1758–1829), Alexandre, Abbé d'Antigny (1762–1811), and Gaston de Damas (1771–1808). During the American war Charles had been aide-de-camp to Rochambeau. The Comte de Rochechouart was the maternal grandfather of the sick man.

ought to acknowledge in person and perhaps plan to cultivate. He did not, however, consider taking Adrienne with him. In his absence, she alone could keep an eye on his interests, on Chavaniac, and on Morizot. Indeed, she was better suited than he to do so. Furthermore, much though she wished to meet Washington and to be introduced to America, she could not bring herself to leave her children. In the end his only traveling companion was a young aide-de-camp, the Chevalier de Caraman. Though a very rich man, Gilbert was—not for the first time—short of funds, and before setting out he was obliged to borrow 12,000 livres from his father-in-law, the Duc d'Ayen. He carried with him an affectionate message from Adrienne to Washington. In it she spoke of her grief at being once again parted from a husband setting sail for America, but added that this was to some extent softened by the hope she had of some day seeing the Washington family, either in Paris or at Mount Vernon. Little Anastasie, then seven years old, also wrote to her "dear Washington."

From Rambouillet, the first stop on his journey, Gilbert sent a more than affectionate letter to his wife by special messenger:

The vicomte will give you my news, but of my heart's news only your heart can speak. I am very unhappy, dear heart, and it is with feelings of profound regret that I have torn myself from you. With all my heart and soul I love you, and your feeling for me and the charming way in which you show it are my delight. Farewell, farewell, dear heart.[5]

He was to embark at Lorient on the New York packet, but the winds were contrary and the sailing was delayed. He occupied the interval of waiting by loading his wife with messages for his friends:

Forgive me, dear heart, for burdening you with all these commissions, but in sending you this letter I can indulge in the illusion that it is not one of farewell, and that is sweet to me.[6]

On June 28 he was still at Lorient. A fair wind was promised for the morrow, but in his letter to Adrienne he noted that it was by no means certain that the prediction would be borne out:

While waiting for the change, I have taken up my quarters on board and am making acquaintance with our hamacks [sic] and our little rooms. They no longer smell, and I have had them made tolerably comfortable. So long as I remain undisturbed, my sufferings, both mental and physical will be only such as I always feel when I am confined. But once this mousetrap starts to pitch and toss, I shall fortify myself with magnetism, with sachets of camphor and thorium on the pit of the stomach, and lumps of sugar dipped in ether—all new remedies which I am going to try and which will do me no good at all. In telling me to put my arms round the mainmast, Mesmer did not know (and I had forgotten) that it is smeared with tar to a certain height, so that this form of embrace becomes absolutely impossible unless I am prepared to be covered with the stuff from head to foot!

I much regret the time I have spent here, dear heart. If I had foreseen this long delay, I would have brought you with me to Lorient. Still, it would have been wrong for you not to have waited for your sister's lying-in, and I am distressed at having been unable to be present on that occasion. . . . I won't bore you today with commissions, dear heart, but will simply say good night . . . with wishes for as much happiness for you as you give me. Let me say again, with a sense of pleasure always renewed, that I love you tenderly, with the most complete confidence, and a sense of the most perfect happiness in the assurance that we belong to each other.[7]

On June 30 the wind changed:

We are off at last, dear heart, and now nothing can stop this journey. Though I could not but wish for a fair wind, its coming has caused me an indescribable heart-pang. You may rely upon my writing regularly and looking after my health, so as not to add anxiety to all the other cares that I inflict upon you. I like to think, dear heart, that I carry with me a cargo of your good wishes, and that knowledge will ensure my taking good care of myself. . . . But, by the same token, I claim the right to tell you not to neglect your stomach, which stands in great need of a healthy regime. Never forget, dear heart, how great a part you play in my life.[8]

Gilbert's tour of the United States was one long triumph. The young Frenchman had become the symbol of American victory and American unity. Everywhere he went he was greeted with the ringing of bells and the firing of cannon. All New York was at the Battery when he landed. He drove to the center of the city in an open carriage, through streets gay with bunting and crammed with spectators. If only Adrienne could have heard the ovations and shared in the well-merited glory, how happy she would have been! But it was fated that she should never make acquaintance with the New World. Each time her husband went traveling, he always had some perfectly honest pretext for leaving the mother to her children, the housewife to her home, the pious Christian to her devotions. A "dear heart" is best left to beat at the domestic fireside.

At Mount Vernon Washington greeted the marquis like a son and Gilbert spent ten delightful days with him, reviving old memories. He enjoyed the evenings on the veranda overlooking the Potomac, Martha Washington's peach brandy, the Virginia hams, and the dishes of fried chicken served by smiling Negroes. He preached to his host the doctrine, so dear to Adrienne, of the emancipation of the blacks. "That is all very fine," said Washington, "but how are we going to get our plantations cultivated?" Both men were farmers and livestock breeders, and harvests and cattle formed the topics of many of their talks. Fired by Washington's example, Gilbert began to take an interest in domestic matters and sent to Adrienne a number of instructions:

To begin with, dear heart, let me commend to your attention certain arrangements for my study. It must contain a barometer, a Declaration of Independence, and a smoke-machine, which will cost me fifty crowns and Déplaces * an equal number of groans. The addition of a carpet would do no harm.

He also left her to deal with all matters connected with the staff. In future, Déplaces would live permanently at Chavaniac, where he would be admirably suited to superintend the charitable enterprises.

Le Blanc [Gilbert continued] can take over the duties of hall-porter without ceasing to be my valet and Madame le Blanc can replace Madame Déplaces. . . . If your people were rather more presentable, Le Blanc would be quite sufficient on nights when there is company, and, as a result of arranging things as I suggest, it will be possible to run the house very much more cheaply. As to our cavalry, Le Blanc must find me four or five old horses for the month of December, as well as a strong and active supernumerary instead of the one we have

* For many years, La Fayette's faithful servant.

got at present. It will be quite unnecessary to increase the number
of our people. If, however, we must keep Courtois or Demanche in
the house, I would very much rather it were the latter, in which case,
he would remain all the time in Paris.... There, dear heart, you
have the fruit of the profound reflections in which I indulged during
thirty-five days on shipboard, where, as you may well imagine, these
projects kept me fully occupied.[9]

This sincere democrat, though he did not realize it, still had
aristocratic ideas about how a house should be run. But problems
concerned with the domestic staff were not his only preoccupation. His Egeria had another part to play:

Be sure, dear heart, to give news of me to all my friends. . . . I like
to think that when I return I shall have reason to be satisfied about
Madame de Tessé's health: that Madame d'Hénin will at last have
turned away from the appalling precipice on the brink of which she
is at present walking; that Madame de Simiane will have realized
that it is better to go to bed at midnight for six months than to run
the risk of enduring sufferings which are no less horrible for her
friends than for herself.[10]

To Adrienne's care Gilbert entrusted not only the Rue de Bourbon but Chavaniac as well. She spent the summer of 1784 in
Auvergne. She had just lost her Daguesseau grandfather, and had
the great happiness of taking with her to Chavaniac the Duchesse
d'Ayen who, after her period of mourning, needed to get away from
the city. The peace of the countryside, the joy of being with her
daughter and watching her grandchildren growing up, the company of Mme de Chavaniac (to whom she was greatly drawn) all
contributed to the rapid recovery of her spirits. For Adrienne, the
companionship of her mother added to her enjoyment of everything. Rosalie, too, throve in the homeland of her absent brother-in-
law. Far away in America, La Fayette was seriously thinking that
it was time to see about getting Rosalie married.

I was talking the other day to young de Caraman [he wrote Adri-
enne], and he told me that his brother would be immensely rich
and that his father would be overjoyed at the idea of his marrying
into your family. I know very little about them in the matter of
birth, but since we have two to settle in life, I thought it as well to
mention this to you.[11]

The two were Clotilde (a widow) and Rosalie. The first very soon took a second husband, the Vicomte de Thésan; the second became Comtesse de Grammont.

Each of Gilbert's letters contained new instructions and requests:

I must not forget, dear heart, to commend to your attention Mr. and Miss Jefferson. The father, an admirable, cultivated, and charming man overwhelmed me with kindnesses when he was governor of Virginia during the war, and I very much hope that he may like France well enough to wish to replace Mr. Franklin, which will not be difficult to manage should he consent. As to the daughter, she is a very attractive young woman, and I here and now appoint you to be her mother, chaperon, and anything else you can think of. I beg you to take them under your wing and to do all you can for them. . . . It would be no bad thing if you took them to see Madame de Tessé.[12]

The modest magician acquitted herself of these many tasks without fuss, without self-importance, and to everybody's satisfaction. News of her husband's continuing successes reached her from America:

OCTOBER 4, 1784
Here I am, dear heart, among the savages, surrounded by Hurons and Iroquois, and much bored at having to play the part of paterfamilias, which I am constantly compelled to do. I have already told you that my influence may be of some use in the treaty negotiations now proceeding with all the Indian nations.[13]

The astonishing thing is that his visit was in fact very useful, that the redskins received him as a friend, and that his American companions were very much surprised to find him as much at home there as he would have been in the Faubourg Saint-Germain. Good manners and tact can overstep frontiers and differences of race. He mounted the orator's platform and made the Indians an excellent speech in their own style. The Representatives of Congress were not a little jealous of his prestige, but nonetheless had to admit that he had done them a great service. He also began negotiating to take a young Iroquois of twelve or thirteen back with him to France, where he planned to raise him into his own household.

I must, dear heart, while I remember it, tell you of a famous plant in these parts called genzing, of which I can send you only one specimen. It is addressed to you, but I should like you to share it with Monsieur le Maréchal de Noailles and Madame de Tessé. Since this is probably the only time in my life that I shall talk botany to you, let me add that I have discovered here a climbing plant that stays green all year and would make a fine showing on the two walls of our terrace. When it reaches you, I beg that you will have it sown and planted in great quantities at the foot of the two walls. I also send something which in summer will cover them with beautiful red flowers, so that if my study is ready, nothing will be lacking to make our house charming. . . .

I am much distressed to learn that poor Poirey is suffering with his nerves, but if he is better, do prevail upon him to learn that contracted form of writing which is as quick as speaking, and get him to arrange my library. I have so bored you with all this talk of arrangements that I will stop. Let me say this only: that I should like to find on my return that the workmen have been paid their money.[14]

Husbands have a way of thinking that everything is easy when they have loving and efficient wives. The confidence of this one was more than justified, inasmuch as even the ministers did not hesitate in his absence to consult Mme de Lafayette.

When bidding farewell to the American Congress, Gilbert uttered these bold words: "May this great temple of liberty stand as a lesson to the oppressors, an example to the oppressed, a sanctuary for the rights of mankind." Several of the states had made him a citizen of the Union in perpetuity.

At Mount Vernon Gilbert took his leave of Washington. The American general wrote a number of letters for his "adopted son" to take back with him to France. One was to Adrienne:

The pleasure I received in once more embracing my friend could only have been increased by your presence. . . . The Marquis returns to you with all the warmth and ardour of a newly inspired lover. We restore him to you in good health crowned with wreaths of love and respect from every part of the Union.[15]

To the seven-year-old Anastasie, who had written to him in very passable English, Washington sent a kiss "which might be more agreeable from a pretty boy."

The parting was a sad one. Washington had a presentiment that he would not see La Fayette again. The twenty-seven-year-old Frenchman, on the other hand, was confident that he would again visit his "general-father."

The frigate *Nymph* carried Gilbert into the port of Brest on January 20, 1785. He might have hastened to Paris, but chose to make a stop at Rennes, where the States of Brittany were in session. Owning, as he did, great properties in this province, he had a right to a seat in the assembly. This he duly occupied, and was greeted with much applause by his peers.

He wrote to Adrienne on the evening of January 23.

Here I am, dear heart, at no very great distance from you, impatient to arrive, and glad that the vast spaces which separated us are behind me. What sets the coping-stone on my joy is the knowledge that my aunt [Mme de Chavaniac] is now established in Paris. . . .

I shall reach Versailles on Wednesday evening, but since I have to see several ministers next day, I am wishful to stay the night there and take this opportunity of paying my respects to the king. So on Friday we will go and dine with my aunt, sup with Madame de Tessé, and resume our old way of life. Or, if it would suit you better, I could drive to Paris after dinner on Thursday. That will mean that I shall put in an appearance much later, so as to find you alone. In that case I hope to embrace you about eleven o'clock or midnight, provided always that we are not delayed upon the road. . . .

There follows the usual Homeric catalogue:

Pass on this news of me to Madame de Tessé, your sisters, your father and mother. I have instructed Le Brun to go to Charlus, Poix, and the vicomte. I am sending a line to Madame d'Hénin and Madame de Simiane . . . also a note to my aunt. Give news of me to Madame de Boufflers as well. . . . I love you very much, and am eager to tell you so by word of mouth.[16]

III

THE SWEET WINE OF GLORY

*Youth is a charming thing. It sets out
at the beginning of life, crowned with
flowers like the Athenian fleet.*

CHATEAUBRIAND

The young general was overjoyed, on his return to the Rue de
Bourbon, to find that Adrienne had furnished and arranged his
study with the greatest care, exactly as he had wanted it. On the
wall hung the American Bill of Rights with an empty frame next
to it. Asked what that meant, he would reply: "It is intended to
contain a similar document for France." Some of his visitors
smiled, others were indignant.

The young Iroquois, Kayenlaha, was now a member of the household. Adrienne heard from Gilbert of the honors paid him by the
United States, and the tale of his successes filled her with delight.
Americans came often to the house. Franklin and Jefferson were
practically part of the family circle. John Adams was less of a success in Paris. He was suspicious of French charm, French manners,
French cleverness. Since he did not know the language, he could not
communicate the one thing of which he was certain—his own
superiority. Franklin, he thought, was too much of a diplomat.
He, Adams, prided himself on being brutally outspoken. Nevertheless, Adrienne found favor in his eyes. She had succeeded in
taking the Adams to the Te Deum in honor of the birth of the

dauphin. It was nothing less than a triumph to have introduced so
fanatically Protestant a family into Notre Dame.

Young Abigail Adams decided that the marquise was "sprightly
and very pleasing. I had always heard she was handsome; I do not
think her so; she was not painted, and very little dressed." After
dining in the Rue de Bourbon, she expressed herself as being
struck by the youthful general's modesty, reserve, and agreeable
manners. She was appreciative of the friendliness of the marquise
and impressed by the obvious affection shown by the couple for
their three children, which is "the more remarkable in a country
where the least trait of such a disposition is scarce known." [1]
Adrienne was more ready than her husband to exhibit their brood,
for, unlike him, she was not afraid that the youngsters would prove
an embarrassment to guests little accustomed to the presence of
children in the drawing room. The Monday dinners, at which
Americans predominated, were renewed. Anastasie (seven) and
George (five) sang songs in English, and Kayenlaha sometimes
danced in his tribal costume—that is to say, almost naked.

Correspondence with the Washingtons was resumed. Presents
were exchanged: dolls for the children, animals for breeding purposes, seed. Mrs. Washington sent Adrienne a whole barrel of Virginia hams.

I do not know [Washington wrote] that they are better, or so good
as you make in France, but as they are of our own manufacture (and
you know the Virginia Ladies value themselves on the goodness of
their bacon), and we recollect that it is a dish of which you are fond,
she prevailed on me to ask your's and Madame de la Layette's acceptance of them.

I wanted to have accompanyed them with an anchor of old peach
brandy, but could not provide any which I thought of such a quality
as would do credit to the distillery of this liquor, and therefore sent
none; and after all, both perhaps would have been better furniture
for your Canteens on a long wet march, than for your table in Paris. [2]

But the hams of Virginia are worthy of being served at the best
tables, and Adrienne was proud to offer them to her guests.

La Fayette was not the man to remain long contented with
domestic happiness. Accustomed to cutting a figure in the world,
he was greedy for fame and dangers. Vague ideas of political
reform were floating in his mind, but abstract theories did not

greatly interest him. What he needed was some concrete object, capable of arousing his feelings, on which to concentrate. It was not long before he found one, which had the additional advantage of meeting the approval and securing the cooperation of his young wife. He wished to take a hand in the education of an American, John Edwards Caldwell, but at once came up against difficulties because the boy was a Protestant. Ever since the revocation of the Edict of Nantes, Protestants in France had been exposed to humiliation. Deciding to attack these abuses, Gilbert told Washington of his plans.

MAY 11, 1785

French Protestants are the victims of an intolerable despotism. Though at the moment they are not openly exposed to persecution, they are dependent on the whim of the king, the queen, the Parliament, or a minister. Their marriages are not legal, their wills have no force in law, their children are looked upon as bastards, and they themselves are liable to be hanged. I wish to bring about a change in their status. With this end in view, I propose to visit, under some pretext or other and with the consent of Monsieur de Castries, their principal places of residence. I shall then try to enlist the support of Monsieur de Vergennes and of the Parliament, together with that of the Garde des Sceaux, who performs the functions of the chancellor. The work will take time, and it is not going to be an unmixed blessing for me, because no one will want to give me anything in writing or any support. Still, I must take my chance.[3]

Adrienne shared his feelings in this matter. Though she was a declared and fervent Catholic, "enlightened zeal for religion," said her daughter Virginie, "made her especially anxious that no injustices should be committed in its name. The more devoted she was as a daughter of the Church, the more did she detest the persecution which alienated people from it and was so foreign to the spirit of the Gospels. My mother's tolerance was founded on the basic principles of religion. She regarded as a great crime any attempt to obstruct the working of that freedom which is God's gift to men, or even to provoke, for interested reasons, resolutions which the individual conscience alone should dictate. She wished to draw people to Catholicism, but for reasons that were high and noble." [4]

Though Adrienne's dearest wish was to see her husband return to the faith, she refrained with the greatest possible tact from bringing any pressure to bear on him. She gave her full support to the action he was taking in behalf of the Protestants.

That action was energetic and well planned. The most considerable of the Protestant communities were situated in the south of France, in the country around Nîmes and Montpellier, and in the Cévennes. La Fayette was resolved to make contact with them, and took advantage of a visit to Chavaniac to see the most eminent of those who had insisted on remaining in holy orders at the risk of their lives: Paul Rabaut and his son, Rabaut de Saint-Étienne. He told the latter in confidence that Malesherbes, Minister of the King's Household, a man of great power and influence, was privately working for this just cause. La Fayette hoped one day to see young Rabaut in Paris, and himself to present him to the king—a hope that was later realized.

There was something else too in which both Adrienne and her husband were passionately interested: the emancipation of the Negro slaves. "An ardent desire to contribute to this good work and a horror of injustice in any form burned in my mother's breast," wrote Virginie. "She was delighted when my father set himself to work for the abolition of the slave trade." [5] Before deciding to embark on an experiment in enfranchisement which would be both onerous and difficult, La Fayette wrote to the Duc de Gastries, Minister for the Navy, suggesting that a beginning might be made by liberating the king's slaves in Guiana and distributing a certain amount of land among them. If the first generation of freedmen did not make a success of the experiment, then an effort would have to be made to train their children.

The minister declared himself to be in favor, but only if the undertaking was private. Gilbert therefore bought from certain creditors of the Jesuits in Cayenne two plantations, Saint-Régis and La Belle Gabrielle, and forty-eight Negroes, at a cost of 125,000 livres, for the purpose of providing an example of progressive emancipation. He left this enterprise to a great extent in the hands of Adrienne, who was more methodical and persevering than he. In her a wish to instruct the blacks in the basic principles of morality and religion was combined with a desire, which she shared with Gilbert, to show them the way to freedom. She chose as manager a certain Henri de Richeprey, who had all the qualities necessary for such an employment and gave himself heart and soul to the work. She made contact with a number of priests belonging to the Seminary of the Holy Spirit, which had a house in Cayenne. "Her charity was raised to a white heat by the hope that she might instruct the Negroes in the knowledge and love of God, and so be able to prove to the philosopher-champions of the blacks that the success of the experiment had been to a great extent due to religion." [6]

The undertaking gave every sign of being a success. The Minister for the Navy blessed it, and the manager appeared to be competent. On his arrival in Cayenne, he found that the first purchase was unsuitable, reported this by letter to Mme de La Fayette and, while waiting for her answer, acquired a small parcel of land well adapted to the growing of coffee and cocoa and not far from La Belle Gabrielle. This he called L'Adrienne, and settled twenty-one blacks on it. Though he did not immediately free them, he showed himself a kind and gentle master and suppressed the punishment of flogging. Adrienne took an interest in every detail, and urged him to establish a state of complete emancipation as soon as possible. In 1787 Richeprey died and his successor, Lescallier, advised the exploitation of La Belle Gabrielle, a plantation on which clove and cinnamon trees flourished. The number of blacks had now risen to sixty-five. Lescallier, like Richeprey before him, declared that total emancipation would be a slow business (the other planters threatened to intervene and the Negroes themselves were mistrustful), but that the process of humanization would be easy. Each worker received a wage, the sale of slaves was forbidden, an effort was made to provide some sort of education, and it was laid down that punishment should be the same for them as for the whites in the case of similar offenses. La Fayette hoped that as a result of these improved conditions the birth-rate would rise and infant mortality diminish. This would spell ruin for the trade in slaves.

Little by little Adrienne assumed complete responsibility for La Belle Gabrielle. Her husband was frequently away traveling. She had more time at her disposal, and had begun an active correspondence with the House of the Holy Spirit in Cayenne. Even in Paris she was active, and was taking in hand the rearing of a young Negro whom she had had baptized. Somewhat later, when an American about to return to the United States had difficulty in obtaining a passport for his "boy" La Fayette offered to buy him and to bring him up in his own family, so that he should not be exposed to ill-treatment. An engraving of the time shows La Fayette as the "Friend of the Black Man."

In July, 1785, traveling alone, Gilbert undertook a long journey through Germany and Austria. The King of Prussia, Frederick II, had the reputation of being a past master in strategy. Gilbert, ever a passionate student of the military art, obtained permission from the French government to attend the Prussian maneuvers in Silesia. Adrienne and the children went to Chavaniac for the summer. The post brought her many loving letters.

JULY 16, 1785

The climate of Germany, though less free than that of America, appears to have a good effect on my health, the more so since I travel with as much care as though I had the life of an Elector to preserve.... I see October 10 [presumably the date fixed for his return] through rose-colored spectacles, and am fonder of each next day rather than of each last, because it brings closer the moment when, dear heart, I shall be able to tell you of my love.

Give affectionate messages to my aunt, and kisses from me to the children.[7]

Gilbert traveled with letters of credit. The bankers of Frankfurt were of two minds about honoring them. They had expected to see "an old rebel," instead of which they found a young man with well-barbered and powdered hair. He spent a few days with the Landgrave of Hesse, "who," he wrote the Prince de Poix, "has the best troops in Germany, which he would have done better not to send to America. There are still to be seen a number of those who have come back from America, and—this makes my blood boil at the thought of Louis XIV and your dear aunt [Mme de Maintenon]—one is always, everywhere in Germany, coming across those miserable communities of emigrants driven from home by their persecutions."

At last Gilbert reached Berlin. On August 2 he wrote to Adrienne:

Yesterday I paid my respects to the king, who received me most warmly. I could not take my eyes off this extraordinary man, the greatest of generals and one of the pleasantest persons imaginable to meet.[8]

Three days later he wrote at more length.

Chavaniac is for me a temple in which are brought together all those objects which my heart holds sacred. It knows so well the road to Chavaniac. Love comes so naturally there, and within its walls are stored all the loving wishes that my heart is forever sending. My last letter told you of my visit to Potsdam, where the king gave me so kind a reception. The house in which he lives is charming, and the palace which he has had built for his amusement is among the most magnificent things to be found anywhere in the world. There one sees the king in a setting of columns, pictures, and statues, dressed in a shabby old blue coat and the high boots which he has worn since time immemorial. But his face can be so gentle when he wishes, and there is so much of intelligence in his eagle eyes that the general effect is one of very great nobility, though he lacks height and his body is slightly bent. I found him less old than he is depicted, and all about him seems to promise a long life. . . .

The last mail has brought me several details of the way in which the Negroes are treated in the West Indies, which increase my zest for the experiment we are making. . . . I hope, dear heart, that the walks at Chavaniac are not being neglected. I set much store on laying out a garden above the orchard, as my aunt and I have planned. Send me a detailed account of how matters are proceeding with her, and do not let her entertain the idea of abandoning us this winter.[9]

While he was with the King of Prussia an English delegation, led by the Duke of York and Lord Cornwallis—La Fayette's adversary at Yorktown—arrived. Frederick II, in a spirit of mischief, arranged for the young marquis to be placed between the two Englishmen at dinner. This encounter delighted Gilbert: "Former enemies," he said, "are pleased to meet one another, though I suspect that the victor's pleasure is the greater." Cornwallis, indeed, enjoyed his visit very much less than did Gilbert. "My reception in Silesia," he wrote, "was not flattering; there was a most marked preference for La Fayette; whether it proceeded from the King's knowing more of France, and liking better to talk about it, I know not."[10]

Nevertheless, though La Fayette appeared to be a favorite, he sometimes served as a target for the king's sarcasm. One day, when he had maintained against Frederick the Great that there would never be either royalty or a nobility in America, and that his own wishes for France in this matter had been forcibly expressed, "Monsieur," said Frederick, "I once knew a young man who, having visited several countries in which liberty and equality were the rule, took it into his head to establish the same way of things in his native land. . . . Do you know what happened to him?" "No, Sire." "Monsieur," said the king with a smile, "he was hanged." Gilbert laughed at the parable and admired the great man's wit. But Frederick II was not joking.

"As a friend of liberty," Gilbert wrote his cousin and friend, the Prince de Poix, "I pray God to save us from having such a monarch." Frederick the Great made him fonder than ever of Washington—and even of Louis XVI.

The French ambassador in Vienna was the Marquis de Noailles, Adrienne's uncle, for whom Gilbert had been a cause of considerable embarrassment in London. The welcome he extended the young man was not enthusiastic. "My uncle advised me to stay only long enough to recover from the fatigue of my journey," Gilbert noted, "which, in plain French, meant that I was not to try to see either the military garrisons or the fortified places. This was not a very avuncular attitude on his part." It must be admitted that the ambassador's previous experience in the matter of his nephew's travels had scarcely been encouraging. All the same, the Emperor Joseph II (the French queen's brother) graciously consented to receive the young and famous globetrotter. La Fayette celebrated his twenty-eighth birthday in Austria.

On his return to Paris, Adrienne and his children welcomed him joyously. The court, struck by the welcome extended to him by so many powerful sovereigns, lavished favors upon him. When the king went to visit the new port of Cherbourg, La Fayette was included in his entourage and invited to ride in the royal coach with the Maréchaux de Castries and de Ségur. In the course of the journey, the king was no less astonished than touched by the obvious signs of his own popularity. In the provinces the monarch was in no wise identified with his government. Toward the end of his trip Louis noted that the warmth of the crowds was markedly less. "I perceive," he said, "that I am approaching Versailles."

In Auvergne, where Gilbert had recently bought the lordship of the Manor of Langeac, close to Chavaniac, he made a happy entry into his new property, mounted on a white horse and loudly acclaimed by the inhabitants. A Te Deum was sung. His enemies maintained that he intended to elevate his new domain to the dignity of a dukedom. This seemed little compatible with his contempt for aristocratic distinctions. Meanwhile, in the capital, the state of Virginia had presented a bust of him by Houdon to the City of Paris. It was to be housed in the Hôtel de Ville. This decision had raised a problem of protocol. No such honor had ever been accorded a subject during his lifetime. But the attachment felt by the king for America and his personal esteem for La Fayette carried the day over all conventions. Louis expressed his approval of the project. To the music of a military band, the likeness of the general was installed on its pedestal in the presence of Adrienne, amid the acclamations of an enormous crowd. The hero himself, slightly embarrassed, had stayed in Auvergne.

On his return, he took an active part in promoting commercial relations between America and France, especially in the tobacco trade. It was at about this time that Thomas Jefferson wrote to James Madison:

The Marquis de La Fayette is a most valuable auxiliary to me. His zeal is unbounded, & his weight with those in power, great. His education having been merely military, commerce was an unknown field to him. But his good sense enabling him to comprehend perfectly whatever is explained to him, his agency has been very efficacious. He has a great deal of sound genius, and is well remarked by the King, & rising in popularity. He has nothing against him, but the suspicion of republican principles. I think he will one day be of the ministry. His foible is, a canine appetite for popularity and fame; but he will get above this.[11]

Later on this remark about Gilbert's love of popularity was frequently used against him. But it should be remembered that Jefferson was a very close friend, that a friend can smile at a friend's quirks, and that he had added: "But he will get above this." Still, the fact remains that the intoxicating love of a whole people is a delicious thing, and he who has once tasted it has great difficulty thereafter in doing without it.

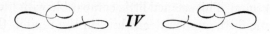

THE HIGHROAD OF LIBERTY

*As to monarchy, men have become too intelligent to
submit to it and not intelligent enough to trust in it.*

PAUL VALÉRY

The Hôtel de La Fayette continued the general headquarters of the Americans in Paris.

In his house [wrote a young officer, Xavier de Schönberg] *there are always to be found many English and Americans, for he speaks English as fluently as he does French. He has a savage from America, dressed in his native habit, who serves him as a running footman and always addresses him as "Father." Everything in his home is eloquent of simplicity. Marmontel and the Abbé Morellet have dined there. Even his little daughters, young though they are, speak English as well as French. They play games in English, and laugh with the Americans. They would form a charming subject for an engraving in the English fashion. I could not but wonder at the simplicity of so distinguished a young man, for there are many persons who have done nothing, that show as coxcombs beside him.*[1]

Morellet, Marmontel. . . . Gilbert was beginning to move in literary circles. He and Adrienne also dined at Saint-Ouen with Necker and his family. This banker, a Swiss and a Protestant, had been Controller-General of Finance. He enjoyed great popularity among the "philosophers," and even with the common people. He was shrewd and honest, but he had so scrupulous a conscience that, like the Chancellor Daguesseau, he could never make up his mind, a serious fault in a minister. Apart from uttering an occasional witticism, he was a silent man and relied upon his wife and his daughter, Germaine, to keep the conversation moving. The latter, who had married when quite young, was a creature of outstanding brilliance, known to history as Mme de Staël. She got on marvelously well with La Fayette, whose ideas she shared.

In this year of 1786 it was obvious to all intelligent observers that the situation in France was becoming dangerous. The incredible and idiotic Affair of the Necklace had badly damaged the reputation of the queen, who was too much upset by it to make any effective move to clear herself of the scandal. As dauphine, she had been adored. As queen, she found herself looked upon as responsible for all the misfortunes of the kingdom. She had many enemies, as clever as they were vicious, among them the king's cousin, the Duc d'Orléans, who maintained that the national deficit was to be explained by her and her circle's prodigal expenditures. In 1781, when Necker had issued his famous *Compte rendu*, the first budget ever made public in France, he had been able to boast that he had established a balance between receipts and payments. His dismissal had shocked all classes of the community. He had on his side those most celebrated for wit, and the devastating power of wit was increasing with every day that passed. Calonne, his successor as controller-general, was unpopular.

Ballad-makers deplored:

> *The Minister of Finance's*
> *Outrageous extravagances.*

The Treasury was empty. Why? Public indignation found a scapegoat in the court, though its alleged prodigality in fact accounted for only 6 per cent of the official expenditure. There were many other causes. The help given to the United States during the war had cost a great deal of money. A country's policies should be adjusted to the state of its finances. Who plans for glory plans too for the taxes necessary to pay for it. But what taxes? The last possible sou had been squeezed out of the people, and the privileged classes refused to pay. In view of the wide gap between the cost of government and the resources available, the only possible step was to fall back on the eternal system of loans. But subscribers were fighting shy. Calonne realized that some more drastic measure must be tried, and that the only thing to be done was to submit a general program of reform to an Assembly of Notables. Henri IV had once made the experiment, with success. "But what you are suggesting is pure Necker!" said the king. The public wanted Necker. On one occasion, when a comic opera by Paisiello, *Tesoro*, was played in the town theater at Versailles (in it a king complains that the finances of his kingdom are in a shocking state), a wag in the pit called out that he had better appeal to the Notables. The queen was present and laughed loudly at the impudent joke.

An Assembly of Notables chosen by the king was not a Congress elected on the American model; nevertheless it was a first step on the road to liberty. At all costs La Fayette must be included. It is not difficult to imagine the sort of conversation that went on in the family circle. It was not ambition that was driving him on, but a sense of duty. Who better than he, with his experience of free government, could act as guide to such a body? But it was no easy matter to be allotted a seat. There would be no more than a hundred forty-four members for the whole country: archbishops, bishops, nobles, mayors, presidents of parliaments. Gilbert's name, appearing on the first list, was struck out then restored after a protest by two ministers, the Baron de Breteuil and the Maréchal de Castries.

LA FAYETTE TO WASHINGTON: JANUARY 13, 1787
You will understand easily enough that the root trouble is the need for money with which to re-establish the balance between receipts and expenses. Profusion has made the gap enormous. But in order to arrive at the desired end, there was no way open to the government more patriotic, more frank or noble than this. The king and his minister, Monsieur de Calonne, deserve the thanks of the nation, and I hope they will be accorded some measure of gratitude and good will as a tribute to this popular step.[2]

Gilbert would have been less enthusiastic had his name not found its way back on to the list.

The Notables (whom an Anglo-French play on words transformed into the *not-ables*) began their meetings at Versailles in the spring of 1787. The most eminent, of whom La Fayette was one, were given quarters in the château.

ADRIENNE TO THE COMTESSE DE CHAVANIAC: MARCH 17, 1787
News of the Assembly is still brilliant, my dear aunt. It is accomplishing marvels, and it will come as no surprise to you that the particular

*Notable in whom you take a personal interest is acquitting himself
well. The members insist on seeing the minister's accounts, and on
being acquainted with the plans for reform before consenting to an
increase in taxation. The land tax in kind has been rejected almost
unanimously.... A law, said to be very wise, on dealings in crops
has been accepted. I am becoming quite a journalist, you see....
Just now I am having one of my periods, which means that I have to
keep to my room in Paris, but I hope to be able to go to Versailles
next week. I cannot observe the Lenten fast, but go to bed early and
take great care of myself.*[3]

This gathering of the Notables had the effect of increasing
Adrienne's admiration of her husband, who was now the leader of
the most progressive of the parties. It also accentuated her concern
for Gilbert's health, for he was having trouble with his chest. The
improvement in the position of the Protestants delighted her. Supported by the Bishop of Langres, La Fayette had proposed that all
their civil rights be restored and that the criminal code be amended
where they were concerned. The Comte d'Artois, president of the
administrative committee of the Assembly, objected that this matter did not form part of the purpose for which the Notables had
been summoned, but that since they seemed to wish it, he would
speak to the king. Support for the measure was voted unanimously
in committee, but there was a good deal of opposition elsewhere.
The Maréchale de Noailles, Adrienne's grandmother, assumed the
leadership of a group of outraged Catholics, and it was reported of
her:

*Madame la Duchesse de Noailles continues to intrigue and to wax
indignant. She is plaguing the life out of the counselors of the
Parliament. She wants them to adopt the odd and ridiculous measures proposed by the Abbés Beauregard and L'Enfant against the
Protestants, and at the same time to stand up for the interests of
Church and State by not allowing these outcasts to produce legitimate children. Her zeal has inspired the following two-edged epi-
gram:*

> Noailles and Genlis are two pious dames
> Who stir up all Parliament.
> If you see them or read them,
> You are surely a Protestant.

... She has been told to keep her enthusiasm within bounds, but of this she has taken not the slightest notice. It is a matter of general knowledge that she is a leading spirit among the visionaries, and used to sup regularly with the Virgin Mary.[4]

Malesherbes, and more especially public opinion, finally imposed a compromise. Once again the Bishop of Langres came out in support of La Fayette. "It is better," he said, "to have Protestant churches than sermons, ministers than preachers." Non-Catholic marriages were recognized as valid and Protestant children were legitimized. Protestant dead, too, could now be given legal burial. Jefferson remarked ironically that all this new law amounted to was the recognition that a Protestant was capable of begetting children, and there was always a risk that a corpse might become embarrassing. But tolerance had made a little headway, and Adrienne could rejoice wholeheartedly in her husband's achievement. In the following year La Fayette had the satisfaction of bringing Rabaut Saint-Étienne, his Protestant protégé, to Versailles and presenting him to the king's ministers. A beginning, even if small, had been made in the battle for religious freedom.

About financial matters, too, La Fayette behaved in the Assembly with commendable courage. There had been a considerable amount of talk about bad bargains made by the state in certain business deals (estates bought at too high a price or sold at too low a one, to the benefit and enrichment of favorites), and His Majesty had observed that when charges of such gravity were formulated, it should be with the utmost clarity and precision of detail, and should carry the names of their authors. Still with the Bishop of Langres behind him, La Fayette went so far as to identify publicly the beneficiaries in a number of scandalous deals, adding: "No matter how great the affection of the people for the person of Your Majesty, it would be dangerous to hold the view that their resources are inexhaustible. The truth of the matter is that they have been very nearly squeezed dry." In his own province of Auvergne he could see for himself that farmers were leaving their fields unplowed and craftsmen abandoning their workshops. Gilbert, in his cold, precise way, was an effective public speaker. He always gave the impression of being convinced of the truth of what he was saying. Calonne much resented his intervention in matters of national finance, but it was Calonne who was discomfited. The Assembly of Notables, said the wits, would be brought to bed either of a mouse or a new controller-general. As a matter of fact, it produced both. Calonne was exiled to his estates. He was ill and spitting blood. "Is it his own, or the country's?" asked his enemies.

The Easter holidays brought an adjournment of the Assembly and enabled La Fayette to give some attention to his chest trouble in the privacy of the Rue de Bourbon. He had also painful reasons of another kind for this temporary withdrawal from public life. The following entry appears in Bachaumont's journal under the date of March 14, 1787: "There is a rumor to the effect that Monsieur le Comte de Simiane, the husband of the celebrated Madame de Simiane, lady-in-waiting to Madame, has recently killed himself in an access of jealousy occasioned by the conduct of the Marquis de La Fayette." [5] The report is confirmed by d'Espinchal: "The Comtesse de Simiane is now a widow. The count, unsuccessful as a lover and unsatisfied as a husband, has found life so unbearable that he has blown his brains out." [6]

An anonymous "open letter" denounced La Fayette:

Letters from America, Monsieur le Marquis, once informed us that you were a hero, and for a long time we believed it. . . . At so great a distance a trifling injury to the leg makes a fine showing in the news sheet, and when one happens to be connected with a powerful, numerous, and scheming family, one can, thanks to the advice of a clever major general, usurp a precocious reputation . . . and without much difficulty concoct a title to renown. Given quite a small dose of common sense, one should remain content with so unhoped-for a piece of good luck, but when at closer quarters one apes the patriot and plays Cato, then those who have eyes to see have some right to demand a stricter standard of behavior in the aformentioned "hero," and rather more discretion in his public pronouncements than you have shown. The despair of a gentleman, your equal, who has taken his life because you have taken his wife's heart, scarcely provides a fitting opportunity for boasting of your austere moral code. Believe me, the pleasure of pleasing this fair widow and a willingness to join the enemy ranks of those who form her set cannot excuse the vile trade of a denunciator—ill-informed at that—which you have been so irresponsibly playing in the Assembly of the Notables. . . .

Finally, Monsieur le Marquis, those who wish to make the grade in their profession should be careful at least not to degrade themselves. That is my considered conclusion, and about what you deserve. A friend of mine who writes the words for comic operas entertained the idea of composing a song for you which would have tickled the public, set to the well-known tune: "He was a little man," but on second thought he has decided to wait until he can celebrate in verse the mighty deeds you will undoubtedly have to your credit when you come to fight your first campaign in Europe.[7]

Anonymous pamphleteers do not deserve to be read, but this was La Fayette's first experience of the breed and such first experiences are always something of a shock.

It is curious to note that shortly after this scandal Adrienne de La Fayette, then twenty-eight years of age, drew up a will for the first time. It is a touching document, full of piety and nobility, and gives us a pretty clear idea of what she was like and what she was thinking in 1787. It begins with a profession of the Catholic faith: "In the name of the Father, the Son and the Holy Ghost, Amen." She then proceeds to express her unqualified love for her husband:

I beg Monsieur de La Fayette to be so very kind as to undertake the duties of executor in the matter of my will. It contains nothing very complicated, but it is a great happiness for me to entrust to him all activities, no matter how small and unimportant, which have to do with my memory. It seems to me that in this way I shall prolong our union, which it will most certainly cost me dear to see broken.

I ask him to accept the box which contains the picture of the child whom we have lost [Henriette], the portraits I have of Anastasie and George, and the ring with the likeness of Virginie. I wish that he should keep them as some evidence of my feelings, and of the consolation I derive from the knowledge that he will remain with them, and they with him. The letter which I attach to this document will tell him more, but I cannot resist repeating in this, the last act of my life, that I have always valued to the full the worth and charm of my lot, and wish only that I might have been as deserving of it in all my ways as I have been in my affection.

She next addresses herself to her children, asking them to see that she is buried in the churchyard of the parish in which she dies, no matter where, since "I do not wish the cost of my funeral to exceed six hundred livres." She forbids all ostentation and display at her obsequies, and expresses a wish that the church shall not be draped in black. After listing the numerous gifts she wishes made to the different parishes of which "Monsieur de La Fayette is seigneur," and to the poor of St-Sulpice, of which parish they were members as householders of the Faubourg Saint-Germain, she mentions a number of personal legacies:

I give and bequeath to Monsieur Frestel, my son's tutor, a diamond of the value of one thousand crowns, and a plaster bust of Monsieur de La Fayette by Houdon. I wish him to accept both as a poor token of that gratitude which my confidence in him has rendered so great that, no matter how long the debt may continue, time could never add to what it already is.

To Mademoiselle Marin, my governess, I leave my rosewood dressing-case with the few objects of porcelain and silver which it contains. I beg her also to accept an annuity of four hundred livres, tax paid. I can only repeat here, and do so with great pleasure, my gratitude for all the pains she took with my education, and for the delight which her friendship has occasioned me. I ask her to continue to bestow on my children all the loving care which she has always given them. That is yet another reason for my gratitude.

I give and bequeath to Madame Beauchet, my personal maid, an annuity of eight hundred livres, my lace, and my linen. (The rest of my wardrobe is to be shared equally between her and the maid next in seniority.) She knows how deeply touched I have been by her devotion during all the years she has been with me, and how sincerely I hope that happiness will be her lot, her husband's, and her children's, for the rest of her life.

I leave to Anastasie, my eldest daughter, my portrait in miniature of her father, and the little picture of Chavaniac made by Madame de Grammont. It has been a great happiness for me to find in the heart of this dearly loved child the seed of all the feelings which are in my own. It is for her to take my place with her father. This duty will, I hope, be a consolation to her and a constant reminder of me in her mind and heart. I hope she will remember all the wishes I have ever entertained for her, and will impart them to her little sister whom I commit, more especially, to her care. . . .

The feelings of Madame de Tessé for Monsieur de La Fayette have made so deep an impression upon me that nothing could ever efface it. I hope she will accept this last acknowledgment of the sincere and tender feelings which she has inspired in me. The in-

terests of Monsieur de La Fayette and of our children will provide her with frequent occasions for remembering the many kindnesses which she showed to me during my lifetime. It is a consolation for me to entertain this hope. With the utmost confidence I commend myself to her memory in all those circumstances which may have to do with the feelings of my heart. Her character and her unceasing goodness to me are an assurance that I shall live on in her memory. I leave her the originals of Monsieur de La Fayette's letters, with the request that she in her turn will bequeath them to my children.

Naturally her mother and her four sisters were each mentioned separately and awarded such legacies as might best please them. The impression left by this testament is first and foremost one of no little astonishment that so young a woman should have felt so certain that she would die before many of her family who were a great deal older than she was, and of sadness too, for one cannot help feeling that she found a melancholy pleasure in the thought of dying and leaving a few happy memories behind her. Her husband's notorious liaison must have been cruelly disturbing. She remained entirely devoted to him, loved and admired him more than anyone in the world, felt no resentment against Mme de Simiane, but regretted with a heartrending humility the fact that she had not been able to inspire so great a passion. Unshakable faith was the dominant feature of her life. It led her to accept without a murmur the will of God and all she might attribute to that will.

I end by renewing to all whom I love the assurance of my deep feeling for them. Once more I give to my children a final blessing. I need not, I hope, commend to them the unity in which they live, of which their love for their father and the memory of their mother will provide two strong and tender bonds, and of which their principles and the hope of an eternal reunion in the life to come should be the center.

Given at Paris, this 15th day of April, 1787, by my hand.

MARIE-ADRIENNE-FRANÇOISE NOAILLES DE
LA FAYETTE [8]

In the years to come the problem for Adrienne was not how to make a good death, but the much more difficult one of how to make a good life.

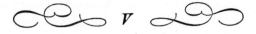

HOPES RUN HIGH

*Never has there been a society at once
so serious and so brilliant.*

MME DE STAËL

When the Assembly of Notables resumed its sittings in May, 1787, La Fayette demanded that the king should consolidate the results obtained by summoning a National Assembly.

"What, Monsieur," exclaimed the Comte d'Artois, "do I understand you to suggest the calling of the States-General?"

"Yes, Monseigneur, and even better than that."

Unpopular though he was at court, Gilbert knew that he was popular in the country. He had behind him his friends the "Americans"—the Vicomte de Noailles, Ségur, Poix, La Tour-Maubourg. His father-in-law, the Duc d'Ayen, was prepared to accept the idea of a general overhaul of the state machine. Public opinion was favorable to La Fayette's hopes. The aristocracy, no less than the prosperous bourgeoisie, realized that the days of absolutism were over and longed for a monarchy on the English model. It seemed so easy. Reform would be carried forward on a great upsurge of good will and idealism. In Paris, fans were being sold with the legend "The Assembly of Notables" on one side, and on the other a song entitled "Joyous Roundelay on the Occasion of the Assembly." Everything began with singing.

One can imagine the emotions aroused by all these happenings among the five serious-minded and generous-hearted daughters of

the Duchesse d'Ayen. Adrienne's lively imagination led her to believe that she would very soon see her husband's principles being
put into practice. She had a picture of him, seen through a rosy
haze, as a French Washington, but at the same time showing due
respect to his sovereigns, who in their turn would be guided by his
wise advice. So radiant was her mood of exaltation that she was
ready to strip herself of privileges that both her heart and her
religion condemned, certain that the people would respect and
understand so great a sacrifice. Liberal leanings and a love of argument made the reputation of many a great lady at this time. Mme
de Tessé showed herself more "advanced" than even her dear
nephew Gilbert. "Those who lived through these years," said Mme
de Staël, "could not but admit that never, anywhere, had there
been such a display of life in ferment and of eager intelligence."

Too brief, alas, it was a time of charm, of intellectual activity and
confident assurance. In the Noailles circle serious political discussions were frequent, though conducted within the framework
of the traditional elegance and good manners. In 1788 the provincial assemblies were convened over most of France, and the family
played a leading part in them. The Duc d'Ayen was president of
the Assembly of Limousin, and took his duties seriously. The Prince
de Poix was one of the members for Picardy, the Vicomte de
Noailles for Paris, and the Vicomte de Beaune (father of the young
Marquis de Montagu) presided over the Assembly of Auvergne,
of which La Fayette was the star performer and stormy petrel.
Adrienne, the "angel in the house," stayed in the Rue de Bourbon.
Her duty was to administer the family fortune with the help of
Morizot.

The Assembly of Auvergne sat at Clermont-Ferrand. From the
very first session La Fayette drew attention to himself by voicing
what one of the other members described as "revolutionary principles." He was reprimanded by the Vicomte de Beaune, and the
general view was that his chief occupation was that of flattering
the Third Estate (the Commons), and doing all he could to arouse
enmity against the government. But when, after the session, Gilbert toured Auvergne, he was received everywhere with signs of
affection. He was the first hero its inhabitants had seen, and they
never seemed to grow tired of staring at him. The parish priests
saw to it that an armchair was placed for him in the choirs of their
churches, and at night he was the chief guest at balls where the

ladies were disappointed because, instead of dancing, he talked politics with the men. Not everybody was pleased at his success. The Comte d'Espinchal commented sourly that:

He went out of his way to woo the poorer nobles and the more obscure members of the bourgeoisie, among whom he enlisted a considerable number of supporters, and was careful to let it be known well in advance when he was to visit those towns—Riom, Clermont, Brioude, Saint-Fleur, and Aurillac—in which he knew that he would be received with honor, and was, with a degree of pomp which was as ridiculous as it was extraordinary. He thought of nothing but making an impression and being talked about.[1]

This is unfair. Gilbert thought, in fact, of nothing but propagating his ideas, though certainly he had no aversion to being talked about. These assemblies, all this public criticism of abuses, produced an intense reaction throughout France. There was no lack of combustible material, and it duly took fire. The king, in a mood of increasing uneasiness, read Necker's reports and made careful notes of their contents. La Rochefoucauld, La Fayette, and their friends argued in favor of refusing subsidies because they were demanding the summoning of the States-General and the granting of a constitution. Prices were soaring. Bread rose from one to seven sous a pound.

To Madame de Tessé La Fayette wrote an account of what he and his friends were hoping to achieve:

A sufficient degree of fermentation to produce a threat of civil war, though without letting it materialize: in the army, enough of patriotism to worry the government, without causing actual disobedience: in the collection of taxes, a sufficient number of obstacles to lead to capitulation, though not to bankruptcy. The general effect of all this will lead us, by the shortest possible road, to the winning of that constitutional liberty for the attainment of which other countries have not thought torrents of blood and a hundred years of wars and misfortunes too high a price to pay.[2]

It was the program of a sorcerer's apprentice, but it was the way in which his thoughts were shaping. In the eyes of the court and the ministers, they had the color of treason. Gilbert was particularly blamed for having signed a letter of protest against the arrest of twelve Breton deputies and their imprisonment in the Bastille. He was told that the queen had said, "What has Monsieur de La Fayette got in common with Brittany?"—to which he replied, "My contacts with Brittany are the same as the queen's with Austria." Only a few years had passed since Marie-Antoinette had received him graciously on his return from America, and now this. The government dared not imprison him on the strength of his letter about the Breton deputies, but he was relieved of his army inspectorship and treated by the court as a social outcast.

This disgrace brought him numerous letters of sympathy. Adrienne knew that her husband was the center of much argument, but gave him her wholehearted support. She was more than ever proud of him. He took care that she should have every reason to be so. Attaching, as he did, great importance to the moral nobility of the character he had elected to play, he faithfully maintained it at a high level. He felt certain that he could establish a proper balance between his American principles and a due respect for the monarch, on condition that Louis XVI on his side should realize that the days of absolute power had passed.

But was such a solution possible? The Duchesse d'Ayen, Adrienne's mother, was one of the first to be alarmed. "She did not share the confidence of her circle in the wisdom and enlightenment of the age." [3] One day, when the malady from which she was suffering at this time was more than usually violent, she gathered her daughters around her bed and spoke to them gloomily of the future. She thought that terrible misfortunes were on the way, and was distressed by the active part Louis and Gilbert were taking in public affairs. Her daughters (with the exception of Pauline de Montagu) shared the hopes and expectations of their husbands. These wise young women devoted most of their time and thought to their children, their family duties, and the poor. They visited the prisons and returned with impressions which La Fayette immediately transformed into plans for reform. Their political outlook was dominated by their all-absorbing concern for their duties as daughters, wives, and mothers.

Meanwhile, the older generation was already sniffing danger and thinking about how to escape. The Vicomte de Beaune, Pauline de Montagu's father-in-law, though he had shown considerable independence as president of the Auvergne Assembly, was becoming more and more guarded in expressing his opinions. "As one who

had so constantly railed against abuses, he could scarcely now have
the effrontery to defend them. All the same, when he saw people
setting the ax to the root of the tree on the pretext of pruning it,
he shook his head in a irritable way, and, if he happened to be in
the *salon*, took his seat at one of the card-tables, there to discharge
his ill-humor on his partner." [4]

The ministers' distrust of La Fayette resulted in his being more
often at home in the Rue de Bourbon than formerly. The house
swarmed with "philosophers" and Americans. The frequent presence of her husband made Adrienne very happy. The affection of
her sons-in-law La Fayette, Noailles, and Grammont was a very
precious source of comfort to the Duchesse d'Ayen and her surviving daughters when, at the end of July, 1788, Clotilde de Thésan
died in childbed at the age of twenty-five.

In the outside world events were moving faster than thoughts.
The queen had become universally unpopular. Pained and surprised
by the coldness shown her by the Paris crowds, she asked despair-
ingly, "But what harm have I done them?" At the Opéra there
were some who dared to hiss when she made her curtsy to the house.
She was nicknamed "Madame Deficit." At a performance of
Athalie, the public wildly and rudely applauded a passage dealing
with "the schemes of this cruel queen."

Bankruptcy appeared imminent. The provincial assemblies were
saying "No taxes without reforms." The king recalled Necker, who
had a certain amount of credit, scraped together a little money, and
left the responsibility of convoking the States-General to the famous
Notables. Writing to Mme de Simiane, at that time living at some
distance from Paris, Gilbert was reticent:

*I do not believe that the Notables can handle the constitutional
question with sufficient skill.*

The fair widow must have been an intelligent woman who, like
Adrienne, was interested in serious matters, for Gilbert took great
care to justify his conduct in her eyes. His love letters always contained more of politics than of emotion. For Adélaïde, however, he
managed to find a number of graceful clichés:

*I am oppressed by your absence; my heart counts the days that have
gone and those that still remain; they grow in number toward the
end of an absence, as shadows lengthen at the end of a day.* [5]

With his political friends, Gilbert had established a society, known as the Thirty, which met at the house of Adrian Duport, a young and brilliant counselor of the Parliament who had been completely converted to the new ideas. La Rochefoucauld, Lauzun, Talleyrand, and the Vicomte de Noailles were members. It was there that La Fayette first made the acquaintance of the Abbé Sieyès, a forty-year-old and highly intelligent priest; the Marquis de Condorcet, a mathematician and man of the world; and Mirabeau (whom he had already met in the Society of Friends of the Negroes), with his enormous and impressive head, pock-marked face, and powerful gift of eloquence which amounted to genius. La Fayette felt a deep distrust of Mirabeau. His life had been stormy in the extreme and he had a bad reputation where money was concerned. He was never invited to the Rue de Bourbon.

The Society of the Thirty became a sort of constitutional club, an open conspiracy, with its main purpose the support in the Assembly of Notables of reforms as extensive as public security permitted. The chief of these was the doubling of the number of representatives of the commons. That was the key reform, since, should the principles of the three orders (Nobility, Clergy, and Commons) be maintained without it, the bourgeoisie and the people would be proportionately less well represented than the privileged classes, a state of affairs which the Thirty considered with good reason, to be nothing less than scandalous.

The Assembly of Notables was a sad disappointment. Only one section of it, that under the leadership of Monsieur, the king's brother (the Comte de Provence), voted for doubling the representation of the Commons. Such apathy was a serious matter in the circumstances, and there was no counting on the people to remedy it. Discontented though they might be, they showed no sign of reacting. Gilbert voiced his disappointment in a gloomy letter to Washington:

MAY 25, 1788

Our French affairs are reaching a crisis, the good results of which are the more uncertain since the people in general show no inclination to proceed to extremes. "Death for Liberty" is certainly not the prevailing motto on this side of the Atlantic. Seeing that all the classes are more or less dependent, since the rich want to be left alone and the poor have become lacking in backbone as a result of

ignorance and destitution, there is but one road open to us: that of
public discussion and an attempt to inspire in the nation a sort of
negative discontent or passive resistance, which may in the long run
have the effect of killing irresponsibility through sheer exhaustion
and baffling the plans of government. . . .

"And what of the people?" you will ask. The people, my dear
General, are become so dull and sluggish, and disgust has made me
so ill, that the doctors have been obliged to freshen up my blood.[6]

Then at long last Necker roused himself, and, with the courageous
backing of the king, managed to get the Council of Ministers to
adopt a seemingly enlightened program. This consisted of revised
distribution of deputies, so as to bear some relation to the population; the doubling of the representation of the Commons; the en-
titling of each order to choose its representatives from among persons not strictly belonging to it; the restoration to the nation of
the right of granting taxation, with a regular annual budget; a
periodic summoning of the States-General; the discussion by them
of all questions relating to arrest warrants and the freedom of the
press. This program, published on December 27, was hailed as
"France's New Year Gift."

For La Fayette it was a prodigious success. Two years earlier he
had been among the first to raise the question of convoking the
States-General and had caused much scandal by so doing. Now,
the convocation was an established fact and he himself was a candidate. At Duport's the advisability had been discussed of members
of the nobility offering to stand as members of the Commons, but
the majority opinion had been that young aristocrats with liberal
views would be more useful within their own order. The Third
Estate would have enough ardent supporters in any case, without
having to look elsewhere for them. La Fayette therefore decided to
offer himself as a candidate to the nobility of Auvergne, which
was due to meet in March at Riom. Adrienne would stay on (as
usual) with the children in Paris.

Before setting out, La Fayette entertained Gouverneur Morris,
who was later to hold the post of United States minister in Paris. In
his journal Morris noted that "La Fayette is full of politics; he
appears to be too republican for the genius of his country." Morris
had little sympathy with revolutionary ideas. When La Fayette
showed him his projected draft for a Declaration of Rights, the

American advised him to tone down the exuberance of his language. "It is not by sounding words," he said, "that revolutions are produced."

But the American was charmed by the generous and sincere welcome given him by his host's family. He found Adrienne as pleasing as she was good. One of the little girls sang for him, in English, a song of his own composition, and he was deeply touched by the attention. Morris had no liking for Neckcr, who seemed to him to be forever posturing as "the man," though his embroidered velvet coat contrasted unpleasantly with the simplicity of the La Fayette household. "If Necker is really a very great man, I am deceived" was Morris' summing-up in his journal.

In March Gilbert left Paris for Chavaniac, which was within easy distance of Riom and the election. Aunt Charlotte was happy to have him with her. The fashionable ideas of the moment filled her with horror, but she adored her nephew.

GILBERT TO ADÉLAÏDE DE SIMIANE: MARCH 8, 1789

I am very much better here than in Paris, and am quietly preparing myself for the heavy responsibilities which await me. There is division and jealousy here between the orders, the cantons, and individuals. It is to my disadvantage that my audience consists of people with an ax to grind, hopelessly prejudiced and already stubbornly opposed to my opinions. Some of my friends among the nobility have already told me that if only I were willing to do a bit of toadying, I should be elected unanimously, but that otherwise I have not a hope. My reply is that I wish to convince, not to flatter. The Third wanted to go to pretty extreme lengths, and that has given me a chance of acquiring celebrity. I have preached moderation at the risk of displeasing, and it may well be that instead of a nomination, all I shall get will be a great deal of quarreling and a great deal of esteem. Well, be that as it may, I shall do my duty and be moderate, though between ourselves their oppression revolts me and their characters make my blood boil.[7]

The nobility was as unhelpful as possible. Nevertheless, he got his nomination, though with a very small majority—198 votes out of 393. He returned to his aunt "elected, but far from contented." The program of the nobility, which he had been obliged to accept, seemed to him "a hodgepodge of popular and feudal ideas. In it, we say that nature has made all men equal, yet in the same breath has forbidden commoners to carry arms. . . . These conceptions are two hundred years apart." Still, it was a question either of making concessions or of retiring from the fray. Of two evils, Gilbert chose the lesser. The "squalid persecution" and the intrigues by which he found himself surrounded made it "a sort of a duty to be victorious." He campaigned too for his friend and neighbor, Colonel César de La Tour-Maubourg, for whom the Polignacs had made things difficult at Le Puy. He was always ready to fling his purse into that pan of the political scales which contained his own views.

The devoted Morizot complained to the marquise about the new holes her husband was making in the family fortune, but Adrienne, careful though she was in all matters concerning herself, loved Gilbert's acts of folly. La Fayette set off for Paris on April 11 and found his wife much distressed by the rumors reaching her from Versailles. The court, it seemed, was accusing him of preaching revolt. Nothing could have been farther from the truth. He was reckoning on the States-General to bring about reform in an orderly manner. Gouverneur Morris, who saw him on April 17, made the following note of their talk: "He gives me the history of his political campaign in Auvergne. . . . We consider of a revolt in Paris and agree that it might occasion much mischief but would not produce any good."

It had been a hard winter and there was a shortage of flour. Adrienne, her mother, and her sisters devoted such time as they could spare from their children to helping the numerous poverty-stricken families who were dependent on them. In the evenings they sat in their gilded *salons* and talked with confidence about the future.

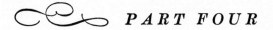 *PART FOUR*

1789–1792

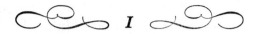

I

HONEYMOON

And he that sat upon the throne said,
Behold I make all things new.

REVELATION 21:5

You French know how to put up bar-
ricades, but not barriers.

LORD CHESTERFIELD

In the spring of 1789 the Noailleses, like most of the great families, opened their house at Versailles and moved into it from Paris. The Duchesse d'Ayen had only recently recovered from a serious illness, and it was thought that at this season the air of Versailles would be beneficial. The States-General were to hold their first meeting on May 5 and two of her sons-in-law would be taking part in it. It would be convenient for the young households to be able to make use of the family mansion. The daughters accompanied their mother, with the exception of Pauline de Montagu, who did not share her sisters' optimism in the matter of the expected reforms.

For Adrienne, however, it was a time of great hopefulness. Her husband had foretold and longed for these events. She felt sure that he would play an important and salutary part in them. His aunt, Mme de Tessé, was enthusiastic. She too had reopened her Versailles *salon*, where she brought together Jefferson and the young liberal aristocrats. Gouverneur Morris went there and predicted disaster. In Paris, wandering gangs of men armed with clubs were becoming a menace to peaceful citizens. The Palais-Royal swirled and eddied with highfalutin talk. An abbé who had spoken disrespectfully of Necker was shot. In the Faubourg Saint-Antoine, a ragged mob broke into the premises of a papermaker named Réveillon and destroyed his entire property, on the baseless grounds that he had said something derogatory of the workers. There was a feeling of violence in the air, and it was being said that the Duc d'Orléans, from reasons of personal ambition and because he hated the king, his cousin, was supplying the ringleaders with money. The La Fayettes neither liked nor respected him, and believed that he was capable of any baseness.

On May 4 the king, the queen, the ministers, and the deputies attended the Mass of the Holy Spirit. The procession was magnificent, and windows and roofs along the way were crowded with spectators. At the head of the column walked the five hundred and fifty deputies of the Commons, dressed in black, with silk capes and cambric jabots. Among them was Mirabeau with his great head of hair—a lion whose very ugliness had about it something both powerful and impressive. Next in order came the contingent of the Nobility, with their lace ruffles and their broad plumed hats looped back in the fashion of Henri IV. La Fayette, much to his annoyance, had to appear in this dazzling costume. He and at least forty of his friends felt themselves to be much more at one with the representatives of the Commons, who were greeted with loud applause by the crowd. Only the Duc d'Orléans (among the nobility) and, later, the king, were accorded a similar reception.

There was some show of hostility when the queen passed. For a moment she seemed about to faint, but recovered herself and moved on with head held high. Adrienne felt profoundly sorry for her. Gouverneur Morris recounts a story to the effect that when Marie-Antoinette, in a sudden flood of resentment, exclaimed "Oh, these disgusting French!" Madame Adélaïde, the king's aunt, replied, "Say rather, *disgusted*, Madame"—one of those witticisms invented by journalists, spread by idlers, and in times of civil unrest frequently responsible for bloodshed.

The Royal Opening took place next day in the great Salle des Menus-Plaisirs. From a gallery Adrienne saw Louis XVI seated on a gold and crimson throne, wearing his plumed hat with a marked lack of grace, and, two steps below him and to his left, the queen, looking very beautiful, with a diamond tiara in her hair. The Commons were respectful but determined not to let themselves be humiliated. Contrary to protocol, they put their hats on when the king put on his. Louis XVI immediately uncovered. Among the younger representatives of the Nobility, the "Americans" attracted a great deal of attention: La Fayette, Noailles, Lameth, and Ségur, as did also the "Anglomanes": La Rochefoucauld, his cousin Liancourt, and the Comte Stanislas de Clermont-Tonnerre. On the very next day battle was joined over the question of voting by heads and of the unification of the three orders. If the voting was to be by orders, separately, then the double representation of the Commons would be without effect.

La Fayette was at once confronted with a problem of conscience. In his heart he was a republican—or rather a Washingtonian—but he realized that France was in no mood to accept so radical a change and was therefore prepared to support a constitutional monarchy. He earnestly desired the unification of the three orders and voting by heads. On the other hand, at Riom, when he had been chosen to represent the Nobility, he had been compelled to give his word that he would uphold the separation of the orders unless unanimous vote decided otherwise. He now deeply regretted having given a pledge so much at variance with his own feelings, but as a man of honor he intended to keep his word. When the Commons declared themselves to be a National Assembly and called upon the two other orders to rally round them, La Fayette strongly supported this idea at the meetings of the Nobility and hoped that the king would follow suit.

Louis XVI was a good and worthy man, but irresolute and dullwitted. Was he capable of playing the part of arbiter? He was surrounded by diehards whose attitude was diametrically opposed to the real necessities of the situation, and, said the royalist Comte de Rivarol, "constituted a clique of fools." They took the view that the Commons could be silenced by shutting the Hall of Assembly against them, thereby showing that they had completely failed to understand the determined mood of the Third Estate. Its representatives found another place of meeting in the tennis court, where they took a solemn oath not to disband until constitution of the realm should have been established. Two days later four bishops and one hundred forty-four priests and two deputies of the Nobility threw in their lot with the Commons in an atmosphere of wild enthusiasm.

La Fayette was in a turmoil. His ideas, his hopes for the future, and his concern for his reputation combined to drive him into the arms of the Commons. The fateful oath now tied him. On June 23 the king came down in person to the tennis court. The session was disorderly. "I order you, gentlemen, to disband immediately," said the king. Nothing is more dangerous than to give orders when one does not have the means available to see that they are carried out. The president of the Assembly, Bailly, a famous astronomer and scientist, one of La Fayette's friends and a kindly but strong-minded man, replied, "It is my view that our assembly cannot accept orders." The Assembly disobeyed and the king capitulated.

That evening La Fayette, dining with Adrienne at the house of Mme de Tessé, found that Gouverneur Morris was one of his fellow guests. He reproached the American whose views, hostile to the patriots and loudly proclaimed, were harming the cause.

I seize this opportunity [Morris wrote later] to tell him that I am opposed to the democracy from regard to liberty. That I see they are going headlong to destruction, and would fain stop them if I could. That their views respecting the nation are totally inconsistent with the materials of which it is composed; and that the worst thing which could happen would be to grant their wishes. He tells me that he is sensible that his party are mad, and tells them so, but is not the less determined to die with them. I tell him that I think it would be quite as well to bring them to their senses, and live with them. He says he is determined to resign his seat, which step I approve of, because the instructions by which he is bound are contrary to his conscience.[1]

Adrienne shared Gilbert's scruples and longed for him to resign his seat in the assembly. Adélaïde de Simiane, whose opinion carried great weight with La Fayette, was more critical. He hit back:

I ask your forgiveness for my momentary impatience yesterday: but your concern had so much the appearance of blame that I cannot but feel somewhat embarrassed in giving free course to the impulses of a tender heart and a preoccupied mind, which, useless though it may be, lacks nothing of energy.

At the age of nineteen I dedicated myself to the liberty of mankind and the destruction of despotism, so far as an individual as weak as I am, could venture upon such a task. I took my departure for the New World, thwarted by all and helped by none.

He recalled his pleasure at witnessing the triumph of the revolution in America, and his hope that it would "serve as a lesson to the oppressors and as an example to the oppressed":

I have tried everything but civil war, and that I could have provoked but did not because I feared its horrors. It is a year now since I drew up a program, the simplest points in which seemed at that time the wildest extravagances. Six months from now it will be carried out in its entirety, without the alteration of a single word. I have also prepared a Declaration of Rights which Mr. Jefferson finds so excellent that he has insisted on having a copy of it sent to General Washington. This declaration, or something very like it, will become the catechism of the French nation.

Gilbert could not resist the temptation of pointing out how right he had been when the whole world was against him, and wrote, with a somewhat timid show of tenderness:

It is only to you that I can write of all these fatuities, not because I think that you will judge them favorably, but because I know that you will keep them to yourself. I swear to you that in the whole course of my twelve years of public life, though I have committed many faults, I have never once failed to approve of my actions and to realize that many of the faults to which I refer were due to the prudent advice given me by others.[2]

To his mistress he confessed his eagerness to go to Riom, there to hand in his resignation to the nobility of Auvergne and to get himself re-elected as a representative of the Commons, one of whose deputies would make way for him by resigning his seat.

It is natural that when twelve hundred Frenchmen are at work drawing up a constitution I should wish to be one of them. . . . I cannot rest content with the position of a county councilor in Auvergne after having contributed to the winning of liberty in another world. You must realize that I cannot stop dead in full career without falling from the eminence which I have reached, and that, no matter how anxious I may be to do my duty, that duty must be in the forefront of the political battle.[3]

But on June 27, at Versailles, the whole of the order of the Nobility rallied to the Commons. Gilbert's problem was solved. On the Fourth of July, the commemoration day of American independence, the Marquis and Marquise de La Fayette dined in Paris at the house of Thomas Jefferson. The company on that occasion contained a great many Americans. Gouverneur Morris solemnly called upon La Fayette to preserve, at least in part, the authority of the Nobility. Should it be entirely destroyed, he feared the worst. Morris was sufficiently naïve to believe that the torrential waters of a river in flood can be turned back. Four days later La Fayette burned his bridges by making a sensational speech in the Assembly in which he demanded the withdrawal of the foreign troops (mercenaries in the king's service) who were patrolling Versailles and Paris. The Comte de Saint-Priest, the Minister for War, spoke severely about La Fayette to Mme de Simiane in the belief that she could bring some influence to bear on him. Adélaïde was one of the queen's ladies-in-waiting. But even she could do nothing with La Fayette where his principles were concerned. At court proscription lists were being passed around, and La Fayette's name figured on them.

On July 11 he presented his Declaration of the Rights of Man and of Citizens. He was filled with pride when he thought that it would take its place in his study alongside the American Declaration. This July 11 was in his opinion the greatest day of his life. On the same day the king dismissed Necker. Both in Paris and in the Assembly this measure produced the worst possible impression. Actually, Necker's presence had settled nothing, but it was generally considered that his absence would disarrange everything. Parisians were much disturbed on seeing their city occupied by Swiss and German regiments. Citizens flocked to the Palais-Royal, carrying busts of Necker and the Duc d'Orléans.

At Versailles, on the thirteenth, the National Assembly declared that Necker took with him into retirement its esteem and its regrets, after which it decided that a proportion of the deputies should remain in session through the night. Since such an exhausting duty would have been beyond the power of the president (the old Archbishop of Vienne) to endure, he nominated La Fayette vice-president. In this way it came about that the thirty-two-year-old Gilbert quite suddenly found himself in the front line, directly threatened by the fury of the court. His brave young wife accepted the danger, though she did not, as he did, have the consolation of satisfied self-esteem. By education and tradition she was loyal to her sovereigns, and she could never forget the many kindnesses she had received from them.

La Fayette, for his part, had a naïve faith in *his* Declaration of Rights, in equality and liberty. As a great admirer of Washington, he hoped that all Frenchmen would turn out to be Washingtons. His intentions were good, but he had two weaknesses: a craving for popular applause, and a too-optimistic credulity. All the same, when he believed that he had taken the measure of a bad man he never changed his opinion. He had put both the Duc d'Orléans and Mirabeau beyond the pale.

Gilbert felt sure that he had been born to govern. But had he? Morris considered that there was too much of the knight-errant about him, that he was more interested in striking noble attitudes than in grasping the realities of a situation. His speeches, cold and disdainful, were delivered with an air of aristocratic authority. Noailles and Ségur maintained that had he been born in the Middle Ages he would have founded a religious order. He had courage in its every form. He had shown physical courage on the battle field, and its moral counterpart within his own social class, and even in his dealings with his family. He always felt more at ease on a horse, prancing at the head of his troops or before a friendly crowd, than on the rostrum.

On July 14, at 6 A.M., after spending all night presiding over the Assembly, he wrote to Mme de Simiane:

The vice-presidency has cost me a sleepless night. I put the question of adjourning to the vote, but it was made quite clear that the view of the chamber was that we should not disband. A considerable majority demanded that we should stay where we were. Many of the Commons, together with several members of the Nobility and Clergy, spent the hours of darkness pacing up and down the assembly hall while I dozed on a bench.

The information from Paris is that all is quiet and the bourgeoisie under arms. I imagine that a deputation from the city will wait on us this morning, and there could be nothing more strange than the situation in which we find ourselves. It will be an interesting day. I hope that we shall get to bed, because the only excuse [for an all-night session] was the possibility of further disturbances in Paris. But these seem now to have died down.[4]

It had become the fashion in Versailles to disbelieve all rumors of riots or unrest in Paris. But on that same July 14 a mob looted the armory at the Invalides and stormed the Bastille. The news was brought to the Assembly by the Vicomte de Noailles. At two o'clock in the morning the Duc de Liancourt woke the king with word that the heads of de Launay, the governor of the fortress, and of de Flesselles, the provost of the city guilds, had been stuck on pikes and paraded through the streets. La Fayette and his wife had a horror of cruelty in any form, and after this day Adrienne was never happy except when she saw Gilbert "throwing the weight of his authority into the scales of Justice to ensure the triumph of Charity."

There were some in the king's entourage who wanted him to withdraw to Metz, where he would be with his loyal troops. "We can certainly go to Metz," agreed the Maréchal de Broglie, "but what shall we do when we get there?" Louis XVI judged it more prudent to bow before the storm and to hope that time would eventually rally all men of good will to their proper place around the throne. He gave orders that the troops should be moved from the capital, and went to the National Assembly, which for the first time he officially referred to by that name.

Following on this reconciliation, a deputation from the Assembly, led by its young vice-president, was sent to Paris. La Fayette was received at the Hôtel de Ville, where he made a speech in which he congratulated the citizens on having conquered liberty by their courage and brought happiness to a benevolent monarch who had now seen the error of his ways. At each sentence he spoke, the crowds shouted "Long live the king! Long live the nation!" La Fayette did not yet know that on the same morning (July 15) he had been appointed commander of the bourgeois militia. In the terror and confusion then reigning in Paris, efforts were being made at the Hôtel de Ville to find a military leader. The president of the electors had pointed to the bust of La Fayette presented to the City of Paris by the state of Virginia in 1784. This gesture was loudly acclaimed, and the shouts were renewed when La Fayette appeared in person. But he insisted on having his appointment confirmed by an election in due form in the sixty districts of the city. At this same time his friend Bailly, the astronomer, became mayor of Paris. The Duc de La Rochefoucauld went to see the king and informed him that both men were remaining in Paris to see that public order was maintained.

Next day, it was decided that the militia should be called the National Guard, that each commune in France should have its own, and that from now on La Fayette should be commandant-general of the National Guard of Paris. It was a heavy responsibility. A rebellious people, conscious of its strength, had tasted blood; on the day of their appointment, La Fayette and Bailly had to exert themselves to save a number of unfortunates from being hanged by the mob. Just as La Fayette was trying to get a certain Abbé Cordier de Saint-Firmin out of the hands of a bloodthirsty gang in the Place de l'Hôtel de Ville, he caught sight in the distance of Frestel, his son's tutor, bringing the boy to him. Seizing hold of him, the general turned to the crowd, and called out. "Messieurs, I have the honor to present my son to you." There was a moment of surprise, and the general's friends who were with him on the steps of the Hôtel de Ville, taking advantage of this, managed to get the wretched abbé to a place of safety inside the building.

As soon as Adrienne heard of Gilbert's appointment, she left Versailles and returned to the Rue de Bourbon. Here, through a series of terrible days, she was to render many great services to her husband. It would have been easy for her to remain aloof, but she wanted to show publicly that he had her full approval and support. She responded to all the demands made upon her by the sixty districts in the matter of collecting money at the blessing of the colors and other patriotic ceremonies. She had very little rest. La Fayette kept open house. He had refused the salary of 120,000 livres offered him by the municipality, and this meant a heavy drain on her resources now that she was the domestic minister of finance.

She did the honors of her home [Virginie wrote] *in a way that charmed her numerous guests, but what she suffered in her heart was known only to those who heard her talk of her experiences. She saw my father at the head of a revolution, the end of which nobody could foretell. Every misfortune, every occasion of disorder she watched with a clear and disillusioned eye. All through that time she was sustained by my father's principles, and was so wholly convinced of his power to do good and to prevent evil that she* endured with unbelievable strength of character the constant dangers to which she was exposed. Not once in those days, she told us, did she see him leave the house without the feeling that she might be saying good-by to him for the last time. No one was more terrified of the perils which threatened those she loved, but she rose above herself and, with my father, lived always in the hope of being able to prevent crimes from being committed.[5]

II

THE KING OF PARIS

Young man, exalted principles and sublimity
are not the same thing.   MIRABEAU

With an armed guard to do his bidding, La Fayette was in so strong a position that for several weeks he could be looked upon as the virtual king of the capital, though a king constantly being challenged by the turbulent clubs of the Palais-Royal. It was he who, on July 17, when Louis XVI drove to Paris in "a very simple carriage," guaranteed the safety of his sovereign in the midst of a howling mob bristling with pikes, guns, and sticks. La Fayette was on horseback at the head of two hundred thousand men. The king said to him, "I wished to see you, to let you know that I have confirmed your appointment as general commanding the Paris guard."

Whether for confirming or rejecting, Louis XVI on that particular day had more of dignity than authority, but a French gentleman does not easily forget the long centuries of respect for the throne. The knowledge that he had protected his sovereign aroused a genuine emotion in Gilbert's breast. Bailly handed to the king the revolutionary cockade, made up of the colors of the City of Paris—red and blue. Louis XVI fastened it in his hat next to the white cockade of the Bourbons, and so the tricolor was born. La Fayette had the new cockade adopted as the national emblem. Parisian tradesmen turn everything to account, and very soon the market was flooded with snuffboxes and fans adorned with portraits of Louis XVI and La Fayette. The latter's white horse became famous. As soon as Gilbert felt that he was popular, he was ready to believe that everything was going well. In a mood of happy confidence he wrote to Mme de Simiane: "Today I am too strong for teasing." [1]

The thoughts of the Duchesse d'Ayen, who had stayed on in Versailles, were divided between her two daughters whose husbands were so deeply involved in the revolutionary adventure and her "Benjamin," Rosalie de Grammont, who was with child. For her she dreaded the possible effects of shock, as event followed event at breakneck speed.

The king might be resigned, but the princes, his brothers, considered that honor (and prudence) made it necessary for them to take refuge in flight. The Comte d'Artois was the first to leave, at dawn on the seventeenth, with his children and his household. The Condés and the Polignacs followed hard on his heels. Other fugitives made their way to Switzerland and the Low Countries. Soon there were two camps: the *emigration*, the symbol of determined hostility on the part of the privileged to reforms accepted by the king, and the *revolution*, represented for the most part by the "people," though their leaders were still drawn from the ranks of the younger members of the nobility. Between the two were many women torn by conflicting interests—like Pauline de Montagu, whose father-in-law did all he could to steer his family along the road to emigration while her brothers-in-law were in the forefront of the opposition movement. With Adrienne, there was no hesitation. What Gilbert was doing was well done. Nevertheless, on July 20, when Gouverneur Morris again dined with the La Fayettes, he found both husband and wife uneasy. Morris suggested that the scope of La Fayette's command should be extended to cover the whole of the Île-de-France.

He tells me [Morris wrote] *that he would prefer that of Paris simply, that he has had the utmost power his heart could wish, and is grown tired of it; that he has commanded absolutely an hundred thousand men, has marched his Sovereign about the streets as he pleased, prescribed the degree of applause which he should receive, and could have detained him prisoner had he thought proper. He wishes, therefore, as soon as possible to return to private life.* [2]

This also was what Adrienne wanted. She and Gilbert had reached the limits of physical fatigue and moral disgust. The groups of the Palais-Royal were usurping the functions of the National Assembly. France was being exposed to the danger of mob rule. Paris was threatened with bloody anarchy. When, on July 22, La Fayette saw the Councilor of State, Foulon, and his son-in-law, Bertier de Savigny, strung up before his eyes on a lamppost opposite the Hôtel de Ville, he tendered his resignation. Two days later he wrote to Mme de Simiane:

My difficulties are increasing every day. You cannot imagine the consternation caused by my resignation. Deputations from all the districts have waited on me, begging me to stay at my post. They flung themselves on their knees, wept, and swore to obey me in everything. What am I to do? I am in despair.[3]

He was not exaggerating. We have the written reports of these deputations. In every case he was implored to stay on.

Things being as they are, the City of Paris needs the services of an officer with eloquence at his command and a character known for its virtue.[4]

Gilbert withdrew his resignation, and was on the whole glad to do so. Bailly embraced him. So La Fayette retained his position as the Hero of Two Worlds and genius of liberty. The appointment suited him. He was at one and the same time citizen and soldier, and thought that he could still hold the balance between two manifestations of excess: reaction on the one hand, demagogy on the other.

It was undeniable that he still had sufficient prestige to enable him at times to save the innocent, and sometimes even the guilty. On July 30, accompanied by Adrienne, he went with Necker and Mme de Staël to a meeting of the representatives of the Commune to speak in favor of the Baron de Besenval, a difficult man to defend since he had commanded the Swiss regiments sent against Paris and had adopted an attitude of bantering persiflage toward the new regime. They managed to get him off with his life.

La Fayette no longer attended the Assembly meetings at Versailles except when matters of especial interest to him were being debated, such as his Declaration of Rights or the constitution. He was therefore not present on the night of August 4 when his brother-in-law, the Vicomte de Noailles, put forward his proposal for the voluntary surrender of privileges. Noailles himself (the younger son of an impoverished family who was known to his friends as "landless John") was not risking much since he possessed next to nothing, but La Fayette characteristically abandoned everything without a twinge of regret. Many of his political colleagues (Lameth, Duport, Barnave) were hoping for a parliamentary form of government, with a single all-powerful chamber and no more than a suspensive veto for the king. Others (Mounier, Lally-Tollendal) wanted the two-chamber system as in England and an absolute veto.

GILBERT TO ADÉLAÏDE DE SIMIANE

It seems to me that the famous veto is a matter of no very great importance. All parties are agreed that the absolute veto never works and is little more than an addition to the crown jewels.... Still, should it go through I should not break my heart, for there is much to be said for it.... But on the subject of two chambers I have no doubts at all; not that I favor a hereditary upper house, but a senate appointed for six years, or even longer, composed of members chosen by the provincial assembles. This senate would have a suspensive veto.[5]

There was good sense in this, but Mme de Simiane, who was in closer touch with the court than was her lover, felt uneasy about the part he was going to play. He made gentle fun of her: "I was delighted to know that you are chief of the king's advisers, and in command of his armies." He protested his complete disinterestedness:

I feel a great need to talk with you: we must arrange to meet on Tuesday. Meanwhile, here are my answers to all your points. Do not think about what I could do: that is no manner of use to me. Do not think about what I have done: I want no reward. Think only of the common weal, about the well-being and liberty of my country, and please believe that there is no burden I would not shoulder, no danger I would not face, provided that, when peace and tranquility are restored I can again be a private individual. I have only one ambition now—to go back to zero.

My situation is truly extraordinary. Here I am, at the very center of a great adventure, and the only thing I really want is to get out of it, free from all reproach of having indulged any thought of personal ambition, and, having put everything to rights, to withdraw into obscurity with a quarter of the fortune which was mine when I came into the world.[6]

It was true that the French revolution had already cost him a great deal more than the American one had. Morizot warned the Marquise de La Fayette of this danger, but Adrienne accepted without argument all her husband's decisions about money. She also accepted Mme de Simiane and sent her news of the general when he could not write. She received the delegations which came to the house and calmed their exacerbated nerves. She put in an appearance at the meetings of Gilbert's friends and at the blessing of the colors of the National Guard in Notre Dame. She loyally played her part as the wife of a leader.

It was under Jefferson's roof that a meeting took place, in September, 1789, at which the future constitution was discussed from four in the afternoon till ten at night. Jefferson always maintained that on this occasion he heard speeches worthy of Plato and Cicero. The majority inclined to a single chamber and a suspensive veto. In Paris the patriots were growing restive at the dilatoriness of the Assembly, and talked of marching on Versailles. There was reason to fear a schism between the two-chamber monarchists and the single-chamber patriots. La Fayette was begged by his friends to act as negotiator and arbiter. The attempt was a failure. Guile, or at least feinting, is sometimes a justifiable form of tactics and a duty. But he was too chivalrous to employ such methods, and for that reason was never a skillful politician. The champions of the single chamber won the day but accepted the principle of the suspensive veto.

Mirabeau, a realist, came out strongly in favor of the royal veto and against a regime of unbridled parliamentarianism. "The members," he said, "might form an oligarchy which would endanger the liberty of the subject. It is as a weapon against such an oligarchy that the veto is necessary." But in Paris the demagogues and the agents of the Duc d'Orléans worked up a popular agitation against the veto. Nothing can do more harm than words imperfectly understood. Paris was short of flour? The agitators threatened the city with obscure dangers: "The king will say 'veto' and you will have no more bread." This strange new word frightened the citizens no less than the word *deficit* had frightened them earlier. In times of trouble it is well to beware of Latin. La Fayette knew that a section of his National Guard wanted to march on Versailles and bring pressure to bear on the Assembly. He said as much to Gouverneur Morris. "Would your troops obey you?" asked the American. "They do not like doing guard duty in the rain," said La Fayette, "but I think they would follow me into action."

Gilbert spent most of his time away from home, at the Hôtel de Ville or in the districts. His house was filled with petitioners and he still entertained lavishly, but he was seldom present for long. It was Adrienne who presided at his table. She was his second self. The National Guard had as much, if not more, respect for her than for their general. On the morning of October 5 a mob armed with pikes invaded the Hôtel de Ville, shouting "To Versailles!" It had reached their ears that on the previous evening the Regiment of Flanders, which was loyal to the king, had arrived at the château, that the officers of the household troops had given a banquet in their honor, that the royal family had been present, and that the soldiers had trampled the tricolor cockade under foot and replaced it with a black one while the band played "O Richard! O my king! The universe abandons you."

A crowd of women, infuriated by the food shortage, began marching to Versailles. A number of ill-shaven men wearing petticoats mingled with them. Bread was scarce, was it? They would look for some at Versailles. "We will bring back the baker, the baker's wife, and the baker's boy!" In spite of La Fayette, at whom the mob shouted "To Versailles or to the lamppost!," the National Guard hesitated. La Fayette had hurriedly sent messengers to the court with news of the rioting. Twenty times the fatal rope was lowered from the lamppost, twenty times muskets were leveled at him. His prestige saved him. After standing his ground while the march on Versailles increased in numbers—men with muskets had joined it, and it now contained even a few pieces of artillery—Gilbert decided that the time had come for him to set about defending the king. Mounting his white horse, he placed himself at the head of several batallions and then "marched by compulsion," Gouverneur Morris noted, "goaded by his own troops, who suspect and threaten him." But Morris was a prejudiced observer. In point of fact, La Fayette still exercised considerable authority, at least over the National Guard.

On reaching Versailles, he halted his men and made them repeat their civic oath of obedience to the nation, the law, and the king. He then went, with two commissioners of the Commune, to the grill of the great forecourt. At first he was refused entry. When, however, the officer with whom he was parleying learned that he wished to enter the château alone, he was much surprised and opened the gate. La Fayette found the apartments filled with courtiers, many of whom were related to him and had been his friends.

"Here comes Cromwell!" said someone.

"Monsieur," retorted La Fayette, "Cromwell would not have come here unaccompanied."

Those who were doubtful of his loyalty were completely mistaken. Though he was not a "believing monarchist," he held the view that constitutional monarchy was at that time the only possible form of government for France. Furthermore, he thought that he owed a personal allegiance to the sovereigns, and knew that all those he loved, men and women alike, considered him to be bound by his oath. He had too high a view of his role not to play it with honor and courage. About midnight, while he was in the royal apartments talking with the Marquis Daguesseau, a major in the king's guard and Adrienne's cousin, a frightened messenger brought the news that the people were marching on the guards' barracks. La Fayette drove there immediately. His carriage was stopped by a drunken mob armed with pikes.

"What is it you want?" he asked.

"We wants the guards' heads!"

"Why?"

"Because they have insulted the national cockade!"

La Fayette gave them some money, calmed them down, tried in vain to see the king, paid a visit to Minister Montmorin, then, exhausted and scarcely able to stand, took a few hours' rest at the Hôtel de Noailles.

Early next morning he was awakened and told that the château had been broken into during the night. Several of the guards had been killed. It had been impossible to halt the rioters until they reached the door of the queen's bedroom. The National Guard had behaved with courage and loyalty. La Fayette hurried to the château. The king and queen showed themselves upon a balcony, from which the king promised that from then on he would live in Paris. He was not too badly received, but several women of the lowest class booed the queen and made gestures of cutting off her head. Gilbert behaved supremely well. He stood beside the queen on the balcony and respectfully kissed her hand. In the hysterical and capricious crowd anger gave way to emotion. All of a sudden, the queen and the general were acclaimed by the women, who had now turned tearful.

On this occasion La Fayette's love of the somewhat theatrical gesture and his chivalrous fervor served him well. He had saved the lives of Louis XVI and Marie-Antoinette. Madame Adélaïde, Louis XV's daughter and the king's aunt, said to him: "I owe you more than my own life: I owe you the king's, my poor nephew's!" The young Madame Elisabeth pressed his hands with emotion. At one o'clock in the afternoon Louis XVI and his family took their places in a coach. A hundred or so of the deputies followed behind it in carriages, for the Assembly had declared itself to be inseparable from the person of the king. Thirty thousand armed men, with loaves of bread and garlands of poplar leaves stuck on their pikes, marched behind.

All the way to Paris Gilbert rode at the window of the royal coach. Louis XVI was taken first to the Hôtel de Ville, then to the Tuileries Palace. He was in fact the prisoner of the Paris Commune, though still supported by the majority of the people who claimed that they were doing no more than removing him from the influence of the court and the queen, who, as she entered her room at the Tuileries, told her ladies-in-waiting that it had been her duty to follow the king to Paris, but that she was very sure that she would never again leave it. The little dauphin, when he saw the dark and dilapidated palace which had long been uninhabited, exclaimed: "How ugly it is here, Mamma . . ."

"My son," said Marie-Antoinette, "Louis XIV managed to live here. It is not for us to make more difficulties than he did."

Gilbert now sent a reassuring note to Mme de Simiane:

No doubt Madame de La Fayette has sent you news of me. Things have turned out better than we dared hope. The solidarity of the troops prevented what I feared from happening. Our army, before arriving at Versailles, took an oath of loyalty to the king, in spite of scheming and plotting. The king and queen behaved very well. . . . Good morning to you.[7]

One of his major concerns was to retain the esteem of his beloved. Notes reached her in rapid succession.

Good-by until eight tomorrow morning. Your feelings make me very happy, but I know that for the next six months I must ask forgiveness of anyone who has the misfortune to love me. Speak of me to all who, animate or inanimate, serve to remind you of those dear days which I long to see renewed.[8]

Then follows this heart's cry of a man in love:

This has been a very busy day, though empty, all the same, since I have not seen you.[9]

RUE DE BOURBON

To play at chess is no laughing matter.

CHAMFORT

On the evening of October 6, his day's work done, La Fayette returned to the Rue de Bourbon. He knew that with Adrienne he
could be certain of finding unfailing support, occasional advice, but
never a word of blame. He was exhausted, but pleased with himself.
If he remembered the time when Marie-Antoinette had treated him
as a figure of fun, he must have had some faint feeling of revenge
in the knowledge that she owed her life to him. Gouverneur Morris, who had come for news, found him in conference with his wife,
Clermont-Tonnerre, and M. de Staël. After events of such gravity
it looked as though there would have to be a complete change of
government.

The general was now the arbiter. Of that there could be no
doubt. Morris told him that he could not be both minister and
soldier, and still less, occupy all the ministerial posts. He would
have to choose men in whom he could have confidence. Some of
them, such as Mirabeau, aroused feelings of moral disapproval in
the La Fayette household. Adrienne could respect only men
whose lives were pure. A smell of money hung about Mirabeau.
Morris made the point that men are moved by ambition and that
no one enters an administration with the idea that he will find
in politics a short-cut to Heaven. What was going to happen to
La Fayette himself? Some wanted to make him generalissimo. The

ministers were proposing that he should be given the baton of a marshal of France. "Just between ourselves," he wrote to Mme de Simiane, "I rather think that ingratitude will save me from the embarrassment of being rewarded."

There were two questions that had to be settled without delay: his relations with the Duc d'Orléans and his relations with Mirabeau. For a long time he had been on bad terms with the first (once his rival for Algaé d'Hunolstein). Rightly or wrongly, Gilbert regarded him as one of those who had been chiefly responsible for the crisis at Versailles, and he felt sure that the Duc d'Orléans would be a pretender to the throne. He had an interview with him at the house of the Marquise de Coigny and insisted on his leaving for London on the pretext of some mission. The Duc d'Orléans, timid and vacillating, at first accepted this suggestion but went back on his word when Mirabeau, his political adviser, dissuaded him from obeying La Fayette, who was, he said, "assuming the airs of a mayor of the palace." La Fayette then persuaded the king to send for the Duc d'Orléans. Louis XVI pointed out to his cousin that the confidence inspired by the general made it essential that he should remain at his post. But it was quite out of the question that the Duc d'Orléans and La Fayette should both be in Paris at the same time. Accordingly, d'Orléans set off for England with his mistress, Mme de Buffon, and Choderlos de Laclos. Those who knew him well were of the opinion that he was more a man of pleasure than of affairs of state.

Mirabeau was indignant at the duke's departure, which he regarded an act of weakness. "People are fond of maintaining that I belong to his party," he said. "Why, I would not have him as one of my footmen." Trying to get the backing of the king's brother, the Comte de Provence, and finding him to be "just as pitiful a creature" as the Duc d'Orléans, he wanted to come to terms with La Fayette, the conquering hero of the moment. Never have there been two men less likely to get on with each other. Gilbert was above all things a thrifty guardian of his fame and his virtue. His moral prudishness, his everlasting scruples, got on Mirabeau's nerves, for Mirabeau was a man overflowing with vitality, possessed of the hide of a rhinoceros, a complete lack of scruples, and a wide-ranging and creative brain. La Fayette seemed to him to be more in love with praise than power. He accused him of talking his way out of everything, dodging difficulties and being incapable of anticipating them; of being without the strength of character to form a good ministry or the courage to make a bad one.

La Fayette was no less exasperated. Mirabeau's murky past of debts, scandals, and the insides of prisons filled him with horror. The heavy figure, the immense head made even more outsize by a great mane of hair all frizzed and powdered, made him feel physically sick. Mirabeau wore a coat with exaggeratedly large buttons of colored glass—the very reverse of the good taste and exquisite simplicity of the Noailles set. La Fayette would have ruined himself rather than accept a salary or a gift. Mirabeau, crippled with debts, borrowed from anyone he could persuade to lend. He always maintained that he had never taken a penny from the Duc d'Orléans, but he had cadged at court for subsidies with which to finance a political program of constitutional monarchy—the only one in which he genuinely believed. Now, in order to be rid of him, La Fayette suggested that he should be given an embassy, but Mirabeau wanted to form a ministry. With whom? That he regarded as a minor matter. "I will excommunicate nobody: everyone is grist to my mill."

Unfortunately for him, the Assembly decreed on November 5 that no member could hold a ministerial post. This was a fatal error. It meant condemning the king to seek support in Necker, Montmorin, and other has-beens. Mirabeau would have liked the king to leave Paris, and establish himself at Rouen, from which place he could have sent out a rallying cry to the whole country, while the provinces would have been solidly behind him. A La Fayette-Mirabeau government could have saved the monarchy, with La Fayette contributing popularity and Mirabeau genius. They would have had the whole country with them. Now that the king had come to Paris, everyone had once again become a monarchist.

But how does one bring together two men who despise one another? Where mutual esteem is lacking there can be no friendship and no collaboration. At a later date La Fayette blamed himself for his own attitude at this time. "La Fayette," he wrote in his memoirs, "was wrong about Mirabeau, whose immorality shocked him. Though he found much pleasure in his conversation and felt great admiration for his outstanding gifts, he could not help adopting toward him an attitude of wounding contempt."

Gilbert had several interviews with the queen at this time, and these gave the pamphleteers an excuse for spreading the absurd rumor that they were lovers. Several scurrilous publications appeared, among them, "The Nights of Love of General Motier and the Beautiful Antoinette, Written by Her Little Spaniel." Another writer, in a lampoon entitled "The Confession of Marie-Antoinette, Former Queen of France, Concerning Her Intrigues with Monsieur de La Fayette," credited her with this admission:

Having every reason to fear La Fayette, it was necessary for me to employ in my dealings with him every trick of which a woman, and more especially a German woman, is capable. Prayers, promises, tears—I left nothing untried. It is at moments of tender intimacy that a pretty woman can best make her influence felt, and it was at such times that I snared my simpleton and got him on my side. . . . Having become my acknowledged lover, he paid passionate court to me and was forever lavishing kisses on me, night and day, which made him more my slave than ever.[1]

Gilbert found opponents even in his own family circle. Adrienne, the Vicomtesse de Noailles, and Mme de Tessé proudly maintained that he had saved both his king and his country, but Pauline de Montagu and her father-in-law, the Vicomte de Beaune, could think of nothing but the dangers inherent in the ever-increasing disorders for which they held him responsible.

The Vicomte de Beaune no longer wished to see either La Fayette or Louis de Noailles. Only very grudgingly did he let Pauline de Montagu receive her sisters. If he happened to be at home when the Marquise de La Fayette was announced, he would take his hat and leave the room, slamming the door behind him. When that happened, Pauline would raise her lovely eyes to heaven and embrace Adrienne. For sisters so closely united, it was a wretched situation. M. de Beaune was eager to emigrate at the earliest possible moment, taking all his family with him. His daughter-in-law would willingly have followed him abroad. She thoroughly approved of the emigration, regarding it not as flight but as a declaration of war. Gentle and submissive where she herself was concerned, Pauline did not regard resignation a civic virtue. To emigrate and to fight was, she thought, the only possible way of saving the king and France. Perhaps the *émigrés were* prepared to accept foreign aid, but had not the American rebels accepted help from France? Joachim, her husband, and Adrienne, her sister, looked on emigration as a crime. Montagu still hoped that moderate men, like his brothers-in-law Noailles and La Fayette, would eventually impose their leadership on the masses. To this Beaune replied that such quibbling merely had the effect of "lulling to sleep those who had been asleep for far too long." Having failed to convince his son, he set off alone into exile.

Just when these family storms were at their height (February, 1790), Mme de Montagu saw her daughter Clotilde die before her eyes. This was the second child she had lost. As she knelt in prayer beside the lifeless body, news was brought that her younger sister, Rosalie de Grammont, who was living in the Hôtel de Noailles, had been brought to bed. This produced a fresh access of grief, but she got to her feet, dressed, and told her husband that she was going to see her sister. Montagu tried to dissuade her, but in vain. "Rosalie would not understand my not being with her. The death of our daughter would have to be broken to her, and at such a moment the shock might well be fatal." She made her way to the Hôtel de Noailles, kissed the newborn child in its cradle, and showed a tranquil face to the young mother. But as she was preparing to go home, her powers of resistance gave way and she fainted. The daughters of Mme d'Ayen were nothing if not tender and stoic.

Meanwhile the Assembly was trying to draft a constitution on the American model, "quite forgetting," said Gouverneur Morris, "that France had not got American citizens to support such an institution." The financial situation was worse than ever. Talleyrand, the Bishop of Autun, suggested that the immense resources of the clergy should be transferred to the nation. The property thus obtained could be used as security for treasury bonds. Bishops and parish priests would be paid a regular salary by the state. This measure scandalized a great number of believers, but the general mood of the moment was to accept anything and everything.

In those early months of 1790 French society had seemingly changed little. When Louis XVI went to the Assembly the Parisians cheered him. "I have been lied to," he observed. "I am still king of the French." On the other hand, the Vicomte de Ségur, La Fayette's uncle and friend, on his way home from his Russian embassy after an absence of five years, was struck on his way through towns and villages by the new behavior of the peasants, tradesmen, and artisans. When he had gone to take up his foreign appointment, he had left behind him a people at peace but with the bent backs of humility. Returning, he found a passionate spirit of independence, and people so intoxicated by their new freedom that they could not enjoy it wisely. In Paris he found that politics had become the sole topic of conversation. Everyone talked loudly and listened scarcely at all. Gallantry and the arts were things of the past. Ségur formed the opinion that the change had been detrimental to the women, that politics, with its accompaniment of moodiness and ill temper, had altered their looks for the worse. For his father, and for most men of middle age, what was happening seemed nothing more than an uprush of hysteria. Forgetful of the abuses which had brought about the downfall of the Old Regime, they were conscious only of an attack upon the throne and a deliberate attempt to destroy ordered living and discipline. Ségur's nephew, La Fayette, on the other hand gave him the impression that he had his heart's desire, "since he seemed to think that the whole country shared in his views." Nevertheless, even La Fayette showed signs of being disturbed by the excesses of the revolution.

In Ségur's view, La Fayette's position was dangerous. On one hand, he was a leader of the popular party; on the other, as commander of the National Guard, he was responsible for the protection of the king and his family. "I am afraid that one of these fine days the resentments of both parties will combine against you," he told his nephew.

"I am not unaware of that danger," Gilbert replied, "but, having done what it was my duty to do, I have nothing with which to reproach myself."

That too was how Adrienne saw the part played by her husband. Her life was a tangled web of hard work and anxieties. She kept alive the contact with Washington:

JANUARY 14, 1790

Monsieur, in the midst of the agitations of our revolution, I never cease to share in Monsieur de La Fayette's happiness at having followed in your footsteps, in having found in your example and your lessons a means of serving his country, and in picturing the satisfaction with which you will learn of his success.[2]

She had to welcome all and sundry to their house, feed her guests, find the money with which to meet so many fantastic expenses, and keep the family together in spite of the divergent opinions of its members. The affection that bound her to her mother was a source of great happiness to her, but the Duchesse d'Ayen now belonged heart and soul to the aristocratic party. All the same, she looked upon every detail of her son-in-law's conduct fairly and honestly, and never said anything that might have put her daughter in the painful position of having to choose between them.

In 1790 Anastasie, Adrienne's eldest daughter, made her first communion. In matters of religion La Fayette's attitude was still one of respectful condescension. For his wife, on the other hand, her child's first communion was an event of major importance at a time when there was no lack of important happenings. With Anastasie she prayed that Heaven might bless husband and father.

And in fact it looked as though the general's position had grown stronger. Mirabeau was still, even after having been rebuffed so often, offering his support.

You have a number of friends (though fewer than you think) [he wrote to La Fayette]. . . . Not one of them but has value and virtue of a certain kind, and they all respect you as a private individual. But they are one and all completely ignorant of human nature and of the real feelings of the country. They know nothing of practical affairs. . . . I am a great deal more necessary to you than all of them put together.[3]

Mirabeau was casting himself for the part of the Gray Eminence, but La Fayette was no Richelieu.

Mirabeau was a man of politics. La Fayette, the eternal undergraduate, wanted to bring about a reconciliation between the reality of the political situation in France and his own idealistic moral code. But at any given moment, a country is a tough and pitiless entity. Gilbert wanted to be loved, but Mirabeau knew that nobody can be loved always, nor by all, and that the essential thing is to lead: to make up others' minds for them.

Rebuffed, Mirabeau did his best to turn the court against La Fayette, calling him "the one citizen in the realm on whom the king can least rely" because he derived his power from the Paris masses, the most excitable element in the whole kingdom. He had a number of secret interviews with the queen in the gardens of Saint-Cloud, hoping that she would persuade the king to say to La Fayette: "I insist on your joining hands with Monsieur de Mirabeau. We must be able to say: these two are one man." His friend La Marck wrote to him: "The queen was much pleased with the letter that reached her yesterday evening. If this impotent blusterer goes on beating about the bush, he must be told plainly 'I *insist*.' "

"Impotent blusterer" was unfair. La Fayette had at least been powerful enough to snatch the queen from the hands of an uncontrollable mob. All the same, about the basic facts of the situation Mirabeau was right. Had he and La Fayette been able to work in harmony, they could have saved the monarchy. But Mirabeau's threats and attempts to exercise pressure merely had the effect of exacerbating La Fayette: "I overcame the might of the King of England, the authority of the King of France, the unleashed fury of the people. I shall certainly not surrender to Monsieur de Mirabeau." Modesty was never Gilbert's strong point. How, indeed, could he have remained modest, with the sweet savor of popularity rising like incense to the nostrils of the Hero of Two Worlds?

Federations were becoming the fashion. The national guards in the various departments were joining forces. The Paris Commune proposed a federation of all the departments so that there should be only one National Guard. The whole of France was called upon to unite in a great symbolic gesture of federation. Courtiers, friars, and Freemasons worked shoulder to shoulder at the task of building great turfed banks of seats in front of the Altar of the Nation in the Champ de Mars. La Fayette, who had a weakness for symbolic gestures, put in two hours digging with a spade.

His glory was at its peak. He was the sole buttress of his king. He was at the center of everything. When Adrienne was unwell, the Assembly, as a token of its concern for all that had to do with M. le Commandant-Général, deputized two of its members to inquire after her health.

There were, however, certain patriots who protested against this cult of personality. "We are of the opinion," wrote the *Chronique de Paris*, "that we should praise those of his actions which deserve praise, disapprove of those which merit disapproval, but never on any account adore his person. We believe that those who raise their hats when he passes and kiss his horse's hooves do him more harm than they realize." "I am quite sure," said the queen, "that Monsieur de La Fayette wishes to save us, but who is going to save us from Monsieur de La Fayette?"

July 14, 1790—the first anniversary of the fall of the Bastille. A great day of celebration, and very well organized. Talleyrand, who had neither illusions nor faith, said Mass. The family tutor, Frestel, took George-Washington de La Fayette to see the sights. Adrienne overflowed with admiration of her husband, when, as major general of the Confederation, he stepped up to the Altar of the Nation, laid his sword on it, and swore to be faithful to the country, the law, and the king. The queen showed her son to the assembled thousands. Sensitive hearts were touched. The king refused to go to the altar and took the oath from where he was sitting—which was held against him.

There was a torrential rainstorm, but what did that matter? It was merely the tears of the aristocracy. Once again the revolution was at an end.

It was just beginning.

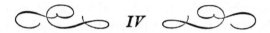

IV

LET SLEEPING DOGS ...

Woe to those who stir the dregs of a nation.

RIVAROL

Adrienne's family was beginning to scatter. Her father, the Duc d'Ayen, a skeptic and an epicurean in whom his son-in-law and the revolution inspired no confidence, was now settled in Lausanne, Switzerland, where he lived in close intimacy with the Comtesse Golovkine, a gay, affable, and prepossessing lady who provided him with light relief from the austere virtues of his wife, who was both saintly and deaf. The Grammonts had taken refuge at their estate of Villersexel. They were good landlords and had made themselves much beloved by their tenants. Pauline and Joachim de Montagu, after taking a cure at Aix, shut themselves away in their Château of Plauzat in Auvergne.

The Vicomte de Beaune, Joachim's father, was lord of the manor of Plauzat, and his son and daughter-in-law were welcomed with the ringing of bells and the carrying of cross and banner in procession. It was as though, so far as ceremonial and manners were concerned, nothing had changed. Pauline's simplicity touched the hearts of the village folk. Dyed-in-the-wool aristocrat though she was, she refused to retain any privileges, and instead of hearing Mass from the manorial pew, knelt on a straw-bottomed chair in the nave among the peasants. In the great hall of the château, hung with crimson damask (like the doves' nest in Paris), were rows of family portraits: bishops, cardinals, barons, ministers, and

183

grand masters. When she looked at them and watched her daughter Noémi (the only one left), dancing the *bourrée* with the village children, she found it hard to believe that a whole society was in its death throes.

But now, throughout France an agonizing case of conscience set Catholic hearts—especially Adrienne's—in a turmoil. Ever since the confiscation of church property, bishops and parish priests had been paid by the state. They had become public functionaries and were now elected by their parishioners and diocesans. Such had been the decision of the Assembly under pressure from the Jansenists and the "philosophers." All priests had to take an oath of allegiance to the nation and the constitution. It meant an open breach with the Roman Church. Pope Pius VI condemned this civil organization of the clergy, which denied all authority to the Vatican and deprived it of the right to appoint bishops. The electoral body, which now had the duty of doing so, contained non-believers and members of other denominations.

All the bishops except four had refused to take the oath, and a great number of parish priests followed their example. From then on there were two sorts of priest in France: those who had "conformed" and the "nonjurors." Talleyrand, Bishop of Autun, consented to consecrate the first of the elected bishops. All over the country the conformists claimed the monopoly of officiating at baptisms, marriages, and funerals. But among the faithful there were many who, refusing to recognize the validity of their orders, had recourse to the nonjuring clergy now in hiding. The king, a devout Catholic, refused to receive the sacrament at Saint-Germain l'Auxerrois from the hands of a "constitutional." Until then he had tried honestly to cooperate with the Assembly, but he valued his salvation more than his throne, and this religious conflict forced him back into the queen's camp and numbered him among those who were resisting the revolution. It is always dangerous to lay hands on religion, because it inspires heroic opposition by setting the transitory at odds with the eternal.

Adrienne, a sincere believer, found herself involved in a network of scruples. Her husband, though tolerant and respectful in all matters deserving of respect, had to remain on good terms with men who were the very embodiment of intolerance, for the simple reason that on them depended his position as a soldier.

Adrienne fully understood the difficulty of his ambiguous position, but thought it her duty for that very reason to stress her personal devotion to orthodox Catholicism. She happened to be present when the curé of Saint-Sulpice—whose parishioner she was—announced from the pulpit that he had refused to take the required oath. On April 21, 1791, the following statement appeared in *L'Ami du Peuple*: "On the pretext of respecting religious opinions, Louis XVI has authorized the rebel priest of Saint-Sulpice to preach revolt. Motier's wife is his abettor." Those who did not like La Fayette always referred to him as Motier.

Adrienne was a regular communicant at the chapels in which the persecuted clergy officiated in secret. One day there was a hostile demonstration in front of the former church of the Théatins: someone had spread a report that Madame Bailly and Madame de La Fayette were to take communion there. Adrienne received in her house many nonjuring priests whom she encouraged to exercise their sacred ministry. La Fayette had too much respect for his wife to insist on her behaving in any other way, but she was afraid of doing him an injury and of diminishing a popularity of which the country stood so desperately in need. Nevertheless, she was pleased to have this opportunity of giving Gilbert a chance to prove his attachment to the doctrine of freedom of worship.

Meanwhile, he had become an object of attack from both right and left. At the Palais-Royal, a young orator declared in stentorian tones: "As I always told you, Messieurs, the general is an aristocrat who ought to lose his head; a rascal who plays the patriot that he may the more easily serve the king!" The *Journal de la Cour et de la Ville* gave prominence to a paragraph attacking La Fayette and his family:

It is being said that the king, bored with having nothing to do, has asked Monsieur de La Fayette to find him employment, and that the general told him plainly that the only way in which he could obtain this was by putting on the uniform of the National Guard. He even promised His Majesty promotion.

It was Adrienne's dearest wish to appease—on both sides— passions that were political rather than religious. But how could she hope to succeed? The nonjurors called the constitutionals thieves and intruders. There were cases of angry demonstrations in the churches. On one occasion La Fayette invited certain members of the constitutional clergy to dine at his house. In their presence Adrienne declared with the calm fervor of a martyr her attachment to the cause of the former bishops, but she spoke with such sincerity, intelligence, and tact that it was impossible for them to take offense at what she said. It was enough for her husband to express his wishes in the matter for her to receive in the Rue de Bourbon a man whose opinions she by no means shared, and that without any loss of dignity because she reserved to herself the right to express her own. Only once did she depart from this rule. The constitutional bishop of Paris, recently enthroned, went to dine at the Hôtel de La Fayette, where the commandant-general of the National Guard of Paris was in duty bound to ask him to sit at his table. Adrienne, not wishing to receive him as one of his diocesans, was conspicuously absent. The incident was reported in the *Journal de la Cour et de la Ville*, on April 13, 1791:

Monsieur Gobel dined with Monsieur de La Fayette two days after his installation in the See of Paris. Madame de La Fayette stayed in her own room, though she was in perfect health. After dinner the new bishop informed the general that a great number of rich women had installed chapels in their own homes, so as not to have to go to their parish churches and hear the praises of the Lord sung by constitutional priests. He mentioned in particular Madame de Noailles, Madame de Mouchy, and Madame de Poix, all of them related to Madame de La Fayette. He asked the general to give him his support in closing these chapels as well as the religious houses. Monsieur de La Fayette replied that Monsieur Gobel must be aware that his nomination to the See of Paris was entirely owing to his, the general's, representations; that, the appointment having been made, he was not going to say whether he was or was not sorry, but that he was astonished at being asked to persecute in the name of the constitution citizens whose opinions did not happen to be the same as his own, and that if he, Monsieur Gobel, intended to act in this manner, he would always find in his path a general who would be firmly opposed to him.

Gilbert wrote a testy letter to Adelaïde de Simiane:

I am deeply grieved to have to say this but when one has become, as I have, the trustee of all the religions in the world, and is com-

*pelled to adjust the fervor of one's family to the ifs and buts of the
various administrative bodies and the ecclesiastical commission, one
is apt to get home rather later than usual. For the last two days I
have spent the whole of my time in discussions and arrangements
which have to do with the complete and immediate exercise of religious freedom.*[1]

The situation of her husband was causing Adrienne increasing
anxiety. He was being harassed from all sides. First and foremost by
Mirabeau, who now hated him and swore that he would "pursue
him relentlessly, even to the foot of the throne, and even *on* the
throne, should he succeed in getting there"; second by the aristocrats and by the members of the Duc d'Orléans' set; and third by
the group which gathered around Lameth, with whom he had
formerly been so closely connected.

The Lameths came of a noble family related to the Broglies. The
four brothers were all colonels, a distinction they owed to the king's
favor. At the beginning of the revolution Charles and Alexandre
de Lameth had been elected deputies. Alexandre, notorious for his
successes as a Don Juan, his wardrobe, and his debts, was more
likely than La Fayette to appeal to the Comte d'Artois. All the
women of the demimonde quarreled over him, and all decent
women spoke ill of him. He was very jealous of La Fayette.

Finally, there were the extremists, Camille Desmoulins and
Marat, who circulated filthy and stupid libels about him.

*But all honest folk [La Fayette wrote the Marquis de Bouillé], from
the least comfortably-off sections of the people to those who are not
out-and-out aristocrats, are for me. I am on good terms with the National Guard, except for a few Jacobins of bad reputation, for the
decent Jacobins are on my side in spite of my obstinate refusal to go
near their club.*[2]

This famous club had established its headquarters in a former
religious house belonging to the Jacobin (Dominican) order in
the Rue Saint-Honoré immediately opposite the Hôtel de Noailles.
At first many liberal-minded aristocrats and bourgeois had belonged
to it. Later on these broke away and founded another club—the
Feuillants—with the result that it fell into the hands of the more
virulent Jacobins, who launched violent attacks against La Fayette.
They represented only a minority of Frenchmen, but a majority

which observes the rules of the game almost always loses to an unscrupulous minority.

Of what did these Jacobins accuse the general? Of the most unlikely crimes, and, of course, of having been the lover of Marie-Antoinette. A new "Confession of Marie-Antoinette to the People of France" was now being hawked in the streets of Paris. In this the queen listed, among other lovers, the Comte d'Artois and the Cardinal de Rohan. After the outbreak of the revolution, having reason to fear La Fayette, she had, according to this scurrilous publication, set out to conquer him:

My lover, my dear La Fayette, brought over to our side Bailly, the greater part of the Paris municipality, the headquarters staff of the Paris guard, and most of the district leaders. . . . I conquered and seduced all of them. The only two I failed with were the two scatterbrained Lameths. Neither Charles nor Alexandre would yield.

Of the warfare now raging between the two great rivals, Mirabeau and La Fayette, Gouverneur Morris wrote on March 3, 1791:

I incline to think . . . that La Fayette will hold a good tug, being as cunning as anybody. Mirabeau has much greater talents, and his opponent a better character.[3]

The problem was suddenly resolved by the death of Mirabeau, after a short illness, on April 2. Men wrangle and death steps in. The monarchy lost its most intelligent adviser. When he was buried at the church of St-Geneviève, La Fayette as commandant-general of the National Guard did him the last honors. Destiny made of the situation a posthumous revenge.

A few days later, on Easter Monday (April 18, 1791), the king, having refused to take communion from the hands of a constitutional priest, expressed a wish to go to Saint-Cloud—where he knew that he could find a nonschismatic one. La Fayette, with the full support of Adrienne, urged Louis XVI to stick to his guns, and undertook the duty of seeing that he make the journey in safety. Was the king distrustful? Whether he was or not, he gave up the idea, and La Fayette placed his resignation in the hands of the municipality. Consternation reigned. The mayor, accompanied by numerous guardsmen, waited on the general and begged him to reconsider his decision.

LE MONITEUR UNIVERSEL: APRIL 21

The municipality, headed by Monsieur Bailly, called upon Monsieur de La Fayette at eleven o'clock at night. It conferred with him behind locked doors. The rooms of the house, the courtyard, and part of the street were swarming with members of the National Guard. It was raining in torrents. Madame de La Fayette appeared and, addressing herself to those who were outside, expressed her regret at not being able to provide shelter for all of them, and made it clear how deeply touched she was by their zeal. The crowds then dispersed. It was midnight, and still Monsieur de La Fayette had given no answer.

JOURNAL DE LA COUR ET DE LA VILLE: APRIL 25

Monsieur de La Fayette is unshakable. . . . Much attention is being given to the speech made by Monsieur de La Fayette to the general council of the Commune. Here is what it amounts to: he much appreciates the approach made to him by the National Guard, but does not think that he ought to resume command of them because he has no assurance that the law will be any the more respected in the future than it has been in the past.

. . . It is being said that Monsieur de La Fayette has expressed his willingness to resume the command, but that he insists on the soldiers renewing their oath of obedience to him. As we have already said, Monsieur de La Fayette is treading a path between two abysses, and sooner or later will be a victim of one party or the other. Retirement alone can save him. That solution may not be the most heroic one, but it is at least the safest.

JOURNAL DE LA COUR ET DE LA VILLE: APRIL 26

Monsieur de La Fayette, after the customary smirks and smiles, has at length yielded to the gentle violence of the fifty-seven battalions (out of sixty) which sent representatives with a request that he should once again consent to fill a position which he alone can occupy with dignity.

He agreed to stay on, but his prestige had been sapped, on the right no less than on the left. Marat and Desmoulins abused him, called him "an ambitious nobody, the vile tool of a despot," and denounced the "shameful twists and turns of the said Motier."

Lacking as he did, said Desmoulins, the vision of a Washington, he was merely waiting until he could play the part of a Monk. Meanwhile, it was clear that the court also regarded La Fayette an enemy. "I got the impression that the queen was soured," La Fayette said; "that she would rather make a fine showing when danger threatened than take steps to ward that danger off; that she hated me, though, at the same time giving me a degree of grudging respect."

This was a shrewd piece of observation. The queen, like La Fayette, stuck to the part she had chosen to play—which is sometimes the best method of ensuring human dignity.

To Louis XVI Gilbert said: "If I have to choose between the people and the king, you know well enough that I shall be against you. . . . I am, by temperament, a republican, but my very principles make me a royalist at the moment." And, to the queen: "Your confidence in me should be the greater, Madame, seeing that I am completely free from anything resembling a superstitious feeling for royalty. . . . It is better to rely upon a friend of liberty who acts from conviction than on an aristocrat who follows the dictates of blind prejudice."

But the die had been cast. The royal family no longer believed in the possibility of living in a peaceful state of coexistence with the revolution. Across the frontiers the *émigrés* were loudly proclaiming that it would not be long now before they took action.

Meanwhile, they were looking around for foreign aid. In France itself there were already signs, especially in the south, of a counter-revolutionary movement. The king thought that he could count upon the loyalty of fifteen regiments. At Montmédy and at Metz General de Bouillé, La Fayette's cousin, was ready to receive the king and queen and was preparing a plan of escape. Up to the moment of Mirabeau's death, he had advised the court to keep on good terms with him. On ambition and cupidity, the two strongest traits in his character, one could always count, said Bouillé, whereas La Fayette was a fanatic and a fool. Even Mme de Simiane told her lover more than once that she was heartily sick of the disorders and misfortunes which had been the result of his undermining operations. But Gilbert was as much a professional champion of hope as Adrienne was of fidelity. Both continued to believe in reconciliation.

Meanwhile the king had already made his choice. He had decided to flee to Montmédy, where troops under Bouillé's command would be waiting for them. The Austrian ambassador, Mercy-Argenteau, and a young Swede, Axel Fersen, who was in love with the queen, were involved in the plot. In Paris La Fayette commanded the troops stationed in and around the Tuileries, where the protective duties were divided between the National Guard and the regiment of Swiss Guards. Under pretence of sending a treasure to a place of safety, the king had had a passport prepared for Marie-Antoinette under the name of the Baronne de Korff, traveling to Frankfurt with her two children and a number of domestics. Bailly, the mayor of Paris, had received several warnings of what was about to happen, but had paid little attention to them. All the same, it was decided to strengthen the guard, and on the night of June 20 La Fayette went to the Tuileries to see that the necessary steps were taken. Just as he was leaving the palace, the queen, who was going on foot toward where a carriage, driven by Fersen, was waiting, passed close to him. She was wearing a hat with a long veil. The night was very dark. She treated herself to the pleasure of touching one of the wheels of La Fayette's carriage with her riding-switch.

Between six and seven o'clock on the morning of June 21 the king's flight was discovered. La Fayette, roused from his bed, rushed to the Tuileries. His responsibility was terrible, for he had given his word that Louis XVI should not leave Paris. He at once dispatched officers of the National Guard along all the roads leading from the capital with orders to intercept the fugitives. His aide-de-camp, Louis Romeuf (the son of one of his Auvergne neighbors, a prosperous farmer of Brioude, and devoted to the general), was instructed to bring the royal family back to Paris without a moment's delay. The streets were soon filled with excited crowds, determined to lay the blame at the door of the young general. Courageously, however, Gilbert went on foot first to the Hôtel de Ville and then to the Assembly. On June 22 a man was arrested for saying that it was surprising that La Fayette, who had answered for the king with his head, and then let him get away, had not had his head cut off and paraded on a pike.

That evening it was learned that Louis XVI had been recognized and arrested at Varennes-en-Argonne. The Assembly sent three commissioners, Pétion, Barnave, and La Tour-Maubourg, to bring him back. On June 25 the royal carriage made its entry into Paris. Strict orders had been given and were displayed everywhere: "ANY-

ONE WHO CHEERS THE KING WILL BE BEATEN: ANYONE WHO INSULTS HIM WILL BE HANGED." National guardsmen lined the streets, with arms reversed as for a funeral. La Fayette in person saw the royal family safely into the Tuileries. The Vicomte de Noailles and the Duc d'Aiguillon were present, according to protocol, to hand the queen from her carriage. The sight of them frightened her, for she knew that they were sympathetic to the revolution. She was wrong to be frightened: their only concern was to defend her in case of danger.

La Fayette, bowing to the king, said respectfully: "Sire, you know how attached I am to the person of Your Majesty, but I have never concealed from you that, should you separate yourself from the cause of the people, I should be on the people's side."

"That is true," answered Louis good-naturedly. "You have acted in accordance with your principles. It is all a question of party. And now, here I am."

Then, La Fayette having asked for orders, the king said with a laugh: "It seems to me that I should receive orders, not give them."

Adrienne, a woman of inflexible conscience but a loyal wife, said that no other action of her husband's life had caused her to feel so great an admiration for him. And indeed he had behaved like a man of honor. On one hand, Gilbert had suppressed his republican feelings in order to be true to his oath of allegiance to the king; on the other, in the painful situation which his position forced upon him, he took great risks and assumed complete responsibility for what had happened, in order to spare the royal family as much as possible from having to endure painful humiliation. Adrienne made a great point of going to the Tuileries as soon as the queen began to see a few visitors. The occasion cannot have been a very agreeable one for her, since she was the only woman present of her own political persuasion and knew that she would be cold-shouldered; but she agreed with La Fayette that in such a situation politics should not be allowed to override the claim of protocol.

Each day suspicious deputations visited the palace, wishing to see with their own eyes what precautions were being taken against any further attempt at flight. La Fayette was constantly being roused from his sleep to be told that the king and queen had again made good their escape. There was no grain of truth in these stories. In the early days of her return Marie-Antoinette had been compelled to go to bed at night, get up in the morning, and dress and undress in full view of the guards. La Fayette, however, managed to bring these men into a better frame of mind and to persuade them of the impropriety of what they were doing.

The queen saw La Fayette frequently: in fact, he visited her more often than was strictly necessary. She was polite though distant, and talked with him freely and without bitterness.

THE BEGINNING OF THE END

It is the privilege of the great to watch
catastrophes from a balcony seat.

JEAN GIRAUDOUX

From then on the sovereigns were prisoners. The Assembly, however, decided on July 15, 1791, to admit the principle of the king's
irresponsibility and to support the dynasty. A thousand citizens
signed a protest and took it to the Champ de Mars on the seventeenth. Two "suspects" who, according to La Fayette, were merely
a couple of unfortunate army pensioners, were found hiding under
the Altar of the Nation and were lynched. The municipality proclaimed martial law. The National Guard had to fire on the rioters,
and on the second anniversary of the fall of the Bastille the Champ
de Mars was dotted with corpses, the number of which was as usual
exaggerated by political passions.

It is difficult to imagine the intensity of the torments suffered
by Adrienne while Gilbert was at the Champ de Mars, exposed to
the fury of a mob thirsting for his blood. One part of it broke away
and made for the Rue de Bourbon, yelling "Kill his wife and take
him her head!" The children never forgot those horrible voices,
the terror of those who lived in the house, and, in contrast, the joy
felt by their mother at the thought that the brigands who had
come to threaten her were at least not at the Champ de Mars.

She took us in her arms with tears of joy [Virginie wrote], *and saw*
to all the necessary precautions against the impending danger with

impressive calm and a tremendous sense of relief. The guard had been doubled and was now drawn up ready for action in front of the house. But the brigands were on the point of breaking in upon my mother by way of the garden, which looked on to the Place du Palais Bourbon, when a body of cavalry which happened to enter the Place dispersed them.[1]

The popularity of La Fayette and of Bailly was spattered with the blood shed on that day. Camille Desmoulins was bent on doing away with both of them. "What! are we to keep our hats on before the king's wife and doff them to the white horse—to say nothing of Bailly's great nose and La Fayette's *toupet?*" * He called the general the "Don Quixote of the Capets" and the "Fine Flower of the Janissaries." This was tantamount to setting up the scaffold.

Gloomy news was reaching Adrienne from the country. In Auvergne, at Plauzat, her Montagu sister was noting the disaffection of the people. The wind of revolution was blowing over a canton that so far had been tranquil. Clubs and national guards were being organized; here and there in the countryside a château was burned. From the room where she sat knitting gray woolen dresses striped with black for the poor girls of the village, she could hear violent harangues in the Auvergne dialect. The same people who, a short six months earlier, had cheered their lords and masters, now kept their hats on when they passed them and whistled the *"Ça ira!"* When the Montagu parents went walking with their little Noémie, unheroic patriots shouted from behind the hedges, "To the lamppost!" Since there had never been any street lamps in Plauzat, this made the whole wretched business ridiculous as well as painful.

The parish priest changed sides three times a day. They would leave him after dinner staunchly orthodox, only to find him next morning turned schismatic. Such weakness in a man of the church so disgusted Pauline that, for all her piety, she gave up going to Mass. She tried to persuade her husband to join the Vicomte de Beaune, who had emigrated. But Montagu, like La Fayette, was still hopeful. His idea was to rally all Frenchmen of good will. Finally he agreed to go to England, yet he kept on putting off the fateful moment from day to day.

* *Toupet* has the double meaning of hair or wig, and effrontery. (Translator's note.)

On September 4 the drafting of the constitution was completed. The king went to the Assembly, where he publicly signified his acceptance of it. The people, delighted by this gesture, thought that reconciliation had been achieved. "We have reached the end of the revolution," said Louis XVI. "May happiness return to our country." But passions are not so easily demobilized. On the twentieth the Assembly broke up, having finished its labors. Before doing so, however, it decided, on a motion put forward by the "incorruptible Robespierre" (who considered his colleagues too lukewarm in their revolutionary ardor and wanted to see the personnel of politics entirely changed) that none of its members should sit in the new legislative body. This meant depriving the country of all the experience gained in the last few years. "There was only one tremendous blunder left for us to make," said the royalist Baron Malouet, "and sure enough we made it."

The constitution had been accepted by the king, and its makers had disbanded. La Fayette decided that his task was ended and that he could now make his final bow with good grace. He had in mind the great example set by Washington, who, when victory had crowned his efforts, had chosen to retire and live quietly on his estate. When Gilbert sent in his resignation, Adrienne was delighted. She had fearlessly faced danger with him, and she did not want him to be led into taking responsibility for measures of which no doubt he would disapprove. He seemed in these last days to have won back his popularity. Bailly said to him: "We shall never forget the Hero of Two Worlds, who has played so great a part in the Revolution." The National Guard presented him a gold-hilted sword engraved with his motto, *Cur non?* Petitions were circulated demanding that after his death he should be accorded the honor of the Panthéon.

Gilbert had the wisdom, at the very beginning of this new honeymoon between the nation and himself, to leave for Chavaniac. Perhaps he would have liked to be mayor of Paris now that Bailly had resigned from that office, but the queen, who could no longer endure him, put up a rival candidate in the person of Pétion (whom she had got to know during the return drive from Varennes), and Pétion won. This was the height of folly on her part, because La Fayette would have put up a very much better defense of the royal family. But Marie-Antoinette preferred a simple-minded bourgeois to a noble who had played the schoolmaster. The journey into Auvergne was flattering to Gilbert's self-esteem.

My journey has been a long one [he wrote Mme de Simiane], but, being obliged to stop at every place I came to, to parade on foot through towns big and small, to receive enough civic crowns to fill a carriage, I could not travel as quickly as I usually do. I left Clermont at night; the whole place was illuminated. We were accompanied by the National Guard and men carrying torches, which made a truly charming spectacle. At Issoire, which you know well, there is an excellent brand of patriot. I need not tell you that I was well received there, as also at Lempdes. Brioude paid me every imaginable honor.[2]

Adrienne, who followed with her daughters in another carriage, had written to her sister Pauline to say that she would make a halt at Plauzat to rejoice with her over the happy termination of the Revolution. Wrote Pauline's biographer:

Madame de Montague can scarcely have restrained her tears when she read this letter, for nothing is sadder than the illusions of those one loves when one knows in advance how empty they are. So far was the Revolution from being finished that the promised visit made her tremble. Monsieur de Beaune was quite capable of shutting his door against her, even in a foreign land, if by chance he learned that she had received General La Fayette in his house at Plauzat. So with an aching heart she wrote to her sister to say that she could not, without incurring the displeasure of her father-in-law, offer her the hospitality for which she had asked. But she would go secretly to meet her on the road, at the stagehouse of Vaire through which place she knew that she must pass. It was there, hidden away in an obscure inn, that they said good-by to each other. The meeting was brief and touching. The two sisters promised, with tears, to write to each other often, and Monsieur de La Fayette, though much blaming his brother-in-law's determination, embraced the young emigrant with redoubled affection.[3]

When passions obscure judgment it is pleasant to find personal affections getting the better of public conflicts. Pauline de Montagu no longer understood either her sister or her brother-in-law, but she did not love them the less. To her father, the Duc d'Ayen, she had written to say how greatly relieved she was at the news that La Fayette had sent in his resignation. Then, from the stagehouse at Vaire, she wrote again:

Since I love to share everything with you, my dear Papa, and because I know how incredulous you will be of the facts which I am now going to impart, I do not want the mail to leave without my inform-ing you that Monsieur de La Fayette arrived here this evening, where he will sleep since, on my own authority, I have refused to receive him at our customary place of residence. My own I have, for the past two days, taken up here.... It was a pleasure indeed for me to embrace the traveler, who, with his usual simplicity and kindness, has made this journey with his wife who is well-nigh intoxicated with joy and happiness.... What will surprise you is the kind of life he intends to live in his retirement. Not one single secretary has he brought with him into the country. He will install his library and his furniture. Books, Swiss cows, Spanish sheep, and a Maltese don-key will provide him with his sole occupations. Those in which he has been involved over the last twenty-seven months have really and truly exhausted him.[4]

At Chavaniac a maternal welcome awaited Gilbert. Aunt Char-lotte (now sixty-two) held in horror all the innovations that had penetrated even as far as Auvergne, but her affections for her nephew remained unimpaired. He was quite convinced, as he wrote to Madame de Simiane, that his decision to be nothing but a gentleman-farmer was irrevocable:

Here I am, installed in my place of retirement.... I take as much pleasure and perhaps self-pride in complete repose as ever I did over the past fifteen years in that activity which, always directed to the same end and now crowned with success, has left me no role to play but that of a plowman.[5]

He had imported from England a certain Mr. Dysson, an expert in farming, to instruct him in the latest methods of cattle-breeding. Soon he surprised the villagers by introducing English herds and pigs. The architect Antoine Vaudoyer came from Paris to make the château habitable, and Gilbert embarked on a monumental renovation. He established his own quarters in the treasure tower. Here he installed his mementos of the American Revolution. The

walls of his bedroom were hung with Aubusson tapestries, and his
austere camp bed was moved to the dressing room which was
adorned with *toiles de Jouy* representing scenes of American life.

The alterations, the furnishings, and the purchase of livestock
cost a great deal of money, and to provide it he had to sell some
of his land. After paying his principal debts, he was left with an
income which, though it had amounted to 128,000 livres in 1788,
had now fallen to 57,000. The American war and the French
Revolution had run away with more than half his fortune. It was
Adrienne who, with the help of the faithful Morizot, had to meet
the most urgent demands. In December, 1791, she wrote Morizot
that she was going to try to borrow 2000 écus locally. If she failed
in the attempt, she would have to ask him for the money required
in January and February.

We live here in a world of profound peace [she continued]. Mon-
sieur de La Fayette revels in its delights as though he had never
known a more active existence. His land, his house, Mademoiselle
his aunt, his children, and the writing of a few letters now fill his life
completely. Only a war against the émigrés could tear him away, and
I hope that nothing of the sort will happen.[6]

The Duchesse d'Ayen had promised to go to Chavaniac for a
rest. On her way there she spent two weeks at Plauzat. For fear of
disturbing the happiness of this reunion, Pauline de Montagu
refrained from telling her that she was making preparations to leave
France. Her mother saw that she was worried but did not ask the
reason. The calamities of the times were quite enough to engender
a mood of melancholy. Again, Pauline's biographer:

So terrifying was the obscurity in which the state of public affairs
was then buried that the Duchesse d'Ayen had chosen what she
considered the better part, and kept her eyes carefully averted from
the gloomy spectacle of revolution, fixing them instead on higher
things. In the general state of disorder then prevalent, her faith had
never been so firm, and she spoke of it to her daughter in language
which had never been simpler, clearer, or more beautiful. Madame
de Montagu listened entranced while the duchesse, sitting beside her
at her work, explained with the help of remembered passages from
the Bible and elsewhere how God's loving mercies are made mani-
fest even in His anger, and so teaching her to adore His ways....

In those stormy autumn days, whenever there was an uninterrupted hour of fine weather, mother and daughter took advantage of it to walk in the surrounding country, though never venturing too far beyond the ancient towers. In this way did they spent fifteen days together, without once communicating to each other, or at least not directly, the sad thoughts that were troubling the secret places of their hearts. The absence of the master of the house, the sight of the church into which they never went, the sound of the bells which they pretended not to hear, served to remind them of what by tacit agreement they were trying not to remember.[7]

So it was that the Duchesse d'Ayen arrived at Chavaniac without the slightest idea that Pauline was about to emigrate. Her eldest daughter, Louise de Noailles, joined her there. Adrienne, happy to find herself living in a more peaceful world at last, with a husband who seemed to have resigned himself to a life of retirement, with her three children, her mother, and her sister, was able to enjoy their period of tranquility without thinking too much about the future. Gilbert said that the Revolution was over, and it was only right and proper to believe him.

The electors of Haute-Loire unanimously appointed him to act as administrator of the department. This he refused to do, saying—no doubt sincerely—that he had made up his mind to live as a simple citizen and to concern himself only with domestic problems. In December, rumors of war and the provocative activities of the émigrés and their foreign friends led to the mobilizing of three armies of 50,000 men in north and northeast France. Narbonne, now Minister for War (thanks to Mme de Staël, whose lover he was), suggested to the king the names of the three men best suited to command them: Luckner, who had been a German general in the Seven Years' War, a man of limited intelligence and sordid avarice, but with a high reputation as a strategist; the Maréchal de Rochambeau, and La Fayette. The king objected only to La Fayette. "If Your Majesty refuses to accept his nomination today," said Narbonne, "public opinion will compel you to do so tomorrow."

So eager was La Fayette to resume his profession of soldier, this time with a major French command, and so sure was he that he could be of service to his country and to his ideas, that he accepted the appointment at once. Adrienne, despairing, decided to remain at Chavaniac. She loved the old aunt, with her sharp tongue and passionate enthusiasm, and did not wish to abandon her just when Gilbert was about to go away. La Fayette left in a great hurry, saw the king in Paris, and was escorted as far as Gonesse by detachments of the National Guard who greeted him enthusiastically. The man on the white horse still retained a certain amount of prestige. One of his aides-de-camp, Pillet, wrote to Mme de La Fayette:

PARIS, DECEMBER 24, 1791

Madame, Monsieur de La Fayette has arrived here loaded with the blessings and marks of affection of the people who eagerly saluted him in all the towns through which he passed. Anxious to arrive on the appointed day, he sacrificed his moments of rest to these complimentary exchanges, but fortunately, though he has been on the move night and day, his health seems not to have suffered at all from the fatigues of his journey, and those friends who saw him leave Paris as a sick man are overjoyed by the freshness of vigor and the increase in girth which he has acquired at Chavaniac.

All faces here light up at the mention of Monsieur de La Fayette. He is seen everywhere and is welcomed by all as the liberator of his country and the one man in whom they can place their hopes, and he seems happy to know this. The general opinion, especially in government circles, is that we shall not have a war, but that in order to put an end to the state of anxiety in which the country has been for some considerable time and especially to rally the friends of order and to heighten public morale, it is necessary to adopt vigorous measures and to make an imposing show of strength. So, as you may see, the future presents no cause for alarm.

Throughout his journey, Monsieur de La Fayette seemed deeply affected by the condition in which he had left you. He hopes that, once the rumors of war have been dissipated, Madame de Chavaniac will recover her peace of mind, and that her fondness for him will enable her to exercise sufficient self-control to prevent any deterioration in her health.[8]

From her husband's headquarters in Metz Adrienne received letters the chief burden of which was politics and the tactical situation. It was not lack of affection that made him thus concentrate on the realities of the moment, but his confidence in the intelligence of a wife who was clear-sighted enough to take an interest in everything. He prided himself on being a good soldier. He had found the armies in a deplorable state, well below the average of efficiency. A third of the officers had emigrated; another third, hostile to the Revolution, deserted when fighting became imminent; veterans and volunteers got on badly together. It was thought that a revolutionary general would be more indulgent than the old marshals. In fact, it was just the contrary. The old marshals felt it to be incumbent on them to frequent the clubs, whereas Gilbert never set foot in them. His disciplinary measures were stricter than those of the Old Regime.

But Paris did nothing to back him up. The new Assembly wanted a war, though it did not have the means for winning one. In March Narbonne was dismissed and a Girondin ministry came into power (Dumouriez, Roland). Dumouriez, the lover of the sister of the celebrated *émigré* Rivarol, was a man of intelligence and a brave soldier. But he was irresponsible and venal. La Fayette had no confidence in him, but all the same retained him in his command. He did not like the men who dominated the new Assembly. To his confidante Adrienne he sent a secret letter:

METZ, APRIL 18, 1792

I cannot hide from you my opinion that war is becoming more and more probable. There is still hope, but I should be much more inclined now to put my money on a war. We go under canvas about May 10. The parties are at present divided as follows: Robespierre, Danton, Desmoulins, etc., form the hard core of the Jacobin rabble. They are puppets manipulated from behind the scenes, and do the court good service by creating a general state of confusion, shouting that we are beaten and without resources, and attacking La Fayette, who, so they say, has deceived people and court alike, has led Monsieur de Bouillé (who is a great deal less blameworthy) by the nose, and, in his own person, constitutes a far more serious danger than the aristocrats. Duport has rather ingenuously informed me that the party has been accusing me of republicanism, and that if only I could come to terms with it he would find himself, somewhat to his surprise, a good deal closer to me. I don't give a button for Duport's frank speaking and guilelessness, and rather think that he will get a good scolding for saying all this. I am also being blamed for being anti-Austrian. The other party, known as the upper-crust Jacobins, is composed of the Bordeaux faction: Abbé Sieyès, Con-

dorcet, Roederer, etc. They fear and hate Robespierre, but dare not risk losing their popularity. They think that war is inevitable, feel that Rochambeau is on the way out, have a high opinion of Luckner, and, though they hate me personally, have for some time been of the opinion that they must put complete confidence in me as an unshakable friend of freedom and equality and an incorruptible defender of the Constitution.

I have, through the good offices of my friends, been able to have things out with the two ministers who mostly concern me, and this explanation will lead to another with the leading figures in the Assembly, though not on my initiative. I have renewed my profession of faith to a friend charged with the duty of finding out what precisely my views are. I have put forward certain demands: that civil and religious freedom shall be respected, that everything possible shall be done to maintain public order, and several other matters of the same sort about which you know my feelings. I have an idea that they have been adopted. As to personal questions, I have no complaints to make about the present ministry, or, to be more accurate, about the two Ministers of War and Foreign Affairs, who will, I think, give me all I want. To sum up my position: as I have already made clear, the French nation is my only party, and my friends and I are at the disposal of anyone who will act for the best, defend liberty and equality, uphold the Constitution, and reject everything that might tend to give it either an aristocratic or republican coloring. When the will of the nation, expressed by the elected representatives of the people and by the king, shall have declared that war is inevitable, I shall do everything in my power to bring it to a successful conclusion.[9]

This is a curious letter to have been written by a husband and father separated from his family, but one worthy of the woman to whom it is addressed. Like her husband, Adrienne was concerned above all else in holding her head high. The attack on the Low Countries, ordered by the government, was a complete failure. The Austrian hussars spread panic through the French army, which retired in disorder on Lille and Valenciennes. Paris was in a state of hysteria. The king dismissed the Girondin ministry. Robespierre, denouncing the generals, organized street demonstrations. On June 20, 1792, the king was treated in the Tuileries as he had been on October 5, 1789, at Versailles. The mob invaded the palace. No defense was put up by the guard. To cries of "Down with Monsieur Veto!" several men armed with pikes brought Louis XVI to bay in a window embrasure. He put the red cap on his head, drank to the health of the nation, but stood firm on essentials: "I have received the sacraments; I fear nothing. . . . I shall do what the Constitution orders me to do."

La Fayette was furious when the news of this riot reached him. He immediately left his headquarters and presented himself at the bar of the Assembly, where he denounced the faction which had "invaded the national sovereignty" and demanded that action be taken against those responsible for the invasion of the palace. He was loudly applauded. Public opinion rallied to him. He proposed to take advantage of a review of the National Guard to lead it against the Jacobins. In these decisive days he gave proof of a steadfastness and resolution worthy of the highest praise. But the queen, strangely obstinate in her attitude, did not wish under any circumstances to owe her safety to him, and warned Pétion, who canceled the review. La Fayette went back to his army. The monarchy had been given its last chance, and had rejected it.

At Chavaniac Adrienne was gloomy. There was no one with whom she could share her anxieties. Her mother, and later her sister Louise, had been obliged to return to Paris. Mme de Chavaniac's violent political feelings and her resolute hostility to a revolution, the reasons for which she completely failed to understand, made it impossible for Adrienne to find in her either consolation or support. The only comfort she had came from Anastasie, then fourteen. Virginie, ten, was too young, and the Montagus' decision to emigrate soon separated them from Adrienne.

They left France without saying good-by to anybody except Rosalie de Grammont. The process of deliberate expatriation was becoming dangerous and difficult. Together, Pauline and Rosalie made the necessary purchases for the journey in Paris, and, early on the morning of December 7, in spite of a heavy snow, went to hear Mass in one of the clandestine chapels. They went on foot, making use of back streets so that their footsteps in the snow should not attract attention. The improvised chapel was on the third floor of a house, and the only light came from a single candle. That evening the two sisters packed clothes and linen, unknown to the servants. Outside the wind was howling. Montagu came to tell his wife that everything was ready, and shook his sister-in-law's hand as though he were merely setting off to spend a few days in the country. Mme de Grammont drew her sister aside to where a fire was burning, and asked whether she had her diamonds with her.

"What purpose would there be in that?" Pauline asked with a sigh. "We are not going to a party."

"That, my poor dear, is why you must take them."

Mme de Montagu got her jewel case and hid it under her cloak. Then the two sisters sadly exchanged locks of hair.

Next evening the couple reached Calais and embarked for England.

The declaration of war filled Adrienne with the most dismal forebodings. The disturbed state of the country added to her anxieties. Even at Chavaniac there were echoes of the increasing dissension between Girondins and Jacobins, the forerunners of storms to come. But her conscience brought her some moments of happiness. A courageous letter written by her husband to the Assembly, and his appearance there brought to her troubled mind the joy she was accustomed to find in his conduct. She alone saw Gilbert as he wished to be seen: a knight *sans peur et sans reproche*. But she suffered much from her knowledge of the many dangers to which he was exposed. He suggested her joining him at Metz, and and this was sweet to her because it showed how much he wanted to have her with him.

But she was afraid that, with feelings running so high, the journey might give rise to calumnies, since a rumor could easily be put about that he wanted to send his family to a place of safety [so wrote Virginie]. She feared too that her presence might prove to be an embarrassment to him, since his movement depended on so many unforeseeable events. After deliberating for several days, she decided to sacrifice herself and to remain at Chavaniac. About this time a battalion of Girondin volunteers passed through the village on its way to join the army. The men were in a highly excitable state of mind, and some of them went so far as to threaten to set fire to the château. [She] entertained the officers at dinner and provided food for the detachment which was billeted in the village. Her noble and patriotic behavior inspired respect and preserved the château from all harm.[10]

Shortly afterward news reached Adrienne of the insurrection of August 10. A motion in the Assembly, demanding that La Fayette should be put on trial, was defeated by 406 votes to 224. But out in the streets there was much booing of him and of the Assembly. "I verily believe," Gouverneur Morris wrote Thomas Jefferson, "that if M. de La Fayette were to appear just now in Paris unattended by his army, he would be torn to pieces."

In point of fact, without the support of the king La Fayette was powerless, and the king refused to make common cause with his followers. He was counting on the weakness of the Assembly, in which he was right, and on that of the Jacobins, in which he was wrong. On August 10 the great bell of the Cordeliers summoned the rioters to arms. The legal Commune, as opposed to the insurrectionist Commune, wished to protect Louis XVI. It had strengthened the Tuileries with a detachment of Swiss Guards, a number of militiamen, and the National Guard. Danton, in order to get the commander, Mandat-Grancey, out of the way, had him summoned to the Hôtel de Ville, where he was arrested and later, killed. The busts of Bailly, La Fayette, and Necker were mutilated, much to the delight of a cheering crowd. Popularity is as fragile as the statues it produces.

On August 10 the Tuileries was attacked. Within the palace a number of gentlemen offered their swords to the king. The Duc d'Ayen, having heard about the events of June 20, had left Switzerland to resume his duties as captain of the guard, though that office had been abolished. His son-in-law Grammont and the Prince de Poix spent the night in the Tuileries. They had both supported the new ideas, but now refused to do so any longer. The queen was in favor of resisting but Louis, when the first insurgent bands showed themselves, sought safety for himself and his family with the Assembly. The assault cost six hundred Swiss their lives. Two hundred of the king's servants were also killed, and four hundred of the assailants. The Duc d'Ayen, the Marquis de Grammont, and the Prince de Poix came out of the affair unharmed. A price was set on their heads. They went into hiding and, thanks to a number of faithful servants, managed to escape from Paris. The victorious rioters invaded the Assembly building and clamored for the king's deposition. They succeeded in having him temporarily suspended from the exercise of his functions and imprisoned in the Temple. A new Jacobin government was formed. The second stage of the Revolution had been completed: constitutional royalty had followed absolute monarchy into limbo.

La Fayette, who heard of these events from an officer who had escaped the massacre, was not the man to accept the ruin of his work. Like his friends Noailles, La Rochefoucauld, Clermont-Tonnerre, and Broglie, he had dreamed of a constitution on the English or American model—of a free and ordered realm. But the French people were now less interested in institutions than in insurrection, less concerned about the state than about society, less eager for liberty than for equality. For such a misunderstanding there was no cure.

La Fayette called upon his army to remain loyal to their constitutional oath. He would have liked to march on Paris and give battle to the insurgents. The old Maréchal Luckner, however, was strongly opposed to any such idea. La Fayette managed to get the municipality of Sedan to order the arrest of the commissioners sent by the new government to the army, but when on August 15, having paraded his men for inspection, he asked them to renew their oath "to the nation, the law, and the king," he was met with hostile mutterings. The Hero of Two Worlds had lost his prestige. His charm no longer worked. The National Assembly, informed of his act of rebellion, ordered him committed for trial.

All was over. The wonderful fame and splendor he had won with his sword at so young an age and at the peril of his life had fallen from him. What should he do? Put up a fight? With what? Take some rash and headstrong step? He was neither sufficiently cynical nor sufficiently powerful. Surrender to his persecutors? The sacrifice would have been purposeless, to say nothing of the fact that the eternal optimist in him still hoped some day to see liberty triumphant. Go over to the enemy? The idea filled him with horror. No, his only course was to seek asylum in a neutral country. With a few of his staff officers (La Tour-Maubourg and his two brothers, and Bureaux de Pusy and Romeuf) he crossed the frontier of his homeland and entered neutral Belgium.

At Chavaniac, on August 24, the whole family was assembled in Adrienne's room after dinner. In silence they waited for Michel, who had gone to Brioude for letters. Only Adrienne knew of the terrible decree that had been issued by the Assembly against her husband. The parish priest, who was one of the company, was waiting impatiently for the arrival of the gazettes before ringing for vespers. Anastasie, feeling ashamed because she had been play-

ing battledore and shuttlecock for a moment, was leaning against
a chest of drawers, looking dejected. George and Virginie were
talking together in a corner. M. Frestel, George-Washington's
tutor, was stretched out in an armchair reading some old numbers
of the *Logographe*. Vaudoyer, the architect, had assumed a suitable
expression and dared not make a movement for fear of losing it.
The priest, after looking two or three times at his watch, tiptoed
out of the room. Vespers must be rung, no matter what was going on.

With each moment that passed hearts beat faster. "Mamma's
face became paler and paler," Anastasie said later. "At last she got
up and we followed her to Mademoiselle Marin's room. We had
scarcely reached it when Monsieur Frestel appeared with some
letters." There was one from the Vicomtesse de Noailles, who wrote
to tell her sister that La Fayette was across the frontier. "Mamma's
joy was in proportion to the anxiety she had been feeling for the
last few days." Her children shared her happiness. At this moment
Mme de Chavaniac came into the room.

"Is there any news of my nephew?" she asked.

"Yes," replied Adrienne. "He is out of danger. He has left the
country."

"Left the country!" exclaimed Mme de Chavaniac. Then,
shaken by sobs, she went into a corner of the room, plucking at her
dress and her cap. She had completely failed to grasp the gravity
of the situation. She was conscious only of her own personal drama
and kept on saying "I shall never see him again!"

M. Frestel and Mlle Marin begged Adrienne to conceal her joy,
since it might become dangerous. Already the whole of the domestic staff had come one after the other to congratulate her. These
demonstrations were more than usually touching and courageous,
since Michel had brought word that people were coming from
Paulhaguet to loot and burn the château. Adrienne quickly signed
promissory notes for all her creditors, hid such compromising papers as she knew about, and made up her mind to get the children
away. She was racking her brains to think of some safe refuge
for George when the son of the curé of Conangles (a widower who
had turned priest, taken the constitutional oath, and so was left
in peace by the authorities) arrived with a message from his father
to the effect that the boy would be welcome should he wish to
take refuge in that remote mountain parish. Adrienne accepted

the offer, and at the same time decided that her daughters should go to the Château of Langeac (bought by La Fayette before the Revolution but never lived in). Anastasie and Virginie protested. They wanted to stay with their mother, but she was determined and packed them into the gig with Mlle Marin. Off they went, to the accompaniment of sobs from several women of the village.

PART FIVE

THE GODS ARE THIRSTY

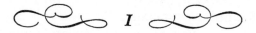

THE JACOBINS AT CHAVANIAC

> *Though the injustice of the people has*
> *not lessened my devotion to their cause,*
> *it has destroyed for me the delicious*
> *sensation of basking in the smiles of the*
> *multitude.* LA FAYETTE

Chaos piled on chaos! Only a month ago Adrienne had been the wife of a general in command of an army, of a man who was in a position of power and enjoyed throughout Auvergne the respect of those authorities who had been set up as the result of a revolution he had fathered. Now she was the wife of a man proscribed, herself a hostage, and fated perhaps to be a victim. Once, to the sound of cheers and clapping hands she had passed under triumphal arches in the towns and villages of the province. Now she was suspect. No doubt some honest folk would still remain loyal to her. All who knew her personally loved her: many revered her. But public opinion is a strumpet who gives herself to the strong. The countryside was alive with brigands. Battalions marching from the southwest to join the armies were filling Auvergne with men who were complete strangers to the district. Almost everywhere the municipalities had turned Jacobin. Danger was imminent and deadly. But Adrienne was firm in her determination to sacrifice none of her beliefs and principles, to bear her husband's name proudly, and at least to save her children.

Anastasie and Virginie had been driven to the Château of Langeac, where they had been welcomed by the keeper's wife. The sisters shared a bed. Next morning the little girls learned that the municipality had officially taken them under its wing. Terror and cowardice had not smothered all other feelings.

At Chavaniac, as soon as the gig left with her daughters, Adrienne had helped her son and his tutor to disguise themselves as peasants. After a night in the woods, they reached Conangles, where the priest offered them hospitality. He had a hidden loft into which George and his tutor climbed by ladder whenever there was an alarm.

Next day, Adrienne was awakened by two cannon shots. She thought the brigands had come, but she was wrong. The cannon had been fired in honor of St Julien, the patron saint of Brioude. Soon visitors came with terrifying news. A woman from Le Puy told them that a crowd was assembling with the intention of marching to the château and setting it on fire. Adrienne made sure that a carrying-chair and two sturdy men would be available, should necessity arise, to move her old aunt.

She then wrote to the president of the tribunal at Brioude, asking him to affix his official seals to Chavaniac. This was an ingenious move to protect the château, since looters would be intimidated by the seals of an administrative body. Adrienne carefully did not take any action under the law as it applied to émigrés, for she did not wish her husband to be considered one. Accordingly, she had an inventory made to "safeguard the rights of her creditors." The commissioners turned up next day, as requested, and affixed the seals. Everything was done in the most respectful manner. The word émigré was never once mentioned, and Gilbert was spoken of as simply being absent.

Some days later Adrienne was preparing to drive to Brioude, where she wanted to take a lodging in order to prove that she had no intention of emigrating, when Michel arrived with letters. There was one from Gilbert, the first since his departure, and it filled her with joy to learn that he was at least safe. Having crossed the frontier with a group of his officers, he had been arrested by an Austrian patrol at Rochefort, not far from Namur. He had hoped to reach Holland and from there to take ship for the United States, but it soon became clear that he and his friends were to be regarded as prisoners. The Marquis de Chasteler, an Austrian general who was in command at Namur, had told Gilbert that Prince Charles of Lorraine was coming from Brussels for the express purpose of "consulting with him about the situation in France." This was intended to make things easier. La Fayette replied sharply that "he could not suppose that anyone would have the effrontery to put questions to him which it would not be proper for him to answer."

His letter to Adrienne was pure La Fayette. A specialist in pleading his own cause, Gilbert set himself to justify his conduct to France, to his children, and to his wife. He would present to posterity that picture of an honorable man:

No matter what the vicissitudes for fortune, my dear heart, you know that my spirit is not of the temper to acknowledge defeat. But you know it too well not to feel pity for the sense of heartbreak I now suffer at having to leave my country, to which I have devoted my every effort and which would have been free, and worthy of freedom, had not private interests combined to corrupt the public mind, to disorganize the means of resisting attacks from without and of achieving liberty and security within. Proscribed by my country for having served it courageously, I have been compelled to cross into a territory which is subject to an enemy government in order to flee from France, in whose defense I should have found so sweet a happiness.

An Austrian post lay on our road, the commander of which thought it his duty to arrest us. From here we are to be taken to Namur, but I cannot believe that our captors will have the dishonesty to confine for long foreigners who by a patriotic and constitutional declaration have been careful to dissociate themselves from those Frenchmen who have emigrated because they held opinions very different from ours, and have openly announced their intention of making their way to some neutral country, Holland or England....

As to myself, there are many who have long sworn to bring about my ruin. I could, with more of ambition than morality, have had a very different sort of life; but there shall never be any connection between me and criminal activities. Up till the last, I have supported the Constitution to which I swore allegiance. You know that my heart would have been wholly republican, had not my reason contributed a touch of royalism, and had not adhesion to my given word and to the national will made of me a defender of the king's constitutional rights. But the weaker the will to resist grew, the more loudly did my voice make itself heard, with the result that I became a target for attacks from every quarter. It was as obvious as a mathematical demonstration that I could no longer usefully oppose one crime and at the same time be the victim of another. I was therefore compelled to withdraw from a struggle in which it was evident that I should lose my life to no purpose.

I know not for how long I may be delayed, but I shall eventually go to England, where I wish all my family to join me. I should dearly like to think that it might be possible for my aunt to undertake the journey as well. I know that the families of those who have emigrated are held, but only those émigrés who have taken up arms against their country, and God knows that only a monster would dare believe that such should be the case with me. Such few letters as I shall write will be read in both the imperial and Jacobin post-houses, but that is all the same to me, provided they reach you. I have never had a feeling which I needed to conceal.

I offer no excuse either to my children or to you for having been the ruin of my family. There is not one of you who would have wished me to owe prosperity to conduct of which my conscience could not approve. Come and join me in England: let us settle in America. There we shall find the liberty which no longer exists in France, and my love shall try as best it can to console you for all the happiness you have lost. Farewell, dear heart.[1]

Gilbert next wrote to the Princesse d'Hénin, who was in England, telling her about the events that had led up to his departure, about his troops "torn to pieces by the artillery of dismissals," and about Adélaïde de Simiane—for his correspondent knew all about that affair. "I shall go to England," Gilbert asserted, "and hope that our friend may be able to go there too. I could almost wish that she were here." He wrote again to the Princesse d'Hénin on September 3. "I would rather suffer in the name of the despotism against which I have fought than in that of the people whose cause is dear to my heart. . . . Since leaving France, I have had no news of our friend; she will be glad to know that I am across the frontier, though at the moment she must be feeling very uneasy. A letter from me, if it were opened by the Jacobins, might compromise her and let those monsters see what pain they could cause me by tormenting her." Two days later, another letter: "Good-by, my dear Princesse. I do not write to our friend, whom a letter might compromise, nor to Madame de La Fayette, who is probably on her way to join me." [2] Gilbert knew his wife well enough not to doubt her wish to join him, but Adrienne was no longer free to come and go as she pleased. Madame de Chavaniac took charge of Gilbert's letter, intending to hide it, and begged her niece not to change her mind about the trip to Brioude. Adrienne was reasonably well received in the town. A young national guardsman gave her his arm when she went in search of a lodging. On the way he suddenly said: "That, Madame, is where our fellow townsmen put up a triumphal arch for Monsieur de La Fayette. All real patriots would gladly do the same today."

There was much excitement in the streets because it was the day of the primary elections to the Convention. Some of the electors were Jacobins, and Adrienne's friends warned her to be careful. They made a special point of advising her to go the following Sunday to hear Mass said by the constitutional parish priest. She replied that if her peace of mind could be bought only at the price of a base action, she would at once leave Brioude. She added that she would regard as an insult any attempt to persuade her that it would be to her advantage to adopt an attitude at variance with that of her husband, who was *not* an *émigré* after all but a prisoner of the *émigrés*. There was actually a rumor going about Brioude to the effect that Adrienne had said, "I would like to see all *émigrés* hacked to pieces." This was not at all like her, but all the same it deeply shocked the old members of the nobility in the neighborhood.

She found a few faithful souls, but there were others whose feelings were decidedly mixed. They were afraid of the Jacobins and the brigands, but no less so of the aristocrats, who would recover their power should the Prussians invade France and enter Paris. One of the electors, Aulagnier, said violent things about Adrienne: "What are we to think of a municipality which has the wife of La Fayette within its walls and lets her go free?" On Sunday she went early to hear Mass said by a nonjuring priest, after which she received several visitors. Some of them she found rather pathetic, but others made her impatient—for instance, an abbess who expressed aristocratic opinions.

This tragic Sunday, September 2, was the day on which savage massacres in Paris set the prisons running with blood. All that happened at Brioude was that the *sans-culottes* danced around the Tree of Liberty. A number of decent folk, fearing for Adrienne's safety, offered to hide her, but instead she drove to Langeac, where she dined with her daughters, for whom her coming was a great happiness. She then returned to Chavaniac.

The gazettes were filled with items of news about La Fayette's defection and arrest. Mme de Chavaniac had also received a letter from Gilbert, written at Nivelle on August 25, 1792.

I am in good health, my dear aunt, but that is the only consoling information I can send you. You have doubtless learned by what concatenation of fatalities and proscription the most loyal friend of liberty has been compelled to abandon his country which it would have been such a joy for him to defend.

They have arrested us, and, contrary to all justice, took us first to Namur and then to this small town to await, they say, the decision of the emperor, who is at Vienna. I said that I would very much rather have to complain of the injustice of an arbitrary government than of that of the people, and that imperial persecution seemed to me more natural than the proscription decreed in Paris against me.

Madame de La Fayette and my children are probably no longer at Chavaniac, and I should have liked to hear that you had consented to go with them. In any case, show them my letter, or send it to them. I beg you to speak kindly of me to the sisters, and to all who still live at Chavaniac. Tell the inhabitants of the commune of Aurac that it would be very wrong of them to feel hostile to the Constitution simply because a fellow citizen whom they love is suffering persecution. . . . Good-by, dear aunt. I love you tenderly.[3]

Gilbert sat unmoved among the ruins, awaiting with a confidence at once artless and sublime the coming of his wife and children.

Adrienne, feeling reassured, though it is hard to understand why, brought her daughters back to Chavaniac. All the village children escorted them. Would it be necessary to send them to Langeac again? It was being said in the neighborhood that a contingent from Marseilles would pass that way. Adrienne did not want to alarm Mlle Marin, the governess who had brought her up in the Hôtel de Noailles and for the last thirty years had been one of the family. To spare this kind-hearted but weak and tired old woman, Adrienne kept her anxieties to herself, or rather, confided them only to Anastasie, a young heroine who was far more proud than fearful at being trusted in this way. Adrienne told her elder daughter that brigands might turn up at any moment, even in the middle of the night, and that in such a case the only thing to do would be to take refuge in the woods. Somebody would have to carry Virginie.

On the morning of September 10 a party of soldiers suddenly appeared at Chavaniac. They had come from Le Puy. With them was Commissioner Alphonse Aulagnier, a sinister-looking man in a rust-color riding coat. Adrienne, who had heard him described in Brioude as a fanatic Jacobin, thought that perhaps she now faced death. Forcing his way into the château, Aulagnier showed Adrienne his orders, issued by the Committee of Public Safety: *"The woman Lafayette is to be arrested, together with her children, if they are found with her, and confined in a house of detention."* A letter from Minister of the Interior Roland made Aulagnier responsible for carrying out these instructions.

Not for a single moment did Adrienne lose her head. She realized that the essential thing was to get the soldiers out of the château as soon as possible, before they discovered Virginie— Anastasie had already been recognized. Adrienne hoped that the municipality would be reasonable and consent to hold Virginie prisoner and be responsible for her. While Aulagnier and his men were rummaging through drawers looking for incriminating papers, Adrienne managed to get away for a few moments, and see that Virginie hid herself with Mlle Marin.

Mme de Chavaniac, sixty-three, "whom nothing in the world could have persuaded to leave Chavaniac for her pleasure," declared that she would never be separated from her niece and insisted on being taken off to prison. This favor was granted.

At last Aulagnier gave the signal for departure. In his hands were Adrienne, fifteen-year-old Anastasie, and the elderly mistress of Chavaniac.

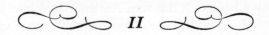
A HIGHLY RESPECTED
PRISONER

One does not go to heaven in a state coach.

SPANISH PROVERB

The party proceeded slowly. The great traveling-coach, in spite of its four horses, was too heavily loaded for the mountain road. The first night was spent at an inn in Fix. Soldiers were posted at the ladies' doors. Adrienne kept telling herself how much happier she was now than during those terrible days when she had not known whether Gilbert was alive or dead. Anastasie, delighted at not being separated from her mother, felt that she was safer than Virginie probably was. Aunt Charlotte was irritable but not in the least afraid.

Mercier, a devoted servant who had followed on foot with the escort, went to ask the ladies whether they were in need of anything. He said that the soldiers did not seem to be too ill disposed, and that Aulagnier had asked him to dinner. Adrienne, with tears in her eyes, thanked him for his zeal and devotion. "That is not difficult!" he replied, deeply moved. He looked earnestly at all the prisoners, one after the other, before withdrawing to wait and watch. He did not seem to realize that what he was doing might cost him his life.

Some officers came to ask at what hour the ladies would be ready to leave next morning. Would 2 A.M. be convenient? Mme de

Chavaniac thought this rather too early, but Adrienne was of the opinion that it would be well to give the soldiers as little time as possible in which to get drunk. She therefore agreed. Then, before settling down for a few short hours of sleep, the three ladies knelt together.

"Let us try," said Adrienne, "to put ourselves into that state of mind we would wish to be in at the moment of our death."

They slept little. At two o'clock, Aulagner, by this time all politeness and consideration, once again put his prisoners into the coach. Anastasie thought this a likely moment for assassins to attack them, but all three remained very calm. On their arrival at Le Puy, Adrienne asked to be driven straight to the town hall. The outskirts of the town seemed quite unsafe. Only a few days before, a prisoner had been lynched quite close to where they were.

"If your father knew you were here he would be very uneasy," Adrienne told her daughter, "but also very proud of the way you are behaving."

At the town hall the councilors were hastily summoned. As soon as they were all assembled, Adrienne announced that she placed herself with complete confidence in their hands and relied on them to protect her. She recognized them as the representatives of the people's authority, which she respected. "You gentlemen take your orders from Monsieur Roland or from whomever may be in a position to issue them. I wish to receive them only from you." Then she asked that those of her husband's letters which had been impounded at Chavaniac should be copied before being forwarded to Paris, "since lies are frequently told in the Assembly." She wished to read the letters aloud herself. When somebody objected that this might be painful for her, she answered: "On the contrary, Monsieur; the sentiments expressed in those letters are my support and consolation."

She noticed everything and thought of everything. Having found the mayor so kindly disposed toward her that he ran a considerable risk of being compromised, she was careful to make a few protests so that things should look better. After her reading of the letters, which moved all her listeners, she asked to be permitted to stay in the town hall for so long as she was kept at Le Puy. A journey to Paris she regarded as pointless and dangerous. If she was to be held as a hostage, why not confine her at Chavaniac as a prisoner on parole? It was decided that the local authorities should forward this request to the Minister of the Interior. The savage Aulagnier, now completely tamed, wrote personally to Roland: "Monseigneur, I have punctually discharged the mission which Your Excellency did me the honor of entrusting to me...," adding that in the matter of transporting the prisoners to Paris he had thought it better not to act strictly in accordance with the orders he had received. "The events of September 2 and 3 give me only too clear an idea of what might happen to my illustrious prisoner." Put to the test, Commissioner Aulagnier showed himself to be a man of decent feelings and considerable courage.

By the same courier Adrienne sent a letter to the deputy Brissot, who was one of Roland's most intimate friends. She had known him first when, on the point of starting for the United States, he had come to the Rue de Bourbon for letters of introduction. Later she had seen a good deal of him when, with La Fayette and Mirabeau, he had helped to found the Society of Friends of the Negroes. He was highly thought of in the Girondin party, which had recently come to power. He owned a journal, *Le Patriote Français*, and was a republican. An emotional letter of entreaty would in all probability have touched Brissot's susceptible heart, but the Marquise de la Fayette possessed, as did her husband, a form of pride which demanded an attitude, and the letter she sent was composed a little too much in the high Roman fashion:

LE PUY, SEPTEMBER 12, 1792

Monsieur, I believe you to be a true fanatic of liberty, and at present that is something I would say of few persons. I do not propose to consider whether this fanaticism, like that of religion, produces as a rule results which are the very opposite of its intention, but I cannot believe that so zealous a friend of the Negroes can be a willing instrument of tyranny. I feel convinced that no matter how enthusiastically you may support the aims of your party, the means it employs to achieve them must be repugnant to you. I feel sure that you esteem, nay, I would go further and say respect, Monsieur La Fayette as a faithful and courageous friend of freedom, even at a time when you are persecuting him because he holds opinions contrary to your own as to the manner in which it may best be established in France. That these, the courage with which he supports them, and his unswerving fidelity to his sworn word, may be opposed to those entertained by the party whose cause you have embraced and to your new revolution, I fully believe, and it is for that reason that I am addressing myself to you, since I scorn to approach others in the matter.

What your answer will be I do not know. It is easy to see that if it is dictated by the spirit of justice, it will restore to me an unconditional liberty. If it is in accordance with my heart's desire, it will permit be to join my husband in England, as he wishes, so soon as he may be released from captivity, in order that we may together settle in America when traveling to that country becomes once again practicable. But should it be decided that I am to be held as a hostage, then my imprisonment might be sweetened by my being allowed to choose Chavaniac as my place of enforced residence, on parole and on the responsibility of the municipality of my village. If you wish to be of service to me, you will have the satisfaction of having done a good action by softening the fate of one who has been unjustly persecuted, and who, as you very well know, has no longer the means or the wish to harm anybody.

I am willing to be beholden to you for such a service.[1]

This last sentence was harsh, tactless, and in no way like Adrienne's usually gracious and charitable manner of expressing herself. But humility ceases to be a virtue in the eyes of those who think that honor is a stake.

While waiting for an answer she lived in the administrative headquarters of the department. Well-wishing members of the National Guard requested the honor of being allowed to keep watch on her. News was passed to her of George and Virginie, hidden near Chavaniac. The information arriving from Germany by way of the Princesse d'Hénin was bad. Instead of being set at liberty, Gilbert had been handed over to the King of Prussia and taken to the fortress of Spandau. Adrienne was in despair at having given her word not to leave Chavaniac. She would so much have liked to join Gilbert in his captivity.

In Paris a republic had been proclaimed on September 22. Brissot had often talked of this possibility to La Fayette, whose answer had always been, "It is not yet time for that." When Brissot received Adrienne's proudly worded letter he showed it to Roland, who not unnaturally took it in bad part. Nevertheless, the minister wrote to the authorities at Le Puy saying that the prisoner might be permitted to be interned on parole at Chavaniac.

At the same time, Roland sent a severe letter to Adrienne. In it, he said that the expression " 'willing to be beholden for a service' smacked of the outmoded pride of what used to be called the nobility." This reprimand was much applauded by the departmental authorities. All the same, seeing that the required authorization had been given, the municipality of Aurac, in which Chavaniac was situated, was instructed to take over the duty of guarding the prisoner, for whose safekeeping the commune would be held responsible. The municipal authorities were not a little uneasy about the precise meaning of this expression. One of the officials asked whether Mme de La Fayette had *promised* to remain at Chavaniac. "If that is so," he said, "I am prepared to stand surety for her in my own person, for she is a good woman." The department decided that the commune should provide six men, every day, to guard the prisoner of Chavaniac. Adrienne at once confronted the council in session.

"I declare, gentlemen, that I shall withdraw the word I have already given if guards are stationed at my door. You can choose between these two guarantees. I cannot be shocked that you should not believe me to be an honest woman; my husband has given far better proof that he is a good patriot. But you must allow me to have confidence in my own integrity, and realize that I have no bayonets with which to support my word."

It was agreed that the guards should be withdrawn. This energetic woman made herself respected, and the Auvergne revolutionaries were not a bad lot. Adrienne had a faithful messenger in Paris: Nicolas Beauchet. He was a public servant (a clerk in the Court of Bankruptcy) who had married Adrienne's former maid. Marie-Josèphe Beauchet was Mme de La Fayette's fond and devoted friend. Several times a month letters were dispatched from Chavaniac, addressed to "The Citizeness Beauchet, at the house of a grocer, Rue de Courty, Faubourg Saint-Germain."

Adrienne now wrote to Brissot, taking him to task for having shown her confidential letter to the Minister of the Interior:

LE PUY, OCTOBER 4, 1792

I ought never again to write to you, Monsieur, after learning the use you make of my letters, but since I received news yesterday, which occasioned me much alarm and pain, of the far worse captivity of one who deserves more than I do to be set at liberty I have overcome the feeling of revolt aroused in me by an unjust captivity. . . .

A certificate of residence in an enemy prison for no better reason than that of having devoted himself to the cause of liberty, must inevitably carry, for the wife of Monsieur de La Fayette, the same advantages as would, for the wife of an artist, a certificate stating that he was traveling for the purpose of better instructing himself in his art. I will say nothing of the barbarity of holding wives as hostages, but this I will say: that my husband is powerless either to injure or to serve any cause whatever. Allow me to repeat once again that it has been necessary to reduce him to his present condition so that he might no longer serve the cause of freedom.

I confess, Monsieur, that I could not have believed it possible to think that one who for so many years has worked for the abolition of Negro slavery should refuse to employ his eloquence to free from slavery a wife who asks no other liberty than that which would allow her to get herself confined within or near the walls of the fortress of Spandau. Monsieur Roland has been so good as to assure me of his conviction that I can neither do, nor wish to do, any harm. . . . If that is so, he must needs give me my freedom, since, according to the principles to which he has himself subscribed, one ought to ensure the good of all with the least possible harm to each. My freedom would do no harm at all to anybody.[2]

Then she wrote a confidential letter to Roland:

I can, Monsieur, attribute only to a feeling of kindliness the change which you have brought about in my situation. You have spared me the tribulations of an extremely perilous journey and have consented that my chosen place of retirement shall be my prison. But I can no longer endure any prison of this nature at all since learning today from Monsieur Brissot's gazette that my husband has been transferred by the enemies of France from one town to another and has now been taken to Spandau. No matter how repugnant I may feel it to be indebted to those who have shown themselves to be the enemies and accusers of one whom I revere and love as he deserves to be loved, it is with an overflowing heart that I shall express my everlasting gratitude to him who, by relieving the administration of all responsibility for my person and by freeing me from my promise, shall make it possible for me to join my hus-

band when, France having become more free than she is at present,
it may be possible to make the journey without risk.

It is on my knees, if need be, that I ask this favor of you, from
which you may judge of the state I am in.[3]

This time she had struck the right note. Beauchet had the courage
to deliver in person Adrienne's letters to these two powerful individuals. Brissot received his with a caution which he expressed
in obscure phrases. He hoped, he said, that it might be possible
"to confide the Citizeness Lafayette to the workings of that feeling
which animates her."

The style was that of the age. Roland, for his part, appeared to
be touched, and replied at once:

I have, Madame, submitted your moving request to the Committee.
I should, however, point out that it seems to me scarcely prudent
for one of your name to move freely in France, because of the unfortunate feelings to which that name at present gives rise. But circumstances may change and I ask you to wait until they do. I shall
be the first to take advantage of any such alteration.[4]

This was all very polite, but Adrienne had to face the facts. It
would be a long time before she would be able to join Gilbert. So
aunt, niece, and grandniece returned to Chavaniac, escorted by
commissioners who were surprised and disturbed by the welcome
the villagers gave to the ladies.

"Monsieur Roland," Adrienne told the commissioners, "thinks
that it is because of my aristocratic background that I feel some
reluctance to be indebted to him for a service. Nevertheless, it is
for me a great pleasure and a great honor to be under the protection of these gentlemen of the commune of Aurac, whom I greatly
esteem."

After her escort had gone back to Le Puy, she invited to supper
the municipal officials who had been awaiting her arrival at the
château. La Fayette's health was drunk.

Frestel arrived in the middle of the night with news of George.
Being unable herself to go where Gilbert was, Adrienne very much
wanted to send George to him. She advised Frestel to procure a
merchant's license, armed with which he could then go to the
Bordeaux trade fair. Once in that city, he could embark with his

pupil on a ship bound for England. Mr. Pinckney, the United States ambassador in London, would be sure to give a warm welcome to the son of La Fayette. She refused to see George before he left. The agony of farewell might have weakened her determination to send the boy abroad.

She wrote to Washington, begging him to intervene with the powers who were holding La Fayette prisoner and to get them to consent to his being allowed to go to America.

If his family [she added] could make the journey with him, you will readily understand what a happiness it would be to them. But if that should raise any obstacle or cause any delay, then I beg you not to think of us. We shall be far less unhappy when we know that he is with you.[5]

In Paris, Roland and the Girondins were now sitting on the right in the Convention. The former extremists had, without any change of program, become the moderates. The Girondins were trying to build up a provincial federalist party against the insurrectional Commune of Danton, Robespierre, and Marat. Roland was demanding an armed force which should belong to the Republic as a whole. Robespierre replied that one could not have a revolution without revolution or mark the precise point at which the waves of popular insurrection should break and subside. Gouverneur Morris wrote to Washington that the violence of the factions terrified him. The French character seemed to him to be one of inconstant fickleness. "They adopt without examination, and reject without sufficient cause," he said.

The trump card in the Jacobin hand was the stupidity of the *émigrés*. As for La Fayette, "His enemies are as virulent as ever," said Morris, feeling that any action taken on his behalf might do more harm than good. Dumouriez called La Fayette "the little Sulla"—and in such matters he knew what he was talking about. The Commune decreed that the public executioner should smash to pieces on the Place de Grève the medal bearing the likeness of the Hero of Two Worlds. The Assembly ordered all his property in France and in the colonies to be confiscated.

The family was still getting news of Gilbert through the Princesse d'Hénin. It could scarcely have been worse. The coalition powers had imprisoned him at Wesel, in Westphalia. He invoked his standing as an American citizen in vain. He had been captured while serving as a French officer, and the Americans could do nothing for him.

Once, during La Fayette's stay at Wesel, Pauline, his sister-in-law, happened to drive past the fortress in a carriage. She knew that Gilbert was confined there, and, in the hope that she might get a glimpse of him behind one of the barred windows, she had chosen a seat next to the door of the vehicle. The tears were streaming down her cheeks, but she did not dare to say anything because her father-in-law, a fierce antagonist of La Fayette, was at her side. The Vicomte de Beaune pretended to have noticed nothing. "He did not complain of the cold air coming through the window, as he would have done at any other time, and drove past the fortress of Wesel without saying a word." [6]

In England, the Montagus had seen their daughter Noémie die of the same ailment that had already cost them the lives of two other children. To escape from his grief Montagu had joined the Army of the Princes, as his father had hoped he would, but he had had the courage to add that many of these misfortunes would never have happened if only they had stayed in France.

La Fayette's arrest had added a further bitterness to the family dissensions. No one dared express sympathy for him in the presence of M. de Beaune. Pauline, having exhausted the money produced by the sale of her diamonds, lived in extreme poverty, sometimes at Liège, sometimes at Aix-la-Chapelle. The war was becoming more active. The French, under the command of Custine, Montesquiou, and Dumouriez, drove the coalition forces before them. "More than one émigré, retreating sick at heart, could not help watching with a wry smile the Austrians and the Prussians fleeing before French bayonets. A Frenchman is always a Frenchman, no matter what the circumstances." [7] Montagu took pleasure in the victory of his countrymen, even though he himself was among the defeated.

Pauline trembled even more for the fate of her sister Adrienne, whom she knew to be under arrest in France, than she did for that of her brother-in-law. At Chavaniac, Adrienne tried every conceivable means of getting news of her family. It was more than one's life was worth to write, except with the greatest secrecy, even to those still in France. In Paris, her relatives had left the Hôtel de Noailles, which was too close to the Tuileries, and taken refuge in an obscure house in the suburbs. But even there the roars and shouts of victory reached them. The Duc d'Ayen had succeeded in getting back to Switzerland and his beloved Comtesse Golovkine. Mme de Tessé was also living in Switzerland. Being a far-sighted woman, she had bought the Lowenberg estate in the canton of Fribourg, where she was making a success of cattle-breeding.

Adrienne was without news of her husband. She took every imaginable step, even writing to the Duke of Brunswick, commander-in-chief of the armies of the coalition. Lebrun, the Minister for Foreign Affairs, promised to get the letter through to him, but no reply ever reached her. The invaluable and levelheaded Beauchet went to Chavaniac for a day, and advised Adrienne to take her courage in both hands and write directly to the King of Prussia, who had known Gilbert and once entertained him. This was also the advice of the American minister, Gouverneur Morris, who went so far as to draft a suitable letter for her to sign. She, however, thought it too humble in tone, and rewrote it:

Sire, Your Majesty's well-known sense of loyalty encourages the wife of Monsieur de La Fayette to write to Your Majesty, without, however, falling short of what she owes to the character of the man she loves. I have always hoped, Sire, that Your Majesty would feel respect for virtue, irrespective of opinions, and would in this set a glorious example to all Europe. In the appalling state of ignorance in which I have been living for the last five months, being entirely without news of Monsieur de La Fayette, I am in no position to plead his cause. But it seems to me that both his enemies and I speak eloquently in his favor: they by their crimes, I by the excess of my grief. They are a living proof of his virtues and give a clear example of the dread he arouses in the breasts of wicked men, and I of how worthy he is of being loved. They impose upon Your Majesty the necessity of not persecuting those whom they persecute. Shall I have the happiness of giving to Your Majesty the joy of restoring me to life by restoring his freedom?

Permit me, Sire, to entertain such a hope, and the further one of offering at a not too distant date the homage of my gratitude to Your Majesty.[8]

Gouverneur Morris did all in his power to help her. He had sent instructions to the banker of the United States in Amsterdam to place 10,000 florins at the disposal of La Fayette, and had himself lent 100,000 livres to Adrienne with which to settle her husband's debts. No matter how severely he might judge the revolutionary general, his gratitude to the friend of America remained unchanged.

In Paris the king went on trial. Morris fully expected the death sentence. Though it was contrary to the wishes of the majority of Frenchmen, it was eagerly desired by the extremists in both camps. "The Monarchic and Aristocratic parties wish his death," Morris noted, "in the belief that such a catastrophe would shock the national feelings, awaken their heriditary attachments, and turn into the channels of loyalty the impetuous tide of opinion." Eternal folly of the politics of disaster! On January 21, 1793, the unhappy king was executed. Morris observed that the great mass of the people of Paris seemed as sad as they would have been at the loss of a beloved parent. Adrienne was overwhelmed. She could not get out of her mind the memory of the fat, kindly man who had always been so good a friend to her family.

Roland had not forgotten his promise, and in mid-December had had the order of arrest rescinded. But the long-hoped-for liberty was illusory, since a constant watch was being kept on all former nobles. Now freed from her parole, Adrienne dreamed more than ever of joining her husband. But she wanted her son to be out of the country and in a place of safety before she took any steps on her own account. In any case, she would have to stay on for some time in France in order to get her own affairs straightened out, and the rights of her husband's creditors legally recognized. Should the general's property be confiscated, the law would at least authorize the payment of sums due to third persons and arrange for the necessary money for this to be earmarked out of the property seized. Adrienne went several times to Le Puy to argue her case.

The remarkable Morizot was still carrying out his duties as administrator, as though there had been no revolution. On January 5, 1793, he again wrote to the marquise.

You will perhaps be astonished to learn that, after all debts have been settled, there will still be a balance left of nearly two million livres. This confirms me in my belief that, but for the decrees and in spite of the revolution, you would now have been in possession of three million. This is indeed a pleasant thought, and should be some small consolation to you in the midst of your trouble and distress. May I venture to say, Madame, that it affords proof of the fact that though in the course of the last fourteen years I have not succeeded in preventing Monsieur de La Fayette from running through more than 1,500,000 livres and largely diminishing his capital, I have at least employed care, vigilance, and often skill in keeping the ruination of his fortune within bounds.[9]

But the decision to treat La Fayette as an *émigré* and to confiscate all his property made nonsense of Morizot's devoted labors. Adrienne's letters to Madame Beauchet show her constantly struggling with a host of small debts.

MARCH 17, 1793

Since what is in question is a money matter, I rely entirely on your tact.... You have too elevated a nature not to feel with me and for me as though these concerns were yours.

MARCH 30

Scarcely a day goes by but I realize, my dear friend, how much reason I have to be grateful to you for giving so much thought to my little business problems.... Your accounts are miraculously accurate.... Not only is it brought home to me that I am completely ruined, but I realize that, after being compelled to treat with the Paris Commune, I shall still not see justice done.... Send me the names of those who are active in the department of the municipality which will be handling this business of mine, and if you can do so without imprudence, let me have some notes on the character of each of them....

We here have now come to the end of all our newspaper subscriptions. I should like to renew those to the Patriote Français and the Débats. I also wish to substitute Thermomètre for Les Feuillants. My aunt begs you to renew hers for Nouvelles politiques et étrangères. I cannot send you any money, and think you cannot have much.[10]

The excessive injustice of the whole situation was driving Adrienne nearly frantic. Even if the authorities *did* confiscate all La Fayette's property, in spite of the fact that he was not strictly an *émigré*, she thought that she had a right to her own personal fortune of 200,000 livres, that being the amount of her dowry. But argue though she might, all she was allowed was a provisional payment of 8000. "Good-by, my dear friend, and do not be too much shocked at seeing me in a temper," she warned Mme Beauchet. "I pray God to give me patience."

Washington considerately placed 2310 guilders at Adrienne's disposal in Holland. "This sum is, I am certain," he wrote her, "the least I am indebted for services rendered by Mr. de la Fayette, of which I never yet have received the account." On May 14 Adrienne admitted to Mme Beauchet that she was in urgent need of a hundred louis with which to settle her debts and pay the wages of her servants. That done, she would be wholly dependent on the charity of her parents:

That will be in no way repugnant to me, for I know how good they are and that it would be the height of ingratitude in me not to trust in them. . . . I embrace you fondly. I see little hope of any consolation in this world, and so little capacity in myself for relishing that of which I should not despair that I do my best to cling to the comfort of doing my duty.[11]

This methodical saint drew up a memorandum indicating how her claims and those of Aunt Charlotte should be set against one another:

. . . Article 3. It is a matter of general knowledge that one can bring off excellent deals by buying back one's own property in return for a few years' revenue, and need put down only a small amount in cash. We must not lose sight of the probability that a time will come when Gilbert will be struck off the list of émigrés and reinstated in his property. This can be done in three ways:

1. Such property as has not been sold can be returned to him in kind.

2. Those portions which, having been bought and paid for, can be bought back by us.

3. Those for which, if they have been bought from the nation but not paid for, we shall be compensated in cash.

. . . Article 5. If we succeeded in buying back the whole or a portion of the land which has been sold, we should be careful not to buy isolated or scattered parcels, for these always bring a higher price because there are competing bidders, and because a neighboring landowner, administering them without cost to himself has a great advantage over us, whereas, in buying parcels of considerable size and importance, one finds less competition, and the purchaser who

has acquired them from the nation has almost always strained himself beyond his means and is prepared to accept an arrangement which is much to the advantage of the original owner.[12]

Adrienne foresaw everything: Gilbert's name being struck off the list of *émigrés* and his reinstatement in his property; what was best to be done in Cayenne to preserve Gilbert's rights and those of the Negro workers; the rights of the creditors (to whom, in fact, they would owe nothing, since if the nation confiscated the property, it must be responsible for the debts contracted on the surety of that property), some of whom were in straitened circumstances and needed to be paid in part. No businessman could have done better.

Adrienne was especially anxious that she should not be thought to be in danger at Chavaniac:

TO MME BEAUCHET: APRIL 28, 1793
I am much grieved to think that you should have been made uneasy by the troubles in our department. Our small municipal council, which is very honorable and very patriotic, keeps order in our villages, and we have seen nothing of the troubles.

MAY 14
I feel myself to be possessed of a courage which is not far removed from stupidity. . . . But it has this advantage, that it enables me to judge sensibly and calmly.

JUNE 10
Honestly, my dear friend, you must be mad to be so concerned about the troubles in Lozère. I beg you to be persuaded once and for all that the peace of our canton is unbroken . . . and that, since all my neighbors know perfectly well that my patriotism is genuine, I am safe from all suspicion.

JUNE 15
If Paris becomes impossible, let me assure you that this department can offer a place of refuge for all good patriots who are not involved in the current intrigues.[13]

Paris was indeed becoming impossible. More attacks were being leveled at Mme Roland than had ever been directed against Marie-Antoinette. There was no Girondin member of the all-powerful Committee of Public Safety. The treachery of Dumouriez had sounded the death knell of the party. He had entered into negotiations with the enemy for the purpose of overthrowing the Convention. The La Fayette household had always been suspicious of this man, who was completely without moral standards, who, though amiable enough to his friends, was prepared at any moment to play false with all of them, and was far better suited to court intrigues than to the frank dealings of liberty. Adrienne was therefore not surprised by what had happened, though the treason of which he had been guilty and the threat of a foreign invasion filled her with new anxieties. The Revolution, menaced from every side, must protect itself by all and every means. A revolutionary tribunal had been set up in Paris. The departments had received orders to check the papers of all the erstwhile nobility. The search now was not for the guilty but for the suspect. Danger had made terror the order of the day.

LA FEMME LAFAYETTE

*Fortune had no power over her: not the
evils which she had foreseen, nor those
by which she had been surprised, could
bring her courage low.*   BOSSUET

Jean-Baptiste Lacoste, a representative of the Convention, made a tour of Haute-Loire. Throughout the length and breadth of the department he distributed a printed denunciation of La Fayette. On his way through Aurac he said that the former marquise ought to be arrested. Always ready to take the bull by the horns, Adrienne hunted him out at Brioude, where he received her politely.

"I am informed, Monsieur," she said, "that there is a movement afoot to imprison all former nobles, in connection with the treacherous behavior of Dumouriez. I come now to tell you that though I declared my readiness at all times to stand surety for Monsieur de La Fayette, I most certainly have no intention of doing so for his enemies. Furthermore, whether I live or die is a matter of supreme indifference to Monsieur Dumouriez. You would do far better to leave me undisturbed in my retirement. When I was dragged from it, the only result was to awaken sympathy for me and to revive the memory of a great many injustices. I ask to be left with my children in the only situation I can find tolerable so long as my husband is a prisoner of the enemies of France."

"Citizeness," replied Lacoste, "such sentiments are worthy of you."

"I do not care to know, Monsieur, whether they are worthy of me," was her reply. "All I wish is that they may be worthy of him."

Lacoste then told her in his most honeyed tones that it was merely a question of establishing in that department a rule similar to that in force in the Ardèche, where no more than three ex-nobles were allowed to congregate, whether when walking in public places or when meeting in private houses.[1]

Exasperation and persecution were the order of the day. The parish priest of Aurac was arrested, but, thanks to representations made by Adrienne, acquitted by a jury of peasants over whose deliberations the mayor, Guintrandy, a surgeon and a friend of the lady of the manor, presided. At Brioude the verdict was held to have been too lenient. Adrienne went to see the priest in Brioude and found his affairs to be in a bad way. Even his friends said that the least he could do was to take the constitutional oath. She saw each official in turn. As always she knew how to act with energy and skill. The curé was sent home, but the whole business was turned into a grievance against Adrienne by several malicious persons.

For many months now she had been without news of Gilbert. He had been moved to Magdeburg, separated from his friends and confined in a secret place. Such was the hatred felt for him by the *émigrés* and the coalition governments alike that he was not even allowed to know whether his wife and children were alive or not. Adrienne's every attempt to get the prisoner freed was in vain. At last, on March 13, 1793, he managed to write to the Princesse d'Hénin:

I am still alive . . . and in a condition to tell you so, but those are the only two things you may expect to learn from my journal. This letter is intended for you, my wife, and my children (though where they are I do not know), and those of my friends to whom you and Madame de La Fayette my think proper to show it.

Let me describe my lodging and the life I live in it. Imagine an opening contrived in the rampart of the citadel and surrounded by a strong and lofty palisade. It is by way of this passage that, after successively opening four doors, each one of which is fastened with chains, padlocks, and iron bars access can be obtained . . . to my place of confinement, which measures three paces in width and five and a half in length. The wall on the moat side is covered with mold. The one opposite allows me to get a glimpse of daylight, though not of the sun, through a small barred window. In addition, there are two sentries who can look straight down into my subterranean dwelling, but they are stationed on the farther side of the palisade and so cannot speak to me. You may judge, therefore, that what with walls, ramparts, and ditches both within and without the citadel of Magdeburg, the foreign powers neglect nothing that may keep me safe and sound in their territories.

I have books, but with the blank pages torn out; no news, no gazettes, no means of communication, neither ink nor pens nor paper nor pencils. It is only by a miracle that I got hold of this piece of paper on which I am writing to you with a toothpick. . . .

Felix * *has been put in a cell apart. My bodyservant, a native of Chavaniac, attends upon me. I should like their families to know that they are not dead. If you knew my aunt you would realize how anxious I am about her health. I embrace my wife and my children. Good-by. I send a thousand fond messages to my friends.*

I do not know what they have done to my house in Cayenne, but hope that my wife has managed so to arrange things that the Negroes who work on the land there have retained their freedom.[2]

Gilbert may have been guilty of many errors, but one cannot fail to admire him for having spared a thought in his dungeon for the liberty of the Negroes. Even though his jailers withheld all letters addressed to him, he nevertheless learned of the assassination of his friend La Rochefoucauld and of the execution of the king. But the only news he had of his family was what he had gathered from Charles de Damas, Mme de Simiane's brother, whom he had seen for a few moments at Ham. Damas was an *émigré*, and therefore an adversary of La Fayette, but he had given proof of humanity when he met the prisoner by reassuring him about the condition of his nearest and dearest. In June, 1793, Gilbert read once again the handwriting of Adrienne and of the Princesse d'Hénin.

I was not allowed to keep the letters [he wrote the princesse] *but I managed to read them. My first reply was allowed to pass. The sec-*

---

* Felix Pontonnier, a lad of sixteen, who acted as secretary to La Fayette, had followed his master into captivity, along with the bodyservant, nicknamed Chavaniac.

ond was returned to me once, twice, three times: once because I had used the word liberty, once because I said how I am and that the king does not wish it to be known, and the third time because they wanted me to write only that I was very well. . . . I will not go into details about the precautions with which I am surrounded. These people must really think they have the Devil in person under lock and key! Every day one is being made constantly aware of the truth of what Cardinal de Retz called "the ridiculous in the abominable."

The French victories filled him with pride:

You must at least admit that those simple civilians fight well, and that I was right when I said that the setting up of a system of national guards would bring the calculations of Europe to nothing. . . . "He is incorrigible!" Is that what you say? I freely admit it, my dear Princesse: delivered over to the most violent of passions, the liberty which commanded my earliest devotion and has made all my life stormy is here the perpetual object of my solitary meditations. It is what one of the ladies of my acquaintance used to call my "blessed lunacy," and whether, as the result of some miracle, I get out of this place, or whether I end on the scaffold, liberty and equality will be my first and final words.[3]

A month later he wrote: "Good-by once more. Your democratic and imprisoned friend embraces you." Victim of demagogy though he was, Gilbert prided himself on remaining faithful to democracy.

The summer of 1793 was a very restless period in Auvergne. Many wives of *émigrés* thought it necessary to bring divorce proceedings in order to protect themselves and to provide for the future of their children. Though divorce under these conditions was nothing but a sham and a formality, Adrienne refused to violate the law of the Church. So far was she from lending herself to any such feigned denial of her husband that she made a point of beginning all the demands made by her to various administrative bodies with the words "*La femme* Lafayette." Beginning in 1791 Gilbert had ceased to use the title of marquis, and soon afterward he began signing his name Lafayette, in one word.

The mill of Langeac having been put up for sale as national property, Mme de Chavaniac, who was one of her nephew's creditors, was determined to bid for it. Before the auction began, Adrienne, who went with her to Brioude, made a declaration with all her customary forcefulness of her own position.

"Citizens," she said, "I feel obliged, before this sale takes place, to protest against the enormous injustice of applying the laws governing *émigrés* to one who is at this very moment a prisoner of the enemies of France. I demand that this protest be put on record."

Those present were much struck by the justice of her argument and suggested that her protest should be inserted in the official report of the proceedings.

"No, citizens," she replied. "That might get you into trouble, which would deeply distress me. No one who will not compromise himself for the sake of seeing justice done should run the risk of doing so for the sake of politeness. I thank God that I have never been involved in any form of collusion, and I do not wish my silence to imply that I am being so now. I would therefore request you to report my protest in a separate document." Her wishes in the matter were respected.

At Chavaniac, Adrienne gave much of her time and attention not only to the education, but even to the games and amusements of her children—as she would also have done in happier times. She found respite for her troubled heart in acts of piety which she shared with her daughters. Every Sunday she had a little gathering of all the devout women of the village for the purpose of communal prayer.

At long last she received firsthand news of her husband:

MAGDEBURG, OCTOBER 2, 1793

So, my dear heart, the five persons in whom the whole of my affections are centered still live together at Chavaniac, and in conditions of tranquillity which they so richly deserve that I scarce dared to hope that they would be fulfilled! I was sure that not even your wish to bring about my freedom would ever persuade you to take any action or to speak any words which would be unworthy of you, but the way in which you tell me of all this so echoes my own feelings that I feel a need to thank you. I have associated you with stormy destinies which have turned out sadly; but I know that you find some satisfaction in the knowledge that your love and esteem are the happiest memories of my life, the consolations of my solitary

confinement, and the proofs of a future that, if it returns me to my
family, will allow me to enjoy it more than ever.[4]

This was high praise and Adrienne had well deserved it, but
Gilbert was wrong in his belief that his wife was secure in an in-
violable sanctuary. A decree issued in September, 1793, on the subject of house-to-house visitations had laid it down that "suspects
must be run to earth in their burrows by day and by night." These
"suspects" were on one side the ex-nobles to whom a certificate of
citizenship had been refused, and on the other all persons who were
related to *émigrés*. In the administrative centers of the various districts prisons were set up in which all such persons were to be
confined. Committees were appointed to name the suspects. A representative, Solon Reynaud, a native of Le Puy, was sent from Paris
to make the necessary investigations in Auvergne.

Needless to say, everybody did his best to obtain a certificate of
citizenship. The municipality of Aurac issued these with its customary good will to all who were living in the Château of Chavaniac.
But the haughty Aunt Charlotte insisted that "not too much stress
should be laid upon her *patriotism*," and Adrienne, from a feeling
of loyalty, demanded that her certificate should be identical with
her aunt's, with the result that both were entirely ineffective for-
malities. A sense of honor was the vulnerable spot in this family.
Adrienne took the certificates to Brioude to be countersigned by
the revolutionary committee. Those of the servants were held to
be valid, but only after a deal of discussion and with bad grace. The
atmosphere was so obviously hostile that Adrienne was careful to
say nothing of her aunt, and still less of herself.

Some days later a member of the committee went to the château
for the purpose of burning all papers "in any way tainted with the
spirit of feudalism" (i.e., deeds and the like). Adrienne's lack of
concern took the commissioner charged with the duty of conducting the incineration completely by surprise. In the surrounding
countryside it was not only aristocrats who were being arrested, but
also the staunch patriots who had been sheltering them. On November 12 Adrienne received reliable information that she was to
be taken in charge next day. She decided to say nothing to the
children before the morning of the thirteenth. On that day the
commissioner, having completed his sorting of the papers, had
them all loaded on to a cart, together with Gilbert's busts of Louis

XVI and Mirabeau. He intended to have a bonfire made of them around which the villagers could dance. But the inhabitants of Chavaniac refused to take part in any such merrymaking on the very day when Adrienne was to be arrested. The cart took the road to Aurac.

A detachment of the National Guard accompanied by Commissioner Granchier of the revolutionary committee arrived at the château in the course of the evening. It was in her bedroom that Adrienne, surrounded by all the dwellers in the house, listened while the order of arrest was read to her. She showed Granchier the certificate of citizenship issued to her by the commune.

"It is too old," he said. "Besides it has not been countersigned by the Brioude committee and is therefore worthless."

"Is it forbidden for daughters to go with their mother?" asked Anastasie.

"Yes, Mademoiselle."

Anastasie pressed her point. She insisted that, being sixteen, she came under the law. The commissioner seemed inclined to relent. To cover his embarrassment, he embarked upon a recital of all the arrests he had carried out in the neighborhood. All the suspected ladies had been placed under lock and key in the church at Aurac for the night. He was willing that the Citizeness Lafayette should not have to sleep in the church, provided she gave him her word that she would be there at nine the next morning, preparatory to setting off for Brioude with the convoy. During those few hours of respite Adrienne kept up everybody's spirits. She would not, she said, be separated from them for long. On November 14 the convoy set off, amid the tears of her children and the consternation of her former servants.

The prison at Brioude was already full. All the same, the new arrivals were piled in. The "aristocratic ladies" with whom Adrienne had had nothing to do since the outbreak of the Revolution at first treated her with a show of impertinence. They gloried in the knowledge that she had been caught in the storm which her husband had so largely contributed to unleashing. She could, had she so wished, have spoken of the faults and follies of the other camp. As it was, she preferred to have no dealings with them and settled down in a passage which had been made to serve the purpose of a cell. She shared this accommodation with the pious wife of a baker and two bourgeoise of Brioude. Such was the attitude and behavior of *la femme* Lafayette that she soon won the unanimous admiration of all her fellow inmates.

She realized that any attempt on her part to persuade the authorities to give her back her freedom would be useless. The orders from Paris were categorical. She did, however, venture to put forward several requests on behalf of the other prisoners. The committee showed rather more consideration to her than it did to anyone else. She had, in all conscience, reasons enough for anxiety. She knew that in Paris her mother, the Duchesse d'Ayen, and her elder sister, Louise de Noailles, were, as suspects, being kept under house arrest. Presently it was Mme de Chavaniac's turn, though by reason of her advanced age she was allowed to stay on in the château with a strong guard. Anastasie and Virginie saw to it that their mother's linen was laundered, and returned it to her each week with the bill sewn on to the bundle. They used the back of it for writing short notes, which she answered in the same manner. The daughter of a Brioude innkeeper, who brought the prisoners' dinner, sometimes caught a glimpse of her and gave the children news of her health.

Now and again Adrienne even managed to get the committee to censor and forward a letter. But she was not allowed to say much.

TO THE CITIZENESS ANASTASIE, AT CHAVANIAC, NEAR BRIOUDE: 27TH FRIMAIRE OF YEAR II OF THE FRENCH REPUBLIC ONE AND INDIVISIBLE [DECEMBER 17, 1793]

*A thousand thanks, my dear Anastasie, for your sweet little letter, and for the melancholy details contained in it. I will not repeat all that I feel for you, for your aunt and your governess. You will easily judge of the state of my heart by your own.... Good-by, my darlings; I send you a kiss. Love makes me one with you. The next décade * will bring us together even more closely. I do not suppose that you will spend it any more agreeably than we shall.*[5]

In January, 1794, the girls learned that it would be not impossible to win over the jailer and have themselves smuggled into the prison. Frestel, George's tutor (who had not managed to get to England with his charge), undertook the perilous negotiations and succeeded. It was arranged that every fortnight one of the children

---

* The ten-day "week" of the revolutionary calendar. In this instance it would include Christmas.

should go to Brioude. Anastasie, as the eldest, was the first to do so. She went on horseback at night as far as the inn, where she spent the whole of the next day and the one after in hiding. In the evening she was taken to her mother, and was able to spend all night in the prison. This was a tremendous source of happiness to Anastasie and to her mother. Virginie and George had their turns later.

It was at this time that the whole of the property of "the *émigré* Lafayette" was disposed of by forced sale. His wife insisted on being present, if necessary with an armed guard. Frestel promised to pass on this request to the government representative. Solon Reynaud, the representative, poured abuse on La Fayette, "whose guts I would like to tear out," on the former marquise—"Noailles arrogance personified"—and on their daughters, "serpents which the Republic had nourished in its bosom." Naturally, the demand was refused. Shortly after this Reynaud was recalled to Paris and replaced by Guyardin, who was reputed to be less violent.

In the Brioude prison Adrienne was the good angel of her fellow unfortunates. She served them at meals, did the cooking, and persuaded even the poorest to pool what money they had with her. This made it possible for Adrienne to pay for practically everything herself, at the same time leaving them the illusion that they were contributing their share. Life in the prison was hard. The inevitable quarrels between persons of different social standing all herded together in this way were a source of constant irritation. But what did such trivial misunderstandings matter to Adrienne? Now she was suffering torments of anxiety over the fate of her grandmother (the old Maréchale de Noailles), her mother, and her sister Louise. Word had come that all three had been transferred to the Luxembourg prison.

The Terror was then at its height, bloody and hideous. Many heads of those Adrienne had loved, revered, or known only slightly had already fallen. On October 16 the queen perished on the scaffold. On November 6 the Duc d'Orléans, regicide though he was, was guillotined. Brissot (once a correspondent of Citizeness Lafayette) shared the fate of twenty other Girondins, all of them "shortened by a head," as their executioners put it, on October 31. Before being dispatched, Mme Roland had exclaimed, "O Liberty! what crimes are committed in thy name!" Next day Roland, who had fled to Rouen, committed suicide. But Camille Desmoulins,

who was in love and therefore in a kindlier state of mind, demanded
the release of 200,000 citizens. "They have been given the name
of suspects," he said, "but this is a term completely foreign to
the spirit of justice, for there are no such persons as suspects, but
only those charged with offenses defined by the law." Desmoulins
wanted to have a committee of mercy set up. Robespierre's answer
to this suggestion was: "The Terror is Justice—prompt, severe, inflexible."

The struggle between the revolutionary factions had become so
pitiless that men had now to kill or be killed. "The gods are thirsty,"
observed Desmoulins. The number of new prisons was multiplying.
It was decided that arrested persons accused of conspiracy should
be brought from all points of the Republic to appear before the
revolutionary tribunal of Paris. This meant condemning them to
death. The best of them, being known and esteemed in their own
departments, had at least a chance of acquittal if they were tried on
the spot. In Paris they would lose their heads, unheard. On the 8th
Prairial, Year III (May 27, 1794), an order reached Brioude that
the Citizeness Lafayette was to be transferred to the prison of the
Petite Force in Paris. Gissaguer, the police captain charged with
carrying out these instructions, was the brother of Montfleury,
who, as president of the department, had saved Adrienne from
being sent to Paris at the time of her first arrest. Gissaguer knew
and admired Adrienne. He went to see her, and without uttering a
word showed her the order of the Committee of Public Safety.
It stipulated that the prisoner should travel in a cart and be passed
on from detachment to detachment. To spare her this indignity,
the worthy police captain offered to go with her in a post chaise.
Adrienne was tempted to try escape, but, fearing to compromise
Gissaguer and to bring further stringencies on the heads of her
fellow prisoners, renounced the idea. She even reassured her companions:

"I am not being summoned before the revolutionary tribunal,
ladies. I am merely being transferred to Paris."

Having succeeded in getting her departure delayed for twenty-
four hours, she was able to send a hasty note to her daughters.
Then she went upstairs to where the parish priest of Chavaniac
was confined, and made her confession. She had already sent a petition to Representative Guyardin:

I was hoping to be tried by you, and, having heard of the way in which you see justice done, was counting on a term being set to a captivity to which I have been condemned by no decree. But just as I was expecting from day to day to see you here, the Committee of Public Safety saw fit to have me transferred to Paris. It is a matter of no little distress to me that my conduct should be investigated in the one place of all others where it is least known. I should have counted it a great gain to have gathered around me those who have been in a position to observe, since those days when I believed that I might be of some service to the Republic, whether the violence of my personal sufferings had changed for the worse those feelings of mine which were well known to all with whom I have come in contact.

But separated though I am from those places in which I have lived since misfortune came upon me, it is my duty to hope that truth will triumph. I beg you, therefore, Citizen Representative, to collect honest testimonies in my favor, so that even though it is no longer possible for you to decide my fate, you may at least be able to enlighten those into whose hands I am to be committed on the facts. It is my children who ask justice of you.[6]

Guyardin did nothing. Not that it very much mattered. The revolutionary tribunal no longer even read the evidence submitted to it, and those brought before it were not allowed to be defended by a lawyer.

It is easy to imagine the children's despair when their mother's letter was shown to them. The devoted Frestel set off immediately with a new certificate of citizenship, which had been courageously furnished by the municipality of Aurac at the request of Mme de Chavaniac. It read, in part:

After mature consideration of the aim and object of the petition, and in accordance with the sure and certain knowledge it possesses of the behavior and civic sense of the said Noailles-Lafayette during her residence in this commune; of acts of charity and fraternity which she has performed or suggested in the interests of her fellow citizens; of the zeal which she has shown at all civic and republican ceremonies, and in view of the general feeling of the people of this commune to the effect that her attitude has never fallen below the level of the Revolution, this council here in session has unani-

mously agreed that the evidence hereabove quoted is genuine proof of her conduct and her sentiments.[7]

The housekeeper and the maids at Chavaniac had entrusted to Frestel all their little odds and ends of jewelry, with a request that he should sell them in order to spare Mme la Marquise the horror of being transported in a cart. At Brioude he found everybody in a state of consternation, not excepting the Jacobins, who, however, dared not disobey. Adrienne had been moved to the common prison where convicted criminals served their sentences. When her children arrived a little later, they found her lying on a straw mattress. It was agreed that Frestel should follow the prisoner's conveyance, should seek out Gouverneur Morris in his country residence at Melun, and beg him to intervene. Anastasie's despair was so terrifying that permission was granted her to accompany Frestel and join with him in seeking the help of the United States minister. Then, in a moment, the child passed from the bitterest grief to joy, since it seemed to her that her mother was not going away at all, inasmuch as she would be going with her.

So that Anastasie might leave the department, a permit was necessary. In the face of innumerable obstacles, Anastasie managed to gain admission to the presence of Citizen Guyardin. She handed him her mother's petition, which he refused to read on the grounds that a prisoner who had been ordered to Paris was no longer any concern of his. Anastasie returned to Chavaniac in despair. At Aurac, she obtained from the municipality a certificate of citizenship for her mother, in which mention was made in the most moving language of the good wishes sent her by all the inhabitants of the village. But the municipality did not have the authority to issue an interdepartmental passport to an ex-noble. The young girl was taken back to Chavaniac in a state of complete prostration.

Meanwhile, in Brioude, Adrienne was saying good-by to George and Virginie. At noon Gissaguer came to tell her that it was time to start. She made the children promise that in the event of her death they would make every effort to join their father.

Frestel had got his passport countersigned by the district authorities. The journey was uneventful. Adrienne guessed from the tone of her guard's voice that it would not be difficult for her to get away and leave him free to abandon a duty which in the circumstances filled him with horror. But that would have put

Gissaguer's brother (who had remained at Le Puy) in a dangerous position. She was careful, therefore, to say nothing that might have the effect of strengthening the feelings which, so she thought, were already causing Gissaguer a good deal of uneasiness. It was not until they reached Fontainebleau and hostile crowds began to gather round the carriage that they confessed their thoughts to each other.

At Melun Frestel had his last conversation with Adrienne. She gave him several letters, the longest of which was for Anastasie. Adrienne begged her daughters to forgive their tormentors from the bottom of their hearts. Frestel then left her, and went to see Gouverneur Morris.

The prisoner arrived in Paris on the 19th Prairial (June 10), the eve of the Feast of the Supreme Being at which Robespierre was to address the Divinity without mediation of priests. He had just been elected president of the Convention and wished to be regarded as both a political leader and sovereign pontiff. The Terror was proceeding in a succession of hecatombs. The verdicts of the revolutionary tribunal were sending victims to the scaffold to the tune of sixty a day. Adrienne seemed doomed to certain death. Gissaguer, profoundly shaken, made no attempt to conceal his grief. He delivered her at the gate of the Petite Force and then hastened to tell Beauchet that Adrienne forbade any attempt to approach the authorities in her favor.

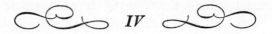

IV

THE GLOOMY BUTCHERY

I plunge with my subject into deepest darkness.
MICHELET

The saints pray for their tormentors.
ALAIN

In August, 1793, the Duchesse d'Ayen was at her father-in-law's deathbed at Saint-Germain. The Maréchale de Noailles, now seventy and stone deaf, was no longer aware of what was going on around her. As soon as the maréchal was dead, the two women, with the Vicomtesse de Noailles and her three children (Alexis, Alfred, and Euphémie), moved to the Hôtel de Noailles-Mouchy in the Rue de l'Université in Paris. The Duc d'Ayen and the Vicomte de Noailles had emigrated. Three women, all alone, who never went out, and three children, the eldest of them eleven, seemed scarcely likely to endanger the Republic.

Nevertheless the law of September 17 was applicable to them. All that had ever been tainted with nobility was now guilty by definition. At first, because of the condition of the old maréchale, who had sunk into second childhood, the family was kept confined to the house. The two *sans-culottes* detailed to act as their guard, seemed harmless enough, provided they were well fed. Grelet, the children's tutor, was a man of exemplary loyalty. Père Carrichon, a nonjuring Oratorian priest, and the confessor of the duchesse and her daughter, came to see them once a week, wearing lay clothes.

Many such clandestine priests were to be met with in the city,

and some managed to penetrate, disguised, into the prisons, sometimes even wearing the red cap and the carmagnole. Père Carrichon had little reassuring news of the outside world to give his
penitents. The war against the Church was being intensified. The
revolutionary calendar recognized neither Sunday nor the Catholic
feasts. The Maréchal-Duc de Mouchy (Adrienne's granduncle),
his wife, and their daughter (the Duchesse de Duras) had been
arrested on October 16 at the Château de Mouchy in the Department of Oise. Since all the Paris prisons were glutted with "suspects," the officers in charge of the convoy, not knowing where to
dump this last little lot, had delivered them at the door of their
town house, the Hôtel de Noailles-Mouchy. There they found their
sister-in-law, the Maréchale de Noailles, their niece, the Duchesse
d'Ayen, and their grandniece, Louise. They all took their last farewell of one another and exchanged the solemn words of those
about to die. No matter how soon death might come, they were
ready.

Père Carrichon, who was present at this meeting, said: "If you
go to the scaffold and God gives me strength, I will be with you.
So that you may recognize me in the crowd, I will wear a dark blue
coat and a red waistcoat."

The Mouchy trio were transferred to the Luxembourg, now
doing duty as a prison. Mme de Mouchy said, "Do you not think
it strange that I should be a prisoner in the palace from which I
was married?" She almost rejoiced in the change of scene, having
treasured an image of the Luxembourg as a place of splendor with
a wonderful garden. At first they were given a comfortable room
(formerly occupied by Brissot), but they were very soon moved to
a kitchen in the attics. They were able to take exercise in the
corridors, where they found many friends, and to pay their respects
to the Duchesse d'Orléans (the widow of Philippe Egalité), who
was also confined to the building.

The jailers spoke roughly and in familiar terms to these prisoners,
who such a short while ago had been Monseigneur, Monsieur le
Duc, and Your Highness. The Duc de Mouchy, who had been very
hot-tempered in the days when he had been governor of Versailles,
put up uncomplainingly with the coarse manners of the turnkeys.
Food was brought in from the Rue de l'Université. The Duchesse
d'Ayen and Louise de Noailles, having sold what remained of their
wardrobes, had hardly a sou to bless themselves with. But the young

tutor Grelet found enough work to keep the whole family alive, and the servants waited on them without wages.

So passed the winter of 1793–1794. Gradually a little hope revived. The great grief of the Mouchy couple was that they were separated from their daughter, the Duchesse de Duras, now incarcerated at Chantilly. At the Luxembourg, a number of political prisoners (including Danton and Camille Desmoulins) were lodged in the more sumptuous apartments for a brief period on their way to the scaffold. Then a fresh batch arrived, and among them were the Maréchale de Noailles, the Vicomtesse de Noailles, and the Duchesse d'Ayen.

The turnkey put the newcomers in a single room with three wretched straw mattresses. All three were deaf, the maréchale completely. At night the vicomtesse fastened a piece of cord to her arm, the other end of which was within reach of her grandmother. The beautiful Louise had always had an angelic disposition; now she made a great effort to keep up an appearance of gaiety. She made the beds and did the cooking, since the new official in charge of the Luxembourg had put a stop to the sending in of food from outside. It was not long before he instituted a communal system of messing. The old maréchale, frightened out of her remaining wits by the elbowing and pushing of those eager to get good places at the table, groped her way around the walls and usually arrived too late.

This community living on the very threshold of death might be rough, but it was certainly not boring. Actresses and members of the Convention, ex-presidents and ex-duchesses rubbed shoulders in the great court, which had now been turned into an exercise ground. There were games of football in the Rubens Gallery. All joined in a conspiracy to make fun of the guards, and there was much laughter, too, from patriots at the spectacle of aristocrats in rags, from aristocrats at the sight of Convention members brought low. There were many who no longer believed that danger threatened them. After all, what had the revolution to fear from octogenarians and solitary women?

On June 26, however, the court ushers of the revolutionary tribunal came to transfer certain prisoners to the Conciergerie (the last stage before the scaffold). They read out the names of the Maréchal de Mouchy and his wife. The other prisoners lined the corridors to see them go. A voice cried "Be of good heart, Monsieur le Maréchal!"

"At fifteen," he said, "I mounted to the assault for my king. At eighty I am about to mount the scaffold for my God. There is no need to pity me."

All that remained was to face the gibes of the revolutionary tribunal, and to cross Paris bound and corded like cattle going to the slaughterhouse. On the 9th Messidor (June 27, 1794) the two white heads fell under the blade of the guillotine.

In the prison of the Luxembourg Louise de Noailles, for all her courage, had now abandoned hope. Killing had become a means of emptying the prisons. A point had been reached when there was no longer room for those awaiting trial. Either a halt had to be called in the routine of arrest and imprisonment, and certain "suspects" set at liberty, or a thinning-out plan had to be put into operation. Guilt or innocence now mattered little. Any head would fit the guillotine. A "prison conspiracy" was invented to give some color to the proceedings. The overcrowded Luxembourg was expected to produce a hundred fifty victims. On the 18th Messidor (July 6) one hundred fifty-six took the fatal road to the Conciergerie. The Noailles ladies were not among them, and the Duchesse d'Ayen breathed again. The old maréchale was quite beyond grasping the situation. Only the charming Louise, so lovely, so delicate, so pale, recited the prayers for the dying.

She had lost everything: her king, her parents-in-law, her friends, her servants. Her husband was in America. Her three children alone remained to her. She consigned them to the care of Grelet, the twenty-three-year-old tutor who had shown such great devotion. Him, too, she called "My dear child." She drew up a tragic little will: "Made in the prison of the Luxembourg, this 24th Messidor, Year II of the French Republic, One and Indivisible— LOUISE DE NOAILLES, femme Noailles." [1] Among its provisions: "I beg Citizen Grelet to accept a watch and a diamond valued at one thousand écus, as a very insufficient mark of my lively sense of gratitude. I ask him to remember me. The greatest consolation I take with me to the grave is the knowledge that I am leaving my children in his hands."

On the 3rd Thermidor Grelet went to the Luxembourg with certain items of linen and clothing for which the prisoners had asked.

From the far end of the Rue de Tournon he saw a crowd of men and women in front of the entrance to the palace. The fatal cart was clearly visible with benches along the whole of its length. He slipped into the crowd and made his way to the main door.

Soon Louise de Noailles came out, followed by two guards. She passed close to Grelet and pressed his hand. Then she climbed into the cart. Her mother and grandmother were close behind her.

When the cart moved off, Grelet went with it. Louise never took her eyes from him. At the point where the Rue de Condé narrows, she made three times with her hand the gesture of benediction. Why had the "Noailles women" been picked out? Their deafness made all converse with them impossible. The idea that they could have been involved in a conspiracy was the very height of absurdity. The fact remains that the gatekeeper had brought them that morning a document signed *Fouquier-Tinville*, stamped with the hatchet and the pike crowned with the Phrygian cap, and summoning before the revolutionary tribunal the wife of Noailles, Louise Noailles, and Daguesseau, wife of d'Enghien (a mistake for d'Ayen). At the moment of being handed the fatal paper the Duchesse d'Ayen was reading the *Imitation of Christ*. She hastily scribbled on her bookmark, "My childen, courage and prayer," slipped it between the pages which she had been reading when interrupted, and gave the volume to the Duchesse d'Orléans with a request to see that it reached her daughters. It was sent to them after the 9th Thermidor.

The Conciergerie was unlike any other prison. It was the antechamber of death, the last of all waiting rooms, "a morgue forever filled with movement and murmuring like a corn exchange on market day," [2] a hideous factory which was expected daily to transform sixty innocent persons into prisoners in the dock, sixty prisoners in the dock into condemned criminals, and sixty condemned criminals into corpses. Those who entered it knew that all hope was gone. Some prayed, others sang, many dreamed. On the threshold of the registrar's office the new arrivals passed friends about to start for the scaffold and realized that their turn would come next day.

The three Noailles ladies arrived at a late hour and were bundled into a cell already occupied by three other women. They asked whether they could have something to eat and something on which to sleep. So far as eating was concerned, there was nothing doing:

tradespeople were not allowed in after dark. Wretched mattresses could be provided at a cost of fifteen francs a month, paid in advance, even if they were going to be used for one night only. The ladies had no more than twelve francs between them. One of the three in residence had a kind heart and offered them a glass of gooseberry syrup and water; another gave up her bed to the old maréchale; the third surrendered her mattress to the Duchesse d'Ayen. The vicomtesse said: "It is not worth while to sleep when one is as close to eternity as we are." She made her mother and her grandmother as comfortable as possible, and then read a devotional book by the light of a tallow candle.

They spent a restless night. Each time the maréchale woke up, she read the charge sheet over again but entirely failed to understand it. She was accused of having "conspired in the Luxembourg." "No, no," she said repeatedly, "I am not going to die for a plot of which I know nothing."

The Duchesse d'Ayen fondly believed that she was to appear before a bench of judges. Her daughter Louise knew that the revolutionary tribunal consisted only of executioners. The maréchale complained because her dress was crumpled.

At nine next morning the bolts were drawn and the door opened. Fouquier-Tinville's dogs had come to round up their flock. The presiding judge that day was Louis-François Dumas, a bloodthirsty fanatic. The Maréchale de Noailles, with her trumpet in her ear, heard herself accused of "planning to dissolve the National Convention and to assassinate the members of the Committee of Public Safety."

Dumas turned to her: "You took part in the Luxembourg conspiracy?"

"What is that you are saying? You must forgive me, Citizen, I am extremely deaf. I cannot hear you."

"So you were a deaf conspirator."

Jurors, clerks of the court, guards, and members of the public all roared with laughter. There is something more odious even than a venal judge, and that is a waggish one. The jury, after deliberating for a few moments, declared it to be their "sincere and honest opinion" that the three Citizenesses Noailles were enemies of the people and deserved the death sentence. Two of them had not even been questioned.

Père Carrichon, who had promised to go with the victims to the scaffold, was warned by Grelet. He made his way to the Conciergerie, where he had to wait a long time, since the tumbrils were not ready to start until six in the evening. In the first of them he saw the maréchale, very ill at ease on the miserable bench which served her as a seat, and with her hands tied behind her back. The back of her neck was shaven. In the second he could just make out the Duchesse d'Ayen in a blue-striped wrap, and the Vicomtesse de Noailles, wearing a white dress. To Carrichon it seemed that they had both grown younger. He walked ahead of the convoy. It was stifling hot, and he was in a sweat. Rain began to fall. The abbé managed to get close to the second cart. At last his penitents caught sight of him. At the Bastille "circus" (a secondary guillotine had been set up on the Place du Trône, renamed Place du Trône Renversé), he gave them absolution, and when he had pronounced the sacred formula, "was struck by their look of content, serenity, and cheerfulness." He reached the Place at the same time as the tumbrils.

The scaffold stood under the trees. There was a crowd of idlers, all making jokes, roaring with laughter, and insulting the condemned. A red-painted wagon was waiting in readiness for its load of headless corpses. The executioner was standing on the platform. His assistants helped the victims get out of the cart and arranged them in several rows, facing the Faubourg Saint-Antoine. There were forty-five of them that evening. Beggars slipped in and out between the guards, asking those about to die for their shoes. The abbé noted that the foppishly dressed executioner had put on a blood-stained overall to protect his clothes.

Carrichon saw the three assistants seize an old woman and fling her face downward on the hinged plank. Three dull sounds were clearly audible: the slamming down of the plank; the neckpiece falling into position; the drop of the knife. Body and head were pitched into the red wagon. The abbé would have liked to run from the scene of butchery, but the diabolical precision with which death was distributed held him fascinated. The old maréchale was the third to mount the scaffold. With a pair of scissors one of the assistants ripped open the neck of her black dress. She was seized by the legs, flung violently forward, and cut in two.

Madame d'Ayen was the tenth [Carrichon wrote later]. *She looked to me as though she were pleased to know that she was to die before* her daughter. When she reached the platform the chief executioner snatched off her cap. It was held in place by a pin which had not been removed, and her hair was dragged forward, causing her, as I could see from her expression, considerable pain. The mother gone, the loving and dignified daughter took her place. What were my feelings when I saw that young woman, dressed all in white and looking much younger than she was, like a sweet little lamb about to have its throat cut! I felt as though I were watching the martyrdom of one of those virgins or saintly women we see in pictures. What had happened to her mother happened to her: the same blunder with the pin, the same expression of pain, and then, immediately, the same calmness, the same death. What an abundance of bright red blood poured from her head and neck! Now she is in bliss, I said to myself, when they threw her body into that dreadful hearse.[3]

The abbé returned home very late, completely exhausted. He slept badly.

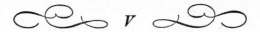

THE PRISON OF PLESSIS

*To Christians, no matter what their sex,
cowardice is not permitted.* FÉNELON

Waiting in the Petite Force, Adrienne learned of the horrors that
were being committed. It was agony for her to think that bloodthirsty madmen were committing these crimes in the name of the
ideas and ideals on which she and Gilbert had fed, drugging themselves with dreams. The ideas had been distorted; the words turned
from their proper sense. Gilbert's ideals were being defiled by the
masters of the moment. She knew that her husband's name would
have marked her out for death, had not the murderers ceased by
this time to attach any importance to names. They did not care
whom they killed: all that mattered to them was to supply the daily
ration of victims. She trembled for her grandmother, for her
mother, for her elder sister. She knew that they were confined in
the Luxembourg, but dared not attract attention to them by associating them in any way with the detested name of which she herself was still so proud.

After a time Adrienne was transferred to Plessis. The college
where once the young Marquis de La Fayette had pursued his
studies, Plessis had been made a prison. There she found her cousin,
the Duchesse de Duras, whose aristocratic ideas had estranged
them at the outbreak of the Revolution. Two days after her arrival
Adrienne heard that the Maréchal and the Duchesse de Mouchy,
father and mother of Philippine de Duras, had been guillotined. It

fell to her to break the news to her cousin. This she could not do without admitting to herself how great was her fear that the three prisoners who were among the persons she most loved in all the world would turn out to have suffered the same fate. Later the Abbé Carrichon was able to tell the Duchesse de Duras that at the very moment when the fatal cart was bumping over the cobbles, some wretch in the crowd had shouted to the old maréchal, who was sunk in prayer: "The *sans-culottes* will drink of your wine and eat of your goods!" Raising his eyes and looking at the speaker, the doomed man had replied with astonishing serenity: "May God grant that in a year from now you may have bread, and not be reduced to eating one another."

The prison of Plessis acted as a sort of depot for the Conciergerie. Every morning twenty names were called out. Their owners then left in a cart for the revolutionary tribunal—in other words, for the guillotine. "The thought that I shall soon be one of them," Adrienne wrote, "gives me the strength to watch this daily spectacle." She was fortunate in being by herself in a fifth-floor attic. There she could meditate, and there she made a will:

From the bottom of my heart I forgive my enemies, if I have any, as also my persecutors, whoever they may be, and even the persecutors of him I love. I pray God to fill them with good things, and to pardon them as I pardon. . . .

I declare that I have never ceased to be loyal to my country; that I have never taken part in any intrigue likely to disturb it; that my most sincere wishes are for its happiness; that the principles on which my love of it is based are unshakable and that no persecution, from whatever quarter it may come, can change them for the worse. A model, very dear to my heart, serves as an example to me. . . .

I give to my children my most loving blessings, and I ask of God that in return for the life which I should dearly have liked to dedicate to their happiness, He will ensure it by making them worthy of its gift. . . . O God, have mercy upon me.[1]

Every other day the good Mme Beauchet, her former maid and her best friend, went to the side door of the prison to make sure that Adrienne was still alive, and being satisfied, reassured her children by letter. They, in distant Auvergne, knew about the Paris massacres, and kept expecting to hear that the worst had happened. The Château of Chavaniac and its contents had been auctioned. Mme de Chavaniac had been able to buy her bed and a few household articles, but had been forcibly deprived of the portrait of her dearly loved brother, the colonel who had been killed at the battle of Minden. The peasants of the commune saw to it that she and her young relatives were supplied with food.

We live [wrote Virginie] off the money which the village people have lent with such touching eagerness to my aunt. Every day we were told that she and my sister were to be sent to the house of detention at Brioude, and that my brother and I would be confined in the poorhouse.[2]

It is very probable that Adrienne owed her life to Gouverneur Morris. As soon as he learned that she was a prisoner in Paris, he approached the authorities. He did not, he said, wish to overstep the limits of his official functions, but felt entitled to point out that the family of General La Fayette was much beloved in America and remembered with gratitude for the services which he had rendered to the nation; and that the execution of his wife would much impair the friendly feelings entertained by the Americans for France. England, he added, would find in it an excellent argument with which to support her distortion of the situation in France. In short, far from profiting the Republic, such a sacrifice would give great happiness to its enemies.

This letter, written shortly before James Monroe succeeded Morris as United States minister, did not bring about Adrienne's liberation, but it doubtless saved her from the scaffold. That she knew of his activities on her behalf seems clear from the fact that she presently wrote to Morris that he had "saved her from the frenzy of a monster," and that "he had prevented the commission of a crime." Later still, speaking of the money she owed him, she said:

It is but a small obligation compared with that other of owing my life to you. Permit me to remember both of them for as long as I live, with a sense of gratitude which it is truly a pleasure for me to feel. The life which has been restored to me is a gift very dear to my heart if it can bring consolation to the man I love.[3]

Morris, it is true, had not always approved of La Fayette, but he unreservedly admired Adrienne's courage and devotion. He behaved very well toward her.

It was the custom to have the list of the latest victims read aloud in the proximity of the prisons and in the exercise yards. But means were found to conceal from Adrienne, and even from the Duchesse de Duras, the news that the three "Noailles women" had been decapitated on the 4th Thermidor. Nobody then could have dreamed that they had formed part of one of the last groups handed over to the Terror. Robespierre appeared to be all-powerful, though in fact he was on the brink of destruction. There was no longer any justification for the hecatombs. The armies of the Republic were winning triumphs in every theater of war. Their victories were, like Furies, hot on the heels of Robespierre. He had threatened the lives of members of the Convention, and this encouraged even the most cowardly of them to combine in an effort to overturn the Incorruptible. Among the people the number of his adherents was diminishing. Widows and orphans were now so numerous that they formed round him a world of enemies. Tradesmen now put up their shutters when the death carts drove past their shops. Paris was sick of the guillotine. On the 7th Thermidor it would have been difficult to find a hundred persons prepared to condemn aloud the excesses of the Terror. Three days later Robespierre had not a single defender. One hundred thousand suspects emerged from their hiding places. The accusers were now the accused. Those who had sent victims to the guillotine were now in their turn victims.

As soon as the death of Robespierre was known at the prison of Plessis, Adrienne's first thought was to send to the Luxembourg for news. But because the poor woman feared that the name of La Fayette might compromise those she believed to be still alive, it was Philippine de Duras who wrote the letter. The jailer's reply informed them of the appalling truth. No worse misfortune could have struck at Adrienne: an adored mother, the most charming of sisters, her grandmother—three generations had been brought low by three blows of the Terror. "You must give thanks to God," she wrote to her children, "who has saved my life, my head, my strength. Feel no regret that you were far from me. God has kept me from rebelling against Him, but I should not for a long time have been able to endure any show of human consolation."

For several weeks after the 9th Thermidor those still in the prisons found great difficulty in grasping what had happened in the world outside. Was the Revolution over? Was it returning to the principles which had marked its beginnings? There were times when Adrienne found the thought of the losses which she had suffered intolerable, and almost regretted that she had not been handed over to the executioner. "The knowledge that she was following in the footsteps of those dear ones would have changed the final scene to sweetness for her," wrote Virginie. But the fall of Robespierre did not mean the end of the revolutionary government. The Jacobins, now no longer threatened, could not allow the position they had gained to be called in question. The Convention felt strong enough to be indulgent without danger. It sought to find a middle way between royalism and terror, and so it moved to empty the prisons.

In September, 1794, Representatives Legendre and Bourdon de l'Oise were instructed to visit the prison of Plessis and decide what should be done about the inmates. The majority they liberated at once. Certain difficulties were raised in the case of Philippine, Duchesse de Duras, the friend and lady-in-waiting of Marie-Antoinette. But Legendre said that she had "suffered so much that the fact of her being an aristocrat should not be held against her as a crime." This Legendre was a master-butcher of Paris, a rich bourgeois of the prerevolutionary days. He was a small man, strongly built, brutal, uncouth, almost illiterate, who had made his underlings tremble. He had been one of the conquerors of the Bastille, one of the pilgrims to Versailles on October 5, one of the rioters on August 10. When, last of all, Adrienne was brought before him, the prison staff announced her in trembling tones, for Legendre hated her, having more than once, in his wilder moods, found himself up against the former commander of the National Guard. This woman was *la femme* Lafayette and gloried in the name. The two representatives declared that "her husband had too glaringly betrayed his country" for them to take upon themselves to settle what should be done with her. They advised her to send her papers to the Committee.

Adrienne was cast down when she found that her captivity was to be prolonged—not on her own account, for she was beyond feeling any further affliction—but for the sake of the children and of her husband, who was waiting for her to go to him in a different prison cell. She had received very little news of him. James Monroe, the new United States minister, who went to see her at Plessis, knew no more than that the King of Prussia, tired of having on his hands prisoners whose liberation was being constantly demanded by

Charles Fox in England and by the American ministers, had handed them over to the Emperor of Austria, whose chief minister, Thugut, had given instructions that they were to be treated harshly. La Fayette, La Tour-Maubourg, and Bureaux de Pusy were now confined in the fortress of Olmütz, where they had been separated from one another and forbidden to correspond.

Now that the number of suspects in Paris had been so greatly diminished, it was found administratively desirable to concentrate them in fewer prisons. Adrienne was moved, first to the Rue des Amandiers, and then to the Delmas house in the Rue Notre-Dame-des-Champs. In the first of these she found that she was the only woman among twenty West Indian colonists, who gave her a very bad reception because of the campaign she had waged in favor of the Negroes. But they were soon won over. In the Rue Notre-Dame-des-Champs her fellow prisoners consisted of former terrorists, who were now very much more numerous in the jails than were the aristocrats. "There, as elsewhere, she gained the respect of all," her daughter wrote.

The winter of 1794–1795 was severe and Adrienne suffered much from the cold. The hope of being very soon released, however, gave her new courage. On the 10th Frimaire, Year III (November 30, 1794), she wrote to Aunt Charlotte, the Citizeness Chavaniac:

The thought of being restored to my children, of embracing them once again, of being able to attend to their needs, will give me intense delight when the moment of my liberation comes.[4]

Père Carrichon, who had accompanied the three Noailles ladies to the scaffold, disguised himself as a carpenter and gained admission to Adrienne's prison. He gave her many moving details of the deaths of those "angelic beings," and she took advantage of his visit to make a general confession covering the whole of her life.

Monroe repeatedly approached the authorities in an attempt to speed her release. The courageous Mme Beauchet endlessly importuned Citizen Colombel, the chairman of the Committee. But the name of La Fayette seemed to inspire terror. Some excuse for delay was always found. At last all the signatures of the Committee were obtained except that of the pig-headed Legendre. Philippine de Duras took him by surprise one day when he was dressing. She reminded him that he himself had pleaded her cause by stressing the losses she had suffered. Mme de La Fayette, she argued, had endured as many misfortunes as her cousin, and was no less entitled to ask for clemency. There was a trace of kindliness in Legendre. He signed the papers, and the prisoner was liberated on January 21, 1795.

Of her husband Adrienne now knew little more than that he was interned at Olmütz. In London, the Princesse d'Hénin, with the help of Lally-Tollendal, had raised funds for an attempted escape which was to be organized by a young German doctor named Bollman, a devoted admirer of La Fayette. Bollman had succeeded in the most romantic manner in getting a note to La Fayette. Then, having fallen in with a young American (the son of Major Huger, in whose house Gilbert had stayed when he first arrived in America), he made him privy to his plan. Together they made the attempt, almost succeeded, and then at the last moment came to grief. La Fayette had been recaptured and placed in solitary confinement. The more Adrienne learned how harshly he was being treated, the more she longed to share his fate.

From Erfurt, Germany, on June 4, 1795, Pauline de Montague wrote her a letter of advice:

Blessed be the author and the moment of your deliverance, my dear, unhappy sister. Forward, my poor sister! It is the duty of all of us to survive and to accomplish with courage what it is incumbent upon us to do in this world. It is exactly a year ago today (alas! I have no later news of you) since you entered the prison of the Petite Force, a victim marked for sacrifice. Judge then whether I can envisage that cruel period without a deep disturbance of the heart. It is with your dear children, whose griefs I have profoundly felt, that I now kneel to offer thanks to Heaven. . . .

You must expect and be prepared for the thousand trials of every description, to which you will be exposed in a world that can only be a strange new place to you. . . . It is impossible, confined as you have been for several years, that you should have been informed about a multitude of matters of which I am going to tell you.

Monsieur de L.F. (to whom I should be glad if you would always refer under a pseudonym—Roch, if you like), two of whose letters I am sending to you, which I have long kept by me and would not forward so long as you were in France, is now at Olmütz in Moravia, in close confinement. Madame de Maison-Neuve, née

Maubourg (it is thus that she is called in Germany), will be able to give you more information than I can about the cause and result of this captivity. She will also explain to you the nature of the great obstacles you will find in the way of reaching him. As for me, dear sister, I have been unable to make any contact with him.

It is even essential that no one shall know of the letter, which came into my hands I cannot say how. The only way in which I can be of use to him and to you is to speak honestly, simply, and courageously of the opinions of all the French émigrés, insofar as their tiresome attitude concerns him. I cannot conceal from you that the progress, the fresh storms, and new atrocities of the Revolution have in no way effaced the memories or lessened the hostility of those who, it is only fair to say, have in their different ways been its victims. . . .

I think it most important, my dear sister, that I should draw your attention to this, in order that you may conduct yourself with the greatest circumspection in every country in which you may be and with everyone you may meet. (1) You should never make use of your name when traveling, when staying in any one place, or in writing letters. It is for you to decide what name you use. Regnac would, I think, be preferable to Chavaniac. But a Christian name would be suspect. (2) In spite of this precaution, it would be unwise for you to stay long in any town where there is a considerable number of émigrés. (3) Do not visit, make approaches to, or ask anything of our compatriots, for, though you may be personally liked and though your situation may arouse sympathy and interest, your name and your habit of identifying yourself with your husband might expose you to unpleasantness.

But the same care and caution is not necessary in dealing with Swiss or Germans: we have had good evidence of their state of mind. They are, if anything, prejudiced in favor of your husband and of all who bear his name. With a little tact and skill you may manage to make friends among them, and contrive useful contacts.[5]

Bollman and Huger had been handed over by the King of Prussia to the Emperor of Austria, who had imprisoned them. But a well-disposed magistrate had freed them, and now they were once more in touch with the London "triumvirate": the Princesse d'Hénin, Lally-Tollendal, and a journalist named Masclet. Prompted by the princesse, Masclet managed to get articles favorable to his cause published in the *Morning Chronicle* and ultimately in all the liberal papers of England and Germany. His friends Charles Fox and General Fitzpatrick made insistent demands for the liberation of the prisoner of Olmütz. But it was obvious that nothing would be done so long as Pitt was in power. Adrienne therefore decided that duty left her no alternative but to join Gilbert. It looked, however, as though such a journey would be impossible. How was she to get out of France? How was she to reach Austria? How, if she did so, was she to persuade La Fayette's jailers to let her live in the prison? The whole project seemed mad. But Adrienne brought to it the patient tenacity, the inflexible determination, and the calm assurance which make it possible to overcome all obstacles. To want is also to believe. Who, if he has doubts about succeeding, can hope to succeed? Adrienne had no doubts. She knew that she would reach the dungeon of Olmütz, just as Joan of Arc knew that she would reach the king and raise the siege of Orléans.

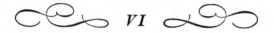

VI

MY LIFE IS LITTLE MORE
THAN DEATH

Leave me, for I would be alone with my dead.
COMTESSE DE NOAILLES

The first person Adrienne went to see after leaving prison was James Monroe, the American minister. Thanking him for the part he had played in procuring her release, she asked him to complete his good work by getting passports for herself and her two daughters. She was eager to join her husband, but if she left France secretly she would be classed as an *émigré*. All three of them would need official documents.

To Madame de Chavaniac she wrote:

I find it very hard to endure the thought that reasons of prudence which do not concern me personally, make it impossible for me to join you in your present place of residence.[1]

She was anxious to send her son to America with his tutor, Frestel, and to entrust him to General Washington. It would be hard for her to be parted from him, but she knew that this plan would be in accordance with her husband's wishes.

While awaiting the result of her passport application, she went to stay with her aunt Ségur, née Daguesseau, who was living at Châtenay, not far from Paris. Mme de Ségur's gentle charm and sweet face worked wonders on Adrienne, whose spirit had been broken more by grief than by captivity. "In my life, which is little more than death," Adrienne wrote, "she has revived a great and tender interest." Six days after her release she had her son brought secretly to the house of two Jansenist ladies at Chilly. This meeting gave her a happiness which she had thought herself incapable of feeling.

Her longing to see her daughters was no less intense, but she did not want to leave Paris until she had George's passport for America in her hands. Her uncle Ségur, a man of resourcefulness under no matter what regime, introduced her to Boissy d'Anglas, an extremely influential member of the new Committee of Public Safety. A member of the Convention, he was a lawyer and a Protestant. His opinions at the outbreak of the Revolution had been almost identical with those of La Fayette, with whom he had worked for the liberation of the Negroes. Later, Protestant though he was, he had fought courageously for the freedom of the Catholic priests. A silent but active opponent of Robespierre, he had found himself, after the 9th Thermidor, in the political front rank. He received Adrienne with expressions of esteem and good will, and procured for George a passport made out in the name of Motier, which, being less well known than that of La Fayette, did not attract the attention of his colleagues who had to countersign it. Frestel had also obtained a passport, but thought it wiser not to travel with his charge. A Bostonian, Mr. Russell, was charged with taking George to Le Havre and putting him aboard a small American ship. On arriving in the United States, he was to wait for Frestel in the house of Russell's father. Then would he seek out Washington, for whom Adrienne had given him this letter:

Monsieur, I send you my son. Though—because your views and mine were not in agreement—I have not had the consolation of gaining your ear and of getting from you the kind of help I thought necessary to free my husband from the hands of our enemies, my confidence in you has been in no way diminished, and it is with that deep and sincere feeling that I now place my dear son under the protection of the United States (which he has long been accustomed to regard as his second country, and which I have for many years looked upon as a place of refuge) and under the especial care of their

*President, the nature of whose sentiments toward my husband I so
well know. . . .*

*My wish is that my son should live obscurely in America; that he
should resume those studies which three unhappy years have interrupted, and that, far removed from places which might either
humble his spirit or too violently arouse his indignation, he should
work with the sole object in view of fulfilling the duties of a citizen
of the United States, the principles and sentiments of which will
always be in harmony with those of a French subject.*

*I will say nothing now about my own position, nor about that of
one for whom I feel far greater concern than I do for myself. I leave
it to the friend who will present this letter to you to express the feelings of a heart which has suffered too much to be conscious of anything but gratitude, of which I owe much to Mr. Monroe. . . .*

*I beg Monsieur Washington to accept all that I feel of duty, con-
fidence, respect, and devotion.*

NOAILLES LAFAYETTE [2]

Adrienne expressed politely the disappointment she had felt at
Washington's refusal to take the steps for which she had hoped.
It was Washington's view that at a time when he was President of a
young republic, he was duty-bound to adopt a neutral attitude to
the domestic concerns of another country.

When George de La Fayette arrived in the United States, Washington recommended him to the good offices of the New York
authorities, where the boy went to live with his father's former
aide-de-camp, La Colombe. Washington did not wish him to go
to Philadelphia (at that time the federal capital). Statesmanship
has reasons of which the heart knows nothing.

In Paris, Adrienne again saw the charming Princesse de Poix, who
had not emigrated with her husband, now in London. Driven
from the Hôtel de Noailles-Mouchy after the death of her parents-
in-law, she was camping out in a few rooms of the Hôtel de Beauvau
with Mme de Simiane, who had also just been released from prison.
Only the 9th Thermidor had saved her from the scaffold. A firm
friendship had developed between the two women. Both had so
high a spirit that their gaiety still shone, in spite of their memories
of the Terror. Adélaïde de Simiane was not only the most attractive
of women, but also the most tenderhearted. Adrienne, when she

saw her again, told herself resignedly that so much charm fully justified Gilbert's passion.

One can imagine the longing felt by Adrienne, now parted from her son, to see her daughters. As soon as possible she left for Auvergne. Anastasie and Virginie went to meet her, and it was at Vaire, a pretty village some eight miles from Clermont, that the three were reunited. Great was their joy, mingled though it was with tears occasioned by so many terrible and recent memories. Next morning was Sunday, and they went together to hear Mass in the mountain hamlet of Montout. Since the 9th Thermidor a few nonjuring priests had emerged from hiding and were once again active.

Adrienne spent only eight days at Chavaniac. She regretted the necessity of leaving the gruff but kindly old aunt who had shared in all their misfortunes, and of having to deprive her of the company of the two girls whose youth had brought a little life to the gloomy château. But she thought it was the duty of the wife and daughters of La Fayette to live with him as soon as the arrangements could be made. The parting was painful.

On reaching Brioude, Adrienne had an unexpected meeting. Her Grammont sister, who was living in Franche-Comté at the Château of Villersexel, where she had been left undisturbed all through the days of the Terror, was waiting for them. With her husband, she had crossed France on foot (having no money for a post chaise) in order to see Adrienne after her release from prison. Not finding her in Paris, she had continued on to Auvergne.

The meeting was heartrending, haunted as it was by three ghosts. The news from Paris was ambiguous. The profiteers of the Revolution were making a vulgar display with their luxury and their balls. In the working-class districts of the Temple and the Faubourg Saint-Antoine there was much clamoring for bread and the Constitution of 1793. A showdown was imminent between the Thermidorians and the more violent Montagnards.

The Thermidorians were taking steps to organize the resistance of the "haves." The National Guard was being reconstituted so as to admit only reliable men to its ranks. Authority was given to move troops into the outskirts of Paris to overawe the Commune. Restitution was being made to the legal heirs of those who had been put to death after March 10, 1793. This measure was of paramount importance to Adrienne and her sisters, for it meant that the estates of the Duchesse d'Ayen—the châteaux of La Grange and Fontenay-en-Brie—would be restored to them. But it was essential to know who would be the victors, the Thermidorians or the Montagnards. If the latter, then Adrienne would have to emigrate: if not, then she must be patient and stay on in France until she could get a legal passport, if she was to save the family fortunes.

The travelers spent three weeks at Clermont, waiting for the outcome of the struggle. Some kind of an explosion seemed inevitable. It occurred on the 1st Prairial, Year III (May 20, 1795), when an armed crowd broke into the Convention. One of the deputies, Féraud, was wounded by a pistol shot and finished off in the lobby. His bloody head was stuck on a pike and shown to the president, Boissy-d'Anglas, who had been so kind to Adrienne when she had gone to see him. He remained completely unperturbed and courageously saluted Féraud's severed head. It was not long before the National Guard from the moderate districts and soldiers summoned in haste cleared the hall of the Convention. Adrienne and her party could now set off again for Paris with hopes raised considerably. She had hired a gig, in which each of the women rode in turn. The others followed on foot with the Marquis de Grammont.

The days of rioting had brought Boissy d'Anglas enhanced prestige and credit, and this Philippe de Ségur managed to enlist on Adrienne's behalf. Passports were very difficult to come by, and while the business of procuring them was proceeding, Adrienne straightened out the family affairs. By virtue of the decree restoring confiscated property, she obtained for herself and her sisters a writ of possession covering her mother's properties in Brie. With the help of a few Grammont diamonds, which Rosalie sold, and a sum advanced by the United States minister, who was happy to be instrumental in saving the birthplace of La Fayette, Chavaniac was bought back from those who had acquired it as national property. The admirable Beauchet, for his part, stood surety for 80,000 livres.

Meanwhile, Adrienne was fully occupied with the creditors, to whom she insisted on giving security for their money—the persons who had come to the rescue of her mother and her sister in their days of destitution. After her return to Auvergne, she had gone with her daughters to live at Fontenay-en-Brie, an estate which had belonged to the Duchesse d'Ayen, where everything was, by a miracle, in order. The young Virginie wrote, in her child-ish hand, to the Chavaniac aunt:

We reached Fontenay yesterday, dear aunt, though we left Cler-mont ten days ago. On Monday . . . Citizeness Marin and we two boarded the mail coach. The journey from Clermont was very bumpy and threatened the coach with disaster. At Riom we were warned that the trunk which was fastened behind was going to fall off. It was made secure. The postmaster told us that we should not find any horses at Aigueperse. We were obliged to wait there for four hours and had to sleep at Ganat.

After much difficulty we started off again next morning. We had scarcely left the town when we had a breakdown and had to return to the post inn, where there was a not very nice couple, an extremely unhelpful husband and the grumpiest wife you have ever seen. There was no blacksmith. The carriage was patched up by three bad far-riers. But at last the work was finished and we asked for horses. (The postmaster was not there, but he had promised us some.) "You will have to wait for my husband," the woman said to Mamma. "You can be sure I am not keeping you here out of interest. I am as anxious to see the last of you as you are to be gone."

The postmaster arrived and refused to let us have any horses. We left next day at three in the morning and had breakfast at Saint-Pourçain. There was another breakdown at Moulins. The carriage was put to rights but went wrong again at Saint-Pierre, so we had to sleep at Nevers, Briare, Montargis, and Fontainebleau, where we separated from Citizeness Marin, who sends you her respects.

So here we are, my dear aunt, at Fontenay. The former château and the park are superb. Mamma hopes to come back here soon. She is working at things here while Monsieur de Grammont is doing the same in Paris, but he will come here often to have discussions with her. The former steward begged so hard and so nicely that we should stay with him that we are now in his house. He is the best man imaginable and the father of a family, with a daughter who is the same age as my sister and charming. This citizen is much loved. The farmers and the inhabitants are very nice to us. The country is more fertile than in Limagne. How happy my brother will be when he can make use of this retreat!

I do not speak of my respectful affection, because I express so *little and so badly what I feel so much. But I hope you will read my feelings in my heart.*[3]

It is curious to find Virginie, after a few years of the French Revolution, quite naturally employing the new vocabulary, speaking of citizeness, and former (*ci-devant*) château, and even using the one-word form of her name, as her father wished.

In July Virginie was able to tell her great-aunt of a "move":

We are going tomorrow to the former château. We have a bedroom with Mamma . . . and a room for when my uncle Grammont comes. Besides the furniture and the mattresses which we got back, we have bought many kitchen things and six chairs.[4]

Business matters, and above all, the question of the passport necessitated frequent visits to Paris. Adrienne made the journey on foot. The days of carriages were long past, but not those of love, and she lived in happy anticipation of the moment when she would set eyes upon Gilbert once again. The passport was issued, not for Germany but for the United States of America, on the strength of a certificate from the American authorities. Nevertheless, Adrienne hoped that it would be the means of reuniting her with her husband. She wrote her farewell to Aunt Charlotte in an affectionate, precise, and businesslike letter:

CHÂTENAY, AUGUST 12, 1795

My little girls [are] enchanted by the news of their brother and by the happy prospect of a reunion of which a year ago there seemed but little hope. . . .

The way in which I do my borrowing is such that I am quite independent of the depreciation in the value of the assignats * and get the greatest possible advantage out of the transaction. . . . I have concluded a loan of 300,000 livres, which costs me no more than a bill for 9000 livres payable in gold. It is Monsieur and Madame de Grammont who are doing me this service, and they are just as satisfied to have my bill as to have diamonds. . . . Now it only remains for you, my dear aunt, to give your orders to Monsieur Beauchet. . . . I do beseech you to make use of your young secretary for your busi-

---

* Paper money, issued 1789; worth less than 5 per cent of face value in 1795.

ness letters. It will spare your eyes, and if you will allow me to say so—those of your readers too.

Good-by, my dear aunt. I am starting shortly for Dunkirk, where I shall lodge in the house of Mr. Coffyn, the American consul.[5]

On September 5, 1795, Adrienne and her daughters embarked for Hamburg on an American ship.

PART SIX

THE PRISONERS OF OLMÜTZ

REUNION IN ALTONA

*It is he who was before me, and it is he
who was behind me, and it is he who
was beside me, like a tower.*

PAUL CLAUDEL

The *Little Cherub* was an American vessel, which was the reason Adrienne and her daughters had been allowed to take passage in her. But her destination was not America—it was Altona, a port not far from Hamburg. Adrienne was hoping against hope that from Germany she might reach Austria, and ultimately Olmütz. During the voyage she wrote a letter to her husband which she believed it might be possible to get smuggled to him. It was both beautiful and passionate. All references to the Noailles tragedy were kept vague, doubtless because she felt that Gilbert knew nothing of it and might have felt responsible for such an appalling consequence of his noble principles. The letter contains only one brief sentence of complaint, the first that its writer had ever expressed: "I am persuaded that you have not always been just to me."

SEPTEMBER 8, 1795

That I am free, my dear heart, is plain, since I am already on the road which will bring me to you. So great is my joy that I can describe it only by saying that I feel guilty at still being capable of entertaining so lively a sentiment after all our miseries. They will poison all that still remains to me of life, but all I can think of now is the only thing which might extinguish the memory of them: namely, that I am on my way to you. That hope alone gave me a renewed sense of life when I was almost at the foot of the scaffold.

Our little daughters, who are with me, share all my feelings, and I bring them to you confident that you will be pleased with them, that you are a fortunate father, and that it would have been sad indeed had not your children resembled you. Our son is in Boston. I have had news of his safe arrival, which makes me happier than I can say. You shall know the reasons for all my conduct, why I took the steps I did, and why I decided on this route, for I myself will explain to you, dear heart, all that has happened. I am persuaded that you have not always been just to me, but entertain a hope of convincing you that in all I have done there is no single detail of my conduct which you would not have approved as wholeheartedly as though you yourself had dictated it. You may judge how necessary it was for me to have this certainty deep in my heart at a time when we were swallowed up in the horrors which have kept us so long apart. Until such time as I can explain these things to you at greater length, the mere fact that I am on my way will make it sufficiently clear that my decision to travel by sea from Dunkirk to Altona and thence to proceed with scarcely a halt to Olmütz, has had but one object: to be isolated from all parties. It seems to me—and the experience of our three years of captivity will bear me out in this—that I can best serve what is most truly you only by devoting to you what belongs to you, and you alone, and seeks always to be not unworthy of you.

I felt that as your wife I ought to seek no other help than what might be afforded me by the United States. It was for that reason that I sought refuge with their consul in Dunkirk, and took passage on an American ship. The passport issued to me in France by the Committee of Public Safety is to enable us to go to America, and my argument, beloved, is this: that one who is condemned to ostracism can best endure that trial in the company of his wife and children. If to the joy of being with you I may be allowed also the added happiness of serving you, then nothing remains but for me to join with you in blessing Him who governs all things, and in whose eyes this miserable life is of so little importance that he has permitted those for whom we mourn to have been so cruelly deprived of it, yet can at the same time make what remains of it for us so truly precious.[1]

Adrienne knew that not far from Altona she would find some part of what family remained to her. When her wise de Tessé aunt had emigrated, she had not let herself be caught napping. There were times when she let argument outstrip reason in the flood of her talk, but when it was a question of taking action her judgment was sound and shrewd. She was strong-minded and great-hearted. Prudent as ever, she had not left France "like a migrating swallow which takes only its feathers with it so as to travel more lightly." She had been careful to see that she was supplied with both money and jewels. In Switzerland, she had made the Lowenberg estate into a flourishing farm with a fine acreage of pasture land, and now lived there comfortably if not luxuriously on her own produce. The running of the estate had given her the work which her active temperament demanded.

She never sat down except to read—preferably Voltaire—and she employed her trenchant mind in brilliant talk. Somebody described her as being like one of those hens which, as they grow older, take on the gait and crow of a cock. She had not lost her sibylline air, her stately and rather pompous delivery, her grimaces and convulsive twitchings. Though expressing her skepticism violently in speech, she nourished three *émigré* priests on the fruit of her kitchen garden and the milk of her cows. She took them vegetables and cheese with her own hands, for the sheer pleasure of joining issue with them on points of theological controversy. But she had also attracted to her rural solitude—in order, she said, to have somebody always on hand who could answer her back—the Marquis de Mun, formerly a fine horseman and still a good talker, a man of scintillating wit, kindliness, and imperturbable composure.

The Duc d'Ayen was still living at Gardane, in the canton of Vaud, with the Countess Golovkine. In July, 1794, his daughter Pauline, an *émigré*, ruined and without resources, paid him a visit only five days after her grandmother, her mother, and her sister had perished on the scaffold—though this she did not know. Taking with her in Mme de Tessé's rickety old chaise the young son of the Marquis de Mun, who improvised comic songs for her amusement, she was approaching Lausanne when she saw a farm cart in the distance, the driver of which had a large green umbrella over his head to give him a little shade. It was the Duc d'Ayen.

He was so changed that it was only by his voice that his daughter knew who he was. He asked her whether she had heard the news. Assailed by a wave of anxiety which made it impossible for her to speak, she leaned against a tree, buried her face in her hands, and prayed. Her father made her get into his cart. At Moudon, in the privacy of an inn room, he told her that he had just lost his mother, the Maréchale de Noailles. Guessing from his disordered speech that he had not told her all, Pauline asked, "And I?" He replied that he was far from easy in his mind about the fate of his wife and eldest daughter. She was not for a moment taken in by this attempt to break the news gently, and cried out "O God! O God! Thy will be done!"

In a voice choked with sobs she added that she wished only that she might have taken the place of her sister Louise. The Duc d'Ayen, himself in tears, begged her to be calm. Suddenly, while speaking of her mother, she remembered how in moments of great sorrow the duchesse had been in the habit of reciting the Magnificat. She began to speak the opening phrase of the canticle, "My soul doth magnify the Lord." Then, falling to her knees and joining her hands, she said the Lord's Prayer, laying particular stress on "Forgive us our trespasses as we forgive them that trespass against us." Pauline felt certain that those words expressed what her mother had been feeling when she was driven to execution.

The Duc d'Ayen took his daughter back to Lowenberg where Mme de Tessé, forewarned by young Mun, ran to meet and comfort her. During the following weeks she did all she could to keep Pauline occupied, in the hope that work, though it could not make her forget her grief, might help her to bear it. Among other tasks, she put her in charge of the kitchen garden. So great was Pauline's eagerness to do her best that she watered everything, including the nettles, never before having seen any in the well-tended gardens of the Hôtel de Noailles. She also accompanied her aunt when the latter visited the three indigent priests with her gifts of terrestrial nourishment.

Unfortunately, the presence of the innocent Marquise de Montagu was a source of uneasiness to the authorities of the canton of Fribourg, who were anxious to maintain an attitude of strict neutrality. Mme de Tessé was "requested" to get rid of "the foreign woman whom she was sheltering in defiance of orders to the contrary." Mme de Tessé explained that "the foreign woman" in question was her niece, now in mourning for five close relatives recently assassinated, and that she was entirely without resources, and homeless. She added: "I do not believe that there is any law forbidding me to receive her, or that, if there were, anyone would consent to enforce it." But be that as it might, this nest of *émigrés* caused the authorities a great deal of worry. Mme de Tessé, having had a Requiem Mass said for the victims of the Terror in the Catholic church of Cressier, found herself threatened with expulsion. The Swiss were very much afraid of the formidable armies of the French Republic.

The little colony soon found itself exposed to vexations of a different kind. A Swiss creditor of the guillotined Maréchale de Noailles tried to make Mme de Tessé refund the money due him, and she was summoned to appear before the magistrates of the canton. Exasperated beyond all bearing, she decided to sell her estate and take refuge in Germany. An accomplished businesswoman, she received a better price than she had paid. In January, 1795, she started out with the whole tribe she was feeding and sheltering, crossed the Elbe, and wound up at Altona, where she set about looking for a suitable property. Land, livestock, and farm buildings were the only investment in which she had any confidence. She would very much have preferred metaphysical conversation in a well-lighted *salon* to agricultural employments, but (as she said), "For one of slender means a *salon* is ruination, whereas it is very possible to live comfortably on the produce of a farm." The difficulty was to find a house large enough to accommodate all her guests. Boutelaud, her manager, pulled on his boots and went hunting for suitable properties in the remoter parts of Holstein and Mecklenburg. Six months were spent in poring over the advertisements of estate agents.

Then, one day in September, 1795, a letter arrived from England. In it the Princesse d'Hénin informed Mme de Tessé that Adrienne, Anastasie, and Virginie were on their way to Altona. Mme de Tessé eagerly hastened to meet the travelers as soon as they had landed. Misfortune and misery had brought about a terrible change in Adrienne's appearance, but in her worn and deeply lined face there was a look of calmness and resolution.

The fragile Mme de Montagu had been overwhelmed by the news of her sister's impending arrival. When the Princesse d'Hénin's letter was delivered, she was knitting a woolen blanket intended for Monseigneur de Bonald, Bishop of Clermont, who had also found refuge in Altona, where he lacked even the simplest necessities and was living in a state of destitution. The needles fell from her fingers. Until that moment she had not even heard that Adrienne was once more a free woman. Why had she come to Altona? Was she in flight from some new persecution? Next morning, when a cannon shot announced the arrival of a ship in the roadstead, Pauline had scarcely strength enough to go down to the wharf to meet the travelers. The two sisters had not seen each other since their hurried interview at the Vaire stagehouse in 1792. Those were the days when Adrienne was not received at Plauzat because of her husband's "advanced" opinions. The reunion was emotional:

Madame de Tessé, so as to give free play to their outpourings, had discreetly moved away, taking her two grandnieces with her. . . . The sisters were so deeply moved that for a long time they could not speak. But they knew well what each was thinking. It was Madame de Montagu who first broke the silence. She controlled her sobs sufficiently to ask: "Did you see them?" Madame de La Fayette replied, without any further explanation, that she had not had that happiness. But she knew almost the whole story of their imprisonment and death. She had seen Monsieur Grelet, she had seen Père Carrichon, and had talked at length with both. She even had with her a copy of her mother's will. During this first meeting they spoke of nothing else, for their conversation had to be cut short out of consideration for Madame de Tessé.[2]

Her aunt made Adrienne give an account of all that she had suffered during her long captivity. The men present (Mun and Tessé) questioned her about the purpose of her journey. She said, as though it were the most natural thing in the world, that she was trying to join her husband. For several months there had been no news of him. After the attempted escape organized by Bollman and Huger had failed, La Fayette had been kept in solitary confinement. It was only through the good offices of Bollman that he knew that Adrienne was still alive. He had heard nothing of her imprisonment or of the Noailles massacre. Adrienne was planning to go to Vienna, where she intended to fling herself at the emperor's feet and ask him to grant her and her daughters the favor of being permitted to share the lot of the prisoner, no matter how hard that lot might be.

Mme de Tessé and the Marquis de Mun, though filled with admiration for this heroic proof of married love, raised a number of objections. They told her of the snubs to which she would be exposed in Vienna and pointed out that, even should she succeed in her request, neither she in her state of weakened health nor her daughters were in any condition to endure prison life, the brutality of jailers, and the lack of air and exercise. But Adrienne had an answer to everything, and her resolution was unshakable.

She saw John Parish, the banker who was the American consul in Hamburg, and from him procured a passport made out in the name of Mrs. Motier, of Hartford in Connecticut, this being one of the states in which La Fayette had been naturalized. It was essential that her other names, and even her nationality, should be kept secret, for no French person who was not an *émigré* was allowed to enter the Austrian territories. She engaged a French-speaking German servant and bought a post chaise, for Parish had generously provided her with money and had even offered to supply her with more should she have need of it. All necessary steps having been taken, she started off.

All those who had spoken with her during her short time of residence in Altona were filled with admiration of her courage, her foresight, her activity, and her sweetness. Her firmness of purpose, her conviction that she would succeed in carrying through an almost impossible enterprise, her faith in divine aid and protection, inspired confidence and respect. Many *émigrés* who were hostile to La Fayette had been to see her, hungry, as was only to be expected, for news of France and of their families. She knew all about their behavior to her husband and the part they had played in the misfortunes which had fallen upon him, and might well have been embittered. But she was incapable of harboring resentment.

It is quite extraordinary [wrote her daughter] that anyone should love with such exalted passion, yet never under any circumstances feel the faintest trace of bitterness against those who had slandered and persecuted the object of her love. She weighed the conduct of those who might well have given her cause to complain with a tolerant and kindly sense of justice. In the whole course of a disturbed and difficult life she never once changed this attitude.[3]

II

ADRIENNE AT OLMÜTZ

Your presence will be an added pleasure.
EMPEROR FRANCIS II

It seemed extremely unlikely that, knowing no German and going to a country the frontiers of which were closed to French travelers, Adrienne would ever reach Vienna. But faith takes small account of obstacles. She made the journey in eight days. We have the notes she kept of her expenses: "Took with me from Hamburg, 1920 livres." Every evening she entered the cost of the inn, and the amount spent on post-horses and repairs to the carriage, which reached an average daily total of about one hundred livres. By the seventh day she was at the gates of Vienna: "Horses, inns, tolls: 252 livres." In all, she had spent 1066 livres. She had 854 left. She was a heroine with an orderly mind.

Now, she was in Vienna with her two daughters. How was she to reach the Emperor of Austria? The aristocratic families of Europe, irrespective of differences of opinion, still formed a freemasonry of caste. Old Prinz von Rosemberg, Grand Chamberlain of the Imperial Household, had known the Noailles family well. Thanks to the intervention of the Countess von Rombeck, a friend of Mme de Tessé, he agreed to see Adrienne. She was introduced to him as Mrs. Motier, but at once revealed her true identity. He was touched by the devotion of a wife whose only request was that she might be allowed to share a prison cell, and, unknown to the ministers, arranged an audience for her with the emperor. The chancellor, Baron von Thugut, who felt for La Fayette a strangely personal hatred, would not have allowed her to be received.

Francis II was a young man. Adrienne's impression was: "He seems to be nothing but a petty crowned head, neither good nor bad." He received her politely. She asked permission for herself and her daughters to join her husband and their father. The emperor said to her: "It is granted. So far as his freedom is concerned, I can do nothing: my hands are tied." By this, no doubt, he meant that his government had made guarantees to England and Prussia.

Adrienne said how envious the wives of several other prisoners (La Tour-Maubourg, Bureaux de Pusy) would be of her good fortune. Francis II replied: "They have only to follow your example. I will do for them what I have done for you." He authorized his visitor to communicate with him personally, should she have any further request to make. Then he added: "You will find Monsieur de La Fayette well fed and well treated. I hope that you will do me justice. Your presence will be an added pleasure. You will be satisfied with the commandant. For the most part, prisoners are referred to only by their numbers, but your husband's name is well known."

ADRIENNE TO MME DE TESSÉ: OLMÜTZ, MAY 10, 1795

Thanks to your good advice, my dear aunt, I adopted the only possible method of reaching this place. Had my coming been announced beforehand, I should never have been admitted into the territories of the emperor, and had I not arranged to lie concealed at Vienna until Monsieur de Rosemberg had arranged my business, it would not have been satisfactorily concluded. I have told you about my visit to the emperor, who, having in the most gracious manner possible given us permission to be shut away with Monsieur de La Fayette, went on to say that the situation as a whole was very complicated, that it did not depend upon himself alone, but that the prisoner was being very well treated, and that our presence would be an added pleasure for him. So far was I from foreseeing how matters really stood, I spoke to him of the way in which Monsieur de La Fayette had been kept in complete ignorance of what had happened to us throughout the first period of his detention in Prussia, but added that, knowing little of the facts, I could not and did not accuse His Imperial Majesty of this act of barbarity. The emperor further gave me leave to write to him in person.

I next saw Monsieur de Thugut, the most influential of all the ministers, and the one most hostile to us. When I remarked that the coalition governments attached a great deal too much importance to a single man, he exclaimed several times over: "Too much importance indeed!" in a tone of voice and with a wry look on his face which was proof enough of the importance he attached to the matter. But Monsieur de Rosemberg had said to me: "I very much hope that everything is going to be arranged, and that we shall have peace," and I confess that we were so happy at having arrived that we saw the situation through rose-colored spectacles.[1]

Adrienne had sent to the Baron von Thugut a brief memorandum on the subject of her husband's case:

It is impossible to deny that the captivity of my husband, who was arrested while crossing the country as a simple traveler with the object of reaching neutral territory (at a time when he was being pursued by those responsible for the crimes of August 10; and because, at the head of his army, he had renewed his oath of allegiance to the king and wished his army to do the same)—it is impossible, I repeat, to deny that his being held in captivity was one of those measures, one of those violent acts, which only a revolution can explain. . . . That, however, does not alter the fact that the emperor was a free agent. It is not easy to see what argument the Allies could have brought to bear on this prince in order to prevent him from following the dictates of his own heart.[2]

She forwarded a copy of this letter to London, so that the "triumvirate" of the Princesse d'Hénin might be in a position to bring influence to bear. But the Baron von Thugut had made no attempt to disguise the vicious nature of his opposition, with the result that, in spite of the emperor's promise, the administrations employed their usual tactics of delay. At long last, however, the Comte de Ferraris, the War Minister, sent Adrienne a "permit of incarceration." At the same time, he said that he thought it his duty to ask her to think very seriously about the step she was taking, to warn her that she would find the results far from pleasant, and that the conditions to which she would have to submit might have serious consequences both for herself and her daughters. But she

La Grange: The forgotten papers were found at the top of this tower. From his study (window with shutters), La Fayette used to call instructions to his farm hands.

René de Chambrun, the present owner of La Grange, makes his preliminary examination of the material in the northwest tower.

LA GRANGE

In this nineteenth-century water color of La Grange the figures in the foreground are said to be La Fayette and his daughter Virginie. At right (above), the La Fayette children: Anastasie, George-Washington, and Virginie. Below, Adrienne (Both pictures at right from Collection Comtesse Amédée d'Harcourt).

HACHETTE

HACHETTE

Au nom du Père, et du fils, et du St Esprit

Seigneur vous êtes mon refuge et ma force, dans les maux extrêmes qui sont venus fondre sur moi, vous êtes mon dieu, tous les évènements de ma vie, sont entre vos mains, venez a mon secours, soyez toujours avec moi, et alors je ne craindrai rien, au milieu des ombres de la mort même

J'ai toujours voulu, et j'espère avec la grace de mon dieu, mourir dans le sein de l'église, Catholique, apostolique, et Romaine; je déclare, que c'est dans les principes de cette religion sainte que j'ai trouvé mon appuy, dans ses pratiques ma consolation, et j'ai la confiance qu'elle me soutiendra a l'heure de ma mort. — Je crois en vous mon dieu, et tout ce que vous avez révélé a votre église, j'espère tout ce que vous avez promis, je mets toute ma confiance dans les mérites de J.C. et dans le prix de son sang, je désire de conformer ma vie a la sienne, et j'unis mes souffrances a ses souffrances, et ma mort, a sa mort. J'espère, mon dieu vous aimer par dessus toutes choses et parvenir par votre grace au bonheur de vous aimer éternellement — j'accepte dans rebisas tous les moyens que votre providence aura choisis pour me conduire a ce heureux terme.

Je pardonne de tout mon cœur a mes ennemis, si j'en ai, a mes persécuteurs quelqu'ils soient, et même aux persécuteurs de ce que j'aime, je prie dieu de les combler de biens, et de nous pardonner comme je leur pardonne — Seigneur, en vous priant pour nos persécuteurs, aussi sincèrement que votre grace me l'inspire, vous ne rejetterez pas je l'espère, mes prières pour ce qui m'est cher, et vous nous traiterez selon la grandeur de vos miséricordes, ayez pitié de nous ô mon dieu

Je déclare que je n'ai jamais cessé d'être fidèle a ma patrie

... justice a ma reconnaissance

Marquis de la fayette

ce lundy 17 9bre 1777

Left, first page of the will Adrienne wrote in the prison of Plessis, 1794: "From the bottom of my heart I forgive my enemies, if I have any. . . ." The signature is from a letter of 1777. Below, seated at Adrienne's desk, André Maurois examines the documents dealing with La Belle Gabrielle, the La Fayette plantation in Guiana.

Above, the Picpus cemetery. Sisters of the Sacred Heart and of the Perpetual Adoration on their way to pray at the mass grave. Below, President Coty of France and United States Ambassador Houghton are among those observing the bicentennial of La Fayette's birth on July 4, 1957. The mass grave is beyond the wall. Among the flags over La Fayette's grave are those of French regiments that fought in the actions at Yorktown.　　　　　　　　　　　　　　　　　LA GRANGE

refused to listen to him, and the three women started immediately for Olmütz in an open carriage, their own traveling conveyance having been damaged. They reached their destination on October 15, 1795.

When the postilion pointed to the distant towers of the town, Adrienne was choked with tears. As soon as she found it possible to speak, she recited for her daughters, just as her mother had been in the habit of doing, the Tobit's prayer of rejoicing: "Blessed be God that liveth for ever, and blessed be his kingdom. For he doth scourge, and hath mercy: he leadeth down to hell, and bringeth up again: neither is there any that can avoid his hand. Confess him before the Gentiles, ye children of Israel . . . extol him before all the living." The Lord had struck her hard blows, but now he had taken her by the hand and led her to where her husband lay in prison. Still speaking to her daughters, she said: "How the ordeal before us is to be endured, I do not know."

She went straight to the commandant of the town, who did not receive her, but sent one of his officers to conduct the three arrivals to the fortress. They were led down a succession of long passages until they reached two padlocked doors which gave access to La Fayette's quarters. He had not been warned of their coming. He was still kept in solitary confinement. Not only were no letters delivered to him, but he was not even told whether the members of his family were alive or dead. The only news that reached him in this terrible solitude was conveyed in a code song hummed to him by Félix Pontonnier, his young secretary, who was put on a diet of bread and water whenever he was caught in the act by the jailers. After a great grinding of bolts, the door suddenly opened and La Fayette saw before him his wife and his daughters. What a shock, and what happiness!

Adrienne was appalled by her husband's physical appearance. He was little more than skin and bone. She had not set eyes on him for four years. Although he was only thirty-eight, he had aged beyond all belief. His lungs, which had always been weak, seemed now to be deeply affected. He too had difficulty in recognizing Adrienne in this gray-haired woman with seamed face. He was still wholly ignorant of the three terrible losses she had had to bear. "He knew," wrote their daughter Virginie, "that there had been a Terror in France, but not the names of its victims. . . . It was not until the evening, when my sister and I were locked into the room next door which had been assigned to us, that she told my father of her loss." He shared her grief and mingled his tears with hers, cursing the monsters who had defiled the Revolution. But what they had done did not change his principles.)

The sweetness of those first transports was interrupted almost immediately by the jailers, who told the newcomers to hand over their purses and confiscated three silver forks that had been found in their baggage. Adrienne insisted on seeing the commandant of the fortress, with whom the emperor had said she would be "satisfied." He refused to see her, but promised that three small requests which she had submitted to him should be forwarded to Vienna: (1) that she and her daughters should be permitted to attend Mass on Sundays; (2) that one of the soldiers' wives should be sent in to do their rooms; (3) that La Fayette's personal servant should be allowed to wait on them. No answer ever reached her. Nor were the forks returned. The three women had to eat with their fingers.

"Your presence will be an added pleasure," the emperor had said. This unconsciously cruel remark became a byword among the prisoners of Olmütz. In the opinion even of the Marquis de Chasteler, who made a report to the Austrian government in July, 1797, on the conditions of their internment, the accommodation provided was disgraceful. An open sewer and the proximity of the latrines made the air foul. In summer a cloud of mosquitoes invaded their quarters. Adrienne and her daughters had to sleep in one room—the two girls in a single bed, even when one of them was ill—and that in spite of repeated complaints. They had to leave their father's room at nightfall. The lights were extinguished at nine o'clock, and the prisoners had no means of rekindling the lamps should it be necessary for them to do so. Gilbert had been badly in need of shoes, and Adrienne had to make a pair from the material of an old pair of breeches.

Adrienne was eventually able to describe their life at Olmütz for Madame de Tessé:

Breakfast is brought to us at eight, after which I am locked up with my daughters until noon. We all meet for dinner, and apart from being twice disturbed by the jailers coming to take away the plates and later to bring us our supper, we are left together until eight o'clock, when my daughters are returned to their cage. Each time the keys are used, they are taken to the commandant and locked away with the most ridiculous precautions. The expenses of all three of us are paid by me. We have more to eat than we need, but the food is indescribably filthy.

The doctor, who does not know a word of French, is brought to us by an officer when we require his attentions. That does not worry us. Monsieur de La Fayette, in the presence of the officer who knows Latin, communicates in that language and translates our needs. While this officer, who would not dare speak to us without witnesses, and a fat corporal-jailer with a bunch of keys in his hand unlock our doors, the whole guard is drawn up in the passage and everyone can see into our rooms when the doors are opened by two sentries. You would laugh to see our two girls when that happens, one blushing to the tips of her ears, the other pulling a face which is sometimes proud, sometimes comic, as they pass beneath crossed swords into our room, the door of which is immediately locked. What is not pleasant is that the small courtyard which is on the same level as the passage is the scene of the only too frequent beatings to which the soldiers are sentenced. We can hear the whole horrible procedure.

It is a matter of great happiness to us that so far our children are standing up well to the hideously unhealthy conditions of our confinement. My own health is, I must admit, not good. I suffer from headaches, and the state of my blood is very much worse than it was before I came here. But there is nothing particularly alarming about that, and you will realize that we should not so much as consider leaving Monsieur de La Fayette. The good our presence is doing him is not confined to the pleasure he has in having us here. His health has been decidedly less bad since our arrival. You know how strong an effect affection has upon him. In spite of the strength of his character, it seems to me a miracle that he should have been able to resist so many torments.

There has been no improvement in his excessive thinness and in his general state of decline since we have been with him, though the guards assure me that there is no comparison between what he is now and the terrible state he was in a year ago. One does not go through four years of this kind of life with impunity! [3]

The good spirits of the two girls did more than a little to make this abominable regimen tolerable. They were filled with admiration and tenderness for their parents, and in spite of everything took an active pleasure in this family reunion. They found something to amuse them even in the life of the prison, in the shifts and tricks of captivity, in the looks of the jailers. At night it was possible to let down baskets from the windows and to buy little extras from the sentries. Anastasie was eighteen, Virginie thirteen, and they could still find much to divert them in thus living the events of a heroic romance.

Though Adrienne was officially entitled to write a few letters, all those containing realistic descriptions of their captivity had to be smuggled out of the fortress. There was always some way of getting them through. Complete strangers were prepared to risk their lives in order to help this wonderful family. Even within the walls of their prison Adrienne and her daughters succeeded in communicating with La Tour-Maubourg and Bureaux de Pusy. One proof of this is that the formula "an added pleasure" appears again and again between quotation marks in Maubourg's letters. But the local authorities, no doubt ashamed of the treatment meted out to the prisoners, censored all complaints sent through the official channels. Anastasie, who had a nice sense of humor, recorded one discussion of this matter with the assistant commandant:

MME DE LA FAYETTE: *So I am to understand that the government will not permit my letters to be dispatched because of certain details contained in them?*

LA FAYETTE: *This base and cowardly refusal of your government to admit the infamy of its conduct is the last straw, Monsieur.*

THE ASSISTANT COMMANDANT: *I have too much feeling not to be aware of what is owing to your situation . . . but there are expressions in this letter which cannot be permitted.*

LA FAYETTE: *There is nothing in it which should anger you, Monsieur. The expressions are not aimed at you . . . nor at your senior officers, who, like you, are merely passive instruments.*

MME DE LA FAYETTE: *I am extremely sorry for your sake, Monsieur, that you should owe obedience to such people.*

LA FAYETTE: *I have never felt anything but pity for the officers and generals of the Austrian army. I reserve my contempt for their government. . . .*

THE ASSISTANT COMMANDANT: As to the complaint about walking-exercise, there is nowhere for you to walk. Even in the officers quarters there is a smell.

LA FAYETTE: That is all the same to me. All I am concerned to point out is that not one single officer, from the major down—and he is about the most stinking creature whom they could have found to fill the position he occupies—that not a single officer, I repeat, but holds his nose when he comes in here.

MME DE LA FAYETTE: What, then, must I write or not write? I beg Monsieur the Commandant to tell me precisely what it is to which his superiors take exception in my letters. . . . Why does he not come in person to see me? Is it that he is forbidden to do so?

THE ASSISTANT COMMANDANT: It is true, Madame, that he is so forbidden. . . .

LA FAYETTE: I am more than willing to believe that the commandant has no more part to play in these matters than my little girl here. . . . What I am saying is aimed at bigger game. What ought we to say? That the court of Vienna is a humane and freedom-loving government? That I love it with all my heart; that it is composed of the most charming gentlemen to be found anywhere?

THE ASSISTANT COMMANDANT: Certainly not! Clearly those are things you cannot say. Besides, in your situation—

LA FAYETTE: My situation has nothing whatever to do with it, for I esteemed them no more highly before I came here.

MME DE LA FAYETTE: They allowed a letter to go through in which I announced the first symptoms of my illness, but stopped the one in which I described the progress of my cure. My friends will be in a most terrible state of anxiety. If I die here they will learn of my death even before they have heard in full about my sickness.

THE ASSISTANT COMMANDANT: That, Madame, would be most regrettable. But it is perfectly possible for you to speak of your health without saying things to which the authorities object.

LA FAYETTE: It is not your fault, Monsieur, if the infamous behavior of your government is such that it is impossible to give a single detail without revealing its barbarity.

THE ASSISTANT COMMANDANT: But, Monsieur le Marquis—

LA FAYETTE: *I am not a marquis, but I am certainly being very badly treated.*

THE ASSISTANT COMMANDANT: *I am instructed only to inform you that certain statements have been found in your letters which are not true.*

MME DE LA FAYETTE: *You had already told me so in the passage, which I did not think very polite on your part.*

LA FAYETTE: *And I, Monsieur, in reply instruct you to tell the wretched little nobody in Vienna who has all along been saying these things that for all I care he can go to— Where he can go I cannot say in front of these ladies ... but I expect you know the French compliment commonly employed in such cases.*

THE ASSISTANT COMMANDANT: *Yes, I know it very well. I have an excellent knowledge of French, and it is very disagreeable for me to have to hear such things. . . .*

MME DE LA FAYETTE: *Perhaps they are angry at my being here at all, because the necessity of having my signature before our expenses can be paid forces them to let me write at least a few lines. But since I am here, they are not going to find it easy to tear me away again. . . . No one is going to take me from this place except in company with Monsieur de La Fayette, unless they carry out my dead body; for I believe that this captivity (which has certainly shortened the life of my husband) has done great harm to my health. But of one thing they may be sure, and that is that nobody is going to make me write lies.*

THE ASSISTANT COMMANDANT: *I agree, Madame, that no one can ask that of you.*

LA FAYETTE: *It is true, Monsieur, that if anyone should flatter himself that he could do so, he would have to be even more idiotic than your court.*[4]

On December 14, 1795, Adrienne again asked to hear Mass, addressing the request this time to the War Minister, the Comte de Ferraris, whom she had met in the houses of the Princess Windisch-Graetz and of Mme d'Ursel. "I have never thought this request of mine to be indiscreet. You would give me much pleasure by sending a favorable answer before the Christmas festival." She hoped too that she might be allowed at last to see La Tour-Maubourg and Bureaux de Pusy. The minister's reply, written *after* Christmas, was unfeeling in the extreme: "I can do no more than point out that, having agreed to share the fate of your husband, you must expect no change in your situation."

ADRIENNE TO THE COMTE DE FERRARIS

I readily agree that we have consented to share the rigors of Monsieur de La Fayette's imprisonment. That was the only favor for which I asked. Our feelings have not changed, and the three of us repeat from our hearts that we are a great deal happier with Monsieur de La Fayette, even in this place, than we could be anywhere else without him.[5]

All the same, she remembered that the emperor had told her that she might write to him direct, although the Olmütz authorities had forbidden her to do so. All that she wanted to ask of His Majesty was permission to spend eight or ten days in Vienna, where she wished to consult some doctors. The sedentary, unhealthy life imposed upon her had brought on a serious illness. Her legs and arms were much swollen and were covered with a rash. She was continuously feverish. But though the prison doctor was uneasy (he had said as much to La Fayette in Latin), the emperor's reply was in the negative. The commandant of the prison went to see her, and, after telling her to send her two daughters out of the room, informed her that she could leave the fortress only on condition that she did not return to it. He demanded a response in writing. This he received. It breathed the very spirit of pride and firmness:

MARCH 4, 1796

The commandant of Olmütz informed me yesterday that the emperor, in reply to my request to be allowed to spend eight days in Vienna in order to consult certain doctors, has decided that I cannot be permitted to leave this prison unless I consent not to return to it. I have the honor to repeat to him the answer I have already made by word of mouth.

I owe it to my family and my friends to seek such medical attention as is necessary in my present state of health. But they know well that the price demanded is unacceptable. I cannot forget that, at a time when we were both of us at the point of death, I as a result of Robespierre's tyranny, and Monsieur de La Fayette from the moral and physical effects of his captivity, I was not allowed to have news of him, nor to inform him that his children and I were still alive. I will not expose myself to the horrors of a second separation.[6]

But sick and badly treated though she was, Adrienne did not think of herself as unhappy at Olmütz.

My mother [wrote Virginie] grieved at not being able to soften the lot of our companions in captivity. But I find it difficult to describe her own feelings of happiness. Something of what these were may be gathered from a knowledge of the sentiments which from the age of fourteen had always animated her. She had suffered much, whether as a result of the frequent periods of separation from my father and the constant claims upon his time which made it necessary for him to be frequently absent from his home, or because of the constant dangers which threatened him. She had spent the last three years almost despairing of ever seeing him again. But now she had the one thing which all her life had been the single object of all her wishes. She saw every day the effect of her presence on his health, and the comfort that it brought him. It was a matter of constant astonishment to her that she could have so far recovered the capacity for happiness, and she blamed herself for being satisfied with her situation while my father was still a prisoner.[7]

It is true that for this woman passionately in love, imprisonment in the company of her beloved had about it something of the taste of paradise. Nothing but death could threaten her happiness.

But the danger of death was only too real. For eleven months Adrienne's legs and arms were so terribly swollen that she could scarcely move. She was suffering from edema and varicose ulcers, complicated by eczema. Her jailers refused her the use of an armchair. During the first months of her confinement she had written a long Notice sur la Duchesse d'Ayen, her mother, on the margins of a volume of Buffon with a toothpick and a little India ink. Later, when she could no longer move her swollen fingers, she dictated her letters to Anastasie. Virginie, deprived of air and exercise during the most important years of her growth, was developing a stoop, which greatly worried her mother.

Adrienne had the belated happiness of finding herself at last judged according to her merits by the man she had never ceased to love. Though Gilbert had always respected her courage and intelligence, he had never before so truly measured the greatness of her character. Now he felt for her immense admiration and tremendous gratitude. Though he did not share her faith, he saw with respectful astonishment the effect it had upon her. It was a matter of amazement to him that his wife and his daughters should be as serene in the fetid atmosphere of Olmütz as they had formerly been in the *salon* of the Hôtel de Noailles, or in the mountains of Auvergne. He felt himself to be supported by their love, and by the love he himself felt for liberty in all its forms. He may not have had religious faith, but he had a great sense of honor, and would rather have died than deny his beliefs. In this he met with the full approval of his wife.

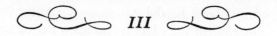

III

THE WORLD OUTSIDE

Such characters should live to posterity,
when kings and the crowns they wear
must have moldered into dust.

CHARLES JAMES FOX

The unfortunate find it only too easy to believe that the whole world is concerned with their sufferings. In the case of the prisoners of Olmütz there was some foundation for this belief. In many cities there were groups of friends taking active steps to bring about their freedom.

At Hamburg, the United States consul, John Parish, not only provided money, but worked on their behalf with Masson and Pillet, formerly aides-de-camp of the general, who traveled endlessly between Hamburg, London, and Paris, rousing all men of good will to take action. In London, the "triumvirate" of the Princesse d'Hénin, Lally-Tollendal, and Joseph Masclet, with the full support of the American consul, Thomas Pinckney, was carrying on the good work. Their efforts were vigorously seconded by Charles James Fox and General Fitzpatrick, largely because they were liberals and friends of La Fayette, and because they were genuinely shocked by the behavior of the coalition governments, but also to some extent because it gave them a useful weapon against Pitt.

In Paris, the fall of Robespierre had left a great vacuum. The royalists and members of the pleasure-loving set had hoped to fill it. A counterrevolutionary "White" Terror had been unloosed in

the Midi and at Lyons. These savage outbursts in no way served
the cause of the king in exile, the Comte de Provence (later Louis
XVIII). France was fully aware that the Bourbons were more likely
to establish a political inquisition than to grant a civil Edict of
Nantes. Had the *émigrés* been less blundering, a restoration might
have been possible. As it was, their uncompromising attitude convinced the Jacobins, now in possession, that they must maintain
their position or perish as a political power. Barras saw clearly that
the old Red terrorists must be mobilized against their White suc-
cessors. The test of strength took place on the 13th Vendémiaire,
when a obscure Corsican general named Bonaparte saved the Convention. Gouverneur Morris, an eyewitness on that occasion, said:
"I have long predicted a single despotism. . . . Chance, or rather
the want of mettle in the usurper, has alone saved them to the
present moment; but I am still convinced they must end their
voyage in that port."

Five directors, all of them regicides, assumed control. They gave
Bonaparte the command of the Army of Italy as a reward for his
services. No one then knew the true nature of the lean general with
the Roman profile, whose tempestuous passion for the overripe
creole Joséphine de Beauharnais, the former mistress of Hoche and
Barras, made the directors smile. Were these men likely to interest
themselves in the fate of the prisoners of Olmütz? It was most im-
probable that Barras, a debauched voluptuary who regarded his
fellow men with contempt, would find much to admire in the
dreamy ruminations of La Fayette. The other four, inflexible republicans, had an uncomfortable memory of the way in which the
Hero of Two Worlds had championed the cause of a constitutional
monarchy. And so it came about that when they exchanged with
Austria the daughter of Marie-Antoinette in return for four pris-
oners-of-war, they chose former Convention members of the stamp
of Bournonville, who had also been imprisoned at Olmütz, rather
than General de La Fayette, his wife, and his daughters.

Meanwhile, from his fortress cell, La Fayette was conducting a
carefully planned campaign. More precisely, Adrienne directed
what he planned. Secret letters were being sent from Olmütz, and
it was just as well that Gilbert's only too familiar handwriting should
not be recognized. On June 20, 1796, Adrienne gave to Pillet a
summary of her husband's views: Contrary to what was being said,
the general was not in favor of royalty. The idea of an hereditary

presidency had always been displeasing to him. Only necessity had at one time made him rally to it. (La Rochefoucauld and La Fayette, said Adrienne, had been the only two genuine republicans in France in the early days of the Revolution.)

It would be as foolish [wrote Adrienne while Gilbert dictated] for the country to re-establish royalty, even on a constitutional basis, as it had been cowardly to substitute for it, with fear and trembling, a Jacobin aristocracy and the arbitrary kingship of their chief. On the question of a Declaration of Rights, Monsieur de La Fayette would never yield an inch. What you have to deal with is a character on which for the last twenty years, the friends of freedom have had their eyes fixed.[1]

On June 22 Adrienne wrote Pillet again:

Monsieur de La Fayette says that there is a Latin proverb: Mitte sapientem et nihil dicas. If that means that we should have unlimited confidence in you, we echo the sentiment with all our hearts.

Adrienne requested Pillet to see Citizen Philippe-Nicolas Beauchet, who knew all about their affairs and would supply him with the addresses of their friends and relations. The deputies whom she thought to be favorably inclined were Dupont de Nemours, Boissy d'Anglas—"honest, sympathetic, and sincere"—and Lanjuinais. There was also Mme de Staël, who was trying just then to reassert her influence:

She has constantly spoken well of Monsieur de La Fayette [Adrienne continued], but her imprudence and the multiplicity of her liaisons makes it necessary to exercise great caution in dealing with her.

This letter, like all Adrienne's, is attractive by reason of its intelligent realism, its almost religious respect for her husband, and its concern not to compromise the noble attitude of the impenitent liberal. It is also important to note, if we are to have a finished portrait of this loving wife who knew nothing of jealousy and was resigned to sharing her husband's heart, that she told Pillet to make contact with Mme de Simiane and to give her news of the prisoner:

Here is another commission for you which has nothing to do with politics but deeply concerns Monsieur de La Fayette's heart. Madame de Simiane is either in Paris or on her estate at Cirey. Should

*the first be the case, see her, but pledge her to absolute silence. If,
however, she should be in the country, then write to her that private
business has taken you to Paris and that you are anxious to give her
such details as you have been able to collect about Monsieur de La
Fayette. Monsieur de La Fayette hopes that Madame d'Hénin has
carried out the commissions he wished her to undertake for her. You
must say that I do not allow myself to write, not even secretly, to
people in France, and that our most devoted friends would run too
great a risk in taking responsibility for receiving so much as a single
line from Monsieur de La Fayette.*[2]

To allay the fears felt by the Directory about La Fayette's political intentions, Masson and Pillet had sent a note on the subject to
the directors and wished to follow this up with a pamphlet. Adrienne supplied them with a text that probably came from the pen
of César de La Tour-Maubourg:

TO MONSIEUR MASSON, MERCHANT, AT HAMBURG

*Your friends have received a letter, undated, containing the note
addressed to the Directory, which is so worthy of you and so touching for them that they have read it with the most tender feelings
of gratitude. . . . They are most eager to know what the answer will
be. . . . You are a truly delightful friend. I enclose with this a small
pamphlet, the handwriting of which you will recognize. . . . I have
told you, dear friend, that we fully approve Pillet's idea with reference to a certain compilation of relevant documents, and leave ourselves entirely in his hands so far as choice is concerned.*[3]

Adrienne pointed out that the pamphlet had been partially
recopied (perhaps by one of her daughters) and that he must keep
a careful watch for errors. For instance, it would be obvious that
for the *civisme* of the Duc d'Orléans he should read *cynisme*. This
was, indeed, self-evident.

What most concerned both husband and wife was not captivity,
illness, or the life imposed upon their daughters, but the preservation of the La Fayette image, without any touching-up or correc-
tions bred of second thoughts.

ADRIENNE TO MME DE TESSÉ: MAY 10, 1796

*You will not be surprised that Monsieur de Lafayette should lay it
down as a rule for his friends that no one must speak for him, on any
occasion or for any purpose whatever, except in a manner consistent*

with his character and his principles, and that he presses even to excess, what you call the weakness of a great passion. This it would be easy to justify. It is not that he is afflicted with that particular form of irritable sensitivity which misfortune so often produces in weak characters. His own is as mild and gentle as ever. But you are aware with what constancy he holds to the sentiments which have animated his whole life, and that it is this unshaken determination which has brought on him so much hatred and so much esteem, so much success and such a mass of persecution, that he has come to see it as the only embankment it is possible to raise against the flood of misfortunes which has flowed in upon us from all sides. Nobody, therefore, should feel any astonishment at the excessive and scrupulous repugnance with which he would view any distortion for the worse, no matter how small, of something which for him has always been the most precious of all possessions, and which, in the midst of so many torments of the heart, has alone served to maintain his courage.[4]

In that month of May, 1796, the military situation was undergoing a rapid transformation. Bonaparte, after his lightning Italian campaign, had entered Milan. The distant sounds of victory had penetrated even the walls of Olmütz. Gilbert did not know Bonaparte, but chose to see him in the guise of a republican general. The two young girls were daily hoping that the prison bars would vanish and a tricolor sash appear. The activities, too, of Gilbert's English friends, Fox and Fitzpatrick, were proving very useful. The prisoners were insistent that full advantage should be taken of the successes of French arms to redouble every effort that was being made in their favor.

ADRIENNE TO THE PRINCESSE D'HÉNIN: SEPTEMBER 15, 1796
Our sojourn here is truly far from pleasant, no matter what the emperor may say, and, quite apart from bugs and stink and filth, we should dearly like a change of bed linen, air, and a female attendant. . . . There could not be more fuss and pother if it were a question of moving wild panthers from one cage to another. All this much diverts our young ladies, whose joy at being once more with their father is as lively now as on the day of our arrival. We have learned with great pleasure that George is now at Mount Vernon with General Washington. . . . Your friend is as he always was: he is much delighted at the spectacle of his National Guard beating all

these famous armies, and of Cadignan's grenadiers outwitting all the great tricksters of Europe. He asks nothing better, he says, than that the prompt arrival of the French in Vienna should be an "added pleasure" for the emperor.[5]

But in spite of all that was being done in London and Paris, the Austrian government showed no intention of liberating the prisoners of Olmütz. On February 20, 1796, Washington had written to Thomas Pinckney, the United States consul in London, as follows:

I need hardly mention how much my sensibility has been hurt by the treatment this Gentleman has met with; or how anxious I am to see him liberated therefrom; but what course to pursue, as most likely and proper to aid the measure, is not quite so easy to decide on. As President of the U States, there must be a commitment of the Government by any interference of mine; and it is no easy matter in a transaction of this nature for a public character to assume the garb of a private citizen in a case that does not relate to himself.[6]

Nevertheless, he did take a further step. On May 15, 1796, he wrote a confidential letter to the emperor in which he made it clear how deeply the American people and himself, grateful as they were for the services rendered them by La Fayette, were concerned for the fate of the prisoner.

Allow me . . . to entreat that he may be permitted to come to this Country on such conditions and under such restrictions, as your Majesty may think it expedient to prescribe.[7]

Mme de Staël, for her part, had written to Gouverneur Morris who, in December, 1796, found himself in Vienna:

Open the prison door of M. de La Fayette. You have already saved his wife; deliver the whole family. Pay the debt of your country.[8]

And Pauline de Montagu, fearing her sister's illness might prove fatal, begged Morris to save her life for the second time. Morris went to see the Baron von Thugut, and showed him Mme de Montagu's letter. The hypocritical Thugut denied the charge of ill-treatment and repeated to him what he had already told Adrienne: that she was free to leave Olmütz, should she wish to do so, but that she could not be permitted to come and go as she liked. As to the general, he would probably be freed when the fighting was ended.

If, meanwhile, England was prepared to take responsibility for him, Austria would be delighted to see the last of him, and if the English wanted to let him loose on London, much good might it do them! Morris then asked Thugut to forward a letter to Mme de La Fayette in which he had put in writing the protests made by Thugut to the effect that the prisoners were well housed and wanted for nothing.

It goes without saying that Morris' letter never got further than Thugut's study, that no reply was received to the request made by Morris, and that thereafter all correspondence between Adrienne and her sister Pauline was intercepted. From this Morris concluded that the description of the horrors of Olmütz was not exaggerated.

Adrienne's health was now so bad that, according to the prison doctor, should her confinement be prolonged, there would soon be no hope for her. In December, 1796, she once again dictated to Anastasie a letter to Parish:

It is now nearly two months since your kind letter reached me. I am, however, deprived of the pleasure of answering it myself. Because of the worsening condition of my blood and of the excessively insanitary conditions of this prison, my arms have been for some time unbelievably swollen, and my fingers incapable of movement. . . . My skin is peeling. . . . The pain, the impossibility of closing my hands, and the spasms in my whole nervous system make my life more than a little disagreeable.[9]

She was not exaggerating. We have the report, in Latin, furnished by the prison doctor. He confirms the sick woman's own account of herself. "*Quamvis Domina de La Fayette excellenti gaudeat constitutione, et sana fuerit dum intraret in carcerum olomuciensem. . . .*" "Though Madame de La Fayette enjoys a good constitution and was in good health when she entered the prison of Olmütz, she is now suffering from crises of a dangerous kind. The nature of her malady demands a thermal cure, as well as other remedies which the prison regime has made impossible. I consider myself fortunate in having been able to prevent more serious developments. The elder daughter, Anastasie de La Fayette, thanks to her excellent constitution, has resisted the effects of captivity for fifteen months. Recently, however, she has been more frequently in ill health. . . ." It was high time for this unfortunate family to be removed from the useless harshness of strict confinement.

On February 12, 1797, Adrienne had an opportunity to write to her son and know with certainty that her letter would reach him:

To be able to exist at all in such bodily discomfort and in the terrible conditions of our captivity is no small an achievement.... I cannot conceal from you the great deterioration in your father's health.... He cherishes the cause of liberty no less in the prisons where he suffers for it than he did when he served it actively.... In this living tomb you are the sweetest and the most constant preoccupation of all four of us.[10]

This very noble letter was intended as much for the eyes of General Washington as for those of George. The cry rose from a deep pit that might well become a grave.

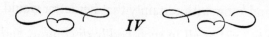

IV

LIBERATION

No transaction is complete until it is concluded.

TALLEYRAND

In Paris, it was not only their friends who took an interest in the prisoners of Olmütz. The injustice of their fate, Adrienne's devotion, and the tender age of her daughters, aroused widespread feelings of sympathy even among complete strangers. A certain Charles d'Agrain published a poem: *The Captivity of La Fayette, a Heroic Epistle, with Characters and Historical Notes Not Yet Known to the Public, on the Illustrious Prisoners of Olmütz, in Moravia.* The preface was a speech for the defense:

There was a time when to speak the name of La Fayette was to be involved in his ruin. There was nothing astonishing in that at a time when Bailly, the queen, and many thousand victims were dragged to the scaffold; when anarchy worked hand in hand with the ambitions of the allied monarchs to tear the French Empire in pieces.... But now that France, for a while confined within a tomb, has emerged from it glowing with an even greater radiance...she has turned her eyes on Olmütz.

Sentimental plates in the manner of Greuze showed the wife and daughters of the hero flinging themselves into his arms. In the poem the hero declaimed:

Within this gloomy prison, the prototype of Hell,
For five years bowed beneath the weight of chains,

Forgotten in the world of man, the world of nature,
Here in the depths where light scarce penetrates,
Thus am I forced relentlessly to suffer pains
And die piecemeal, before the eyes of my oppressor.

In short, public opinion was at work. In 1797 the military situation had become such that France could insist on the liberation of the victims of the harsh Thugut. Bonaparte had crossed the Alps and was threatening Vienna. The armies of Italy, of the Sambre and Meuse, of the Rhine and the Moselle, were converging on Austria. The "Marseillaise" was blowing through the mountain passes. The jailers were afraid, and showed it. On April 7, 1797, the preliminaries of peace were signed at Leoben. England, abandoned by Austria and shaken by a mutiny among her own sailors, was giving way. La Fayette had hopes of immediate liberation, not as the result of representations from abroad, even if they came from America, but of French victories, which he saw as those of *his* National Guard.

Adrienne wrote to Masson:

It is especially to the demands put forward by the French that, from feelings of patriotism rather than from self-interest, he longs above all things to be indebted for his liberty.[1]

It seemed to them inconceivable that the Republic should not demand as a matter of immediate urgency the release of the first of its republicans. La Fayette, Bureaux de Pusy, and La Tour-Maubourg considered that the matter was as good as settled. Adrienne wrote to Madame de Staël:

These gentlemen have great hopes. They know that steps are being taken to provide conveyances and passports to take us all to Amsterdam or Hamburg. The nation must insist, and make of it a national concern. Above all, it must cease from regarding them as émigrés.[2]

Mme de Staël shared these hopes, but it frequently happens that human beings are the pawns of a party, or of several parties of whose very existence they are ignorant. In France the political battle was still raging between Jacobins, royalists, and directors. Another struggle was threatening to set the victorious generals at odds with the government. The Directory, now short of money, had but a limited authority over the young heroes of the military scene, whose reputations were born of success in the field and who followed their soldiers. It delegated commissioners to the armies. At Bonaparte's headquarters General Clarke represented the central power. But Clarke could not long stand out against the prestige of the victor of Lodi and of Arcola. He obeyed to a far greater extent than he controlled. Hence the complexity of the La Fayette affair. Before the general could be liberated, the Directory would need convincing and Bonaparte's agreement would have to be obtained.

The Directory consisted of five men. Two of them, Carnot and Barthélemy, were unreservedly in favor of the prisoners' return. The other three were Barras, an aristocratic Jacobin; Rewbell, whose unintelligent way of seeming to be a man who knew what he wanted and was going to get it could easily turn to the most elementary pig-headedness; and La Reveillère-Lépeaux, an honest enough character, but the high priest of a religion invented by himself— theo-philanthropy—and possessed of a very limited outlook. They were all afraid of the general on the white horse. If he returned, might he not become a leader of the constitutional royalists? Bonaparte, for his part, was decidedly lukewarm. True, he was working amicably with the Directory, but, after Lodi he thought, not without reason, that no ambition would now be beyond his grasp, and he did not want a rival.

Mme de Staël, long regarded with suspicion, had ventured in 1797 to return to Paris. She began at once to enlist the interest of General Pichegru, Supreme Commander-in-Chief, in favor of La Fayette. Her choice was unfortunate. Pichegru, who was secretly intriguing for Louis XVIII, dreaded the reappearance of La Fayette on the scene. Barras received Mme de Staël courteously. "You, at least, dear Barras," she said to him, "are not encased in ice, but have the blood of the south in your veins, which is what I like. You I address as a citizen, a republican, and a member of the Directory. ... Barras, we *must* give La Fayette back to France, to the Republic. I guarantee that he will be the best of citizens—after you, of course." [3] Barras was touched. He convinced his colleagues, and proposed to leave the necessary negotiations in Bonaparte's hands.

This task Bonaparte accepted, but reserved the right to impose conditions. In June, Talleyrand, one of Mme de Staël's great friends and recently returned from America by way of Hamburg, became Foreign Minister. In the faraway days of 1790 when, as Bishop of Autun, he had officiated at the Festival of Federation, he had been on terms of intimacy with La Fayette and would certainly now give his support to any movement for his liberation. To the unfortunate general Germaine de Staël wrote: "Come straight back to France: there can be no other country for you. There you will find the Republic for which you so ardently longed even when you felt in conscience bound to support the royal cause." The faithful Joseph Masclet, however, was less optimistic:

JULY 31, 1797

Your liberation depends at present on the attitude of the Directory, and on Bonaparte, who will follow the instructions and adopt the views of the present majority of the directors.... The Lameth brothers would like to link their names and their interests with those of La Fayette! The Directory lot see in those ranks the fluttering banner of the English constitution, nor have their eyes deceived them. They still believe that our friend will consent to serve with them under those colors, but in that they show a lack of common sense. But stupidity can no more be cured than fear, and I do not doubt that they have given good evidence of both to the very brave and very enlightened republican Bonaparte. Thugut has a pretty good inkling of the unsympathetic attitude of these men. He has a feeling that the councils would be only too happy to ratify a peace which has been so long and so ardently desired, and that he need not, therefore, despair of keeping the locks and bolts securely fastened forever on the prison doors which seemed for a moment to be opening.[4]

This was a terrible prospect for the prisoners of Olmütz. It did not need much demonstrating to prove that Thugut hated them, and that if he found some way of doing so without danger to himself, he would keep them locked away for the rest of their lives. In order to reassure the directors, Talleyrand and Benjamin Constant undertook to promise in La Fayette's name that in the event of his liberation he would agree to stay away from France for six months. Carnot brought pressure on General Clarke:

Get, if you possibly can, a provisional undertaking, to set free La Fayette, Bureaux-Pusy [sic], and La Tour-Maubourg. It is a matter of national honor that they should emerge from those dungeons in which they have been held only because they started the Revolution.[5]

One of Clarke's staff officers was Louis Romeuf. He had once been La Fayette's aide-de-camp, and was devoted to him heart and soul. He was now instructed to open negotiations with Thugut and with the Marquis de Gallo, the Austrian Secretary of State. Victor de La Tour-Maubourg, brother of the prisoner, was sent by Bonaparte to Vienna, where he arrived in advance of Romeuf. No messenger could have been more in sympathy with La Fayette and his companions.

ADRIENNE TO VICTOR DE LA TOUR-MAUBOURG: OLMÜTZ, JULY 18, 1797

We are doubly happy in the prospect of liberation and at the thought of having you as our liberator. . . . What joys await us when we leave this place, and that day, thanks to you, Monsieur, will not be long delayed.

It is precisely three months since the preliminaries were signed. General Bonaparte was already busying himself about us, even before he received the decision of the Directory. Barthélemy's activity on our behalf could not have been bettered. . . . Yet not only are we still here, but we have redoubled evidence of ill will. With the exception of Mr. Pitt, who, having adopted a position of personal antagonism to France, is twice over the personal enemy of Gilbert, there is no court in Europe which detests him so cordially as does that of Vienna.

She advised Victor not to trust Frenchmen like Meilhan and even to go carefully with Gouverneur Morris: "I know he saved my life, but he is very much the aristocrat and would gladly take up an antirevolutionary position. I shall beware of confiding any of our secrets, present or future, to him." It might be necessary to get into personal touch with Bonaparte, she said, and continued:

One cannot help being deeply resentful, seeing that three months after the cessation of hostilities the Austrians are continuing them against the persons of the prisoners of Olmütz. . . . All those people detest both the French government and the victorious general, and will do nothing except under compulsion. . . .

Gilbert has found a heartfelt pleasure in the immense and merited glory of the general who has raised the prestige of the National Guard to so high a point, who has assured the triumph of the French

Revolution and has established in Italy the doctrine of the Declaration of Rights. You know his long-standing and sincere friendship for General Berthier.... He is deeply touched by our dear Louis Romeuf having undertaken this journey.[6]

Prisoners are always apt to be out of date by reason of the state of ignorance in which they live. It was neither true nor tactful to refer to the young Army of Italy as the National Guard.

No matter how repugnant it might be to Thugut, he had to carry out the promise made to the conqueror, or at least to make a pretense of taking the first steps toward honoring it. On July 25 he sent the Marquis de Chasteler to Olmütz. This general already knew La Fayette, having been the first person to question him after his capture in 1792. He was a perfect man of the world and His Imperial Majesty's chamberlain. In his embarrassment at having to treat a Noailles lady as a prisoner, he was so excessively polite that Pusy's old bodyservant, watching him bowing and scraping, said that he had "all the looks of the Devil himself." His instructions were to communicate to the prisoners the decisions reached by the government, and to make a report on their treatment. He did not conceal from his minister that all was not for the best in the best of all possible prisons. "The food is plentiful, but not always clean." All through the interview the two young girls kept on exchanging glances and laughing a great deal. At their age everything was amusing, especially a chamberlain put out of countenance.

When it came to discussing the release of the prisoners, General de Chasteler told La Fayette point-blank that the principles professed by him were incompatible with the tranquility of the Austrian monarchy. Before being set at liberty, therefore, he must give a solemn undertaking never again to set foot on Austrian territory. La Fayette tried to get out of the difficulty by making a joking reference to the honor done him by the emperor in thinking that a single individual could be a danger to so vast an empire, the subjects of which were so devoted to their master. But Chasteler insisted on a formal promise. La Fayette, who was more than ever scrupulous when it was clearly in his interest to be so, declared that he had no wish ever again to set foot in the country, but that his sovereign master was the French people, and that should they wish to send him there, either as a soldier or a diplomat, he should obey them. The proud Adrienne loved him in this mood.

My mother [wrote Virginie] *was well aware of the price they must pay for such behavior. But in the midst of all her sufferings, she would have gladly paid with long months of captivity for the satisfaction she felt in my father's reply to the demand made of him by the Austrian government.*[7]

Chasteler said that he could not accept such an answer. Once again La Fayette's punctilious sense of honor seemed ready to put everything back to where it had started.

But a reservation of quite a different kind affected him much more deeply. In the statement drawn up by Bonaparte and Clarke, which Chasteler read to him, the two French generals demanded that "the said prisoners shall be set at liberty, and given the means of going to America or to any other place they may choose, but not to France." Who was responsible for this prohibition? La Fayette thought it was Bonaparte. He may have been right. The realistic conqueror had no liking for ideologists, especially when they were popular heroes, and the restrictive clause was certainly in his writing. Actually, it is more likely that it had been dictated to him by the Directory. It corresponds very closely with the promise given by Mme de Staël to Talleyrand.

Chasteler returned to Vienna, where the reservation made by the prisoner provided a further excuse for delaying his liberation. From Olmütz, Adrienne wrote to Victor de La Tour-Maubourg: "Nothing as yet. These people seem to delight in always taking the longest and most tortuous of roads." She begged him to be mistrustful of the treacheries of the Austrian court. Perhaps an approach had better be made to Berthier, Bonaparte's chief of staff.

The jailers were already allowing the prisoners to see one another and to receive letters. Perhaps they were beginning to be afraid of what their charges might say about their treatment, once they were free. But would they be free? Everything now rested on the solid shoulders of Louis Romeuf. He was assisted in his efforts by two new notes: one from Carnot to Bonaparte, the other from Bonaparte to Thugut. Romeuf saw the Marquis de Gallo, who informed him of the way in which La Fayette had received General Chasteler.

ROMEUF TO LA FAYETTE: VIENNA, AUGUST 9, 1797

I am filled with admiration for your unshakable character, but must confess that from the way in which he spoke to me about the em-

peror's determination, I could not help fearing that this incident
may have delayed still further the coming of the day for which we
have so impatiently been waiting. I have been trying to base my
defense of you upon the original facts of your detention, and have
done all that it is my power to do in the way of rallying opinion to
your cause.[8]

In this he had been successful. Thugut complained bitterly of
the general's intransigence, but consented to an arrangement suggested by Romeuf. The prisoners should be taken to Hamburg and
there handed over by the Austrian minister to the American consul, who should promise that they would leave the city within
twelve days. A prohibition of any further entry into the territories
of the Empire should be "indicated," but no formal guarantee demanded. Louis Romeuf had taken upon himself to agree to this,
since, had La Fayette been consulted, there would have been considerable risk of still further delay.

It looked as though the game was won. Romeuf, when announcing the happy result of his efforts, had given Adrienne and Gilbert
news of Mme de Chavaniac and had offered to forward a letter to
her. Gilbert duly wrote one:

AUGUST 19, 1797
So now, after five years of silence I can send you a few lines, my dear,
my darling aunt. It is a double joy for me to tell you of my love, and
to know how happy you will be to have a word from my own hand
telling you that I am still alive.[9]

There followed some lines in Anastasie's diminutive handwriting, and a word or two from Virginie. Ah, how they longed to see
the mountains of Auvergne again, the fields of rye, and the friendly
villagers.

Romeuf had already left for Hamburg to arrange matters, but
Thugut insisted on having some assurance that the American
consul would get rid as soon as possible of "the La Fayette caravan." It was for the American consul to export the "caravan," but
where was he to send it? France did not want it. The affair dragged
on for another month. The prisoners, who knew nothing of these
difficulties, grew impatient. Adrienne sent a report of the situation
to their friend Pillet, then in Dresden:

SEPTEMBER 9, 1797

Romeuf and Charles rushed straight off to Vienna and wanted to make a descent on the Vizier in his cabinet, but we stopped them from carrying out this plan for three reasons. The first is that Monsieur de Thugut, who is already thoroughly out of patience with us, with Romeuf, and with the undertaking he gave and now finds it necessary to implement, might try to revenge himself on the two travelers, and, by casting them into prison, cut the thread of these tiresome negotiations. The second is that, should he wish for an excuse to complain of the plenipotentiaries of the Republic, he might turn to his advantage the secret arrival of a citizen known to be in their employment. The third is that, being bound by a positive undertaking, and therefore in no position to do more than delay matters, he might turn such an incident to his own uses by arguing that it constitutes a breach of the reciprocal agreement....

It is our opinion that Monsieur de Thugut's pledged word, given to a French plenipotentiary, guaranteed by Monsieur de Gallo, and known to the imperial minister and the American consul at Hamburg, is the prime fact on which we must base our argument when the moment comes for us to demand the execution of the undertaking.... Could not the ministers of the Republic now assembled in Dresden be of some help to you? [10]

With the same precision of language, the same diplomatic skill, this worn-out and ailing woman with her swollen fingers and crippled limbs added the draft of the kind of "simple and urgent letter" which, in her opinion, ought to be sent to Thugut by Henriette de La Tour-Maubourg and Julienne Bureaux de Pusy. Then she concluded:

We fully realize that we are between two dangers: that of the negotiations breaking down, which, since it must necessarily be accompanied by much bitterness, might have the effect of sealing the tomb for some considerable time; and that of the conclusion of a peace which (as Masclet judiciously observes), comparing the hatred of these people with the apathy of our own, as well as the embarrassments arising from internal dissensions, could very well seal it forever. As to the prisoners, they would do anything in the world to shorten this delay, even by twenty-four hours, except compromise their principles or their friends. If you knew the alarming details (*necessitating* urgent *action*) *which have been given in the last months, and especially in recent weeks, about the state of our health, and in particular about mine and that of my elder daughter, you would be terrified by the barbarity of this court, which, having no reason to doubt the information, would rather leave us to die here than expedite our passports.*[11]

Meanwhile, Romeuf had taken the sensible course of writing direct to General Bonaparte:

SEPTEMBER 16, 1797

It is more than time that your reiterated demands were satisfied. The promise given by Monsieur de Thugut to the man sent under your auspices seems to me to offer a good opportunity for insisting on the implementation of this undertaking, and the loyalty of your character leaves me in no doubt of how you will act in this matter. It is enough for you to know that the long and atrocious persecution exercised against the earliest champions of our liberty is still being rigorously pursued, to be persuaded, I am convinced, to take immediate steps to put an end to it. All that you have done, all that I have personally witnessed, and the friendship with which you have honored me, are sufficient guarantees of this. Malevolence is now at its height, especially since they [the prisoners] have so energetically refused to repudiate the rights which their country can exercise upon them, and for this reason I venture to press upon you the immediate importance of not slackening in your efforts until such time as you may be positively assured that the gates of Olmütz have at last been forced.[12]

At length, on September 19, the "caravan" was able to leave Olmütz in charge of an Austrian officer. An attempt had been made before the prisoners' departure to obtain from them a declaration which would make it possible for the imperial government to punish the subordinate prison officials for the bad treatment of their charges. But the prisoners refused to make such a declaration. They stated, on the contrary, their conviction that the jailers had been acting on orders received from higher authority. "Are they afraid we might take revenge? We despise them far too much for that," said Adrienne. In Dresden they were able to see Louis Romeuf, but only for a moment. "We can no more control our movements than can animals in a traveling menagerie." In Dresden,

Leipzig, Halle, and Hamburg they were welcomed with acclamation. The German patriots flocked in crowds to see these patriots of France, now free at last. The erstwhile prisoners, at first afflicted with dizziness in the fresh air, soon recovered their strength. Only Adrienne, who was a very sick woman, found the strains of the journey hard to bear. She made heroic efforts to play her part in the general rejoicings and to respond to the ovations which were showered upon her.

While on the road they talked a great deal about the *coup d'état* that had taken place in Paris on the 18th Fructidor (September 4, 1797) and had forcibly transformed the government. The first free elections had been hostile to the Directory, and even to the royalists. Bonaparte did not want a restoration at any price, and had sent Augereau, an iron-fisted general, to cow the new Assembly. Barthélemy, as were many other proscribed persons, was shipped in a barred cage to Guiana. Carnot, who had been deeply involved, made his escape. A triumvirate consisting of Barras, Rewbell, and La Revellière-Lépeaux assumed dictatorial power. *Émigrés* and priests were hunted down.

Talleyrand, who had a way of weathering every storm, issued an official declaration to the effect that the 18th Fructidor would in no way change the attitude of the government toward La Fayette.

It is the painful experience of those who are far from their native land to misunderstand completely what is happening there. Mme de Staël, who was on the spot, had to admit that the 18th Fructidor, deplorable though it was, had been necessary if the Republic was to be saved, but she condemned the proscriptions which followed it. "She swallowed the eighteenth but not the nineteenth," observed Talleyrand. La Fayette was more severe. He regarded this forcible intervention as a crime against the Republic. Adrienne, as usual, was on the side of the victims. They heard that priests had been deported. La Fayette, a champion of religious freedom, was eloquent in condemnation.

No sooner was he approaching Hamburg than both political camps tried to annex him. The monarchists said to him: "Restore the king. He will forgive you your mistakes, and you will give the *coup de grâce* to a Republic divided against itself with which France wishes to have nothing further to do." The Fructidorians, realizing that he was deeply respected by the liberals in other countries, made advances to him. They were afraid of Bonaparte, and La Fayette's popularity might restore the balance. But neither of these two extremist positions tempted him. His belief in the Republic was too great to let him take a restoration under his wing: his belief in liberty too fundamental to make it possible for him to accept pro- scriptions, no matter from what side they came.

The La Fayettes reached Hamburg on October 4, and the Aus- trian minister in that city, Baron von Schauenstein, duly handed them over to the American consul "with much dignity," said Gou- verneur Morris, who witnessed the ceremony. Morris was under the impression that his protests to the court of Vienna had been re- sponsible for their liberation. Gilbert, however, preferred to think that it had been brought about by Bonaparte and the victorious French armies. His first concern was to send a letter of thanks to Talleyrand, who fully deserved it, and another to Bonaparte, who probably deserved it less:

HAMBURG, OCTOBER 6, 1797

Citizen General, the prisoners of Olmütz, happy in the knowledge that they owe their freedom to the irresistible might of your soldiers, found consolation while still in captivity in the realization that their lives and liberties were bound up with the triumphs of the Republic and with your own personal glory. They are no less happy today to pay homage to their liberator. . . . It is from the place where we have paid a last farewell to our jailers that we send our messages of grati- tude to their conqueror. . . .

In our remote refuge on the Danish territory of Holstein, where we shall try to re-establish that health which you have saved, we join with our patriotic wishes for the success of the Republic expressions of the strongest possible concern for the illustrious general to whom we are the more strongly attached by reason of the services he has rendered to the cause of liberty and of our country. The gratitude which we delight in owing him is graven forever on our hearts.[13]

Letters were also dispatched to Clarke, who had been out of favor since the 18th Fructidor, and even to Barras, though this second letter was never afterward referred to by La Fayette and was deleted from his memoirs. Together with his two companions, César de La Tour-Maubourg and Bureaux de Pusy, Gilbert at once resolved to give his allegiance to republican France and to declare his loyalty to the principles which had just been violated. The whole family sported the tricolor cockade, which marked them off clearly from the *émigrés*, and went to pay their respects to the French minister, Reinhardt. He was not at home when they called on him, but returned the visit, going with his wife to the inn where the La Fayettes had taken up their quarters. He hinted that some public manifestation of their allegiance would be welcomed. Gilbert responded with a statement about the storming of the Tuileries (now ancient history), about his horror at the *coup d'état* of 18th Fructidor (an explosive subject), and about his feelings of sympathy for all those good citizens who had suffered martyrdom in the course of the two days which had marked the death of liberty.

In Paris, all that La Fayette had been saying was duly reported and rather naturally frowned upon. The Directory, displeased by his behavior, retained his name on the list of *émigrés* and caused the small amount of property which he still owned in Brittany to be sold. Even the faithful Masclet expressed disapproval of so stiff-necked an attitude. "So our friend has thrown down the gauntlet to the 18th Fructidor... which is tantamount to saying that he has sentenced himself to ostracism. I have shown all this stuff to Talleyrand, who agrees with me that such glaring indiscretions can scarcely fail to ruin everything so far as La Fayette is concerned." After such an outburst it would have been quite impossible for Gilbert to return to Paris. Besides, the state of Adrienne's health, which had been completely undermined, would not permit her to undertake a long journey. It had needed great courage on her part to drag herself to the minister's house and to the moving reception given them by the American colony in Hamburg. The obvious solution for the time being was for the family to go into retirement in Mme de Tessé's house at Witmold, in Holstein. Money was not lacking, and the place was large. Mme de Tessé sent the La Fayettes a warm invitation.

The medical Latinist of Olmütz had given his patients a professional report for the guidance of such of his colleagues as might be called upon to attend them: "*Domicilium quietum in aëro puro quaerendum est ubi moderatum exercitium corporis, hilaritas et tranquillitas spiritus, simul cum curis medici habilis eorum sanitatem in integrum restituere debent.*" "What is needed is some quiet place of retirement where the air is good and where a moderate amount of exercise, as well as cheerfulness and tranquility of mind combined with the attentions of a skillful doctor, should have the effect of restoring their health."

Witmold offered a good opportunity for carrying out this program.

PART SEVEN

THE MESSENGER OF THE GODS

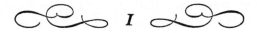

I

WITMOLD

*True forgiveness says: "I pardon you because
I know that such is not your true self."*

ALAIN

Following Adrienne's journey to Altona in 1795, Mme de Tessé
had spent the winter in Holstein, in the little town of Ploen on the
lake of that name. There she had leased an enormous house, for
wherever she went she carried with her an extensive household: her
Montagu nephews, the Muns, and a deported fellow countryman—
an old priest, the Abbé de Luchet, whom this incorrigible unbeliever had taken into her service as private chaplain. For those in
exile a private chaplain was a luxury. In this case the appointment looked like a sinecure. "Never mind," said the old lady with
a laugh, "there is always my niece Pauline, and she can be depended
upon to keep the abbé busy."

Every member of the party was expected to do his share of work.
M. de Mun was detailed to arrange the books in the library, but
found it more amusing to perch himself on top of a ladder and
read them. Pauline de Montagu counted the linen and wrote out
an inventory. Her life was full of things to be done. Meditation,
prayer, reading, charitable works on behalf of the *émigrés*, and
corresponding with her sister Rosalie filled her days. Mme de Tessé
had taken into her employment a number of local seamstresses,
and with them Mme de Montagu worked at making curtains and
learned how to say "Our Father" and other prayers in German—

319

her pious method of acquiring languages. Every evening there was reading aloud, sometimes the novels of Mme de Genlis, sometimes *Clarissa Harlowe, Tristram Shandy*, or Plutarch. The profane nature of these literary pursuits was deeply distressing to Pauline de Montagu, who insisted on sandwiching one of Bossuet's funeral orations between two novels.

The readings were followed by a running fire of critical commentary. The conversation became animated and frivolous. Mme de Tessé and the Marquis de Mun, both typical Parisians of the eighteenth century, had learned nothing and forgotten nothing. Pauline found their philosophy full of disillusionment. She alone had remained royalist and religious. Every day the Abbé de Luchet said Mass in his attic. She was a regular attendant in the company of Mun's manservant and two respectable *émigrés*, Messrs. de Saint-Paul and de Rocquemaurel. On Christmas Eve some peasants came through the bitter cold to pray in the attic oratory. Mme de Montagu could remember the midnight Masses at St-Roch amid the flickering of a thousand wax candles and the booming of the organ. She thought that the office, celebrated at Ploen in a garret by a proscribed priest, was a better reminder of the stable at Bethlehem.

After six months at Ploen Mme de Tessé had bought the Witmold estate, which she had been visiting, coveting, and haggling over for a long time. The move to Witmold was delayed until the month of August, 1796, because Pauline de Montagu, then approaching her time, was as usual having a difficult pregnancy. The child, when it arrived, was a boy—Adrien, known as Attale. Congratulations arrived from the prison of Olmütz and also from Villersexel, where Rosalie de Grammont was living detached from the things of this world. "The expectation, the endurance, and the permanence of misfortune have made me callous," she wrote. The Duc d'Ayen (now the Duc de Noailles) sent a letter from Switzerland to say that he was about to marry the Comtesse Golovkine. Such a move on his part had been expected but it was nevertheless a source of grief to his daughters. It is always difficult to accept the fact that the dead we have loved are being treated as dead.

The "tribe" went from Ploen to Witmold by boat. The new property was an immense stretch of low-lying land covered with pasturage and ponds. The quiet, mist-enveloped countryside seemed at first sight as melancholy as a desert. But there was a farmyard

and cattle sheds; there were meadows planted with apple trees and
bordered with pines; there were fields of hops, flax, and wheat.
Tessé unearthed some boats and nets and turned fisherman. Thanks
to him and to Montagu, there was never any shortage of fish and
game. Mme de Tessé's guests lived a life of plenty on the produce
of the estate, and the lady of the house made money by the sale
of milk (she had a hundred twenty cows). At night, in the *salon*,
Mme de Montagu sat knitting stockings and waistcoats for the
poor of the neighborhood. In silence she endured the talk that
went on around her. It lacked neither charm nor wit, but it was
certainly deficient in religion and charity. She had a horror of the
scandal with which the sallies of her companions were somewhat
too richly laden. Sometimes the look of sadness in her eyes made
the talkers more indulgent.

We live in a state of isolation, and our circle is a very narrow one
[wrote Mme de Montagu to the Duc de Doudeauville]. *We are far
from the events of the great world, far from all human society. We
are in a condition of waiting which nothing disturbs, and we never
enjoy a change of air. It is not a good thing for people to see the same
faces every day, and to be thrown too much on one another's company. This living in one another's pockets sooner or later turns one
into an egotist, a critic, dominating others or being dominated by
them. . . . One ends by treating trivial matters as though they were
great ones. Things of no significance acquire undeserved importance.
We just turn round in circles like the bears in the bear pit at Bern.*[1]

It was to this house outside time, to this countryside the mist
transformed into a fairy bubble outside space, that the survivors
of Olmütz came on October 10, 1797. Their arrival at Hamburg
had naturally been known to the inhabitants of Witmold, and
they were impatiently awaited. Pauline de Montagu, always torn
by scruples, tried in vain to control her joy. She was praying in her
room when she heard the sound of a horn on the far side of the
lake:

*It was the postilion announcing with a fanfare in the German
fashion his arrival in the town: but this postilion was bringing with
him the prisoners of Olmütz. Madame de Montagu, wild with excitement, ran down to the lakeside and jumped into a small boat
which contained a pair of oars and a sail. There was no one but old*

Monsieur de Mun to act as pilot. The sky was lovely, the wind favorable. She had herself conveyed as far as Ploen, and, very soon saw once again the sister who was now for the second time restored to her. She felt that she was seeing in her more than herself—her mother, her Noailles sister, and everything that she had lost. Her nieces were also there, sweet, excited, and charming; the general also, as good, as calm, as friendly as ever. He introduced to his sister-in-law the two aides-de-camp who, like himself, had just emerged from prison: Monsieur Bureaux de Pusy and the Comte de La Tour-Maubourg.[2]

The faithful Pillet and the less faithful Théodore de Lameth were with them.

A flotilla of small boats transported all these poor ex-prisoners to Witmold. The general and his daughter Anastasie, together with Monsieur de Montagu, got into one of them which Monsieur de La Tour-Maubourg offered to steer. Madame de Montagu, her sister and her niece Virginie entrusted themselves to the nautical skill of Monsieur de Mun. The rest looked after themselves as best they could. Madame de La Fayette, seated in the stern, facing her sister, expressed her gratitude to Heaven by reciting the prayer of Tobit.[3]

Mme de Tessé was waiting for her niece at the lakeside. She welcomed her with transports of joy. All the members of the family were accommodated at Witmold; the others lodged at Ploen.

The waters of this poor little lake, normally so calm, were not more agitated by all this continual coming and going than was Madame de Tessé's house by the noise and the unaccustomed ardor of the talk that went on at table and in the salon. What did they talk about? That is a question which it is unnecessary to ask, for of what should they have talked if not of politics? Criticism of things present and things past, of the faults of parties, of the errors of princes, of the wrongdoing of foreigners; of what France wanted, or what she did not want; of what might have happened if the court had taken this or that advice; of weighty conjectures based on hypotheses; of plans of action; of vague and unsubstantial systems. The field was vast, and was worked over in all directions from dawn till dusk. Madame de Tessé, who was in her element, flogged the talk when it grew languid, raised it to new heights when it looked like drooping, prattling away sometimes for a quarter of an hour on end in the middle of an attentive silence, at first mordant, then sententious, strange to see and almost beautiful in the hot fire of discussion.[4]

Mme de Montagu noticed that her brother-in-law's aides-de-camp, and especially Lameth, were more bitter in their references to the *émigrés* than they were about the Revolution. She, who had remained a monarchist, was astonished to find that they would have accepted any form of republican government (provided it were not terrorist) rather than see the king return.

Monsieur de La Fayette was quickly apprised of all that had happened since he had, in a sense, disappeared from the world. He was so little changed that, listening to him, one felt oneself grow young again. He was still as he had been all his life. He showed no bitterness, no hatred of persons or of parties, but there was not the smallest change in his opinions. He felt neither regret nor reproach in his political conscience for any of his actions, for any of his words, for any of his thoughts. With him one was always at the Declaration of the Rights of Man and the dawn of the Revolution. Everything else was just a great misfortune, a tissue of accidents, deplorable, no doubt, but not in his opinion any more discouraging than stories of shipwreck are to good sailors. He had the simple-minded faith and the calm fearlessness of those old navigators who in the sixteenth century set out to explore the world in ill-equipped ships with mutinous crews. He was prepared to go aboard again, should opportunity arise, on the four slightly readjusted planks with which the raft of 1791 had been constructed.[5]

Pauline de Montagu deplored the influence her brother-in-law had exercised at the time of the Revolution. She thought that his ideas were both fanciful and dangerous, but she respected his constancy and his good faith. She loved his character, and was devoted to him as a person.

Gilbert [she wrote to Rosalie de Grammont] is just as good, just as simple, just as affectionate, just as sweet-tempered in argument as when you knew him first. He loves his children and in spite of his cold exterior is charming with his wife. He has an affable manner, an imperturbability by which I am not taken in, and a secret longing for action within his power to direct and control. I avoid, so far as is possible, talking to him about anything that has to do with the Revolution, both what he defends and what he condemns in it. I am afraid of losing my temper, and also of hurting him. I see with pleasure that those around me approve my attitude of reserve. To be patient, and not to become involved, that is my rule of conduct where he is concerned. . . . Poor Gilbert, may God preserve him from ever again playing a part on the political stage.[6]

There were times, however, when Pauline lost control of herself. For instance, one day when La Fayette was explaining that the causes of the Revolution were to be found in the abuses of the Old Regime, she burst out: "I wonder that anyone can find distraction or consolation for so much misery in niggling arguments about the abuses of the Old Regime!" and left the room. But that evening she wrote in her journal:

I was wrong to speak as I did. It is ridiculous to let oneself be carried away like that. After all, what one says in political matters is but the consequence of what one does. One can make only mischief by crossing swords, and certainly no proselytes.[7]

She found an unmixed pleasure in the society of her sisters and her nieces. Thinking that Anastasie and Virginie would grow up to be young women without a penny, she taught them dressmaking and household management. While they sat darning linen she read aloud to them the Book of Job, Fénelon, or Bossuet. Adrienne's comments were sometimes as good as the texts, and Pauline was charmed by the touching diligence with which the young women worked at their humble tasks, their simplicity, and their modesty.

From Switzerland the Duc de Noailles wrote to his daughter Adrienne: "Imagine, my darling child, the happiness I felt at seeing your handwriting, addressed from Brunswick." His letter showed a certain embarrassment. He praised her for having realized with her husband "a unity of being which would have done honor to the virtues and the sensibility of Clarissa," and begged his dear child, together with M. de La Fayette, to accept "those expressions of affection which a century of misfortunes should inspire in me." The new Duchesse de Noailles (whose signature was missing from the letter) added a few very correct words of welcome to this rather clumsy composition.

When her father wrote again, giving the news of his marriage— which he had not dared to do in his first letter—Adrienne replied:

You must have foreseen, my dear Papa, how torn my heart would be on receiving your letter, and I know too well the sensibility of your heart not to pass judgment upon it. There can be no reason, my dear Papa, for you to be afraid of reawakening memories which are present at every moment of my life, and will be until it ends. Painful though they may be, I ever find in them a source of strength, and whenever it fails me, it is by making myself one with my mother that I maintain it. There is no circumstance in my life which brings me closer to her than in sending my every wish for your happiness.

She added a postscript intended for the new Duchesse de Noailles:

You have well judged the deep and painful impression made upon my heart by your letter and by my father's, an impression which will remain as ineffaceable as my regrets.[8]

La Fayette did not stay long under Mme de Tessé's roof with his wife, his two daughters, his numerous retinue, and his companions. The La Tour-Maubourgs and the La Fayettes between them leased a large château an hour and a half distant from Witmold. It was called Lemkühlen. To Mme de Simiane Gilbert wrote at length to explain this decision:

OCTOBER 11, 1797

Holstein is well beyond the reach of the allied powers. In the towns, and especially among the professors, men of letters, etc., are many friends of liberty who for that reason wish us well. The government, I am told, takes very little account of this part of the country, and, though despotic, is not, at least for the time being, either inquisitorial or ill-intentioned. Its tolerance will most certainly be extended to us and we shall be left at peace in our solitude. Holland would have been a suitable refuge, especially for me. It is a republican state and I am a Batavian patriot of long standing, but perhaps I should have had to endure the alternative of approving the despotic acts of the French government, or of being harried by its influence in the retreat which, in that case, we should have chosen so close to it. I need not tell you what the man who drew up the Declaration of Rights thinks of the 18th Fructidor.

Adélaïde must have smiled like Pauline de Montagu when she received this proof of how little Gilbert had changed.

Nothing could well be more public than my life, my conduct, my opinions, and my writing. This ensemble, let me tell you in confidence, is as good as any other. Let us leave it at that, without flattering any opinion of the moment. . . . I risk nothing by saying what I think, since I should not wish to be nor could I be used in the service of what I do not think. From which it results that, unless some great opportunity should arise to serve liberty and my country in my own way, my political life is ended. To my friends I shall be full of vigor, and to the public a sort of museum picture or book in a library.[9]

Mme de Simiane, even while she pretended to be angry with Gilbert, loved him for his simple-mindedness, and from then on did what she could to join him.

To his other "friend," the Princesse d'Hénin, he confided the same projects:

WITMOLD, OCTOBER 24, 1797

I must tell you how profoundly afflicted my heart is by everything that delays the great happiness of seeing you again. I feel that the distance from you at which I am living is a great obstacle to any such delicious hope of a meeting. Not a moment passes but I bitterly regret that I did not choose to take up my residence in Holland, for thither you could have come at once without any embarrassing difficulty, and it is there that I might have looked forward to realizing the unutterable felicity of my heart.

The state of my wife's health made it scarcely possible for me to leave Hamburg on a new voyage, and, after the expiration of ten days, who knows what the princes might not have been tempted to do while I was passing through their territory? The sea voyage would have been tiring for her.

We are going to take the lease of a château called Lemkühlen between Ploen and Kiel. There I shall have little to fear from aristocratic hatreds. The Danish government is for the time being pursuing a wise course. We shall be in Holstein but within easy reach of the frontier of Old Denmark. . . . I do not think that the court of Vienna is likely to start on any trickery, and we are well out of its reach. . . .

I have sent you news of our health. We are all of us improving almost visibly . . . and we look very different now from what we did when we left Olmütz. I believed for a long time that captivity would have a profound effect upon me, but it seems now that my physical condition was no more than temporary. I cannot say the same of my wife. Though her appearance is incomparably changed for the better, and her cure certain, she is bound to be in considerable discomfort throughout the winter. She cannot walk; she is never for a moment free from pain in her teeth, in her stomach, and in the open sore upon her leg. Her arms are not yet well. All the doctors are in agreement about the causes of her illness, and include among them the detestable state of the water we were obliged to drink for so long. They think that she will probably bear the marks of her captivity for the rest of her life, and that her present condition demands the greatest care if it is not suddenly to take a turn for the worse. My young Félix [Pontonnier] is the other victim who needs constant watching. It is only within the last two days that I have been given positive assurance of his recovery. The effects of prison life had got so strong a hold on him that liberation, when it came, could not have the same immediately beneficial results for him as it had for us. He has been getting steadily worse, and his lungs and nervous system are in a bad way. I have a very deep affection for him, and his loss, occasioned by his loyalty to me, would have been a worse tragedy than I can describe.[10]

Mme de La Tour-Maubourg had joined her husband. Charles de La Tour-Maubourg, César's young unmarried brother, had gone to live at Lemkühlen. Bureaux de Pusy was expected from Altona any moment with his young wife and their little daughter. Alexandre de Lameth would very much have liked to be one of the party, but La Fayette had replied coldly to the suggestion:

GILBERT TO THE PRINCESSE D'HÉNIN

The Maubourg-La Fayette family (for, truth to tell, that is what we are) will take up residence at Lemkühlen on the third of next month. It will be some time before we have our friend Pusy with us. He is obliged to remain at Altona for the inoculation of his little girl. But they will turn up later, and then we shall be a delightful trio of households all together under the same roof. Monsieur Alexandre de Lameth, however, must let me give the lie publicly to what he says about being on the point of joining in as a fourth.[11]

II

THE CHÂTEAU OF LEMKÜHLEN

*If you love another woman, tell me, and
we will talk of her together. For all that
happens to you is of interest to me.*

PAUL CLAUDEL

Thanks to the American, Parish, who supplied generously and trustingly all the money needed on the strength of simple promissory notes, the La Fayettes had once more got the wherewithal to meet ordinary expenses. A considerable number of persons had settled into the great Château of Lemkühlen and made a common household: the La Fayettes, the La Tour-Maubourgs (not only César, their comrade in captivity, but César's wife, his younger brother Charles, and his married sister, Marie de Maisonneuve), and the Bureaux de Pusy couple and their daughter. There was also a constant flow of occasional visitors.

The general passed the time writing his memoirs and compiling notes for Bureaux de Pusy, who was planning a great work in justification of the part played by La Fayette's followers during the Revolution, and making quite clear their position with regard to the present French government. La Fayette advised him to be moderate in his criticism of individuals, but to show all possible heat in defense and exposition of the basic doctrine. "We ought, it seems to me," he wrote, "to rise above all considerations of party, and to go out of our way to suppress abusive epithets and expressions of hatred." He hoped through the medium of this work, to rally "all

328

aristocrats who are not possessed of a desire for vengeance; the extreme democrats, or at least those of them who, though Jacobins, had not been involved in criminal activities; and all those peace-loving citizens who at present think themselves divided." [1] It was a fine program of reconciliation, such as wise men draw up after every revolution and time brings to fruition only after they are dead.

Messages of respect and congratulation were reaching the La Fayette family from all quarters. In Paris a one-act play was being given, *The Prisoner of Olmütz, or The Conjugal Devotion*, in which the author, Préfontaine, showed La Fayette, his wife, and his daughters in their Moravian dungeon, and Bonaparte intervening as the *deus ex machina*. Numerous patriots wrote to him from the Low Countries. All associated in their good wishes the name of Adrienne, who had become a popular heroine. The editor of the *Gazette de Leyde* expressed a hope that La Fayette would communicate "to the illustrious companion of your misfortunes the assurance of respect and admiration so well merited by a character which posterity, the true judge of all real piety and virtue, will one day place among the finest examples of Antiquity."

Adrienne herself would have liked to go to France in an attempt to save from the shipwreck of the family fortunes what little remained. She had never been listed as an *émigré*, she held a genuine passport, duly stamped with the Hamburg visa, and, unlike her husband, was entitled to return whenever it should please her to do so. Marie-Josèphe Beauchet was urging her to take this step, and offering her hospitality:

PARIS, DECEMBER 18, 1797

I trust you will graciously accept my expressions of gratitude for the joy your letter brought me. Until it came I could not be entirely happy in your freedom, but now, what happiness is mine! It has come to me like life renewed. I cannot put into words all that it has made me feel, but I am more than ever certain that I can never know real happiness except through you and by reason of the opinion you hold of my feelings. That is very precious to me and proves that you have not forgotten how sweet it is for me to know what a great debt my poor heart owes to you. . . .

My children were no consolation to me. I was resentful because they distracted me from my grief. I blamed myself for having room in my heart and mind for anything but your misfortunes. Do you think, Madame, that if that grief had not been real and deep for me I should so eagerly have waited to have news of you? Could I but have watched over and cared for you, I should long ago have forgotten all my pains and sorrows. We have considered sending the children to boarding school, but the habits and the views they would have learned there are not what I should like for them. Eugène is eight, and very responsive to impressions. I felt obliged to sacrifice the duty which I owed to my heart to that of considering our own problems, and in so doing I was truly meritorious.

Yesterday, Madame de Maisonneuve gave us your news, which is a little better. The bodily humors are changing, and that is a good sign. But that "little better" does not do more than allay my anxiety. I trust, Madame, that you will be so obliging as to send me frequent word about your health. I greatly need to know that the "better" is making progress. That will soften my regret at not being able to look after you. They tell me that Monsieur de La Fayette is perfectly recovered, and I fully participate in your happiness on that account. I am delighted to learn that Mademoiselle Virginie's health has not suffered. . . . I hope that Mademoiselle Anastasie will soon get her good color back again. Have the young ladies grown much? How tall is Mademoiselle Anastasie? I cannot tell you how greatly I long to see them again and embrace them. I beg you, Madame, to tell them how grateful I am for the kind recollection with which they have honored me. . . . I am eager to know that Monsieur George is with you again.

I will not speak to you, Madame, about your affairs (my husband has carried out all your instructions) except to say how greatly afflicted I am by the injustice done to you. I think that as soon as your health will permit you to travel, your presence here would be most useful in more ways than one. That is the opinion of all who take an interest in you and who know the present position. In that case, Madame, allow me to beg you, in the name of all those feelings which attach me so closely to you to take up your residence with us.

You know that we have a very comfortable room where you would be quite undisturbed. When you come you will find a good fire and a good bed. You will not have to bother about anything. This house is well equipped, and you must look upon it as your own. You will find in me a zealous waiting-woman, a cook with whom you will have no reason to find fault, and a secretary of intelligence who is all eagerness to serve you and would have more time and more ways of being useful to you should you condescend to stay under her roof. Besides, you will have with us the good air which you so much need, and you will be close at hand to the Directory and all the administrative offices, as well as near your friends. . . . Nowhere else would you be more free or better looked after. The hope that you will grant us this favor makes my heart leap with joy. Please, Madame, do not refuse us. To do so would be to cause us a pain which would outweigh your many kindnesses, from which you may judge how intense it would be.

We are all very well. Adrien is still a pretty boy. Eugène blushed to his ears when I showed him your letters. He is very much upset at not being able to write well enough to send you his respects. He is a good boy and really quite intelligent. My husband is still in the same employment.

Good-by, Madame. Since my words are too weak to express my feelings or to tell you what a place you hold in my heart, I trust you will be so good as to read what I have written, and to accept my profound respect and veneration which will never change while I live. . . .

Madame de M[aisonneuve] will return six silver dishes and an enamel coffee-spoon of yours which we have. . . . I have put with them two pairs of stockings and some rabbit-skin gloves, thinking they might be welcome in so cold a climate.[2]

Respect, admiration, and affection, when they are thus combined, engender a very high degree of devotion. Adrienne would very much have liked to accept this generous invitation, but her health would not permit her to travel. Meanwhile, Gilbert was eager to get his dear Mme de Simiane to come to Holstein. The good Pillet, who was in Paris, was trying, together with Mme de Staël, to get the necessary permits. Marie de Maisonneuve (La Tour-Maubourg's sister) was to make the journey with Adélaïde de Simiane.

RENÉ PILLET TO THE BARONNE DE STAËL: NOVEMBER 18, 1797

Madame de M [aisonneuve] visited me yesterday morning to ask whether I had any news of Madame de S [imiane], and to impress upon me how impatient she is to start on her journey. She is receiving letters urging her to do so by almost every post from Hamburg. . . . Those which have reached me by the last two couriers repeat the earlier entreaties not to lose a day. It is therefore to Madame de Staël that we are sending on all these messages, with a request that she will inform us of the precise day on which we can set out. . . .

I have read at T[alleyrand]'s house the letter which the three friends have written to him. It seems to have been intended for publication, but the taint of Original Sin which it contains will not allow of its being printed. . . . T[alleyrand] has assured me that the passport for Madame de La F[ayette] has been sent to her. This certificate has been dispatched to the Department of Seine-et-Marne, and will, I hope, put an end to all this shameful caviling. I am impatiently awaiting a letter from Madame de S[imiane] and hope that it will be the last I shall receive dated from Cirey before the great journey begins.[3]

Naturally the impenitent liberal continued to stick to his principles, even to the detriment of his beloved:

GILBERT TO ADÉLAÏDE DE SIMIANE: JANUARY 7, 1798

You will think, I am sure, that I have shown myself in too republican a light. . . . Though I love the Republic more than I loved the Monarchy, I love liberty even more than the Republic, and I am very far from believing that true liberty exists in France today. But some of my friends have given it as their opinion that I am a royalist, and it does not suit me to be saddled with sentiments which I do not entertain. All that remains to be said is that the declaration which contains the whole of my doctrine is dated July 11, 1789.

His political clock had stopped at that date.

You will scold me, too, for not having written to the Directory, but the idea of seeming to abandon friends now proscribed and of being thought to applaud measures of which I disapprove has blinded me to every other consideration.[4]

Coming and going between Lemkühlen and Witmold was easy and frequent. La Fayette's daughters carried on a correspondence with their aunt Pauline, whom they admired.

ANASTASIE TO THE MARQUISE DE MONTAGU: DECEMBER 28, 1797

Though you, in the middle of your stomach pains,* were so fervent, your nieces can scarcely claim that they were so too, my dear aunt;

* The stomach pains were occasioned by her pregnancy. Madame de Montagu was carrying her daughter Stéphanie, who was born May 29, 1798.

but they were very happy and very quiet, and the virtue and uprightness of heart in those surrounding them was the best of examples. . . . Only those communicating were present at Mass. Since Chavaniac had sprained his ankle, it was Felix who served. This he did with much reverence. He is, I am sure, truly religious.[5]

Anastasie was ashamed at having to confess to her aunt that the fruits of grace were scarcely visible in her. "Virginie is much better than I am; she is a little bit more fervent, and is zealous in working and writing." Anastasie's excuse was that she was twenty and in love. The young Charles de La Tour-Maubourg was showing a tender interest in her, but it took the form of silence. Mme de Tessé had noticed his eloquent dumbness, and had put the parents on guard against a "hunger-and-thirst" marriage. The once-rich émigrés (such as Adrienne) could still live in hopes of rebuilding at least part of their fortunes; but Charles de La Tour-Maubourg, being the youngest of a large family, had no personal fortune to rebuild. Mme de Tessé had not progressed beyond the stage of prerevolutionary maneuvers between family lawyers.

For Adrienne the great event of February, 1798, was the return of her son, George-Washington. He had left America as soon as he had learned that his parents were free. Washington had given him a letter addressed to his father. It was full of praise of the young man.

MOUNT VERNON, OCTOBER 8, 1797
This letter will, I hope and expect, be presented to you by your son, who is highly deserving of such Parents as you and your amiable Lady. . . . His conduct, since he first set foot on American ground, has been exemplary in every point of view, such as has gained him the esteem, affection and confidence of all who have had the pleasure of his acquaintance. His filial affection and duty, and his ardent desire to embrace his parents and Sisters in the first moments of their releasement, would not allow him to await the authentic account of this much desired event; but at the same time that I suggested the propriety of this, I could not withhold my assent to the gratification of his wishes to fly to the Arms of those whom he holds most dear; persuaded as he is . . . that he shall find you all in Paris.

M. Frestel has been a true Mentor to George. No Parent could have been more attentive to a favourite Son; and he richly merits all that can be said of his virtues, of his good sense, and of his prudence.

Both your son and him carry with them the vows, and regrets of this family, and of all who know them. And you may be assured that you yourself never stood higher in the affections of the People of this country than at the present moment.[6]

Adrienne had brought up this son of hers with the greatest care. She had given him the best tutor she could find. She had imbued him with her own wisdom and her ardent faith. For all this she was now amply repaid.

ADRIENNE TO GEORGE DE LA FAYETTE: JANUARY 3, 1798

Can it be really true, my dear, my darling boy, that this letter will find you at Hamburg and that we are about to be reunited? . . . Join with us in giving thanks to God who has protected you, preserved us, and has now brought you back. Your sisters, it is true, have during your absence enabled us to enjoy the sweet alleviations of paternal and maternal affection, but our hearts could not surrender to them in peace of mind while being painfully conscious of the great distances which separated you from us. Your return has restored all the faculties of my heart. . . . You will find your father unbelievably improved in health.

George found Paris in a state of considerable agitation as a result of Bonaparte's return. The general, he was told, was not on the best of terms with the Directory. By signing the Treaty of Campo Formio he had acted contrary to the views of the government, which would have preferred the left bank of the Rhine to all his Italian conquests. It was known that he felt strongly about the violence which had followed hard on the 18th Fructidor. Like Mme de Staël, he did not want to have anything to do with the nineteenth. The Fructidorians were persecuting nobles and priests. Bonaparte, in contrast, had said to the Genoese: "Do not exclude the former members of the nobility from the administration; you would have done as they did. It is not enough to treat the Church with tolerance; nothing that might disturb men's consciences should be permitted." Paris was prepared to idolize Bonaparte, not only as a conqueror but as a conciliator. Prudent and seemingly modest, he did his best to avoid all public manifestations of enthusiasm. He rarely appeared at the theater, and lived quietly in the Rue de Chantereine (renamed the Rue de la Victoire). He was a born man of politics, and conducted his maneuvers with astonishing skill. When he was publicly greeted by the Directory, he combined a soldierly bluntness with a charm that was all Italian. In his speech he said that the happiness of France should be based upon laws that were organically new—tantamount to expressing his wish for a new constitution. The directors frowned. Talleyrand, who was attentive to his every word, said: "Oho! promises!" Bonaparte made Barras look anything but pleased (though he owed his career to him), and seemed to be interested only in the Institute. He had just been elected to it, wore its uniform, and signed himself *Bonaparte, Member of the Institute, General in Chief.* This carefully calculated attitude of semiretirement brought him the allegiance of those who had feared that he might prove to be a Cromwell or a Monk.

La Fayette's friends Mme de Staël and Talleyrand would have liked his son George to be received by the man of mystery with whom the future lay. But Bonaparte was still suspicious of everything to do with La Fayette who, should he return, might well become an obstacle or a carping critic. Perhaps, too, the number of those who were soliciting the government in favor of the exiled hero was making him uneasy. "La Fayette," he said, "has the gift of making friends. Should fortune cease to smile on me, I should have no one but my wife—because one always has on one's side the woman one sleeps with—and perhaps my brother Joseph." [8] On the day on which George called, the general was away inspecting troops in the Channel ports. Citizeness Bonaparte was gracious and affable to the nineteen-year-old, and said that "La Fayette and Bonaparte should make common cause," a remark that, when reported by George, aroused great hopes at Lemkühlen. Who could say? Perhaps Bonaparte would return to the *Fayettism* of his youth? United, the two heroes might do great things. Such were the general lines of the Lemkühlen dream.

Adrienne was enraptured with her son, Anastasie and Virginie with their brother. The girls showed their pride in him "to a quite ridiculous extent," said Virginie. The only fault they could find with him was that he carried himself badly and, like Virginie, had a stoop.

GILBERT TO MME DE CHAVANIAC: MARCH 7, 1798

At last, my dear aunt, the admirable George is with us, and I can tell you that we are more than pleased with him. Physically he leaves nothing to be desired: he is tall, and the expression of his face is noble and charming. His temperament too is all that we could wish. He has the same goodness of heart as when you knew him, and his mind is a great deal more developed than is usual at his age. He is really an excellent young man. His character is lofty and in every way interesting. Why cannot I show him to you, and when shall we have the happiness of being all together again at Chavaniac?

My wife has written to you about a most exciting project. I am impatient to hear whether it meets with your approval. What is certain is that there is a complete community of taste and character between them [Anastasie de La Fayette and Charles de La Tour-Maubourg]. My health is very good, as is that of my daughters. My wife's shows a little improvement, but it is a slow business. She has had to make a brief visit to Hamburg for the purpose of getting our accounts in order and for arranging a power of attorney, etc. . . . Her stay in that city will not extend beyond three days, and she will have the opportunity to consult an excellent French doctor. . . .

Send us frequent news of yourself, my dear aunt. Our hearts are always prowling round Chavaniac and you.[9]

VIRGINIE TO MADAME DE CHAVANIAC

It is from under the same roof that shelters my brother that I am writing to you, dear aunt. We missed you greatly at the moment of our reunion, and the thought that the five of us could not be with you prevented us from thinking our happiness complete! My brother is grown so tall that when he arrived we could scarcely recognize him, but we are now finding again all those qualities in him with which we were once so familiar. He is just as good a brother as he used to be at Chavaniac. He is so like Papa that people in the streets can see at once that he is his son.[10]

That same winter Mme de Simiane arrived, much to the delight of her lover. She took up her abode with Mme de Tessé, and from that moment Gilbert frequently took the road to Witmold. Diane-Adélaïde was happy to consider that she had come upon a colony of melancholy exiles in a remote corner of the countryside. She heard of nothing but marriage plans and baptismal arrangements: Anastasie was engaged, and Pauline on the point of being brought to bed.

The Comte de La Tour-Maubourg's feelings for Anastasie were entirely disinterested, it was said, because he was perfectly well aware that she would bring him no dowry but her youth, her virtue, and, as Madame de La Fayette said, "the contempt of riches." He was not himself rich at that time. His only fortune was a bare thirty thousand francs, and even these he did not possess in his own right, but were what his elder brother had agreed to give him.

Madame de La Fayette considered the match to be not only very suitable, but as advantageous as one had a right to expect in those days. The general approved wholeheartedly. But when the subject was broached at Witmold there were loud protests. Monsieur de Mun declared that "only the savages of America get married in that way" and Madame de Tessé maintained that "nothing like it had been seen since Adam and Eve!" But sarcasm was powerless to affect the issue. Madame de La Fayette stood her ground, and when all was irrevocably decided, Madame de Tessé's displeasure melted away in a pleasing concern. She provided part of the trousseau, which was made in the house with much planning and the happiest results. Everyone lent a hand and was prodigal of advice.[11]

Adrienne took it upon herself to keep the revered Chavaniac aunt posted on the family news. She told her that she had found George more charming than words could express, and that Gilbert was planning to go to America, there to re-establish his children's fortune:

The Americans still owe Gilbert the land he refused to accept at the end of the war. He agrees that it would be only reasonable now to take the gift then offered.[12]

As to what remained of the Noailles patrimony, nothing had as yet been settled. Adrienne and her sisters wanted to share the landed property between them and to sell nothing. There were enough people obliging enough to lend them money until such time as their revenues were restored to them.

"I need not tell you, my dear aunt, that nobody believes less than I do that the prospects of a fortune can compensate one for the sacrifices of the heart," Adrienne wrote. "All the same. . . ." Yes, all the same, Adrienne knew that wise administration forms part of the duties of the head of a family, and that parents are under an obligation to set up their children as best they can. So she imparted to her aunt what she thought were sound reasons for Anastasie's marriage. Mme de Chavaniac replied with a number of severe remarks about the unwisdom of any such arrangements with things as they then were. Adrienne hit back, on March 22, 1798, with an argument that knocked the ground from under the old lady's feet: Did she not realize that what was in question was nothing less than *marriage*, the mutual love of two young persons? Anastasie had "a genuine liking" for Charles, and though his extreme shyness and instinctive reserve had not yet allowed him to declare himself, she, Adrienne, felt perfectly certain Anastasie's feelings were reciprocated.

Adrienne reported her health as improving, but in April when the whole family moved to the house of Mme de Tessé, who insisted on providing the wedding feast, she suffered a serious relapse. An abscess had developed in her arm, and there was an accumulation of purulent matter in her leg, which made walking impossible. Nevertheless, she refused to consider any delay.

Never had she been calmer or more determined [wrote Pauline's biographer]. *Her children—her son on one side, the two sisters on the other—carried her on a sofa from her bedroom to the salon, and back again. Madame de Montagu, about to be brought to bed, helped in dressing their mother's glorious wounds. Then, that duty accomplished, [Pauline] gave all her attention to the trousseau, the household chores and the farm, moving here, there, and everywhere, round as a tower but indefatigable. It was impossible not to admire her, and not to laugh at her. Madame de Simiane said that she would most certainly have her child in one of the great wardrobes which she was forever opening and shutting.*[13]

The marriage was celeberated on May 9, 1798, in the finest of the Witmold rooms. The Abbé de Luchet officiated. Adrienne was carried by her son and her son-in-law to the improvised chapel. In spite of her sufferings, she was blissfully happy.

When I think [she wrote] *of the horrible situation in which my children found themselves but a short while ago, and see all three of them now about me, and a fourth, of whom my heart so wholly approves, on the point of becoming one of the family, I cannot be sufficiently grateful to God.*[14]

Mme de Tessé had provided the trousseau: three dozen shifts, six dimity petticoats, three muslin overskirts, eighteen pairs of thread stockings, two pairs of white silk and four pairs of gray silk stockings, six pairs of English leather shoes, dresses, corsets, shawls, a straw hat, and another hat of violet satin.

Ten days later a girl was born to Pauline de Montagu. She was named Stéphanie, mistakingly sprinkled with Eau de Cologne, rather than water, by the enthusiastic Mme de Tessé, and baptized by the Abbé de Luchet.

III

ADRIENNE IN FRANCE

For I am yours, and my passion is to serve.
PAUL CLAUDEL

The position of the family in Holstein was far from secure. Denmark might be invaded by the imperial forces, or might break with the French Republic. In the latter case La Fayette would have refused to stay on as a guest in a country which had become the declared enemy of France. However, as the result of a paradox in his nature, he also feared the arrival of the French armies on Danish territory, having managed by the very consistency of his attitude to make adversaries for himself in both camps. To be sure, Joséphine Bonaparte had accorded a gracious welcome to Gilbert's son, but then George was a young man and Joséphine an incorrigible flirt. The uncomfortable fact remained that Bonaparte did not reply to La Fayette's letters.

La Fayette's friends blamed his attitude, what they called his "doctrinaire intransigence": the way he has of always trotting out his claim to be a good citizen. He quite unnecessarily irritated the men in power. Greater suppleness would have enabled him to be of greater use. To this Gilbert replied that he was *not* supple and that if he was to be accepted, it must be as he was:

It may be held that a different attitude on my part would make me temporarily more useful, or that, no longer being in a position to be so, I should think only of myself and my own concerns. But such is my nature that I cannot accept either of these two compromises.[1]

He declared that all he really wanted was to settle down as a peaceful and philosophic farmer, somewhere sufficiently distant from the capital to avoid being importuned by the politicians, and where he could live a retired life in which he would see only his personal friends. This would have been possible at Fontenay, or better still at La Grange, assuming that Adrienne should have recovered possession of one or other of these properties. Her own fond dream was to live in Brie, far from all scenes of worldly glory, with her husband and her children. But the realization of this dream was possible only if she could go back to France and make good her claims. She had a perfect right to do so: her passport and those of her daughters were all in order. True, she found great difficulty in walking and was still in considerable pain; but Virginie would go with her, and the providential Marie-Josèphe Beauchet would take them in.

Nobody doubted Adrienne's ability to carry through such a mission as this with success. She could argue like a lawyer in a way that was embarrassing to her enemies. She was at her best when confronted by difficulties. Though timid in the ordinary commerce of life, she had shown no sign of weakness in prison or when under the immediate threat of death. She could do sublime things as simply and as artlessly as she described them. Mme de Montagu was of the opinion that her elder sister had too little of "the inner life," that she gave too much thought to happiness, or at least to consolation on earth. Pauline could never have done battle for an inheritance, would not even have thought it worth while to try. Adrienne, on the other hand, was fully equipped to deal with any task that might be assigned to her, material as well as spiritual.

What would she find in France? Bonaparte had left for Egypt, much to the delight of La Fayette, one of whose dreams as a young man had been a French expedition to the East. His former aide-de-camp and devoted friend, Louis Romeuf, had gone too as one of the general's staff, and had tried to speak about his former chief to his new one, but without success. A set face and an icy silence had met his every attempt. Bonaparte and the Directory still feared the return of a popular hero who might be hungry for power. When Joseph Masclet told La Fayette that he was widely distrusted as a visionary, Gilbert had protested:

Do not run away with the idea that I am such a simpleton as to suppose that all difficulties can be overcome, society saved, and a universal reign of sweet reasonableness be assured merely by proclaiming the Rights of Man. Far from it: I know perfectly well that there will have to be an active police force, a vigorous government, and strict laws strictly enforced. But if a true republic is to be set up, then those laws have got to be just.[2]

In July, 1798, Adrienne left Holstein with her son-in-law and her daughters. Gilbert accompanied her as far as the Elbe. She was to enter France by way of Holland. After Anastasie's marriage, Gilbert had given up the expensive tenancy of Lemkühlen and had returned with his son to Witmold, "in the dear and hospitable peninsula." Pusy was at Ploen, awaiting the departure for America of his father-in-law, Samuel Dupont de Nemours, a former president of the Constituent Assembly, banished after the 18th Fructidor. The prisoners of Olmütz were scattering. Anastasie and Charles de La Tour-Maubourg, who had started out with Adrienne, would have to stop at Utrecht for two reasons: Charles's name still figured on the list of *émigrés*, and Anastasie was pregnant. Virginie continued the journey with her mother. One of the numerous tasks entrusted to Adrienne was to get Pusy and the La Tour-Maubourgs removed from the list of *émigrés*. What protectors would she find in a new and hostile world? Providence, she thought, would see to that.

Paris had many surprises in store for her. She had known it in the old days of coaches and great families; she had known it as a city of prisons and *sans-culottes*. She found it now a strange mixture of destitution and luxury. Haunted by her memories of the Terror, she expected to come at every turn on ruins and bloodstains. When she, spoke of these things, she was told: "Oh, that's all ancient history!" The Directory was bent on turning the tragic sites of revolutionary violence into flourishing gardens. The Council of the Ancients met in the Tuileries, where the trees had been carefully clipped; the Chamber of Deputies met in the Palais Bourbon. In the Place Vendôme, not far from the former Hôtel de Noailles, the fine Mansart façades were disfigured with gaudy shop-signs. The monastery of the Feuillants was in the process of being pulled down. Tattered tricolor flags still hung on Trees of Liberty now long dead. The word *saint* was still outlawed, and the Rue Saint-Honoré was now the Rue Honoré. Hackney carriages and gigs had taken the place of coaches and carrying-chairs. Lace, scents, ribbons, and jewels were on sale in the shops. The *Merveilleuses*, half naked in dresses of transparent muslin, exhibited themselves to the public. The *salons* were reopening. In the house of Mme de Staël, "who spun like a top round the seat of power," lists of possible ministers were being compiled. In the Rue Honoré the Voltaire-loving Princesse de Beauvau received her guests in a small apartment filled with the elegant remains of her family furniture. When one left the squalid staircase that was common to all the inhabitants of the house, "one found oneself transported into a different world. Everything in the tiny rooms was well cared for and had an air of nobility. The few servants to be seen were old and feeble; one had a vague sort of feeling that they had been used to good company and that their comments would be worth listening to. These *salons* were crowded every day of the week." [3] The liberal opinions which the old Maréchale de Beauvau had freely aired before 1789, her distinguished lineage (she was a Rohan-Chabot), the crowd of charming, witty women who surrounded her (such as her daughter-in-law, the Princesse de Poix, Mme de Simiane, and the Duchesse de Duras) combined to make her universally popular. To Adrienne, so recently snatched from the nauseating hell of Olmütz, it seemed almost incredible that she should find here, in the heart of a still far from peaceful Paris, such an oasis of easy elegance.

Adrienne and Virginie stayed with the Beauchets in the Rue de l'Université. These good people had put their small lodging at the disposal of the two ladies, and themselves retreated into the attics. No sooner was Adrienne settled in than she set to work. The first thing to be done was to have her rights of succession officially recognized and to get the names of Gilbert's friends removed from the list of *émigrés*. The question of his own return must be left open for the time being. Would the regime last? She had a strong feeling of resentment against the ruling clique: Barras, with his court of glutted contractors and kept women; Rewbell, with his following of commission agents, his upstart arrogance, and his innkeeper manners; La Revellière-Lépeaux, with his hunchback's vanity, his philosophizing pretentiousness, his sectarian intolerance. The Parisians, while waiting for things to change, were content to joke about the situation. In a smoking *salon* where, in order to please the last of the Jacobins, the government had posted the notice: HERE THE NAME OF CITIZEN IS HONORED, the master of the establishment had added AND ONE SMOKES, a play on the double meaning of the word *fumer*—"to smoke" and "to stink."

Mme de Maisonneuve (Anastasie's sister-in-law) wrote to the expectant mother, giving news of the travelers:

Yesterday we had the pleasure of spending some time with Adrienne and Virginie. We found them wonderfully well. Adrienne has as much courage and patience as she has goodness, about which I do not have to expatiate to you. Fortunately she is less fatigued, having a carriage at her disposal. Virginie is as pretty as ever, and looks like a rosebud. She has been a little unwell on two occasions. So far, she has had only one dancing lesson. In spite of her efforts, she holds herself badly. Everyone who has seen her has been much struck by the odd way in which she dresses. In this respect she has improved slightly since her arrival here, but things are not quite right even now.

Evidently, the mode at Witmold was very different from that of Paris.

We were expecting Virginie to go with us today to the Champ de Mars to see the festivities in celebration of the anniversary of the founding of the Republic, but she sent word that she could not come because of her dancing lesson. Her mother writes that she thinks of nothing else, that her master is very pleased with her progress and hopes that her stoop will very shortly disappear altogether. We are sorry not to have seen her: she would have been much entertained this morning. We had places on a fine terrace at Chaillot, just opposite the Champ de Mars, from which we had a very good view of the water tournaments which we watched with great pleasure. On one side, the boats were red and the contestants dressed in white, with red sashes and tricolor streamers. On the other the costumes were the same, but blue. There are going to be superb illuminations tonight all over Paris. Just now there are horse races and running. I think that Charles would have found it all highly entertaining.[4]

In this way did the former nobility take part in the festivities commemorating the establishment of the Republic.

At Witmold, Gilbert was bored to death. His dear Adélaïde had long since left. The lady of the house, Mme de Tessé, was constantly at odds with the local aristocracy, and Gilbert had to be

forever preaching mutual tolerance. He would have liked to join
the young couple in Holland, where he hoped that he might have
found his wife at the moment of Anastasie's confinement. But before the Dutch authorities could grant him right of entry they would
have had to come to an arrangement with the French government,
their ally. He pressed Adrienne to bring this about, and also to go
ahead at full speed with what she was doing for the La Tour-
Maubourg brothers. Though he called her oftener than ever "my
dear heart," and begged her to look after her health, he was not
altogether fair to her (he never had been) in his insistence on quick
results.

Certainly she was not sparing herself, and this he knew.

GILBERT TO ADRIENNE: SEPTEMBER 12, 1798

*You could give me no better mark of your affection than by taking
more calmly what is making you impatient, and by showing moderation in all that fatigues you. . . . Tell your sister [Rosalie] for me that
only someone who has been three years with you and has followed
the vicissitudes of your health can know how seriously it is affected
by any form of restlessness, mental or physical, no matter how slight
and how temporary that restlessness may be. Her great gifts for
looking after and directing young people should extend to you,
though you are the elder of the two. This I can tell her, since I am
forever instructing our dear Virginie to be an intolerable little prig
and to remind you of my sermonizing whenever necessary.*[5]

But he was so naïvely used to seeing everything he undertook
succeed that he was surprised at the slowness of her results. Mme
de Tessé, disturbed by the advance of the French armies, sold Witmold. Gilbert now wanted to transfer himself to Holland, and then,
if France remained forbidden ground for him, to America. For this
Adrienne would have to obtain an authorization from the Directory,
and also find somewhere in France for the children to live while
he was trying to rebuild the family fortunes in the United States.
Another urgent matter was to get for Victor and Charles either a
discharge as *émigrés*, or at least a *surveillance* (the name given the
permit, granted to certain *émigrés* whose names still figured on the
fatal list, to live in France under police observation, and with a
considerable amount of restriction on their movements). "You
must get that *surveillance* at once," Gilbert wrote. At once, indeed!
What government department has ever done anything at once?

Gilbert blamed Adrienne for having left the servant known as Chavaniac in Holland to look after Anastasie, instead of letting the faithful fellow return to Auvergne.

For once, Adrienne answered back. There she was, a sick woman with a temperature, running about from morning till night, and all she got for her trouble were peremptory orders and sharp criticisms! La Fayette, realizing that she was angry, wrote excusing himself.

NOVEMBER 30, 1798

I regret, dear heart, having quite unwittingly caused you pain. . . . You have judged quite wrongly the effect of your correspondence upon me. It has never caused me to feel anything but satisfaction. . . . It would be very unjust of you to think that I have not constantly counted upon the exactitude with which you have taken the steps on which we agreed. But everything then was necessarily so vague that you too may have indulged in illusory prospects. It gives me pleasure to admit that it is I who have been wrong, and you who have been—as always—right. I am much distressed to think that I have caused you worry and anxiety as a result of our Ploen speculations, and caused you to be unfair to me.[6]

Adrienne was saying now that she could not leave Paris before February, 1799. Only then would they all meet again in Holland for Anastasie's confinement. In December she went to Chavaniac. Aunt Charlotte had not changed. She still called Adrienne "Madame" —both to give an added social stature to her nephew, and to show her disapproval of all that was happening in France.

Adrienne's health was improving. An active life was doing her a great deal of good. Victor wrote to his sister-in-law Anastasie:

Madame de La Fayette's last letter made us very happy. Since her health enables her to put up so good a resistance to fatigue and the intense cold, we have good reason to hope that the improvement will continue.[7]

He gave news of Witmold. Pauline de Montagu was suffering from a painful breast abscess but continued by a miracle to collect funds with which to help the poor people in the neighborhood as well as the indigent *émigrés*. The young men went out after deer and wild duck, but without much success. La Fayette, champing at the bit and constantly reiterating his principles, had sent to the Directory what amounted to a speech in defense of his companions in exile.

For himself he asked nothing, but what reason could there be for fearing the Maubourg brothers or Pusy? Why should their native land be forbidden territory to officers who, in circumstances for which their general was alone responsible, had fallen into the hands of the enemy?

The faithful Adrienne, accompanied by George and Virginie, had gone in person to deliver this document to La Revellière-Lépaux, who at that particular moment happened to be president of the Directory. The former regicide did not seem to her to be a bad man but just an "honest booby, saddened by the violence of the age." The Revolution had produced "monsters, generous-minded men, and small fry." La Revellière-Lépeaux belonged to the latter group. Why had he been chosen to be one of the directors? Because the Convention, sick and tired of great men, was athirst for mediocrity.

In his memoirs, written, according to Taine, in the "style of a concierge who has read Rousseau," La Revellière-Lépeaux says that he received with feelings of respect "a woman who had become immortal by reason of her generous devotion, and is the finest example to be found anywhere of conjugal piety. . . . Never have I experienced so deep an emotion. . . . A feeling of admiration was linked with the memory of her misfortunes." He told her that, much to his regret, he could not in the present state of affairs grant her request for the deletion of certain names from the list of émigrés. Nevertheless, he gave Adrienne authority to move freely between her husband's place of residence and France.

This interview made it clear that the Directory was prepared to tolerate, if not to approve, La Fayette's presence in Holland, where the Dutch patriots were disposed to accept him. The whole family could therefore come together at Vianen, near Utrecht. Before leaving Paris, Adrienne resumed her scrupulous correspondence with her creditors. She had always attached the highest importance to protecting their interests. There exists a letter she wrote to a certain Citizen Marchais, to whom she owed a few hundred livres:

Man proposes and God disposes. . . . Our affairs which I came here to wind up have not yet reached that stage. We have not as yet been able to touch any of our revenues, nor consequently to carry out our most sacred duties. I have at present no home of my own, and am lodging with Madame Beauchet who has been so very kind as to *give me shelter. I am about to spend six weeks in Holland with my daughter, who will soon be brought to bed. I hope that on my return we shall be in a position to settle our respective shares in the family inheritance.*[8]

The settling of the problems connected with the winding up of the Duchesse d'Ayen's estate was in fact a matter of great urgency. One of Adrienne's brothers-in-law, Louis de Noailles, was in America; another, Thésan, in Germany. In the eyes of the law Pauline de Montagu was dead, but her sisters had recently succeeded in buying back her part in her mother's succession from the Exchequer. The sooner the three surviving sisters (Adrienne, Pauline, and Rosalie) could meet, the better. They were planning to do so in Holland after the birth of Anastasie's child.

This would not be long delayed. Gilbert was hoping for a grandson.

At the end of January, Adrienne passed through Belgium on her way to Vianen. In spite of her extreme fatigue, she found time in Brussels to console a woman friend in exile. The woman hardly recognized her, so greatly had she changed. Adrienne had no strength left except for acts of charity.

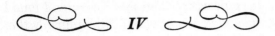

REUNION AT VIANEN

Everybody is afraid of everybody.

LA FAYETTE

*One should never so completely abandon
oneself to God as when He seems to have
abandoned us.* FÉNELON

Anastasie and Charles de La Tour-Maubourg had leased a pleasant country house at Vianen. It was there that, a fortnight after Adrienne's arrival, twin girls were born, only one of whom, Célestine, survived. Gilbert and his companions, delayed by floods, did not arrive until a week after the confinement, to find, not without feelings of relief, that the whole business was over.

ADRIENNE TO MARIE-JOSÈPHE BEAUCHET: MARCH 4, 1799

I do not wish to put off for a moment letting you know that my daughter is well, that the baby still left to her has profited appreciably from having so excellent a nurse, and that there is good reason to believe that God will see to it that this consolation is not taken from her. And now, having reassured you about these two objects of your concern (for I know how necessary to you such reassurance is), let me send you the details for which you have asked and which my heart delights in giving you.

You must have found my letters, since I came here, full of sadness. I felt so great a need of a little peace and quiet after the noise and exhaustion of Paris that I fell into a sort of stupid state from which

I have recovered only with the greatest difficulty. I found my daughter very cheerful and very happy, but extraordinarily thin, worn out, weak and suffering from a slowing-down of all her faculties. I was a great deal happier about her husband, about their mutual tenderness, and about his character, happier, indeed, than I can say, and I sincerely hope that my two other children have such sweet domesticity in store for them. . . . He has made astonishing progress in every way since his marriage, and it is with the strength of a fixed and constant nature that he lives, and will always live, for Anastasie. They are both somewhat reserved, even in the expression of their feelings, and this shyness combines a sort of reciprocal respect with a complete unconstraint in their confidence in each other.

True, the price they pay for this is a lack of demonstrative affection, which those of a more lively temperament might find tiresome, but one would have to be blind not to see how deep a sensibility is theirs.

It was on the twelfth day after my arrival that my daughter was brought to bed. Never can there have been so easy a labor. She did not give us a moment's anxiety. Her very pains were beneficial. From the moment they began we knew that the child was well formed. At the end of seven hours the first of all my grandchildren was put into my arms. I was holding her on my knees, waiting for my daughter to be delivered [of the afterbirth], when the news that another child was on the way came to me as a terrible shock. I did not fear for my daughter, but seeing that the first baby was reasonably strong, I was afflicted by the thought that the other might not be born alive. At the end of three quarters of an hour of violent labor (though the mother cried out very little and bravely did all she could to help) the second child arrived. We heard it utter a little cry. It was pale and weak, but very much alive. Virginie came. We put the elder of the two in her lap at one side of the large room occupied by my daughter, and I took the smaller while the mother was being eased and tended.

Charles was petrified; my daughter very happy, but weak and exhausted. . . . You may well imagine what the arrival of two daughters meant to her! But she was so tired that there was more of sweetness than of liveliness in her feelings. I was not altogether easy in my mind when I went to hear Mass and give thanks to God. It was Sunday, and very cold. We got the curé to come to the bedside and sprinkle the babies. That moment and an hour's good sleep wonder-

fully revived the mother, and I felt completely happy. The babies were in fine condition. No confinement could have been better, though it had left her in a state of extreme exhaustion. Her milk did not come plentifully until the fourth day, and even then not in any great abundance. She showed great courage when it was drawn from her, and it flowed easily. The elder, who was the stronger of the two, sucked only a little, and the younger did not have enough. Still, they partook with pleasure of a mash of biscuit and sugared water, which is widely used in this country.

It was a week later, on the Sunday evening, that the rest of our party arrived. They had been delayed by floods. . . . My husband is very well and putting on weight. He is in an amiable state of mind, extremely happy to be with us all, and is delighted with this country where Dutch and French alike are extending to him the warmest of welcomes. My son is much improved in looks. . . . Join your good wishes with mine, dear friend. After what God has done for us, we may indeed be buoyed up by hope.

I come now to the agonizing ordeal which He has laid upon us. On Tuesday we took our two little pretties to the church. They were both very well. From the moment of her birth the elder had had a very red nose. There were now a number of small white spots on the inside of her mouth, and she did not seem to want to take the breast . . . but she could swallow liquids, seemed to have a marvelously good digestion, and was almost always asleep. On Saturday Charlotte noticed that her feet were swollen. She was given a potion prescribed by the Utrecht doctor and her diet was slightly changed. Her stomach was still working well, but in the evening she appeared to be suffering from a pain in her navel. The swelling in her legs crept higher and she had all the symptoms of an inflamed throat. On the evening of Sunday she found it difficult to swallow, and on the Monday, though she had slept well, she took a definite turn for the worse. At noon she died.

Anastasie thought for a long time that she was suffering from a debility and dared not tend the child herself, fearing lest the milk which she was hoping to keep for the other might have deteriorated. This enabled us to keep her from witnessing the last moments. Her grief is tender, profound, and will last for a long while. Though less violent than it would have been had she been stronger, it has had a bad effect upon her and will delay her recovery. Today, however, I am better pleased with her looks. Her feelings of solicitude for

Célestine (that is the name of the surviving twin) has gone hand in hand with her pain at the loss of the elder. You will fully understand that, having from the first very little milk, she now, after such a shock, has scarcely any. . . . The terror which followed hard on the disaster has made it easy for us to persuade Anastasie to entrust the baby to the care of one of the best wet nurses I have ever met with, whom Providence enabled us to find. . . . This nurse lives at no great distance, and we visit her several times a day. It has been a bitter grief for us to send the child away, even to a place so near at hand, but the fear of losing her has taken priority over every other feeling. I am getting back my courage, dear friend, and have never seen Célestine looking so well.[1]

It was a great happiness for Adrienne to see Gilbert and George again. It was she now who was the real head of the family. She alone knew the political situation at first hand, but this did not keep La Fayette from arguing about it. A new coalition had been formed against France. The Egyptian expedition had brought Russia and Turkey into the field against her. Austria and England were about to resume hostilities. Gilbert and his son had but one desire: to fight for their country. But how was it possible for them to do so? Still a proscribed man, La Fayette did not wish to expose George to ill will and insults. "Can you see yourself, George, seated at the table of your commanding officer and drinking a toast to the glorious Tenth of August, which was the signal for the assassination of our friends?" No, George was passionately attached to his profession as a soldier, but before he could bring himself to serve, liberty would once again have to be the order of the day.

In Holland, the Dutch patriots had given Gilbert a great welcome. At Utrecht, where he paid a visit to his old friend General Van Ryssel, he saw again after so many years French troops wearing the tricolor cockade, *his* cockade. In spite of the injustice he had suffered at the hands of his country, he was proud of her. No doubt the present government was bad, but it was to France that he was loyal, not to a party, and he could praise even his political enemies if they were his compatriots and brave men. Roger de Damas, an *émigré* and an impenitent royalist, was in command at Naples of a corps which the French general, Championnet, had ordered to lay down its arms.

GILBERT TO MADAME DE TESSÉ: FEBRUARY 18, 1799

Roger stepped forward: "Messieurs," he said, "we do not wear the same cockade, but the same heart beats in all our breasts, for I am a Frenchman and you know well that I shall defend myself." And so he did, with no less skill than courage, and in spite of my love of France and the Republic, I rejoice to see him behaving so splendidly.[2]

Roger, it is true, was Mme de Simiane's brother.

To Louis Romeuf Gilbert wrote that he marveled at Adrienne's improved health and was delighted to find Virginie so much grown.

You would not [he continued] recognize Charles, who has become quite talkative, though in other ways you would find him just as he always was, that is to say, formed for the joys of youthful domesticity. I am still extremely satisfied with George.[3]

Adrienne had had to go to The Hague and to Amsterdam with George and Virginie to have their passports stamped, but Gilbert himself wanted to live the life of a recluse and to give no excuse for ill will. Brune, the French general commanding in Holland, at one time secretary of the Cordeliers, the friend of Danton and Marat, took exception to the presence of La Fayette in Utrecht. What would the exile do should the English make a landing in Holland? The most satisfactory solution for him would be to go to the United States, but unfortunately the United States had quarreled with France over the seizure of some ships. La Fayette was hopeful that the matter would be cleared up soon. True, Pusy was going to America, in spite of the official rupture. Adrienne could most certainly find the money for his passage. But what Gilbert, a "displaced person," really wanted was to enjoy French liberty some thirty miles from Paris on the La Grange estate, which would, he thought, form part of his wife's share of the family inheritance.

But was there such a thing as French liberty? The directors, under attack from the royalists on the right, and the Jacobins on the left, were becoming increasingly dictatorial the more powerless they knew themselves to be. They could hope for no support from an apathetic public opinion. Their situation was extremely shaky. "This is a wonderful opportunity for the soldiers to make a change," wrote La Fayette to Mme de Simiane. "A general could persuade

an army to overthrow the existing despotism." La Fayette, himself
a general, thought that in a crisis he could serve his country by
acting as a rallying point for the friends of liberty. But his advisers
told him that out of six hundred thousand malcontents, six at the
most were prepared to take action. So, wrote Gilbert, "if slumber
or crawling is to be the order of the day, if between now and the first
of July there is no immediate hope, I cannot very well get out of going to America. It is my duty to the United States, and to my
family."

Washington, asked for his opinion, advised him not to make the
journey. Pusy had barely left harbor before being captured by the
English. This was a bitter pill to swallow. With the Maubourgs, La
Fayette leased a larger house and prepared to make a long stay in
the Low Countries. At Vianen, Adrienne was awaiting the coming
of her sisters, with whom she hoped to reach a final settlement of
the inheritance problem.

ADRIENNE TO MARIE-JOSÈPHE BEAUCHET: MARCH 18, 1799
*I am anxious to send you a short confidential note by the hand of
my brother-in-law, because I cannot help feeling that you want a
letter in which I can speak more freely than I could in any communication going through the mail.*

*All those dear to me are in good health. Anastasie looks very
much better and is recovering her strength. Her little Célestine is
well, though very delicate. Virginie scarcely coughs at all now. My
husband and my son are in perfect health. They are all very sweet
to me, but the reopening of hostilities makes me exceedingly uneasy. I realize that my son will not long be satisfied with being inactive, and I need not tell you how heavily the prospect of the
unhappy future ahead of us weighs on my heart. My present hope
is that I may be able to persuade the government to allow him to
take service with the Dutch. The very close relations now existing
between the two republics makes this idea of mine, I cannot help
thinking, a possible one. The excellent mood of the Dutch government and the extreme friendliness which is being shown everywhere
to his father, would make this solution comforting to me and agreeable to him. Do not say a word of all this to anyone. Only I can
handle it, and it has been decided that I shall take George with me
to Paris before the end of next month.*

We are expecting Pauline to be here in the latter part of this week. We shall then spend a fortnight with her, after which I shall take the necessary steps for my departure (in company with Rosalie, George, and Virginie).

We are moving from here in two days' time to another house, perhaps rather too nice a one, because it is a great deal more expensive than we should have liked, though we shall be able to save money by running it ourselves. The rent of the charming little place is five hundred florins a month, which we shall not be called upon to pay until the end of six months. We could not find anything cheaper. It is the house about which Anastasie wrote to us. The absolutely indispensable furnishings have cost us between three and four hundred florins. This money I have borrowed from Pauline. All my other money matters have been settled, and I shall send you a detailed account at the first opportunity. . . .

That, my dear friend, is the situation as it affects us. It is pleasant enough for the moment, but my pleasure is much diminished by the thought of what the future may bring.

My husband is constantly preoccupied by the question of choice in the sharing out of our inheritance. His taste for farming is very genuine. . . .

The new house has a delightful little garden. Simon and my children will take full responsibility for looking after it. A love of the country is common to all of us.

My brother-in-law maintains that our respective shares must be settled within the next four months, as also my business concerns in the department of the Côtes-du-Nord. That prospect will make it easier for me to bear out separation. I shall leave Monsieur de La Fayette installed in this young household, in a country which he likes and where he is truly loved.[4]

At last the sisters turned up. Mme de Tessé had kindly made it possible for Pauline and her husband to travel post. They reached Vianen on Easter Eve. Rosalie de Grammont was already there. All of them were guests of the La Fayettes, and because money was short the fare was somewhat Spartan. The three sisters pooled their housekeeping gifts and such money as was available and bought the bare necessities as cheaply as possible.

Monsieur de Montagu said with a laugh that the only good dinner he had had in Holland was in Utrecht, at the house of General Van Ryssel. At Vianen everything went wrong, in spite of the good intentions of the mistress of the house, who had to fall back on making oeufs à la neige when it was a question of adding a substantial dish to the table d'hôte of fifteen or sixteen "lodgers," all as hungry as hunters. But though rations might be short, how happy everybody was! ...

As soon as it was possible to escape from matters of business (as often as not after supper, or what passed for supper), the sisters withdrew in the icy cold to one of the fireless bedrooms. Each wrapped herself as well as she could in a cape to protect herself from the wind which whistled through the partitions that played the part of walls, put her shivering feet on an inefficient warmer, and stayed up talking until midnight, or sometimes until one or two in the morning.[5]

Adrienne, now forty, was going gray. Pauline, at thirty-three, looked a great deal younger than Rosalie, her junior by a year. Adrienne was a heroine cast in the antique mold, though without being in the least aware of the fact. Mme de Montagu lacked anything resembling Adrienne's authority in worldly matters. Which was the best, the most perfect, of the three sisters, who were truly three saints? That is a question Pauline's biographer could not answer:

It may be that one was superior in strength of mind, another in spiritual gifts, the third in sensibility; but it can be said that, allowing for different shades of emphasis, the same virtue showed in all three. Lights placed in china vases take on the coloring of the container. Had each been in the others' shoes, it is probable that her conduct would have been much the same. It is not difficult to imagine Madame de Grammont at Olmütz and Madame de La Fayette at Witmold helping the émigrés. None of the sisters failed in the tasks allotted to them. In each case they showed the same forgetfulness of self. They would have walked on hot coals to fulfill a duty. They had a horror of the useless and the futile, and thought it lamentable that people should do anything for the sole purpose of giving themselves pleasure.[6]

And what did they do in that icy room at Vianen? They prayed together, they chatted in hushed voices, taking great care not to awaken the children and their fathers, already sleeping. They composed a prayer in the form of a litany to the memory of their martyred mother, and promised not to let a day pass without reciting it "at the fatal hour." In spite of sitting up so late they rose early and went to Mass together.

Rosalie said to Pauline: "I have a feeling that you stimulate me to goodness and draw me on to prayer."

"That," replied Pauline, "makes me think of horses on the towpaths that one sees in this part of the world. They are thin and puny, yet they draw great barges after them."

On May 5 they had to separate. Friends had informed them that the innocent family reunion was being talked about in Paris as a "meeting of conspirators," and that there were mutterings in high places. Stupidity not infrequently goes hand in hand with fear. The three households had reached complete agreement about their respective shares. It was the carrying out of their decisions that was going to be difficult. Only Adrienne could take charge of the negotiations. While Pauline returned to Witmold, taking with her two trunks of clothes, one from Auvergne containing the Vicomte de Beaune's outmoded wardrobe, the other brought back from America by George, the courageous Adrienne took the road to France with Rosalie, who was going home to Villersexel. By a miracle the Revolution had left the château intact.

George and Virginie accompanied them. Gilbert stayed on in Holland. During this renewed separation Adrienne would be carrying not for the first time the whole weight of the family's future on her fragile shoulders. What would she find awaiting her in Paris? The war news was bad. Bonaparte, it seemed, was having no success in Syria, whither he had led his army from Egypt. Suvarov, the Russian general, had occupied Milan. In France the elections had given the Five Hundred a majority hostile to the Directory. Adrienne would once again have to live dangerously. But she was used to that.

She found a country of grumblers, more than ever hostile to the government. In the provinces the tradespeople were deliberately and nostalgically closing their shops on Sunday and opening them on the *décadi*, the official holiday of the revolutionary calendar. The profiteers of the Revolution were sending their children to schools in which there were chapels and confessionals. Grammont heard a man sitting beside him in the church of St-Roch say fervently: "O Lord, have mercy upon us and exterminate the nation!" which meant, for the simple-minded speaker: "Deliver us, O Lord, from the regime of the Convention!" The words *citizen* and *patriot* were taking on a pejorative meaning. News of victories and reverses were being received with the same apathy. They might have concerned the fortunes and activities of a foreign people.

This passivity of the masses was a poor augury for the future of the Directory. Nobody believed in the system, and it was to nobody's interest to support it.

George, who had come to Paris to have his passport regularized, wrote to his father: "I have found great changes here, and you will realize that my personal affairs are for the moment in abeyance." There were fears of rioting, of revolt. Adrienne, courageous as ever, had immediately embarked on a thousand and one approaches: "Do not be alarmed for my safety," she wrote Gilbert. "I hope to be with you before there is any danger for women or for the poor."

GILBERT TO ADRIENNE: MAY 16, 1799

I am now back, sad and lonely, my dear Adrienne, and though I cannot look upon this renewed separation as resembling that of last year, still, there is more than enough of it to cause me much suffering. I am already beginning to feel that impatience to see you again which always comes upon me when the moment of our reunion draws near. It has attacked me sooner than usual. . . .

We long for news of you. My confidence in you is too great to let me fear that you are not taking care of your health, as you solemnly promised me to do. . . . Our garden grows more charming every day, but a weasel has eaten my poor wood pigeon and her eggs.

Yesterday, when I went to see the nurse, I met three tinkers from Cantal. They were fellows of sound common sense whose answers to the questions I put to them were better than anything one is likely to hear in the salons. It seems pretty obvious that the Revolution, in spite of the crimes and the acts of violence which have befouled its course and diminished its effects, has nevertheless brought about a great improvement in the condition of the peasants in that department. I pass on to you this piece of consolation, which came to me casually, so to speak, and gave me much pleasure.

Good-by, my dear Adrienne. My heart is with you, longs for you, preaches to you, and loves you very tenderly.[7]

GILBERT TO ADRIENNE: MAY 29

My letter will in all probability find you at La Grange, dear heart, in that place of retirement where I hope we are destined to find rest together from the changes and chances of our life. I trust that this thought will bring some sweetness to mingle with your present difficulties, and will show you that in spite of the successes of the coalition, I do not think it likely that they will have the effect of counterrevolutionizing the Republic. . . . This is a very critical moment, and all true patriots should more than ever before feel it their duty to serve France. . . . I am therefore not surprised that George's enthusiasm should grow in proportion as that of the still undecided diminishes. But of this I can assure you, my dear Adrienne, that I associate myself more with your maternal anxieties than I should have thought possible in the days when you would have shared them between him and his father. . . .

I most certainly agree with you, my dear Adrienne, that if he is to be conscripted in six months' time, it must seem a great deal better to anybody who faces the fact fairly and squarely that he should offer himself as a volunteer here and now. . . . In the whole of this affair and in your manner of seeing it from all angles, your conduct has satisfied my heart and increased, if that be possible, my confidence in you. You say that your head is bowed, but that is certainly not the case with your spirit; my own is at one with you in all that you feel.

You are, I hope, going to send all the detailed information I want about La Grange: first and foremost about the house and about your reactions to my plans for it; secondly, about the farm. I want to know how many animals, large and small, we shall be able to keep, what the cost is likely to be, and how many hands we shall need to look after them. To all this I should like you to add a word or two about the park and the woods. Liancourt has lent me some of Arthur Young's books. I am deeper than ever in my study of agriculture, and it will give much pleasure to compare the details you send me with the current practice in England and Holland. The future is threatening. . . . My general conclusion is that we must be together again as soon as possible. Why are you not with me now? [8]

In his hermitage at Vianen Gilbert was better placed to study the flower beds in his garden than the political situation in the Republic. For the moment it was fluid. By a drawing of lots, one of the directors, Rewbell, had been eliminated. Though his reputation was bad, he was a serious loss to Adrienne, whom he had done much to help. The councils had chosen the Abbé Sieyès to replace him. Then, on the 30th Prairial, a minor *coup d'état* had got rid of La Revellière-Lépeaux and Merlin de Douai. Since Barras was now much discredited, Sieyès would be the tie beam of the edifice.

The La Fayettes knew Sieyès well. They had entertained him in the days of the Constituent Assembly, and Gilbert liked to quote something he had said at that time: "They want to be free, but do not know how to be just." Sieyès was scarcely an abbé. Family pressure rather than faith had turned him into a priest. Before the Revolution he had been the brain of the opposition. Mirabeau had called him "my master." In the Convention he had entrenched himself behind a wall of silence, weighty with contempt, which had later seemed to be heavily charged with wisdom. He had the reputation of being the greatest expert in all that had to do with constitutions and institutions. In May, 1799, he spent several months in Berlin as ambassador at the court of the King of Prussia, Frederick William III. France believed that it owed to him the neutrality of that monarch, and this increased his prestige. He was making his appearance in the last act of the national tragedy as a *deus ex machina*.

Adrienne asked for an audience, obtained it, and went to discuss with the new director the question of La Fayette's eventual return. She feared an invasion of Holland, and even the possibility of a second sojourn in Holstein, since the coalition troops might well advance into the Low Countries. She felt that France was a less dangerous place for her husband. Virginie accompanied her mother. Sieyès received them both with demonstrations of friendship. They drew upon their joint memories in order to set down as accurately as possible what he had said in his southern twang, and sent the resultant document to Vianen:

MME DE LA FAYETTE: *Holland is threatened with invasion. In my view Monsieur de La Fayette will have to choose between the scaffold, Siberia, or a return to France. I have told him that I think the latter course preferable, and want you to know this so that if he chooses it in his extremity, you may attach no other motive to that choice than a feeling of confidence in his country which would make him prefer that danger to others.*

SIEYÈS: You have been deceived, Madame, if you have been told that I am an enemy of La Fayette.

MME DE LA FAYETTE: That I do not think you are is proved by my addressing myself to you.

SIEYÈS: I sincerely desire the return of La Fayette, and of all the patriots of 1789. But I think that it would be dangerous for him to come back to France just now. There are certain laws that cannot be set aside.

MME DE LA FAYETTE: I am asking no favors of you, Monsieur. My sole object in coming here is to declare that of all the dangers I think this to be preferable.

SIEYÈS: If that is merely a declaration, you have made it. But I gather since you have come in person to speak with me, that you wish for an answer, and I repeat that I consider it to be a dangerous line for him to take. I do not believe in an invasion of Holland, but, like you, I regard it as a possibility. La Fayette is still far from any likely scene of trouble. How, by the way, does he come to be in Holland? I know nothing about that.

MME DE LA FAYETTE: He is there by tacit permission of the French government. He has nothing to fear, and I am not in the least uneasy about him so long as the patriots of 1789 remain in power in that country.

SIEYÈS: So far, so good. Should Holland be invaded he could withdraw into the territories of the King of Prussia, who at the moment is definitely neutral. I am careful not to place more reliance on that than I need. I cannot see into the future.

MME DE LA FAYETTE: But I, sir, can see into the past. Monsieur de La Fayette puts no trust in kings. The emperor had him informed at Olmütz that his principles were incompatible with the safety of the imperial government.

SIEYÈS: I agree that it would be terrible for La Fayette to fall into the hands of the powers, and that for the time being it is impossible for him to cross the sea. But as I said before, he can go to the King of Prussia, or to Nijmegen in the Duchy of Clèves, and do there what he is doing now—wait. You know, I suppose, that Messieurs de Lameth and d'Aiguillon managed to get a few leagues into France, and that we got wind of it at once?

MME DE LA FAYETTE: I am quite sure that if Monsieur de La Fayette *showed his nose in a French town you would get wind of it, and you would also be sent several issues of the Hommes Libres in which there would be references to the fact. But you could always have him thrown into prison.*

SIEYÈS: *Worse than that. I should be much distressed should anything happen to La Fayette. I think of him only as a man who once sat with me in the Assembly and has since been unfortunate.*

MME DE LA FAYETTE: *And, you might add, one who for five years suffered in the cause of libetry.*

Note by Virginie: *Mamma more than once asked him "Do you think that I should take your colleagues into my confidence?" The only answer vouchsafed by the director was: "You would do well to make use of any means at your disposal."* [9]

This was not very encouraging. In actual fact, Sieyès, the "mole of the Revolution," was already busy undermining the government of which he was a member. La Fayette's return would have interfered with his plans. The abbé saw clearly that the Directory could not survive military reverses. The directors had taken steps to ensure public safety—a mass levy and an enforced loan—but to attempt to revive Jacobinism in a country sick of the Jacobins would be tantamount to suicide. Should the generals, by a miracle, succeed in restoring the military situation, it would be on them that the government would have to lean. "I need a sword," murmured the abbé—but whose hand was to wield that sword? Sieyès' thoughts had turned to Hoche and to Joubert, but these two heroes were now dead, and only Bonaparte was left. He was less reliable, but more brilliant and more political. Who else was there? Bernadotte? Moreau? Bonaparte would have replied: "The Revolution should learn not to make conjectures about the future."

Might the sword be La Fayette's? Adrienne had not got the impression that Sieyès' mind was moving in that direction, and she knew that her husband did not admire the abbé. "He is timorous, moody, and does not know how to make himself pleasing," Gilbert had said. "He can neither speak fluently nor ride a horse: he is an abbé in the fullest sense of the term. . . . Everybody has expected to see him on a pedestal, and everybody is astonished to see how small he looks." [10] Nevertheless, he was of the opinion that circumstances might put Sieyès in the saddle again, and that it was important not to quarrel with him. Thanks to his wife, he had got a pretty clear picture of what France was like. In the capital and in the provinces alike, the profiteers of the Revolution were determined to hold on to their gains. At the other end of the scale, the ultras, the fanatics, and the adventurers were busy with plots, hoping that in a new court it might be their turn to make their fortunes. "Between these parties lies the nation," said Gilbert, "which dreads an out-and-out victory for the counterrevolution, would like a limited monarchy, could manage quite happily with a free republic, and dreads major shocks more than anything else." [11] A very accurate picture.

Adrienne had succeeded in getting permission for George to return to Holland. He wrote to his father from Fontenay-en-Brie on July 7: "At last, my dear Papa, I am in possession of the much-desired passport, and in seven or eight days I shall be with you." The young man described himself as torn in two, happy at going back to his father, desolated at the thought of leaving his mother. "Mamma is so good that, not giving a thought to herself as usual, she maintains that she derives much comfort from the knowledge of my happiness." On August 5, 1799, Gilbert announced the arrival of their son to his wife:

I was just thinking very sadly but very tenderly of you, my dear Adrienne, when suddenly (this was the day before yesterday) George came into my room. You will not have to make any very great effort to realize my feelings, and I know how generously you partake of my joy. When are we to see a reunion of the whole family? It would be soon and in France if in this final crisis all who took part in the revolution were within measurable distance of being in complete agreement about the one thing that really matters—liberty. Its coming would be much to the interest of those in power: but men only talk about their interests; it is passions that govern their actions.

I shall go to America only when I have lost all hope of serving my country here. When I see the coalition advancing against France and against the whole of humanity, with the most detestable intentions, when I realize that it is my personal enemies who are at the head of this horrible league, I feel that there is nothing for me to do but range myself on the other side and to fight until we have been wiped out. But that cannot be. The other side bears me almost as much ill will! I see no reason to suppose that it is liberty they wish to defend, and I am fully aware of what those motives are that keep me from my native land.

Since yesterday, George and I have been spending our time in planning a farm for you, either in the beautiful valley of the Shenandoah in the back country of the state of Virginia, not far from Federal City and Mount Vernon, or in the prairies of New England within reach of the city of Boston, for which, as you know, I have a special liking.[12]

But for the purchase of this farm not a single dollar was as yet available.

Meanwhile, an Anglo-Russian army had landed in Holland. The commander of one of the English divisions was Gilbert's old adversary, Sir Ralph Abercrombie. Twenty-five thousand Russians were fighting for the English. What the devil were they going to do in this land of polders? Victor de La Tour-Maubourg and George de La Fayette enlisted in the Dutch army. They could not remain inactive when their hosts and their friends were being attacked. La Fayette wrote to his wife:

SEPTEMBER 4, 1799

My dear Adrienne, I hope that you approve of us. You will notice that I have confined myself to the civilian duties of a patriot residing in an invaded Holland. It would have been against my principles to raise any objections to the plans of Victor and George.

They will not, I think, be exposed to those dangers in which they are so anxious to be involved. That will be some consolation to you, and to me also, for I cannot help feeling that sending others to war and waging it oneself are two very diffierent things. . . .

The day after tomorrow I shall enter on my forty-third year. It is high time that I thought of settling down.[13]

He told her of the arrival of the Duke of York, the son of King George III, who was to assume command of the Anglo-Russian forces. Gilbert knew him well: "A poor performer, except in the eating line." Mme de Tessé was badly frightened and begged her nephew to leave Holland. He would not so much as consider the suggestion. The old lady blamed him for having his eyes so constantly fixed on principles that he was incapable of seeing dangers. He answered her proudly: "When liberty is in danger, I am inclined to ignore my own selfish interests."

On September 19, the anniversary of their leaving Olmütz, Adrienne received a sad and tender letter from Utrecht.

It is two years today, dear Adrienne, since we left the prison to which you came, bringing me consolation and life itself. If only, after two years of exile and five of captivity, I could give you some assurance of our being together forever in some peaceful place of retirement! [14]

They were living at a time when "forever" seemed to be a meaningless expression. The situation was changing from moment to moment. All of a sudden the military position seemed to improve. As happens in most coalitions, the English and the Russians were quarreling. The Franco-Dutch armies, as a result, gained a tremendous victory. Two thousand prisoners and twenty pieces of artillery were captured. Holland was saved. In Switzerland, Thugut had most inadvisedly withdrawn the troops under the Archduke Charles, and Masséna had surrounded Korsakov's Russian army.

These astonishing successes brought Adrienne little peace of mind. She had left the Beauchets' house. Winter was approaching. She could not decently confine in a freezing garret the generous friend who had given up her own room to her guest. For a moment she had toyed with the idea of camping out at Fontenay, but it was too far from Paris, where she was engaged in making one approach after another to the authorities. With Grammont, her brother-in-law, she took a diminutive lodging at Châtenay, from which place she could make the journey into the city on foot in spite of her bad leg. There she lived very cheaply, and there Virginie found someone to give her free drawing lessons.

VIRGINIE TO ANASTASIE

Your letters are charming, but then, so are you, always, as Mamma and I keep on reminding each other. I know what a grumpy companion I am, but everybody seems to get on my nerves and the only thing that gives me any pleasure is the half-hour we spend at Madame de Simiane's. [15]

Virginie judged herself severely. Others did not take so hard a view. Marie de Maisonneuve wrote to Anastasie:

I have seen Madame de Simiane and Madame de Poix. They were full of praise for Virginie, which gave me great pleasure. They think, as I do, that she is wonderfully improved in looks, beautifully dressed, and as charming as she could possibly be. They went so far as to say that if she held herself more upright, she might perhaps be less piquant. Her dresses are well made, with short white sleeves. In short, she is a little muscadine in the best of taste.[16]

Adrienne was in continuous correspondence with Gilbert:

I am deeply touched to know that our separation adds so greatly to your melancholy. I wish that I had at least some consolation to give you, but of what kind could it be, my dear Gilbert? I doubt not you would be still more unhappy if you could see into the bottom of the abyss in which we now are, and realize how small is the hope of our ever seeing liberty reborn in the midst of so much filth and after having been so utterly disfigured.

One thing, however, is certain, and that is that the military situation is improved; that Masséna has just won a great victory in Helvetia; that the coalition has not succeeded in drawing in the King of Prussia; that inside France a few persons, unjustly detained, have been freed; and that Fouché and Dubois-Crancé do not look with favor on the Jacobins.[17]

Adrienne, all passion spent and now on the brink of middle age, sent him news of Diane-Adélaïde de Simiane without a trace of jealousy:

We dined yesterday, as I told you we were going to do, with Adélaïde's sister-in-law, who had just left her. It seems that she is going to have a happiness which I much envy her, that of getting some money on the security of her word of honor with which to pay the first instalment of the forced loan which has driven her from her house. You may rest assured that I shall learn the conclusion of this affair and shall let you know what Adélaïde proposes to do about finding somewhere to live. From this sister-in-law, who has been really very kind to her, I have found out all I possibly could about the extent to which this fresh upheaval has affected Adélaïde. She told me that, as you may suppose, she had been very brave, and that with her the troubles of the heart so completely submerge all others that they are felt far less acutely. She adds, however, that this pulling up of roots has been extremely painful, and that for three days everything went so wrong for her that she was positively ill. Her friend is staying on with her until next month. We can only wait and see how her sister-in-law's efforts will turn out, and whether

*what we hope may happen will happen and that this accursed loan
be canceled, or at least its methods changed. Only then can we
know what her next step will be.*[18]

It was only in small sums and with considerable difficulty that
Adrienne managed to raise any money—by borrowing eight hundred francs and selling wood from the Fontenay estate. She sent to
Vianen the amount of the rent which her husband had to pay for
the "pretty house." She explored endless avenues, and by dint of
sheer tenacity, diplomacy, and personal authority, frequently got
what she wanted. Sieyès was now only too glad when she called
upon him, since he had a great belief in her wisdom and found her
advice valuable. More urgently than ever before he was looking for
that "sword" he so much wanted. Except for the crazy ultras and
the confirmed Jacobins, Frenchmen in general seemed disposed to
accept an arbitration of which the country stood so desperately in
need.

There will have to be sacrifices on both sides [wrote Adrienne on
October 9] *and the lessons learned on both have been so hard that
at last they seem to be taking them to heart. . . . In such a situation
there is very little room for virtue.*[19]

Such was the warning of a realistic wife to a husband whose head
was still in the clouds. He, for his part, seemed to be still convinced
that he was immensely popular in France. Carnot, now an exile
in Holland, was, he said, making advances to him. Very soon now
he would be recalled because the country had need of him. Already
he was laying down conditions, the first being the unfettered return
to France of all honest men, whether exiles or *émigrés.*

GILBERT TO CÉSAR DE LA TOUR-MAUBOURG: OCTOBER 17, 1799
*Persuaded as I am that the first step to success is to dare, and seeing
that everybody is afraid of being compromised, I have offered to
make a sudden appearance in Paris; to force the government to
choose between acting or assassinating me; to get Beurnonville and
Lefebvre to mount and ride with me; to proclaim and to ensure
liberty in the capital, and consequently in the whole of France, in
the teeth of all comers. The answer given me is that I should merely
lose my life to no purpose. Pétiet, one of Moreau's most intimate
friends and so far as I am concerned the same today as he was at
Sedan, has begged my wife to send me word that his friend is an*

excellent fellow whose intentions are of the best, but that he lacks the character to turn his back on routine and to make something of himself, and, in a word, that slogging away at a twelve-hour battle is about all he is good for. They must, however, have talked pretty frankly together and I await news of that conversation.[20]

The great news, when it came, had to do with a very much more brilliant and enterprising figure. On October 9 Bonaparte, having secretly left his Army of Egypt, had landed at Saint-Raphaël. What was he up to? Had he been recalled by Sieyès, and acted in accordance with the wishes of the government, or was he playing a lone hand, relying on the support of his two brothers, Joseph Bonaparte in the Council of the Ancients, and Lucien, who was a member of the Five Hundred?

GILBERT TO CÉSAR DE LA TOUR-MAUBOURG

Bonaparte's attitude to us will depend entirely on where his interests lie and on what he may be planning. You know that his first word in Italy was that I must not be allowed to return to France. He told Victor when they said good-by that he very much hoped to be acquainted with me, and you know that later on he declared that he had given me a very proper answer, which in fact was not true. Madame Bonaparte told George how important it was for her husband and me to make common cause. But though Bonaparte said nice things about me to Louis Romeuf in Paris, and appeared to be concerned about the risk I ran of being taken by the English at sea, observing that the only inconvenience in that would be the delay it would cause in my being taken into a French harbor, he ended by saying quite frankly that our political views were so divergent that it had never so much as occurred to him that I should come back. . . .

You must have realized that since the defeats suffered by the coalition, the malcontents are of the opinion that salvation can come only from activities inside France. That being so, this is a very favorable moment for Bonaparte. He will certainly not risk his personal advantage in the cause of liberty. He has already given proof that he would very calmly envisage its violation, and even cooperate in bringing it about. All the same, should his prestige and his ambition seem to demand his coming forward as a champion of the good cause, he will do so. His wish must be to see the Republic firmly established on a foundation of liberty and justice. Perhaps

*he wants to be president for life? I should be very much in favor of
such an arrangement. It would be a curious experiment. The Council of the Ancients would propose certain changes in the constitution, and this would be one of them. In a word, anything is good
except an aristocratic-absolutist monarchy or a despotic republic, and
I must confess that I am personally in favor of a nonhereditary
presidency, though I should be very much averse to putting an obstacle in the way of any other arrangement which might establish
the nation in its rights and allow it to find peace in good and complete liberty, which is the ultimate conclusion of this lengthy scribble.*

    *But let us not plunge into speculation. Rather let us wait for the
first reliable news. I am pretty sure that Sieyès has an understanding
with Bonaparte. . . . Should that not be the case, he must be shak-
ing in his shoes!* [21]

La Fayette himself was not at all frightened. At the worst, if he
could no longer play a part in public affairs, he could always give
all his energies to farming with the enthusiasm which, as a young
man, he had devoted to military and political matters. Adrienne,
whose dearest wish was some such retirement, now concentrated
all her efforts with passion and a scrupulous attention to detail on
the problem of rescuing the properties of Fontenay and La Grange,
both of which had belonged to the Duchesse d'Ayen.

GILBERT TO ADRIENNE: UTRECHT, OCTOBER 28, 1799

*It seems to me that your men of business are being very sluggish. It
is you, my dear Adrienne, who are carrying the whole burden of our
affairs on your shoulders. I can see you do not doubt that La Grange
will be your portion of the inheritance. I very much want you to
take the necessary steps to making the farm a really good proposition, for if we are destined to find our place of retirement in France,
I am pretty sure that my activities will be in the way of agriculture,
which I am studying with all the ardor which in my younger days
I gave to other occupations.*

    *It is ridiculous for a man of the Old Regime to think that he can
be metamorphosed into a farmer merely by purchasing a farm of
the English type, and it is certainly true that there are minor tasks
which are better left in the hands of men who are experienced in the
day-to-day problems of agriculture and have given their whole lives*

to it. But it is going to the other extreme to hold that a broadening of the mind, the power to make useful comparisons between the objects he sees and the knowledge he has acquired, a sensibly organized routine and the discovery of valuable truths, unfit a man for a calling in which practice stands in such great need of theory.

Good-by, my dear Adrienne. I am impatient to be back in France —because of public affairs, because of my friends, and because of my own wishes. I am also—and to an extent I cannot express in words—longing to see you again.[22]

Whenever she came up against an obstacle, Adrienne never hesitated to go straight to the source of power. This she now did with her usual calm courage. Foreseeing that General Bonaparte would soon be all-powerful, she asked him for an interview as soon as he was back in Paris, so that she might convey to him the gratitude of all the prisoners of Olmütz. At that time the general was still easy of access, and when he was visited by Adrienne, accompanied as usual by her aide-de-camp Virginie, he was all affability. He admired the heroine, and from the very first moment realized that he was in the presence of a woman of intelligence. The man she saw was pale and hollow-cheeked, but young and virile. The eyes were magnificent, the mouth well drawn and strong. He had "more the look of a mathematician than a general."

"Your husband's life," Bonaparte assured Adrienne, "is bound up with the preservation of the Republic."

This was as good as an open declaration against monarchy, and was not likely to meet with disfavor in the La Fayette household. As soon as Adrienne had returned from her visit, she advised Gilbert to write Bonaparte a short and dignified letter.

GILBERT TO ADRIENNE: OCTOBER 30, 1799

Here is my letter for Bonaparte. I have followed your advice about making it short. It is, if anything, somewhat dry. But all the letters and all the mutual friends in the world count for very little in comparison with half an hour's conversation. There are things to be said about his ambition and his thirst for glory which cannot be written. Those who are jealous of Bonaparte foresee a future in which I shall be in opposition to him, and in this they are right if he sets himself up as an oppressor of liberty. But if he sincerely wishes to be its servant, then there will be complete agreement between us, for I do not think him such a fool as to want to be nothing but a despot.

Meanwhile, my dear Adrienne, what should I do, or hope that others may do for me? Perhaps those who have my interests at heart have not yet looked beyond my arrival in France as a simple citizen unburdened by any public office, eager to give his support to anyone who wishes to do his best for the country. I ask for nothing better.

To bring the Revolution to an end for the benefit of the whole human race, to lend my influence to the introduction of measures useful to my contemporaries and to posterity, to re-establish the doctrine of liberty, to keep hallowed my regrets, to let my wounds be healed, to pay homage to all martyrs in the good cause, would bring me such happiness that even now my heart would swell with it. But I am more disgusted than ever, invincibly so, at the thought of ever again taking root in the soil of public affairs. I shall have nothing more to do with them, except insofar as I might be asked to lend a helping hand, as the saying goes.

If, quite simply, I am asked to return to Paris and am in agreement with what is going to happen immediately after my arrival there, then, I may hope to see you very soon. There is another possibility, which is that Bonaparte, Moreau, and Sieyès may agree to my going incognito to discuss matters with them. If we see eye to eye, much the better; if, on the other hand, they are not satisfied with me, then I shall come back here.

I am in a hurry, dear Adrienne, to get this letter finished and so cannot reread what I have written. But I must say once again how completely satisfied I am with what you do, with what you say, and still more with what you are. I can read your heart, my dear, my darling Adrienne, and none of its good, affectionate, and generous movements but find an echo in mine. I am more impatient than words can say to see you again, whether here or there, and to grasp that happy moment when we shall never again be parted.

LA FAYETTE TO GENERAL BONAPARTE

Citizen General, It would have been enough for me to love liberty and my country to be filled with joy and hope by the news of your arrival. But to this longing for the common weal I join a deep and lively feeling for my liberator. She whose life I owe to you has told me of the welcome you accorded to the prisoners of Olmütz. I rejoice in the thought of all my obligations to you, Citizen General, and in the happy conviction that to acclaim your glory and to hope for your success is as much a civic duty as it is the expression of my personal attachment and gratitude.[23]

It had given him no pleasure to write this letter, but Adrienne had said it would be useful, and in the La Fayette family it was she who exercised supreme command.

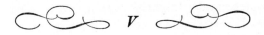

V

THE RETURN

*I have always had a more sensitive con-
science than is convenient for a man
who, like myself, is concerned with great
matters.*   **RETZ**

On the 16th Brumaire (November 6) Gilbert wrote a long letter
to his wife. She was in hourly expectation of great events, but he
spoke only of family and local matters:

*You must have suffered cruelly from that inflammation on your
lungs, my dear Adrienne, for it to have left you so weak even after
it had been effectively treated. I do implore you to take care of yourself. There must be no more going on foot from Châtenay to Paris,
and you must always drive when you have errands to do in distant
quarters of the city.*[1]

He insisted that the return of Anastasie and her husband to France
was a matter of the utmost urgency. "I am the more eager that the
young family should be sent for at once, thus ensuring that their
child may be safely in Paris before the worst period of the year—
so far as roads and traveling are concerned—will have set in." For
himself, he had as great hopes as ever. The news sheets were
loud in their praise of George's campaigning in Holland, and this
was a good sign. "Proofs of Bonaparte's good intentions are reaching me from all parts, and I am deeply touched. I am delighted to

hear that there is complete understanding between him and Sieyès."

The "complete understanding" was not very surprising. Sieyès was sick of the Directory and wanted a strong government in which, shoulder to shoulder with a general, he might liquidate the Revolution. All Frenchmen shared this hope—those who wanted to be left in peace to enjoy what they had got out of it, those who hoped to get back what they had lost, and the population in general because everybody was disgusted by the present state of disorder and because France, a nation with a love of discipline, wanted to be able to feel that there was a strong hand on the helm. Bonaparte was fully informed of Sieyès' plans, and wholeheartedly approved of them. His two brothers, Joseph and Lucien Bonaparte, had drawn up a complete scenario for the Ancients and the Five Hundred. On the 19th Brumaire Adrienne learned that on the previous day the general had taken an oath of allegiance to the Ancients, and that during the ensuing night they had ordered the transfer of the Five Hundred to Saint-Cloud. Three directors of the five (Sieyès was one) had resigned in order to make way for the new regime; two had refused to follow suit and were under arrest.

On the nineteenth matters reached boiling point in the Five Hundred. The Jacobins of the left raised the cry of "Outside the law!" when Bonaparte entered the Assembly. He withdrew, discomfited. Lacking the gifts of an orator, he had been unable to hold his own in a hostile chamber. But Lucien had been calm and collected; the two Bonapartes, on horseback, had harangued the troops and denounced the "knights of the dagger, soldiers in the pay of England," and the grenadiers had dispersed the deputies. The directors were thereupon replaced by three provisional consuls: Bonaparte, Sieyès, and Roger-Duclos. The public had ears only for one name. The legality of the new government was not contested. France was not raped: she gave herself willingly.

Next day Bonaparte drove through Paris on his way to the Luxembourg. It was a *décadi*, a holiday, warm and rainy. On the walls official notices announced the change of regime. The working-class districts failed to come out in support of the Jacobins. The whole city surrendered to a pleasing sense of slackened tension and general joy. In the privacy of family circles there were smiles of contentment. In the theaters that evening anything that could be taken as an allusion to what had happened was loudly applauded. In the streets crowds carrying torches escorted the criers, who, to the sound of trumpets and drums, proclaimed the Consulate, which had taken the place of the Directory. Complete strangers embraced one another and shouted "Down with the tyrants! Give us peace!" Everybody was convinced that the invincible general would triumph over Europe without having to strike a blow. In the confectioners' shops there were figures of Bonaparte in sugar, some inscribed: FRANCE OWES HIM VICTORY: SHE WILL SOON OWE HIM PEACE.

But was it really and truly peace? That was what Adrienne was asking herself. She hoped it was, and put the question to that other woman who, like herself, was longing for the return of the proscribed exile. On the 24th Brumaire, she wrote to Adélaïde de Simiane.

What events we have witnessed since last I wrote to you, Madame.
... I do not doubt that they will lead to Gilbert's return. I am even convinced that had his friends been somewhat more active, it would now be an accomplished fact. His wife has done everything in her power to make them act: she has seen Roederer, who has given her every reason to hope. She is also very much alive to the fact that the manner of it should be—to some extent at least—seemly. All this keeps her in a constant state of agitation. After the recent great happenings she is waiting for news with the utmost impatience. ...
You would like, Madame, to hear from me what kind of a life we shall lead should our efforts be successful. The Brie property is still the only place where we can conceive of settling permanently, but in the meantime we shall have to stay in Paris where there is a certain American (incidentally, when passing through the place where Gilbert is he lent him a hundred louis, which was most timely) lodging with Monsieur Le Ray, the proprietor of the house at Passy that was once the residence of Franklin. There is also just a chance that we may be able to find somewhere to live at Châtenay. ... So much for my gossip, Madame. You wish us well, and so may find it of interest. Do not fail to let me know what impression the most recent events have made upon you. I confess that they delight me. ... I trust that you will permit me to send my warmest greetings to Madame de Poix, and to offer you my daughter's most affectionate homage. I will not attempt to express the warmth of feeling for you with which my heart is filled.[2]

Such was the manner in which, with simplicity, frankness, and affection, Adrienne confided her hopes to the woman of great beauty whom her husband loved. She might have been excused for treating her as a rival: instead, she wished to see in her only a friend.

As things now were, Gilbert's fate depended wholly on Bonaparte, in whose hands the real power lay. Sieyès was more concerned with appearances than with facts. So long as he was entrusted with the task of drafting the new constitution and allowed to give free rein to his virtuosity in matters of political theory, he was completely satisfied. Meanwhile, Bonaparte's situation remained difficult. The greatest care would be necessary in his handling of the army, of the landed proprietors, of the Jacobins, and even of the Institute, whose influence on men's minds was very great. On the 21st Brumaire Bonaparte took his seat in the Academy of Sciences among his fellow members.

At the Luxembourg he regularly appeared in civilian clothing, wearing a frock coat which hung about him in loose folds. He chose, and received, his future collaborators. Luckily for Adrienne, Talleyrand (a close relative of Mme de Simiane) remained in charge of foreign affairs, and Fouché of the police. The general enchanted everybody with his intelligence, his ease of manner, in which there were scarcely a hint of the patronizing, and with his eagerness to acquire knowledge. He knew nothing about the running of a state, but loved asking questions, and since he always directed the conversation, the gaps in his knowledge passed unnoticed. He advanced cautiously. The first proclamations of the new regime might almost have been drafted by La Fayette himself. A speech by Lucien Bonaparte: "Liberty was born in the tennis court at Versailles. Today it has assumed the toga of manhood." A proclamation by Napoleon Bonaparte: "Frenchmen, you will doubtless see in my conduct the zeal of a soldier fighting for liberty and of a citizen devoted to the Republic." Had La Fayette ridden into Paris on his white horse he would scarcely have spoken differently. He therefore learned with delight of the fall of the Directory. When the news reached Utrecht, the officers commanding the garrison gave as the day's password: "Liberty, Paris, La Fayette." "I am assured," Gilbert wrote to Van Ryssel, "that on the very day of the 18th Brumaire and at the most critical moment of that day it was Bonaparte's intention to demand my recall, and that on the 19th instructions were sent to his brother Joseph that I was to be made commandant-general of the National Guard." It is easy to believe what one wants to believe.

Adrienne, who was on the spot and had a clear head as well as informed friends, viewed the situation less optimistically. Of course the Consulate had begun with professions of liberalism; of course the confirmed Jacobins had gone to the ground; of course Bonaparte wanted to be seen as a moderating influence, one that would cancel the past, make the French unlearn the lessons of hate and drink of the waters of Lethe. But a counteroffensive by the Jacobins was still a possibility. Sieyès dreaded it and was frightened at night. Nor was that all. La Fayette's prestige might turn out to be embarrassing. His name was the only one that could compete with Bonaparte's in its power to fire the public imagination. Adrienne had seen the general and spoken with him. She had weighed his silences, and felt certain that if the question were put to him, he would refuse La Fayette a passport.

She was a woman who could, when necessary, make quick and daring decisions. Her husband must return *at once*, taking advantage of the liberal tendencies brought about by the change of regime. Now, when the principles of 1789 were being restated, no one would dare to arrest the man who had been the first to proclaim them. Later, danger would doubtless reappear. She obtained a passport in an assumed name, and got Alexandre Romeuf to take it to Utrecht with a message that if he were still thinking of setting out for France, he must make up his mind at once. Gilbert was certain that Adrienne could not be wrong: "It did not take me two minutes to see what I must do, and a couple of hours later I was on my way."

As soon as he reached Paris he went straight to his friend Adrien de Mun, the son of Mme de Tessé's old admirer, and in a mood of noble confidence wrote to two of the provisional consuls, Bonaparte and Sieyès. There was no point in bothering about the third, Roger-Duclos, whom Mme de Staël compared to a piece of rag put between two precious surfaces to keep them from being dented. Sieyès had every reason for treating La Fayette with tact. Before the 18th Brumaire, he had said of Bonaparte:

"I should like to know what is going on in that young man's head."

"He knows now," Benjamin Constant commented with a laugh.

What the young man with the waxen complexion had in his head was a determination to rule in solitary splendor. Consequently, Sieyès was pleased to think that in La Fayette he had a first-class ally. But to turn the occasion to account, the letter to Bonaparte should have been extremely diplomatic. In fact, it was dignified and imprudent: pure, undiluted La Fayette.

Citizen Consul, Since the days when the prisoners of Olmütz owed their liberty to you until now, when the liberty of my country is about to impose upon me even greater obligations to you, I have been thinking that any further extension of my exile can be beneficial neither to the government nor to me. I have this day arrived in Paris.

I am about to leave for a remote part of the country where I shall be united with my family. Before doing so, however, before even seeing my friends, I have not delayed a moment addressing myself to you, not that I doubt my place to be wherever the Republic rests upon worthy foundations, but because it is not only my duty but my wish to tell you in person of my gratitude.[3]

General Clarke, one of the plenipotentiaries who at Campo Formio had obtained the liberation of the prisoners of Olmütz, took it upon himself to deliver this missive to Bonaparte. He heard a fine outburst of temper. If La Fayette did not return immediately to Holland, said the Consul, then he must suffer the consequences of his folly. Talleyrand, who still had feelings of friendship for La Fayette, at once arranged a meeting with him, at which Regnault de Saint-Jean d'Angély was present.

Both of them [wrote La Fayette], after greeting me warmly, told me of the Consul's fury, warned me that it might be followed by violent measures, begged me not bring disaster on my friends for taking my part, and urged me to go back to Holland. I made them promise not to let themselves be compromised, but added that having judged it proper for me to come into France, it was now for the Consul Bonaparte to decide whether it would be proper in him to leave me unmolested, and that they ought to know me well enough to realize that a menacing and imperious tone was in itself sufficient to determine me to pursue further the line I had taken, and since their fruitless entreaties had lasted until after midnight, I remarked as I left them on foot with Louis Romeuf that it would be a fine thing if I were to be arrested by the National Guard of Paris and flung into the Temple prison next day by the man who had restored the principles of 1789.[4]

This was said with gentle irony, but it contained a veiled threat. Would the National Guard consent to arrest the man by whom they had been founded and from whom they had received their flag?

Next morning Gilbert was visited by another former friend, Roederer, the one-time public prosecutor of the Commune and now one of Bonaparte's intimates. Roederer also advised him to go back to Holland. La Fayette answered him as he had answered Talleyrand, adding that Adrienne would see Bonaparte. To Adrienne he always turned as a last resort. Bonaparte, who was prejudiced in favor of Mme de La Fayette, gave her a friendly welcome, referred merely to the annoyance he felt at what had happened, and explained that La Fayette's sudden appearance in France would prove a hindrance to him in his intention of re-establishing the principles for which her husband stood and might force him to shorten sail.

"I do not expect you to understand me, Madame," he said, "but General de La Fayette will understand me, and since he is no longer at the center of things will realize that I am in a better position to make a correct judgment than he is. Therefore I beg him to avoid anything in the nature of publicity. I rely upon his patriotism." [5]

Adrienne replied that it had always been her husband's wish to avoid publicity. She spoke with a nobility and a precision that much struck Bonaparte. Skillfully she pointed out the favorable reaction that La Fayette's return would produce in honest men and patriots.

"I am charmed," he replied, "at having seen you again. You are a very intelligent woman, but you know nothing of politics."

In fact, Adrienne's knowledge of politics was so extensive and so sound that she won her case. Bonaparte agreed that La Fayette should stay somewhere in France without having to ask leave to do so until such time as his proscription should be officially terminated.

The Consul then left Adrienne in order to go to the council, where he arrived in a thoroughly bad temper and told his colleagues about the visit he had had. Sieyès spoke up in defense of La Fayette, and pointed out that anything in the nature of persecution would have a very bad effect on the country. Meanwhile, Adrienne, who knew from experience how inflexible her husband could be when his pride was touched, made a point in reporting to him the outcome of her approach to Bonaparte of stressing the fact that the Consul had *advised* and not *ordered* his withdrawal from Paris. This made it possible for him to tell Roederer, who went to see him in the hope of putting an end to the quarrel, that he had *voluntarily* decided to go into the country. "I confined myself to saying that I was little disposed to take notice of Bonaparte's threats, but that I felt myself to be bound by his advice," wrote La Fayette. Honor was satisfied, and the family party set out for Fontenay-en-Brie, a château not far from La Grange and in a better state of repair. La Fayette would have preferred Auvergne and said so to Sieyès, but the government had raised certain objections which he explained in a letter to his aunt:

You will be surprised to learn that I am in France, my dear aunt, and I am still more so to find myself there without immediately setting off for Chavaniac. The news of the 18th Brumaire, and the promise of liberty and justice made by the leaders of the movement, one of whom is the generalissimo to whom I owe my liberation, seemed to me sufficient to bring me back to my country. No sooner had I arrived than I wrote to Bonaparte and Sieyès, telling them that it was my intention to pay an immediate visit to you. It seemed to me, however, only proper that my return should remain generally unknown and so might not provoke the effects to be expected of the malevolence of my enemies. It would have been impossible for me to turn up in our department without causing that very sensation I so much wished to avoid. It is not without feelings of regret, as the Citizen Vallette will explain to you, that I have decided to come here instead. I beg you to believe, dear aunt, that this is not what I had planned, that it is not my fault, and that if you were here you would think as I do.

As soon as it is possible, however, we shall all of us set off for Chavaniac. I have turned my back on politics. The idea of staying longer in Paris, stained as it is with the blood of my relatives and friends, was intolerable to me. I could not be induced to go back there except from a sense of patriotic duty, of which there can be no question since the Revolution is about to be terminated by a power with which I am not associated but which has at its disposal all the means necessary to the doing of much good. . . . I hope that my return will make as little sensation as possible, though without compelling me to resort to concealment. You would do well to address my letters to my wife.

We hope to see Anastasie, Charles, and their child here tomor-

row. Virginie has stayed behind in Paris in order to bring them to us. My stay on a property which forms part of the family inheritance, while far from consoling me for not being at Chavaniac, has at least this advantage: that it will enable me to exercise some degree of choice in this matter of our share. I am making an examination of Fontenay, La Grange, the farms, and the woodlands. Since our co-heirs are extremely obliging, I think we shall be able to have what suits us best.

Rejoice, dear aunt, until such time as I shall have the happiness of embracing you, in the thought that I am now in all probability settled once and for all in France, and that if after ten tormented years our country at long last is granted that liberty which we sought to achieve by honest means, although they were disfigured by so many atrocities, I shall be firmly established in my native land for the rest of my life. This is a huge house, but completely stripped of all furniture. It stands in the middle of a fine park and has a number of good farms. I am going tomorrow to La Grange which is in an even worse state of devastation, though from many points of view much more agreeable. . . .

[Postscript in Adrienne's hand] He is here, my dear aunt, and longing to be with you. Together we give thanks to God. He is far from wishing to become involved in public affairs, and looks for happiness only to family life. When shall we all be with you again? As soon as it is at all possible. Anastasie is not yet with us. Her daughter had an attack of toothache on the journey, which meant traveling by very short stages. Her brother, who was acting as rear guard, caught up with them on the road. Good-by, my very dear aunt. Your heart knows full well how closely and tenderly we are united with you.[6]

After so many setbacks, it looked as if a happier chapter was now to begin for Adrienne.

PART EIGHT

WORKS AND DEATH

I

THE SILENCE OF THE MASTER

What, at times, can one do with a good
man?   LA BRUYÈRE

Part of the Noailles inheritance consisted of two châteaux in Brie, Fontenay and La Grange. Fontenay was to go to the Montagus, La Grange, some thirty miles east of Paris, to the La Fayettes. La Grange, because more land went with it, was better suited to La Fayette's farming projects, and the medieval castle, a fine building with its court of honor, its entrance gate crowned with two towers above a drawbridge, its moat and its park, would provide ample space for the children, and later on for the grandchildren. In the seventeenth century the main block and one of the towers had been pulled down, with the happy result that the quadrilateral of the inner yard enjoyed plenty of light and looked out on to greenery. But a great deal would have to be done to make this empty and abandoned castle habitable.

Adrienne had started work on it some time before the arrival of her husband. With the help of their architect friend, Antoine Vaudoyer, who had so admirably transformed Chavaniac, she had drawn up preliminary plans. But the first thing to be done was to carry out alterations at Fontenay, where the family would have to stay while La Grange was being put to rights. The immediate need at La Grange was to get the roofs repaired to keep out the rain. That done, the next consideration would be a suite of rooms and a library for La Fayette, for which furniture would have to be provided. The farm could be rebuilt gradually, and—last of all—a bed-room prepared for Adrienne. And all this had to be done at a time when no money was available, when debts were mounting and little was to be hoped for in the way of credit. But the Rozoy con-tractors—Claude the carpenter, Devolz the painter-glazier, Viret the mason, Denis the tiler, and Martin the locksmith—were all prepared to wait for a settlement of their accounts.

Here are some of the earliest entries on Antoine Vaudoyer's cost sheets:

SUMMARY OF SUMS DUE TO CITIZEN VAUDOYER ARCHITECT TO THE DEPARTMENT OF PUBLIC WORKS

To traveling expenses, plans, drawings, professional fees, and money disbursed by him at the Château de La Grange, near Rozoy, for General La Fayette in the course of the years IX, X, and XI. As follows:

8TH PLUVIÔSE, YEAR VIII: *Left Paris for Fontenay, re-turned on the 11th. Madame de La Fayette paid for the first carriage: four days*   96 livres

8TH PRAIRIAL, YEAR VIII: *Left Paris with Monsieur Rob-ert for La Grange; returned 10th. Three days' absence*   72 livres

20TH BRUMAIRE, YEAR IX: *Left Paris with Citizen Rouet for La Grange; returned 23rd; four days' absence*   96 livres

Over-all plan for park   72 livres

Four plans for layout of rooms in the château   100 livres

Two drawings in color-wash for projected arrangement of the library   100 livres

Plan for the ceiling and cornices for Monsieur de La Fayette's bedroom   5 livres

Design for a chimney piece   6 livres

2ND PLUVIÔSE, YEAR IX. *Two designs for doors of said room*   9 livres

18TH PLUVIÔSE, YEAR XI: *Left Paris with Citizen Rouet for La Grange by diligence. Returned 20th with Mad-ame, Monsieur, and Mademoiselle Virginie*   72 livres [1]

The idea of having the park transformed by the painter Hubert Robert, who had designed the gardens of Méréville and Ermenon-ville, must certainly have come from La Fayette, a man of the *avant-garde* in all things. He had not forgotten how in 1790 he had admired in some exhibition a picture of the storming of the Bastille, and had exclaimed: "Fortunate the man who is going to possess that picture!" A voice behind him had said: "General, it is yours." The voice had been that of the painter.

Hubert Robert gave sinuous curves to the avenues of the park, draped the arches of the drawbridge with ivy, and planted clumps of ilex, American ash, larches, and catalpa trees. Under his hands the park became symbolic.

The financial situation of the family remained precarious. The most pressing debts (those to Gouverneur Morris, John Parish, and others) amounted altogether to 200,000 livres. Gilbert calculated that after the distribution of the inheritance had been completed, the farm would perhaps bring in some 10,000 livres a year, plus 5000 if the value of the timber were taken into account. This was very far from the immense fortune of the old days, but they were so happy to be alive and reunited with a roof over their heads that they saw no reason to deplore their relative poverty. Chavaniac, which had been brought back by his aunt, would ultimately revert to La Fayette or his children. The estates in Brittany and Touraine which he had inherited from the La Rivières had in part been sold as national property. He would have to go there to find out whether he could recover the money they had brought. He was prepared to cede the Cayenne plantation to the state, which had already occupied it. In this way he would obtain liquid assets which he could then use for buying back his Breton lands and for the improvements at La Grange.

Adrienne took charge of all this immense labor of readjustment. She alone was capable of giving to it the necessary continuity and precision. There were also endless matters in Paris which awaited her attention. Gilbert having sworn not to show himself in the capital, it fell to Adrienne to take his place and to act for him. There was no end to what she had to do: conclude the settlement of the succession, arrange for La Fayette and his companions (La Tour-Maubourg, Bureaux de Pusy, and all the officers who had followed him in 1792) to be struck off the list of *émigrés*, and then undertake the same task for the Montagus, the Tessés, and the Duc de Noailles. Then there was the problem of getting a commission in the army for George. Months of applications and interviews were involved. For two winters (1799–1800) Adrienne made the round of the ministries, dragging her bad leg. Nor was there any rest for her in Brie. Never had so sick a woman worked so hard.

In Paris the reorganization of the country was making good headway. Sieyès had given birth to so absurdly complicated a constitution that Bonaparte, who was all for simplification, rejected it out of hand. "What, Sieyès profound?" said Talleyrand. "Do you not mean hollow?" The abbé realized that his role on the political stage was now at an end, and agreed to retire on a pension of 100,-000 écus. Bonaparte was First Consul, with all the executive power and the initiative in legislation in his hands. Cambacérès having been chosen as Second Consul, it was necessary to find a third.

Bonaparte asked Roederer: "Do you know Lebrun?" Lebrun was a man of letters, a fairly efficient financier, and a well-spoken conservative.

"Very well," replied Roederer. "He is a man of outstanding talents."

"Have his books sent to me," said Bonaparte. "I want to get the feel of his style."

It is no bad way of judging a man. Lebrun's style met with approval, and he became Third Consul. On December 15 the new constitution was proclaimed in the streets of Paris. One woman said to her sister:

"I did not understand a thing."

"I did not miss a word," replied her sister.

"Well then, tell me what there is in this constitution?"

"Bonaparte."

She spoke truly, and France wanted nothing more. A plebiscite approved the new regime. Gilbert, still deprived of his rights, did not have a vote. This was fortunate for him, since he would certainly have voted no, because he did not consider that the essential liberties were sufficiently safeguarded. The two assemblies (Senate and Tribunate), which were not elected but appointed by the government, were in Gilbert's opinion neither representative nor democratic. Authority came from above, confidence from below. There was scarcely any opposition. The royalists swarmed and made a great agitation, but in vain. The workers of the industrial suburbs said: "Neither Capet nor Orléans. Long live the Republic!" Was the Consulate the Republic? Benjamin Constant in a violent speech denounced "the dawn of tyranny." Next day Mme de Staël's *salon* emptied rapidly. Bonaparte, however, let a considerable time go by without reacting.

He dealt with La Fayette by ignoring him. After Washington died on December 14, 1799, the First Consul gave orders that there should be a memorial service at the Invalides. Fontanes, on whom fell the duty of delivering the oration on that occasion, spoke as much about the heroes of Egypt as about the hero of the United States. La Fayette and his wife were not even invited. Their son was present as an ordinary spectator, and the sight of him appeared to cause a good deal of annoyance. Next day the First Consul settled into the Tuileries.

"What a gloomy place this is," Roederer said to him.

"Yes, as gloomy as grandeur," replied Bonaparte. Then, to Bourrienne: "It is not getting into the Tuileries that matters: it is staying there."

In order to do that he had to handle some difficult problems. What with the expropriated clamoring for permission to return, and the glutted dreading their reappearance on the scene, Bonaparte had, in his own words, "to take each day as it came."

From Fontenay Adrienne, overwhelmed with business worries, received a great variety of contradictory instructions. Her husband had complete confidence in her ability to get names removed from the *émigrés* list, but it was a point of honor with him that his own should not have priority over those of his companions in misfortune. At the same time he did not wish the prisoners of Olmütz, who were good patriots, to be included indiscriminately in a batch of repentant *émigrés*. For those who could not be reinstated at once Adrienne must demand a *surveillance*.

As soon as the thing is done [Gilbert wrote] *I shall go and see Bonaparte, or if I am not yet thought to be a welcome visitor I shall write to thank him. In any case he will have a note from me, asking for the reinstatement in their full rights as citizens of the victims of August Tenth, of the companions who went with me when I left France, and especially of Alexandre Lameth. I shall include the two sentences I showed you.*

I shall send the few lines of which you approved, not addressed to the consuls, but precisely as you saw and praised them.

Let me end by confirming your full powers to act for me. You

are on the spot and in a better position than I am to judge. I have
complete confidence in you. These letters of mine should be regarded as mere memoranda, and you must not feel yourself bound
by them in any way. I embrace Virginie, George, and you with a
full heart.[2]

Gilbert was indignant when friends for whom his wife was
literally working herself to death had the effrontery to complain:

I send with this [letter], but for your eyes alone, my dear Adrienne,
a strange letter from Maubourg. You will see from it that even the
best of hearts is not safe from the vagaries of a bad head. This injustice grieves and hurts me. You will see that I have answered it with
restraint. Seal it and put it in the post, or better still, enclose it in
a letter from Passy.

This unexpected lesson should be for us a further proof that no
matter how good one's intentions, one has to be careful even with
one's best friends. It never occurred to me that I should have to
point out to Maubourg or even to his wife that it was not my wish
to do the best I could for myself (as he puts it) in this business,
but I realize now that with him, as with everybody else, one has to
dot one's i's and cross one's t's when it comes to explaining one's
intentions.

Nothing is more dangerous than to do a service: nothing more
difficult than to accept one. Most people think that they can discharge one debt by running up another.

I am delighted about the two surveillances which you have managed to obtain, my dear Adrienne [Gilbert's letter continued].
You did not expect any more than I did that you would get credit
for what you have done. . . . Let me repeat my earlier advice even
more earnestly. . . . There are things that cannot be said outright,
but which can be hinted at in a letter. What you have done, the
official protection which is so necessary, my own personal influence
and that of those close to me are facts and it is high time that those
at Witmold should realize it. . . . I hope no less than you do that
you will be able to settle this affair of your father's. When the
worry and fatigue are things of the past, what you have now done
will be happy memories for you. . . .

You will have seen from what I said in my letter of yesterday
that I am far from satisfied with the reception, or rather the non-

reception, which has been accorded you by Bonaparte. All the same, do not be angry with yourself for having written asking him for an interview. The general opinion is that you are the only person who can dare speak bluntly to him. Our friends and companions are as concerned as we are ourselves that he should be shown the proper way to behave and not give way to temper. I think it a very good thing that Joseph should have had a talk with him on this subject. Regnault must keep as keen an eye on the drafting as he would on a saucepan of boiling milk. It is very possible that in this whole affair Bonaparte has been clumsy rather than malicious, and that had he attended to it personally, everything would have gone right for us. . . .

Madame de Cirey * is still delaying her arrival. . . . And when, dear Adrienne, are you going to come back? Could it not be when your father's business is settled? Even if you had only two free days, might you not spend them with me? Or even one day? . . . Vaugeois could pick you up in Paris or at Tournan. I desperately want to see you again, and find your absence insupportably long.[3]

Gilbert had a great wish to pay a visit to Paris, "if only for a pair of boots and a wig," and also to see the American negotiators who had just arrived. But he dared not venture on such a trip until he had been granted at least a *surveillance*. Virginie, chaperoned by her mother, had made her first appearance in "the great world." Gilbert knew that the event had gone off very well, and would have much liked to see her triumph with his own eyes. "The First Consul is certainly in no hurry," he commented gloomily. He would have felt happier if his friend Regnault de Saint-Jean-d'Angély had actually issued the list of those it had been decided to reinstate in their civil rights.

If only they would make a temporary announcement [he wrote Adrienne] if they don't want to be more precise at the moment, to the effect that reinstatement would be granted to "La Fayette, La Tour-Maurbourg, and to the officers who, by the terms of their service, were obliged to follow their general, La Fayette, and were all taken prisoner on the same day". . . and then publish the full list of names later, or include them in this first statement without any mention of their general, if that is what they are boggling at.[4]

* Mme de Simiane, the lady of the manor of Cirey-sur-Blaise.

Gilbert was prepared to agree to any compromise, provided his honor was not involved.

Meanwhile, the work at La Grange was going ahead rapidly, and he wrote to Adrienne:

Monsieur Vaudoyer, Monsieur d'Ouvry, and I are all quite certain that in a week from today we shall have rooms for everybody at La Grange, and two more, which makes a total of three, since Virginie will share with you. A further two rooms will be ready ten days later. But shall we have furniture for them in a week's time? Monsieur Vaudoyer tells me that it is to be had at the Hôtel de Guerre at all prices, some of them quite cheap, and that if you have time and money to spare he will go there with you tomorrow between eight and ten—but I fear there may be doubt on both scores.[5]

Money was a greater problem than time. Gilbert had gone into residence at La Grange as soon as his own suite of rooms was ready. He had appointed as a farm manager his young friend Félix Pontonnier, the faithful companion of the Olmütz days. He asked his neighbors for advice. Vaudoyer built him a number of model cow sheds and sheep pens. He aimed at breeding in a few years' time two hundred sheep, fifty cows, and a hundred fifty pigs. Among the sheep were several fine Merinos from Rambouillet. He imported special breeds of pig from America and even from China. He was the first person in Brie to sow a crop of alfalfa.

But experiments in agriculture cost money, and La Fayette the farmer showed himself to be as prodigal as La Fayette the rebel. In the country, as in town, he liked to shine, even if his purse suffered. As soon as La Grange was in a fit state, he began to entertain on a big scale. "I am all alone here in my fields," he wrote to Masclet, "where I pass my time very pleasantly, keeping four plows fully employed, and providing an admirable example of that much-discussed individual, the gentleman-farmer." In short, he was thoroughly enjoying his new role of Cincinnatus.

In Paris, the wife of Cincinnatus was doing her best to get the lawyers moving. But they were no more to be hurried than was the First Consul. She had also been busying herself, since the reform of the administration, in an attempt to get some of their friends appointed to the posts of prefect and subprefect. There was some hope that Louis Romeuf might be given a prefecture, and Frestel, George's old tutor, a subprefecture.

As to her father, the Duc de Noailles, who was still in Switzerland, there was a rumor, so Adrienne wrote to the Chavaniac aunt, that the lady with whom he had thrown in his lot and whose presence under his roof had caused his daughter so much pain was dead.

She was a great obstacle to our looking after him as we wished to do, but I think that now he will accept our attentions with all his customary sweetness. You must admit, dear aunt, that here again the finger of Providence is clearly visible.[6]

But the rumor was false, and the second duchesse turned out to be in excellent health.

At last, in March, 1800, the publication of the list of those former *émigrés* who might hope to be reinstated seemed to be imminent. Adrienne was already suggesting to her husband that he should come to Paris, to which he replied:

I am of the opinion that as I have not been back there since the arrival of the American commissioners, I ought not to show my face in Paris before the list appears. I should even prefer not to do so immediately after it has been made public. But the interests of my companions, the presence of the United States ministers, the wish to see a few friends and my impatience to read Ségur's manuscript may induce me to put in an appearance not too long after the consular decision. If Bonaparte leaves Paris on the sixteenth it would be difficult for me to call upon him, and the marked lack of eagerness he has shown in all this business fully justifies my delay in paying my respects. It will be three or four days before I know whether my name has been taken off the list, and it might be well if I waited another six or seven before going to Paris. Bonaparte will not be there, and several of the persons whom I have to see will also have left, which will simplify my program of visits. Still, I am very willing to take advice and do not think that a few days more or less are of any great importance. What I do feel very positively, my dear Adrienne, is that in our present state of uncertainty about the list it would be a great mistake for you to stay on in Paris, waiting for news. It would be very much better for us to go back there together.[7]

The Marquis and Marquise de Montagu had left for France on February 19. Since they were still on the black list, they traveled under a borrowed name: M. Mongros, merchant and wife. The French officials who stamped their false passports recognized them but said nothing. On their arrival in Paris, they betook themselves to a furnished house in the Rue de Courty, belonging to a former servant of Mme de Thésan. The Duchesse de Doudeauville and the Duchesse de Duras occupied two poor attic rooms there, the only luxury of which was cleanliness. When these ladies had a visitor, they borrowed a chair from one of their neighbors on the same floor.

The sensitive Pauline suffered more than her sister Adrienne from the spectacle of Paris in its new dress. The "Rue Honoré" shocked her, as did the faded red caps stuck on shabby flagstaffs. They made a pilgrimage of mourning to the "Noailles" prison, then went to spend a few days at La Grange. "The people there," wrote Madame de Montagu, "thought they had firm ground under their feet, but I walked carefully, as though on shifting sand." She found Adrienne absorbed in worldly matters. She was less of a "contemplative" than either Rosalie or Pauline, but her trust in God was more childlike and more complete. She helped herself and knew that Heaven would help her. She wanted to go to Brittany to look after her husband's estates, but the war of the Chouans was not yet over, though the end was in sight. She did a good deal of walking in the Paris streets, and, rubbing shoulders with people of every class, soon realized that in Bonaparte the French had the government they wanted. There was once again an air of pride about the city, and fear had vanished. Though Adrienne might have a few personal grievances against him, she respected the First Consul and was sincerely anxious that he should succeed.

On March 1, 1800, Bonaparte, by a stroke of the pen, reinstated in their civil and political rights all those émigrés who on the night of August 4, 1789, had voted for the abolition of privileges. This condition applied to La Fayette, but not to his companions. This was precisely what Gilbert had wanted to avoid. He wrote at once to Fouché, the Minister of Police, who, with a wary eye on the unpredictable future, showed friendliness toward him and proved it by contriving to have the names of his companions of August 19 removed from the black list at the same time as his own. The nightmare was at last dispelled. La Tour-Maubourg, his peace of mind restored, at once found employment in the Hôtel de Ville at Neuilly as a first step to a seat in the Senate. George de La

Fayette was given a second lieutenant's commission in the hussars.

It looked as though Bonaparte had laid aside his prejudice against the followers of La Fayette. One day, when a Jacobin general attacked the Hero of Two Worlds in his presence, he immediately retorted: "It is all very fine talking like that, but never forget that nobody is more hated by the enemies of liberty and of France. I, who arranged his release, know better than any one the importance attached by the powers arrayed against us to keeping him in prison." [8]

Gilbert was unable to thank the First Consul in person after his reinstatement, since Bonaparte left on May 6 for Italy to take command of the army, which was again in danger from the Austrians. La Fayette sincerely admired what he called the finest act of Bonaparte's career: his leaving the position of supreme power, into which he had only just hoisted himself, to cross the Alps and win battles for the French people. What he did not know was that Joseph Bonaparte, not unnaturally perturbed at seeing the man on whom the security of France depended exposed to the dangers of war, had had a long talk with Roederer about a possible successor should the worst happen. Though he, Joseph, was the heir presumptive and, like all the Bonapartes, believed himself capable of filling any position, he was far from anxious to be saddled with so difficult an inheritance, at least for the time being. He realized that to the country at large he was almost completely unknown. "There are only two possible men," he said, "Carnot and La Fayette." The farmer of La Grange had not been entirely forgotten.

Adrienne was not greatly upset by George's departure for Italy. She knew that her son asked for nothing better. She wrote to him:

Those, my dear boy, who love one another make a pact to look at the moon at the same moment. Let us rather look to Heaven. Be with your mother in spirit morning and evening, and on Sunday at the hour of the Mass, whether or no you attend it.[9]

On his way over the Simplon Pass, George-Washington La Fayette visited Coppet, where he delivered a letter from his father to Necker, who replied:

Imagine my emotion, Monsieur, when I saw the son of La Fayette enter my house and received from him a letter from you. This communication, which has recalled to my mind so many others, both

of historical and personal importance, this letter which has stirred
the memory of your misfortunes and your courage, has touched
me deeply. This son of yours seems to me to be worthy of you.
There is in him simplicity and a modest pride in the name he bears.
I pray that he may emerge with safety from the dangers of his new
employment, and that he may be a constant source of happiness to
you and to his incomparable mother.[10]

June 14 was the victorious day of Marengo. Adrienne congratulated her son "with all the tenderness which is the consolation and
the pain of my every moment, and will be until we have peace. . . .
The prodigious successes of Bp [sic] lead everybody to hope that
it will come soon." To her Chavaniac aunt, who not unnaturally
had no love for the First Consul ("Another of these upstarts who
have risen from nothing!"), she wrote: "A truce has been signed
in Italy, and peace will follow. This war is being fought not for
conquest but for peace."

The return to Paris of the army and its leader was a triumph.
George brought back with him an engraving of General Bonaparte
in the red uniform which he had worn at Lodi. Adrienne hung it
in her bedroom next to that, now famous, of the "Prisoners of
Olmütz."

During the absence of the First Consul, Adrienne and her
sister Pauline had been received in audience by Lebrun, the Third
Consul, who had known them in the days of the Old Regime. He
gave evening receptions at the Pavillon de Flore, and had managed
to have assigned to him as his official residence the Hôtel de
Noailles in the Rue Honoré. Having deprived the family of its
ancestral home, the least he could do was to smile upon its members. When Bonaparte returned, Lebrun took it upon himself to
present La Fayette and his companions to him.

La Tour and I were presented to him at the Tuileries [Gilbert
wrote] by the Consul Lebrun. Bonaparte came to meet us in the
most amiable manner, and I was reminded of the first time that
I had been received by Frederick the Great. After the first mutual
compliments had been exchanged, he replied to our congratulations
on his Italian victories: "But the Austrians are still resentful: it is
Moreau who will make the peace. I do not know what the devil you
did to them," he added very charmingly, "but they made a great
pother about letting you go!" We associated Bureaux de Pusy

with our expressions of thanks. "He will come back," he said, "and so will Dupont [de Nemours]. Sooner or later they all come back to the banks of the Seine. . . ." I appreciated our reception all the more because of the effect it had on some of the state councilors, who were already busy watching the master's face from a distance.[11]

The little furnished establishment in the Rue de Courty was certainly not short of custom. When Mme de Tessé turned up in June with her immense caravan, there was not a room to be had. She rented a house in the Rue d'Anjou, and the Montagus installed themselves opposite. Mme de Tessé had some difficulty in getting a *surveillance*. Her husband was accused of having indulged in some bitter mockery at the expense of the government. Considering that the poor man had not opened his lips for twenty years, this was hard on him, and La Fayette wrote to Adrienne—for husband and wife were once more separated and had to communicate by letter— "It shows that they don't know much about your uncle."

Adrienne, with her aide-de-camp Virginie in tow, had left for Brittany, where she wanted to see the former agent and to recover some of the farm rents. La Fayette had set off for Auvergne: he was in a hurry to visit his aunt and to deal with a number of political matters. Now that he was reinstated, it was hoped in government circles to gain his support, and the new regime was busy throwing itself at his head. He was offered a seat in the general council of Haute-Loire until such time as he should be made a member of the Senate. But he was more intent on integrity than authority and refused all such appointments. At Le Puy he wanted to see the places in which Adrienne had been imprisoned, and to thank all those who had been kind to her. The terrorists who had treated her so badly were careful to stay out of sight so long as her husband remained in the town. To the royalist dowagers, who were still very touchy, "one more yellow than an old lemon, another blacker than a mole," Gilbert behaved with calculated politeness, which so dazzled them that they repaid him in his own coin.

GILBERT TO ADRIENNE: JULY 24, 1800

The prefect gave a superb dinner to which all the local officials were invited. . . . My toast was to the memory of the martyrs who had perished in the cause of true liberty. . . . I was very pleased with the prefect's attitude to freedom of worship. He complains that there are some priests who try to persuade their penitents not to have themselves entered in the civil registers, and several of our local ones have told me that many of their confreres in other cantons are taking this purely personal line, which they themselves condemn. I know nothing more blameworthy than this sort of intrigue which has no official blessing and causes a deal of suffering to a number of poor unfortunate people. It only needs a polite word from the Pope to Bonaparte to put all right. These country curés are no more enlightened now than they used to be, but they are a great deal more moderate, and certainly better-intentioned than in 1792. Their anxiety touches me because today a great number of them are sincere.[12]

In Brittany, Adrienne was working to good effect; but it was not a very safe place, for brigands were holding up the public coaches.

GILBERT TO ADRIENNE: AUGUST 1ST, 1800

Well, my dear Adrienne, so you have stolen a march on George so far as seeing the enemy is concerned! I congratulate Virginie on having been under fire before the second lieutenant of hussars! I congratulate both of you on the prospects of peace, which seems ever more likely. It was not without reason, dear Adrienne, that I disliked the idea of your driving round Brittany in a public conveyance. I know how gallant you and Virginie are, but though the brigands have eyes only for the moneybags and have laid it down that "the travelers are not to be touched," I should prefer that the two travelers in whom I happen to be interested should take precautions to avoid such encounters. I have not concealed what you tell me from my aunt, who would probably in any case have read of your adventure in the news sheets. She is not in the least frightened by it, but joins with me in urging you not to expose yourselves to the risk of running into an ambush. Look after your health and your persons, and remember that the feelings one inspires in others involve a duty just as much as those one experiences. . . .

Did you know that Madame de Tessé, Madame d'Hénin, and Madame de Simiane plan to spend the month of October at La Grange? . . . You are wrong, dear Adrienne, in being opposed to having the downstairs rooms whitewashed. This small expense will make a scarcely perceptible showing in the general settlement of the succession.[13]

Gilbert was also taking an interest in the restoration work at Chavaniac:

I have had the busts put in the great hall. My aunt has hopes of being able to recover the salon hangings. We shall have to arrange for a chimney piece and a mirror for it. I shall leave a few books and engravings here. My aunt approves the removal of the others, as well as of the table which cannot be repaired except in Paris. I have not dared mention the piano. The cost of moving it to La Grange is not so great as you thought it would be.[14]

It seemed possible that Aunt Charlotte's health was beginning to fail:

AUGUST 14, 1800

You know, dear Adrienne, how struck I had been by my aunt's good health. Except for a slight trembling of the head, she was no different from what she was when I left her. She finds the excessive heat and dryness exhausting, but it was not until [Sunday, August 10] —an ill-omened day—that she felt seriously inconvenienced. She took some rather too thick chocolate, I am told, as soon as she left her bed. She did not complain at all before the time of High Mass, to which she went under a blazing sun, but stayed at church in the stifling heat and returned home in similar conditions. There were a great many people here. . . . My aunt left the table, thinking she had a migraine, but returned later and spent a long time with the company, trying—as she admitted to me later—to put as good a face as possible on her indisposition. She felt drowsy and went early to bed. Next morning we still thought that the headache and fever of which she complained were nothing worse than the after-effects of the migraine, but the fever increased, and the drowsiness which accompanied it was so alarming that we sent for Doctor Pissis. I will keep you informed by every post, that is, every other day.[15]

Aunt Charlotte recovered. The prefect and the general dined at Chavaniac. The priests did not put in an appearance, being afraid that they might be asked to give certain guarantees. Adrienne recovered a number of old debts with the skill of an experienced lawyer. Several potential purchasers turned up, quite honestly prepared to close a deal. She was already hoping to carve out two properties in Brittany for Anastasie and Virginie. She also promised to provide funds for equipping the farm at La Grange.

She was corresponding with the admirable Beauchets even more frequently than with her husband.

ADRIENNE TO NICOLAS BEAUCHET

*I spend almost all my days, dear citizen, much as you do in your office during working hours * and it is absolutely necessary that I should. My consolation comes from knowing that I can at last send money for the creditors. This time it is 4800 livres. I shall be sending you very soon the 2200 about which I have already told Madame de Chavaniac. I beg that you will let Monsieur de La Fayette know (I have not had time to write to him) that the need of funds for the repair work at La Grange is ever present to my mind, and that I am doing all I can. If you only knew what it means to squeeze the 61,200 livres which I have already passed on to you from a lot of peasants, not one of whom has a coat to his back that is not patched, you would realize what good reason I have for being discouraged, yet it is only from them that I can get any money at all.*[16]

To Anastasie, Virginie reported:

GUINGAMP, AUGUST, 1800

This business of the Félix family is another blow! But what, my dearest sister, can we do? We can not turn them into the street. We owe everything to the son, and the old father has a right to expect that we will look after him as a former servant of our old parents.... In three days' time we are going to Saint-Brieuc. Mamma is worn out.

SAINT-BRIEUC

Papa has written to us from Chavaniac.... We waited for the public coach from seven in the morning till six in the evening. We had as traveling companion an ailing woman, who fetched her breath so hard that we were afraid she was going to vomit. We ended by having a breakdown and were compelled to flounder through mud and rain for a whole league. Before we leave this place Mamma will have to get payments from a number of peasants, and also come to an agreement with a purchaser.[17]

Adrienne had had a letter from Mme de Simiane who, Virginie wrote,

* A civil servant of high repute, Beauchet was about to be appointed head clerk at the Ministry of Finance.

imagining that Mamma is very rich as a result of this journey, asks her for a loan of at least four or six thousand livres; and a second letter in which she seems almost annoyed at what she said in the first one, and says that the amount she needs is ten thousand. She wants this to be a private arrangement between Mamma and her, and that no one else shall know of it. This sum will enable her to satisfy the most pressing of her creditors, and she expects to be able to pay it back next year, in quarterly installments. Mamma has replied that she will send her four thousand livres before September 10, that she will give her in person another two thousand, and will complete the ten thousand if the objects she has put up for sale find purchasers.

Virginie begged Anastasie to keep all this strictly to herself:

Spare Mamma the distress of thinking that she has written anything that might be unpleasing to Madame de Simiane.[18]

One can detect a barely perceptible note of bitterness. To love Mme de Simiane was a duty, and easy enough since she was charming, but to keep her in funds was becoming a heavy burden.

Then, since there were certain La Rivière assets and some debts to be recovered in Touraine, Adrienne and her younger daughter settled down for a while at Chenonceaux. Her husband wrote to her there that he hoped, after leaving Chavaniac, to meet her somewhere between Orléans and Amboise. He rather timidly pleaded not guilty to certain errors which this strict and impeccable woman of business thought he had committed in Auvergne. He admitted that he had not accomplished much, but:

at least I have not done any harm, and you can be as completely reassured in this matter of mishandling of which you accuse me as I am satisfied with all the good you have done since we parted. . . .

There, my dear Adrienne, you have a rough summary, which at a glance does not seem very brilliant. What you have done is a great deal more satisfactory, though it scarcely justifies the high hopes which our friends have based on it. But if only our debts were paid we could be content with very little, always provided that each of our children has a nice little assured portion. I am waiting, before embarking on any speculations (as you wish me to do) until I have heard your full rendering of accounts, and I will do no more here *than say how contented I am with what little I know. But you must be very tired, my dear, wonderful Adrienne. I want, above all else, that you should have a real rest, and am impatient to embrace you.*

We must have a good talk as soon as we meet about domestic arrangements. I can see you coming to an arrangement with Charlotte; I much regret Garret. We shall have to find a cook who is a good hand at fricassees. Charlotte will look after the household expenses. But will she be a good maid? I insist on you and Virginie being well looked after. Félix or Antoine can do the serving at table. With a good scrubbing-woman, the keeper Mariette and his wife, and your nurse, it seems to me the house will be passably well looked after. Everything, dear Adrienne, will be all right when we are together.[19]

When Gilbert left Chavaniac he traveled by way of Brioude, "the town where you suffered so much with sweetness and nobility, my dear Adrienne." He thanked those who had behaved well to his wife, abused the others, and reported his departure thus:

At last, having embraced all and sundry according to custom, I climbed into my little gray trap, only too glad to say good-by to the squalid walls of Brioude. You had not told me how arrogant and impertinent the local ladies were when you arrived there. I can only suppose it was because you demanded that women and men should not be put to sleep in the same room; in any case I did not feel it my duty to handle the self-esteem of the inhabitants with kid gloves. Poor Grenier, who has been more than kind in all our affairs, is terribly embarrassed when I speak about his town, its people, and your stay among them.[20]

II

FLIRTATION

I have a liking for Bonaparte.

LA FAYETTE

From 1800 to 1802 Bonaparte was busy garnering his harvest of victories. In 1801 the Peace of Lunéville gave the left bank of the Rhine to France; in 1802 came the Peace of Amiens with England.

In October, 1800, Adrienne rejoiced to see her son emerge unscathed from the storm that had muttered around his head. For her these years of France's rebirth were years of hard work. Gilbert went in comfort from La Grange to Aulnay, with all his women round him, while his patient wife roamed the roads of Brittany and Touraine or haunted the antechambers of the ministries.

One day in October, having gone to Paris to see his father-in-law, newly arrived from Switzerland with his wife, Gilbert paid a visit to his old friend Talleyrand. The minister came out of his study with a man who bore a striking resemblance to the First Consul. It was Joseph Bonaparte. Always good-natured and confident, he greeted La Fayette warmly, expressed great satisfaction at the meeting, and begged him to be present at a reception he was giving at his Château of Mortefontaine to mark the signing of the treaty of reconciliation between France and the United States.

Joseph Bonaparte did the honors to perfection [Gilbert wrote]. I found the occasion interesting for more than one reason. Everything about it recalled to my mind the days of my youthful suc-

cesses. *There were present the American commissioners, several of my French colleagues, many generals, the Bonaparte family, and the First Consul, with whom for two days I had an opportunity of talking a great deal. One of the first things he said to me was that I must have "found the French looking very coldly upon liberty." "Yes," I replied, "but they are in a condition to receive it." "They are thoroughly disgusted," he said. "Your Parisians, for example. The shopkeepers want no more of it." I repeated what I had said, and added: "I did not use those words lightly, General. I am well aware of the crimes and follies which have profaned the name of liberty; but the French are perhaps more than ever in a condition to receive it. It is for you to give it to them; it is from you that they expect it."* [1]

Gilbert was determined from the moment of his first unfettered conversation with Bonaparte to make profession of his faith. He was struck by the simplicity which went hand in hand with the man's genius, by the depth of his intelligence, by the wisdom that showed in his face. The First Consul, wishing to please this rebel, tried to bring the talk around to his campaigns in America, but La Fayette said modestly: "In them, matters of the greatest importance to the world at large were decided by the encounters of patrols." Then he in turn spoke about the idea put forward by several Americans of instituting the system of a life presidency in their country, and added that, given a suitable national representation, it might be a good form of government for France. Bonaparte became very attentive, and his eyes gleamed.

This account of the meeting of La Fayette and Bonaparte is taken from a confidential letter Gilbert wrote to General Van Ryssel, whose daughter had married Victor de La Tour-Maubourg. The talks the prisoner of Saint Helena had later with General Bertrand paint a rather different picture. "La Fayette certainly did not pay court to me," Napoleon said, "but he did so with a good deal of determination to Prince Joseph. He was always hanging about his antechamber. *I saw him only once,* when he wanted certain properties to which he laid claim—in Cayenne, I think— returned to him." But Napoleon may quite well have forgotten a few conversations which for him, busied as he was with so many great affairs, could not have been of the first importance.

Gilbert wrote to his aunt of this meeting:

Your little news sheet will no doubt have informed you of the American peace and the reception given by Joseph Bonaparte for the American ministers. I spent two very agreeable days in the country. The First Consul was there with all his family. The ministers of the United States have now left, delighted with all that was done for them. You may judge that I was no less so, on account of harmony having been restored between our two nations and of the government's having adopted the best means of making itself beloved and respected across the Atlantic. I took advantage of the kindness shown me by Bonaparte to say a few words to him about Monsieur and Madame de Tessé. From the way in which he received my request I have good reason to hope that their reinstatement will not be long delayed.[2]

Bonaparte, the realist, tried hard to win La Fayette over. At a later date Gilbert said: "I would willingly have accepted a place in the Senate under a tolerable regime." But he would not, even tacitly, adhere to institutions of which he disapproved. "My withdrawal from affairs of state gave me something like the right of an elder statesman to speak my mind, and to be in some degree a beacon light of liberty. I did all I could, however, to encourage my friends to perform the useful duty of playing a part in the functions of government." In other words, La Fayette wanted to say: "You who are just ordinary citizens should serve the regime. I, who am a symbol, must stand aside in splendid isolation."

Talleyrand urged him as a friend to accept at least the post of French ambassador to the United States. To this he replied that he was too much of an American to play the part of a foreigner, and that not to consider him as a farmer concerned only with his farming was to run counter to his wishes. His friend General Mathieu Dumas paid him a visit and pointed out that all these refusals were having an irritating effect on Bonaparte. Gilbert replied that silent retirement was the maximum proof he was prepared to give of his respect. This was a policy perhaps more satisfying to his pride than to France.

Adrienne, a counselor to whom he always listened, strongly supported this attitude. She knew that if he became involved in public affairs his oversensitive conception of honor would inevitably give rise to fresh dramas. La Grange was for him a place of rest and refreshment. He did not lack companionship. Mme de

Simiane and the Princesse d'Hénin frequently stayed there. George spent a period of convalescence there after having been wounded at the crossing of the Mincio, and Bonaparte, meeting at La Fayette at one of Josephine's receptions, said in the friendliest way: "An admirable debut indeed for this young man of yours. Allow me to rejoice with you."

Of this wound Virginie noted: "Papa, I think, has seldom been so proud and happy." George, like his father, had been blooded in his first engagement.

And now arose the matter of a husband for Virginie. For a moment Adrienne thought that she had found an excellent match for her in one of the Dampierre boys, but his parents considered that the marriage settlement was too uncertain, and also that their son was not sufficiently eager. This was a pity. Gilbert thought his daughter a charmer:

Let me tell you that I spent two hours this morning at Madame de Simiane's listening to her giving an account of Simple Histoire, and rarely if ever have I been better pleased by anything. Her gifts of intelligence and feeling, and her memory which had made it possible for her to absorb the content of those two volumes and to communicate it in such a way as to delight us, were truly remarkable. Her audience was enchanted.[3]

In December, 1800, Adrienne went back to Paris, where she stayed with Mme de Tessé in the Rue d'Anjou, kept at a distance from La Grange by the innumerable commissions laid upon her by her family. The Duc de Noailles was so relentlessly applying the spur to her in the matter of his reinstatement that La Fayette was exasperated beyond all bearing, and wrote to her:

It is my constant thought that the steps urged on you by your family in this business of your father are superfluous, unseemly, and likely to destroy in advance such results as you may be likely to obtain when the time seems ripe to you. I see your being established in Paris in the same light, and am inclined to think that the only effect of the mission entrusted to you will be to make it impossible for you to bring any useful influence to bear, even in the porters' lodges and the antechambers of the great! I may be wrong about this, but up till now you have been placed in a false position. You have married a man whose role it is to live in retirement with his family, and it is unbecoming that his wife should appear to be intriguing in Paris while he plays the philosopher at La Grange. . . .

If you could really be of service to your father, I would gladly sacrifice my own feelings to that duty and would do all this trotting round myself. . . . Knowing that he has in Paris two daughters, two sons-in-law, a brother-in-law and, unfortunately, a wife. . . . I should feel no very great anxiety at your waiting here until the right moment comes for making . . . those visits about whose timeliness those eight persons could surely keep you informed.

You will, I think, agree that by exposing yourself to the ignominiousness of thrice being turned away from Bonaparte's door in an attempt to get something which it is only too obvious that he has no intention of granting, you have still further reduced any chance we might have of succeeding. What it comes to, dear Adrienne, is this: that my happiness depends too much on having you with me for me to consent to your spending the winter tramping the streets of Paris for no better purpose than that of truckling to vague ambitions which cannot be satisfied by such ill-conceived measures as have so far been decided. Madame de Simiane wanted to leave the day after tomorrow with Virginie, but has consented to delay her departure until Monday, as I had originally planned. She will be at Madame de Tessé's by six, and will drop Virginie there without going in herself. I count on her to help you carry out your wish of returning here.

Adrienne was indeed being much missed at La Grange, where Anastasie and Charles now had rooms for themselves and their two little girls, Célestine and Louise.

The work being done here urgently requires your presence [Gilbert continued]. There has been a deal more building than you would have thought either agreeable or useful had Monsieur Vaudoyer first shown you his plans. The doors of my bedroom and the parquet in my library are a great deal too elaborate, and I have a feeling that expenses are gaining on us like flood water. We must make do with what has been carried out already, or what is absolutely necessary as a result of what has been done, which will eat up the money in hand. We must not countenance anything further until we have the means, have seen the estimate, and have made a definite contract. You have done wonders, my dear Adrienne.[4]

The Cayenne enterprise, originally set in operation from a sense of duty and to help in the emancipation of the slaves, now looked as if it might become very useful to the household, since it would be a means of providing ready money. In Frimaire, Year X, the council of state reached a decision that "General La Fayette has an incontestable right to the ownership of the land in question." The minister had issued instructions that the title deeds should be restored to him. Since the local agent had not obeyed, Adrienne had let it be known that her husband was prepared to compound. The Minister for the Navy was empowered to start negotiations and to get the best terms possible for the Republic, and to this end he wrote to "Citizeness Noailles, wife of Motier-Lafayette." Finally, the First Consul decided that the state should acquire La Belle Gabrielle, the Cayenne plantation, for the sum of 140,000 francs, and that the other properties owned in Guiana by the La Fayettes should be surrendered by them. The settlement was not very fair, but, coming when it did, it proved to be of great service—except that where the government is concerned, it does not mean that if a debt is recognized it will be paid.

On December 23, 1800, a bomb intended for Bonaparte exploded in the Rue Saint-Nicaise. This gave La Fayette an honorable excuse for congratulating him on his escape. The First Consul told him that such outrages were, he thought, a consequence of the continuing cooperation of the two extreme parties—the Jacobins and the Chouans. Nevertheless, the Comte de Provence (later Louis XVIII) had written to him disclaiming any part in the crime. "There was nothing wrong with his letter," Bonaparte said to La Fayette, "nor with my answer, but he wound up by asking me for something I could not do, which was to put him back on the throne."

Then, in high good humor [Gilbert wrote], he told me about the various propositions which his wife was asked to pass on to him and which he got her to read aloud in the evenings to amuse him. "They promise me a statue," he said, "in which I shall be represented offering the crown to the king; to which I replied that I should be afraid of being shut up in the pedestal." When I said that they would have him out of it pretty quickly in order to do something worse: "You know," he said, "that the danger means nothing to me, but to restore them to power would be a piece of infamous cowardice on my part. You may disapprove of the government, you may think me a despot, but a day will come when they will see whether I have been working for myself or for posterity. But when all is said and done, I am the master of the movement, I, whom the Revolution, whom you, whom all patriots have put where I am, and if I brought back those people, it would be to hand you all over to their vengeance!" These feelings were so nobly expressed and he spoke so well of the glory of France that I took his hand to show how great was the pleasure he had given me.[5]

And so the flirtation continued. La Fayette obtained places for his friends without difficulty, and reinstatement for his Noailles relatives, though the First Consul complained of what was being said about him in the *salons* of the aristocracy. "They have no importance except that which one gives them," Gilbert replied. "I am astonished that generals who have conquered Europe should condescend to take notice of the grimacings of the Faubourg Saint-Germain."

At each request for a reinstatement the First Consul asked: "Did he bear arms?"—the implication being *against France*—and added affectionately: "My dear fellow, the really fine attitude is yours. To manage the affairs of one's country and, in the event of shipwreck, to have nothing in common with its enemies—that is what matters." A rough sympathy grew up between the two men.

In the spring of 1801 Bonaparte confided to Gilbert his plan for a concordat with the Vatican. He wished to restore Catholicism to its old position as the official religion of the country. La Fayette urged him to proclaim complete freedom of worship. "You had nothing to do," he said, "with the horrible persecution to which the priests were exposed. You have a clean slate: take advantage of it to establish the American system. The really pious will bless you—I know their attitude from my own family. All they want is complete freedom for their own form of worship."[6] It was Adrienne's feelings to which Gilbert was giving expression. She had come out firmly in support of the Protestants; she would have approved the emancipation of all religious confessions. But her Catholicism was a faith: Bonaparte's was a matter of politics. He wanted to tie the hands of the clergy. "With my prefects, my gendarmes, and my priests," he said, "there is nothing I cannot do."

All he wanted was to be a sovereign anointed by the Pope with the sacred oil. La Fayette ventured to say with a laugh: "Confess that all that this amounts to is that you would like to have the little phial broken over your own head."

"You do not give a damn for the little phial, any more than I do," replied Bonaparte, "but what matters to us, inside and outside the country, is that the Pope and all his brood should declare against the legitimacy of the Bourbons."

After this conversation the First Consul said to Bourrienne: "Monsieur de La Fayette may be right in theory, but after all what's a theory? He told me that I wanted to have the little phial broken over my head—a very odd phrase. Well, we shall see, we shall see."

What they saw was the arrival of Cardinal Caprara, the papal legate, and the signing of the Concordat. The curés of Auvergne viewed the whole business with the greatest suspicion.

In September, 1801, La Fayette was back at Chavaniac with George, but without Adrienne. Negotiations were going on with the aunt for the assignment of the property to Gilbert and his children as security for any future marriage contracts. In the old lady's eyes, George de La Fayette, as sole heir to the family name and the family arms, should have a right to the La Fayette lands. She would therefore leave him one half of the Chavaniac domain. An eighth part should go to each of his sisters, and a quarter to his father for life. Thanks to the miracles achieved by Adrienne, the financial position of the family was now decidedly better. In Brittany and Touraine the farm rents were coming in regularly. The old days of expansion were back again. Both at La Grange and Chavaniac money was being spent on the estates. "If you can find three or four thousand francs to put into apple trees," Gilbert told his wife, "the investment will be very profitable to us and our children in ten years' time."

An excellent marriage was being negotiated for George. The young woman was Émilie de Tracy, the daughter of Antoine-Claude, Comte Destutt de Tracy, a philosopher and a member of the Institute, who to a large extent shared La Fayette's political views, with this important difference: Tracy had accepted a seat in the Senate from Bonaparte. Destutt de Tracy was a small man, elegant and punctilious, though apt to be gripped by an abominable temper. The idea of this union delighted La Fayette, but as yet neither the young people nor the lawyers of the two families had met. Nevertheless, Adrienne was already busy with Vaudoyer, planning a suite of rooms at La Grange for her future daughter-in-law. Gilbert let her have her way, though he complained that he was never consulted.

In October Gilbert and George left Chavaniac. Miserable though the aunt was at this separation, she did not get into one of those states which were so bad for her. She was very pleased at the idea of George's marriage. The young man rejoined his regiment in Italy, while La Fayette went to stay with Mme de Simiane in her house at Cirey. From there he wrote to Adrienne:

I took the Burgundy road, which I should not have done had I known it to be so bad—enough to break the carriage and my bones to bits! I was much tempted on my way through Langres to pay a surprise visit on Rosalie, but was warned that in the present state of the roads I should find it very difficult to get to Vesoul within the day, and that from there on it would mean another day of horrible cross-country driving. The weather was detestable. . . .

It is probable that Madame de Simiane will spend part of the winter at Cirey; the visits she is expecting are being continually delayed; this is the only moment at which I can fit mine in. I am being strongly pressed to prolong it, and Madame d'Hénin says that if I am agreeable to spending a fortnight here, I can go back with her. I find Madame de Simiane looking far from well. I have not told her how grieved that makes me, because I know that it would not be of the slightest use. . . . So far we have had no time for talking. That will be for tomorrow after the departure of the abbé [de Damas, Mme de Simiane's brother], Charles, and another guest for Paris, where they will put this letter in the post. Good-by, dear Adrienne. Good-by, dear Virginie.[7]

When Gilbert returned to Paris, Adrienne, the indefatigable woman of business, was once again at Saint-Brieuc. He found the family with Madame de Tessé at Aulnay, and in a state of great agitation. His brother-in-law Grammont and his stepmother-in-law, the second Duchesse de Noailles, whispered to him: "For Heaven's sake not a word, or all is lost!"

"I was like Don Basilio in *The Barber*," wrote Gilbert to his wife. "All the fuss was about some harebrained idea of Madame de Tessé in connection with the reinstatement affair. She wanted to be the first member of the family to have it, and said laughingly, 'Once the head and arms are through, the rest of the body will have no difficulty.'" She did not want her brother, Noailles, to get wind of this, but of course he did. There are orders of precedence even in misfortune. A more important matter was La Fayette's meeting with Tracy and his daughter Émilie, George's bride presumptive. He found her very charming, and worthy of being his daughter-in-law.

He had a pleasant dinner with Joseph Bonaparte, at which his fellow guest was Lord Cornwallis, his adversary in the American War of Independence. No doubt he talked imprudently about the situation in France, for he soon found himself in trouble. Up till now Bonaparte had been consistently gracious. He had listened without any show of impatience to the polite but firm criticisms of the incorrigible liberal. To those who spoke to him of La Fayette as a troublemaker, he always replied: "He would never say anything behind my back that he would not say to my face." But when he saw La Fayette again after the Cornwallis meeting, he remarked with a sneer, "I should warn you that, according to Lord Cornwallis you have not yet seen the error of your ways."

"What error?" was La Fayette's sharp retort. "Is it an error to love liberty? What should have turned me against it? The crimes and excesses of the terrorist tyranny? They have merely made me hate still more all forms of arbitrary government, and have strengthened me in my principles."

"I must tell you, General La Fayette," replied Bonaparte with a look of great seriousness, "that I see with regret the manner in which you express your views on the actions of the government. By talking like that, you lend the weight of your name to its enemies."

"What else can I do?" answered La Fayette. "I live a retired existence in the country. I do my best to avoid talking politics, but whenever anyone asks me whether your regime is in accordance with my ideas of liberty, I say no. I wish to be a prudent man, General, but not a renegade." [8]

Suddenly everything went from bad to worse. The First Consul growled louder, the workmen at La Grange took their pay and did as little work as they could, the Thésan brother-in-law (more royalist and more surly than ever) was being prickly about the inheritance, and the Cayenne affair was at a standstill.

I see with much regret, my dear Adrienne, that the moment of your departure is being longer and longer delayed. The disappointments you have had come as no surprise to me. You have done far more than I thought possible. If you have, as Mirabeau used to say, mistaken hopes for realities, there is enough reality to have made your journey worth while, so far as our concerns go.

How all our troubles would vanish, dear Arienne, if only all our debts were paid! ... You are perfectly right, given the present state of our affairs and our hopes, not to think beyond rounding off our children's properties in Brittany, and to use what is left over in clearing off our mortgages.

I cannot tell you too often what marvels you have achieved, and that even where results have not come up to your expectations, the number of your successes is more than satisfactory.[9]

George was at Monza, some twenty miles from Milan, with his hussars. He rode, fenced, sketched, made music, and was delighted with all that his father and his sisters wrote to him about Émilie. Being so far away, he was unaware of the immense difficulties his parents were encountering in calming the fear of M. de Tracy, the scruples of Aunt Charlotte, and the untimely zeal of Mme de Tessé.

But human affairs have a way of moving in cycles. A period of calm followed storms. Bonaparte developed a better temper. The sharing out of the inheritance was concluded amicably, with no very great warmth, perhaps, but decently. Each of the Noailles sisters found herself with a château and some farms, which was more than could have been expected in the days of Olmütz and Witmold. As to the Duc de Noailles, despairing of ever recovering possession of his house in the Rue Honoré, he returned in philosophic mood to Switzerland, where he bought the Ermitage des Utins, high above Rolle, on the edge of the Lake of Geneva.

At La Grange Vaudoyer had designed an admirable library for La Fayette on the second floor of one of the towers. It was circular in shape and contained three main sections of shelves supported by delicate white columns. The columns were surmounted by medal-

lions painted in oils, representing Dietrich (the Mayor of Stras-
bourg), Van Ryssel (the Dutch patriot), Franklin, Washington,
Bailly, La Rochefoucauld, Lavoisier, and Malesherbes. The books,
many of which had been presented to La Fayette in the United
States, were enriched with handsome bindings. A megaphone installed next to the window made it possible for Gilbert to call his
instructions to his farm hands without descending from his tower.
The chair cushions had been embroidered by Adrienne. In the
drawer of the writing-desk were two seals. One, of cornelian, he
had brought back from America. It was engraved with his cipher
and the family motto, *Cur non?* The other bore Washington's
head in a sunburst. A curious little picture hung by the door. It
showed the old corporal who had behaved so badly to the prisoners
at Olmütz. Anastasie had drawn this caricature at the time on
her thumbnail, so as to save it from being confiscated. The crabbed
old ruffian was portrayed carrying his heavy bunch of keys. His
sparse hair was gathered into a ridiculous *catogan* or knot, and since
he seemed to be moving with the caution of an Iroquois, the girls
had nicknamed him "Cataquais." The prisoners, once they had re-
gained their freedom, enjoyed being reminded of him and having
a good laugh.

PRIVATE UNIONS,
PUBLIC RUPTURE

*O the charm, the immensity of life!
How lovely is this solitude!* PLINY

It is fairly rare for a husband and wife who have a genuine and profound affection for each other to be so constantly separated as were Adrienne and Gilbert. The confused state of their affairs and Adrienne's scruples—she was always thinking that she had not done enough—were, as we have seen, responsible. In February, 1802, La Fayette was busy at La Grange, while his wife was kept in Paris by the need to wind up the matter of the Cayenne property. The government had agreed that an indemnity should be paid and had determined the amount, but the distance between agreement and action was still apparently considerable. Adrienne was harrying Talleyrand and Decrès, the Naval Minister.

Then Adrienne left Paris for Chavaniac where she had to conduct negotiations of quite a different kind with Aunt Charlotte, and Gilbert now moved to Paris to take over his wife's labors in connection with La Belle Gabrielle. A notable piece of domestic staffwork. At last, on April 3, 1802, the deed relating to Cayenne was signed at the Navy Office.

GILBERT TO ADRIENNE

There have been three main difficulties: (1) To decide who shall pay the legal costs, amounting to two thousand francs. It has been agreed that these shall be defrayed by the government in its capacity of purchaser. (2) To assign a mortgage until such time as the property shall be handed over. My advisers tell me that this is customary. I should have liked it to be on the Hôtel de Noailles, but since neither you nor I are the owners this turned out to be impossible. So La Grange has been substituted. Monsieur Tutat * and Monsieur Beauchet have so arranged matters that this will in no way interfere with our other arrangements. The third point, which turned into a wrangle, had to do with a demand that I should cede all my rights insofar as they affected the farm laborers. I declared that I would not cooperate in any kind of slave system. In the long run it was agreed that I should renounce my rights in all property of whatever kind that belonged, or had belonged, to me in Cayenne. So everything is now signed, sealed, and delivered: 140,000 francs cash down.[1]

One hundred forty thousand francs in cash! This was an undreamed-of windfall and would refloat the family finances, at least for a time. The great affair of George's marriage remained to be settled. The bridegroom being still with the Army of Italy, Gilbert made it his business to be constantly at Auteuil. Émilie pleased him more and more by reason of her "sound intelligence and her sensibility." Her parents wanted the wedding to be in May, 1802, but first of all there was the money question to be settled. No compromise about that was possible. Now that order had been re-established in France, the great families were reverting to the idea that a young couple must have an assured income. No money, no wedding.

On the Tracy side, Mme de Chavaniac's donation was held to be satisfactory, but not if La Fayette was to have a life interest in it and not if George's part was to be mulcted of 10,000 francs to provide for each of his two sisters. Aunt Charlotte was determined to "do something" for her grand nieces. The old lady was being difficult. She was very fond of George, but not so fond of him as she was of Gilbert. She strongly opposed the idea of depriving her beloved nephew of a life interest in the place of his birth. Adrienne was hastily summoned to Chavaniac, where it fell to her to reconcile the two points of view. From Auvergne Virginie wrote to Anastasie:

* La Fayette's lawyer.

*My aunt is the very soul of generosity. She is in excellent health, and
I really believe she looks younger. . . . It is dreadful that because of
her wish to provide for us we should have become the final obstacle
to a marriage which we so much desire.*[2]

At Auteuil, Émilie said yes to everything but her father did not.
Adrienne, sick of haggling, suggested that the La Fayettes should
acknowledge a debt of 20,000 francs to Mme de Chavaniac, for
which *they* should be responsible when they came into the inheritance, thus serving to compensate for the liberal gift made to the
grand nieces. To this Aunt Charlotte consented.

GILBERT TO ADRIENNE: PARIS, APRIL 10, 1802

*I went to see Tracy at eight o'clock this morning, after looking in
on Maubourg, who was the more satisfied with my aunt's decision
because yesterday evening Madame de Tracy had confided her
lively concern to Marie. She was afraid that the marriage would
come to nothing if my aunt did not yield to our entreaties. Such an
eventuality she could not envisage without a feeling of despair, and
I think that Émilie, too, would not have been unmoved. I told
Tracy that I had come to inform him of my aunt's kindness in
renouncing her intention of leaving me a life interest in the property, that George's half would be assured, and consequently that
she no longer needed the letter which I had intended to write stating that after her death one half of Chavaniac should be settled on
George and that no mention should be made of a life interest for
me. Tracy fell upon my neck and embraced me ten times over with
a joy which made it more and more clear to me that—as we knew
already—he had raised these difficulties simply and solely as a matter of principle.*[3]

An astonishing spectacle, this of a philosopher and a senator
falling on the neck of an illustrious general over a matter of 20,000
francs! It is still more curious to realize that this same philosopher
had been prepared to break off a highly satisfactory marriage "as
a matter of principle," which principle, in fact, had amounted to
no more than a squalid disagreement about money.

What mattered to Adrienne, a fond mother for whom money
was always a means and never an end, was to reassure her son
that his betrothed loved him for himself and not for the towers of

Chavaniac. She told him that Destutt de Tracy had realized that the girl's heart was set on George, and that

this had put an end to all hesitation and made the decision independent of all monetary considerations. . . . Matters are now being settled between Monsieur Beauchet and Monsieur de Tracy's representative . . . We do not, however, yet know whether Monsieur de Tracy will give his daughter four or six thousand francs a year. I should like it to be six because I know, dear boy, that in spite of your extreme economy unexpected situations are always turning up, especially when traveling, which compel one to spend more than one intended, and that if you have only seven thousand (four plus three) you will never be quite easy in your mind, which does not mean that you will not be happy but only that you will have one pleasure the less.[4]

GILBERT TO ADRIENNE: APRIL 11, 1802

They [the Tracy couple] tell me that they leave the choice of day to you, provided it is as soon as possible. The drawbacks inherent in a lot of aristocratic connections as well as considerations of economy give them a distaste for the sort of ceremomy to which, on my side, Madame de Tarente would have to be invited, and on theirs, Monsieur and Madame d'Uzès. They say that their house is too small to put up the young couple, but that there are objections to sending them off to lodge elsewhere. They think, therefore, that the ceremony had better be as early as possible so that the breakfast can be at Autueil, after which the bride and groom can set off for La Grange—with Madame de Maubourg in the place of Madame de Tracy, to whom her daughter will be brought back four days later. . . .

Since Émilie has said something about a green paper it will not be difficult to find one with a pretty border, but what paper are we going to put in her closet? And what about George's room? True, you will have time when you get back to choose papers and furniture as well. Still, there is not much time to be lost if we are to have everything delivered in time for them, if they are to come to La Grange on the day of the wedding.[5]

In all the transactions having to do with La Belle Gabrielle the La Fayettes had been much aided by the good will of those in power. Gilbert realized that if the Cayenne business were to be brought to a successful conclusion "a definite show of friendliness on the part of the First Consul" would be essential. This was forthcoming, in spite of Lord Cornwallis' ill-natured gossip. General de La Fayette's pension had been fixed at 6000 francs—the maximum figure. Little by little all his friends had been reinstated.

GILBERT TO ADRIENNE: LA GRANGE, APRIL 16, 1802

I am much pleased with Bonaparte.... In thanking him I have wished him every happiness compatible with public freedom, or rather, I have told him that I hope that he will agree with me that only in public freedom will he find glory cut to his measure. Royal and imperial fortunes are by comparison mere jades. You will learn from the papers all about his episcopal nominations, the preparations made for the Te Deum, and the choice of a preacher—whom I have heard only once in my life, and that, as you know, was a very long time ago.[6]

The reference here was to the famous Easter Sunday in 1802 when Bonaparte drove to Notre Dame in the state coach of the kings of France, and Monseigneur de Boisgelin, who had delivered the official oration at the coronation of Louis XVI, saluted Bonaparte in the name of the Church as "this Heaven-sent genius." In front of the cathedral, to the sound of a tumultuous clanging of bells, the archbishop, supported by thirty bishops, received the First Consul. He wore red, which accentuated the yellowish pallor of his handsome face, and was escorted to a seat prepared for him under a canopy. Many of the officers grouped around him found fault with so much display, but the people in the streets sang "Sunday shall be his festival: alleluia!" and rejoiced too because a peace had been signed with England.

Adrienne could not help being pleased for her son's sake that the war was over, and for the Church that the days of persecution were ended. She could not fail to be grateful to the First Consul for so many signal marks of his favor. But in the following month she was a witness, sad and powerless, of an agonizing case of conscience. All of a sudden the French people were asked to pronounce on the question "Shall Bonaparte be Consul for life?" La Fayette himself had suggested a life presidency, *but only if it was hedged about with constitutional guarantees.* None were offered. Nevertheless, the measure was ratified almost unanimously

(3,568,000 in favor to 9000 against). The royalists flocked to give their approval. La Fayette voted no, adding on the register these words: "I cannot vote for such an office until such time as public liberty shall have received sufficient guarantees. Then, and then only, will I give my support to Napoleon Bonaparte." [7] Next morning he sent a sober and dignified letter to the First Consul in which he expressed the same sentiment, accompanied by personal good wishes. This time the rupture was open and complete. Gone were the days of uneasy flirtation. All the same, Bonaparte had sufficient nobility of mind to retain a high opinion of so loyal an adversary. When someone said in his presence that the only persons who had voted against him were the Jacobins: "No," he replied. "There were also some enthusiasts for liberty: La Fayette, for instance."

Though it was now more than ever impossible for Gilbert to play any part in public affairs, his private life was untroubled. On June 6, 1802, George's marriage was celebrated privately so as to avoid the necessity confronting the republican general with his royalist cousins. Mme de Tessé had at first offered to set up the young couple, but on learning that Adrienne and Anastasie had already bought a certain amount of furniture, had flown into a fury. Aunt de Tessé was only too willing to *give*, on condition that she should run the show.

COMTESSE DE TESSÉ TO MARIE-JOSÈPHE BEAUCHET

Madame de La Fayette forgot, Madame, before she left, to order a cot and some mattresses for her daughter-in-law, and the date of the marriage has been fixed for as soon as possible after her return! It is possible that Madame de La Fayette may write in a hurry asking you to buy a great many things without knowing whether they will fit the places they are intended for. Time is short. I have taken it upon myself to look after the furnishings, so soon as I shall have received from La Grange the necessary measurements. I SHALL NOT PAY A PENNY.

I wish Madame de La Fayette to realize from the account I shall send her of the expenses to which she will be put what it costs to furnish a bedroom decently with a quite ordinary bed, and to be persuaded that the so-called luxuries do not amount to 200 francs out of a total of 1800. [8]

The Beauchets, like Adrienne, knew Mme de Tessé's little ways, and took all this quite calmly. The aunt might make a great song and dance, but in the long run she would come around.

Carrichon, the abbé who had accompanied the three Noailles ladies to the scaffold, gave the nuptial blessing, and the bride and bridegroom spent a short honeymoon with the family at La Grange. George's wardrobe, given him by his parents, had cost 840 livres. It came from Lanier, the Paris tailor, and consisted—among other items—of one pair of black silk breeches, one pair of nankeen trousers, and a blue dress coat.

All that was needed now was a husband for Virginie, and as good husbands have a way of doing, he turned up quite by chance.

During the summer of 1802 Pauline de Montagu had paid a visit to Brive-la-Gaillarde, the center of the estates which together had constituted the duchy of Noailles before the Revolution. Her father had written to her from Switzerland, asking her to see whether something could be saved from their one-time properties in Corrèze. She was put in touch with an old gentleman of the neighborhood, Commander de Lasteyrie, a Commander in the Order of the Knights of Malta, who offered to accompany her on her rounds of the countryside. Louis de Lasteyrie, the commander's nephew, some times went with them. He was a handsome young man, gentle, good, and extremely well educated. He had been brought up in Malta, from which island his uncle had removed him to France after the dissolution of the Sovereign Order. Mme de Montagu became very friendly with him, and remarked to the commander (a distant relative) that their relationship might be renewed and strengthened by a marriage. This suggestion was well received, and Pauline wrote to Adrienne to say that she had found her a son-in-law. After her return to the Château of Plauzat in Auvergne, she invited uncle and nephew to stay and drove the latter over to Chavaniac. The first impressions on both sides were favorable, so favorable, indeed, that Louis de Lasteyrie was asked to pay a visit to La Grange in the course of the following winter. Gilbert presently reported to Mme de Chavaniac:

Louis de Lasteyrie is madly in love with Virginie, who reciprocates his passion with all her heart. Everyone thinks her charming in this new role. So, the younger branch is assured.[9]

He praised the young man's character, his manners, and his heart. "All he lacks, and she, too, is a little more money."

La Fayette now went to Paris to meet his English friends who were taking advantage of the Peace of Amiens to renew acquaintances with France. They were impressed unfavorably by the consular regime. These great Whigs were more in sympathy with La Fayette than with Bonaparte. Adrienne met Fox and Fitzpatrick, with whom she had so often corresponded in the old Olmütz days and to whom she owed so great a debt of gratitude. The likable Charles Fox went with his wife to La Grange, where he planted some ivy which still flourishes. "Liberty," he said to La Fayette, "will be born again, not for us, but probably for George, and certainly for his children."

A shadow was cast over the domestic scene in February, 1803, by a serious accident:

GILBERT TO MME DE CHAVANIAC

Virginie has told you, my dear aunt, that through my own clumsiness I have had a fall, which has resulted in a contusion which obliges me to keep to my room for several days. The blow was on the outer side of the thigh. At first it gave me a great deal of pain, and still causes me vexation. I am anxious to tell you this for fear lest the news sheets—which killed me last year when I was in especially good health—might take it into their heads to say now that I have broken my neck.[10]

In point of fact, coming out of the Navy Office, Gilbert had slipped on some ice and broken the neck of his femur. He was at once taken to the house of Mme de Tessé, where he was attended by two famous surgeons, Deschamps and Boyer. They gave him a choice between a simple reduction, which would leave him a cripple, and a new apparatus, perfected by Boyer, which would give him a great deal of pain for forty days but would produce a very much better result. He chose the apparatus and the pain. "We are on the wheel," wrote Adrienne to Carrichon. "Pray God we may be on the Cross." But she was deprived of this consolation. Gilbert maintained that his endurance was entirely philosophic. When the abominable instrument of torture was removed, and with it a portion of his thigh, the foot was found to be crushed. The wounds took a long time to heal, in spite of the enlightened care of Dr. Deschamps, who declared that should he ever be similarly afflicted, he would choose to be a cripple. His patient did not agree with this point of view. As a result of the treatment Gilbert's leg remained stiff, but he could walk with the help of a stick and congratulated himself on having chosen the pain, the risk, and the cure.

Adrienne, Mme de Tessé, Anastasie, and Virginie took turns sitting by his bed. He had a great many visitors. Though he was in disgrace, generals, senators, and state councilors did not hesitate to call on him in uniform. Bernadotte, Moreau, and Kosciuszko were assiduous in their attentions. Others, more timid, were content to ask for news at the door. Bonaparte had the bulletins shown him, but sent no message. On one occasion when George was on parade with his colonel, the First Consul asked his name and, on hearing that he was young La Fayette, said sharply: "Oh, so that is *his* son, is it!" Another day, accosting Destutt de Tracy, he asked him whether it was his daughter or his son who had married a La Fayette, an absurd question which revealed his embarrassment.

As soon as La Fayette was better, preparations were begun for Virginie's marriage. Mme de Tessé had bought for use in the summer months a charming property at Aulnay, not far from Paris. There, naturally, she bred cows, but she did not sell the milk, having only just enough for her guests, who were more numerous even than they had been at Witmold. It was there that Gilbert spent his convalescence. George and his young wife (who had just given birth to a daughter, Nathalie) stayed there for a time.

The pattern of life at Aulnay was much as it had been on the lake of Ploen. Mme de Tessé spent the morning in bed, reading, pencil in hand. In the afternoon there was whist, conversation, and walking; after dinner, piquet or reading aloud. The only novelty was that Mme de Tessé went every Sunday to hear Mass in the village church. She still called herself a disciple of Voltaire, but after all, had not Voltaire himself built a chapel? Tessé, who had always followed his wife, now followed her to church. They were preparing to celebrate their golden wedding: fifty years of silence.

The Peace of Amiens turned out to be no more than a disappointing armistice. England refused to evacuate Malta. "The whole treaty and nothing but the treaty," insisted Bonaparte. "The Continent in the state in which it was, and no less," replied the English. No understanding was possible, and a resumption of hostilities appeared to be inevitable.

In February, 1804, General Moreau was arrested on a charge of conspiring against the state. Though La Fayette had always regarded him a weak character, he considered him a great soldier, a good citizen, and a true patriot. He went to see him in prison. Attempts were made to compromise him in the conspiracy. "How the devil," said Bonaparte, "are we going to track him down in this sort of a business?" It was soon obvious that if there *was* a conspiracy, it had been inspired by the royalists. "No need to fear anything of that kind," said Joseph Bonaparte. "You will never find La Fayette where there are aristocrats and kings." Nevertheless, his American friends were uneasy on his account and tried to find employment for him outside France.

Bonaparte and Talleyrand had just completed the sale of Louisiana to the United States for the sum of 80,000,000 livres. Jefferson, who had been President since 1801, urged La Fayette to leave a country where "the ground is trembling under your feet" and to settle in Louisiana, where he could have 12,000 acres, a happy life, and the chance of laying the foundations of an immense fortune. His presence in that state with his whole family would serve to form a link between the French and Anglo-Saxon elements of the population. He might well be appointed governor. What pleasanter prospect could there be?

Many of Gilbert's French friends, realizing that there could be no political future for him at home, urged him to accept this offer. But neither he nor Adrienne was tempted. He could not bring himself to abandon France so long as there remained "a chance of liberty," and she did not want to leave her children and her three little granddaughters. He replied to Jefferson, saying that his wife was too much of an invalid to face such a journey, that he himself had a permanent limp and tired easily, and finally that he had an old aunt of eighty-three in Auvergne, whom his expatriation would undoubtedly kill. To these strong personal reasons was added the hope that he might some day establish in his own country "a just and generous liberty; in short, liberty on the American model."

Adrienne rejoiced at this decision. Family life was for her a source of great happiness. She had at La Grange three young couples and three grandchildren. Célestine, Louise, and Nathalie were thriving. It was a cause of great grief to Virginie that she was not yet pregnant. Émilie was very happy with her family-in-law, and George patted himself on the back for having so charming a wife. Their little Nathalie was beginning to have trouble with her teeth. No change of regime could alter the established cycle of teething and measles. Destutt de Tracy had increased the income which he allowed his daughter by the terms of the marriage settlement from 4000 to 6000 francs. Mme de Tessé and Mme de Simiane frequently settled down for long periods in the vast house. Louis de Lasteyrie had enlisted as a private in the dragoons and was stationed at Chantilly, from where he came now and again to see his wife.

Gilbert was devoting all his time and energy to agriculture. From his window he could watch the work of the farm. He himself fixed the prices of his produce, and, like a good chief of staff, kept a careful record of all matters relating to the running of the estate:

CASH PAYMENTS DUE FROM THE FARM

On the last Saturday in each month a return shall be made of the quantity of corn required for tax purposes and for the payment of the threshers and day laborers on the estate. These payments, whatever the price of corn, must be discharged on the first of the month following. . . . Care must be taken to distinguish between the daily wage of the men whose meals are provided on the farm and those of the men who find their own food. As little as possible must be a charge on the house. . . . The bread distributed to the poor shall be kept in a special cupboard so that there shall be no confusion between it and what is intended for the consumption of the domestic servants and farm workers.[11]

In Germinal, Year XII, a sad piece of news reached La Grange. The charming Vicomte de Noailles, of whom La Fayette had been so envious when they were both young men, who had taken the initiative in the famous matter of the night of the Fourth of August, and had had to flee to the United States in 1792 after his troops had been disbanded, had just died in the service of France. In capturing an English vessel in the West Indies, he had been mortally wounded.

Adrienne recounted to his three children, whose mother had been guillotined in 1794, the story of his fine and tragic life. Her sister Pauline had succeeded in having his name deleted from the list of *émigrés*.

In spite of the sale of the Cayenne property, the La Fayettes were short of money. Jefferson renewed his offer of a home in Louisiana, where they would have been rich. Once again, in full agreement with Adrienne, Gilbert refused, though the general situation in France fully justified the President of the United States in pressing his point. The air was full of daggers. Bonaparte was preparing to invade England, England was organizing plots against him, and La Fayette, in spite of his efforts to keep out of the limelight, might well be compromised. Yes, the ground was indeed trembling under their feet. But it was the ground of their own country.

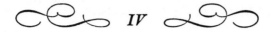

IV

ON THE FRINGE OF THE EMPIRE

*As soon as one begins to change one's
ideas to fit the event, intelligence is no
more than a jade.* ALAIN

Bonaparte, because he had an excessively historical imagination,
wanted to be emperor. His entourage pushed him along the path
he wished to tread.

"Your enemies," they told him, "regard your government as no
more than an interim arrangement."

"I will make it hereditary," he replied. "But it will take a few
years."

He knew that the old members of the Convention, his generals,
and his ministers objected to the idea of monarchy in any form. But
they were intent on keeping the natural frontiers the Revolution had
won by force of arms, and in their view only Bonaparte could maintain them. The execution of the young Duc d'Enghien convinced
the regicides that Bonaparte had now become one of them and
would not provoke a counterrevolution. The Senate, having received
this bloody pledge, offered him a crown. On May 18, 1804, a
senatus consultum ordained the setting up of a French Empire.
A court and a nobility were improvised. The emperor's brothers
became Imperial Highnesses and were addressed as Monseigneur,
which displeased Joseph Bonaparte. The marshals and the great
dignitaries were given titles: Prince, Duc, and Comte. Lebrun became High Treasurer; Cambacérès, High Chancellor; Berthier, who

loved the chase, Grand Master of the Hunt; and Ségur, Adrienne's uncle, Grand Master of the Ceremonies.

He began his duties last Sunday [La Fayette wrote his wife]. *It is now an office under the crown. The salary is sixty thousand francs, and he will retain his position as a councilor of state—which means that altogether he will have an income of a hundred thousand livres.*[1]

Rallying to the new regime was a paying proposition.

At La Grange, where pride of refusal was carefully cultivated, Adrienne watched with melancholy eyes friends and relations rushing down the slope to slavery. Priests, royalists, and Jacobins jostled one another to place their necks in the same halter. La Fayette, persevering in his eccentricity of being consistent, lived a more retired life than ever. In the evenings he had the *Moniteur* read aloud to him in the family circle and there was much laughter at the expense of the new princes.

But La Fayette's silence was not considered by the emperor to be sufficient. He regarded Gilbert as an adversary. When one day Alexandre de Lameth said to Napoleon, not without malice: "I like to think that my enemies are those of Your Majesty," the emperor replied sharply: "You mean La Fayette, eh?"

Napoleon had a low opinion of his fellow men, and thought they could always be won over with money or honors. "I have always noticed that honest men are not good for much," he said. He still hoped to seduce the honest La Fayette, if not with money or honors, then by other means.

Adrienne and Gilbert did not mix in the grand imperial world, nor did they enter the small groups of complainers who represented the critical opposition. Fouché kept a watchful eye on such circles, and sometimes cracked a menacing whip.

Adrienne spent the spring of 1804 at Villersexel, where her Grammont sister was expecting a child. Gilbert was again at Cirey with Mme de Simiane. Their letters contained nothing but family news and were silent about public affairs. Louis de Lasteyrie had been made a corporal in the 3rd Dragoons. It was not very much in the way of advancement, but a son-in-law of La Fayette had to be content with little.

GILBERT TO ADRIENNE: CIREY, JULY 9, 1804

We live here very pleasantly, dear Adrienne. You are daily missed and wished for by the lady of the house and all those gathered here. . . . And talking of the lady of the house reminds me to tell you that it is being said that the great territorial lords are to be re-established under the name of patrons. I presume that for the commune of Courpalay we shall have Monsieur de Boislandry.[2]

From Cirey Gilbert went to Mont-Dore to take the waters with his wife and Virginie, and then to Chavaniac, where he received a most unexpected letter from his uncle Ségur. The emperor had created a new order of chivalry: the Legion of Honor. Joseph Bonaparte hoped that La Fayette would consent to be one of its high dignitaries. "Prince Joseph likes to attribute your withdrawal from public life to the philosophic cast of your mind," Ségur wrote, "but sees with sorrow and disquiet that his brother looks upon it as betokening an attitude of hostility. Prince Joseph's feelings of friendship for you make him anxious to put an end to this situation." Acceptance would not be very compromising, "seeing that your military services both in America and Europe are undeniable facts, and are the reason for this offer being made to you. It is so well adapted to your life of retirement that your refusal of it would indeed be an evidence of hostility. But before proceeding further in the matter, the prince wishes to be assured of your acceptance." Gilbert replied that in his rather curious position he would regard a decoration of this kind as nothing less than ridiculous. He begged Prince Joseph to keep him free from such offers.

And now the republican senators made one last attempt to bring him over to their side. His answer was that he could not understand, and would most certainly not adopt as his own, a plan of senatorial opposition founded on silence and acquiescence. The Bishop of Vannes, Virginie's confessor, asked her why it was that her father refused to be on friendly terms with the emperor. He offered to win her father over to the government, since this would very much improve Lasteyrie's position. She dissuaded him from making the attempt. He slipped in among his arguments "the danger of relapsing into a republic."

"That," replied La Fayette's daughter, "is not what is most feared at La Grange."

Nothing was feared at La Grange except falling short of one's principles, and the life there of the united family was a happy one. The three young couples and their four little girls brought gaiety into the house. Adrienne, her digestion now considerably strengthened by doses of quinine, was better. The sore places on her legs did not trouble her unduly so long as she did not do much walking. The numerous visitors who came to the château were surprised by its isolation, accessible as it was only by poor roads through the surrounding woods. They were charmed by the grassy carpet on the filled-in moat, by the drawbridge, and by the ivy-clad towers. It was a noble setting for noble characters. La Fayette was still vigorous and active in spite of his bad leg. In the fields he was a farmer: in the *salon* he became once more a gracious and attractive man of the world.

Every Sunday evening the household staff were entertained in the great dining hall, where they danced to the porter's fiddling. The young ladies of the family taught them new steps, and they were regaled with cakes and sugared water. La Fayette and Adrienne regularly attended these rustic balls. In summer the patriarchal gatherings took place under the trees in the park. On weekdays La Fayette liked to show his guests the sheep pens, the cow sheds, and the dairy, of which he was justly proud. He was on easy terms with his cowmen, swineherds, and shepherds, addressing them as "My friend . . . My good friend . . . Dear boy . . ." This was not a form of demagogy, but true friendliness. Having outlived ambition, Gilbert no longer wished for that popularity with the crowd which had gone to his head when he was a young man, and he felt no regrets for what he had refused.

The only thing that grieved Adrienne was the knowledge that her son and her son-in-law were paying for her husband's refusals. The emperor would have had to be a saint not to feel aggrieved at La Fayette's attitude of almost contemptuous opposition. Napoleon had more than once taken the first step in an attempt to win over this famous man who still retained prestige and popularity. He had offered everything, and everything had been rejected. La Fayette had wounded him deeply by his haughty and disdainful indifference. To a man who is prepared to risk his son, nothing is impossible. The opponent was invulnerable in his retirement, since his action was entirely negative. Lieutenant George-Washington and Corporal de Lasteyrie, on the other hand, were dependent on the emperor's favor. In spite of their undoubted gallantry, they found themselves denied all advancement. Louis de Lasteyrie would never be more than a sergeant; George de La Fayette would never be promoted to captain. In vain did several generals friends of La Fayette take the eternal lieutenant on their staffs. Whenever they put in a word for him with the emperor, Caesar turned his back.

In 1805 Adrienne went to Switzerland to see her father. In a humble house standing on the hills above Rolle, between Lausanne and Geneva and looking on the loveliest of lakes, she found the man who had once been a great noble and one of the leading members of the leading court in all Europe. Stripped of his dignity and despoiled of his fortune, he had now settled down quite happily to live as a simple bourgeois. Calm, amiable, without bitterness or regrets, he was now studying science, for which he had always had a predilection. The frivolous courtier had become a philosopher, and by sheer strength of will had risen above the blows of fate. Contrary to what Adrienne had long feared, her stepmother turned out to be an ideal companion in a life of exile. Modest and affable, the new Duchesse de Noailles never made the slightest effort to come between the father and his daughters. Mme de Staël's Coppet was not far away, and there the Noailles couple shone resplendent. Adrienne was surprised to find herself so happy at the spectacle of her father in this new home, from which, for her, the ghost of her mother could never be entirely absent. Events have a way of giving the lie to anticipation.

While Adrienne was in Switzerland, Gilbert was at Chavaniac with his daughters, worried to death because war was about to break out again. It was being said that the emperor had in mind a descent upon England.

GILBERT TO ADRIENNE: AUGUST 20, 1805

Yesterday, dear Adrienne, I received your letters of August 7 and 9. They breathe an air of security which wrings one's heart when one thinks that in so short a time it will be shaken. My most recent news of George is dated the 20th Thermidor, at which time General Grouchy and his staff were about to embark in the corvette Iris. I would point out that a vessel of that type is likely to be exposed neither to the dangers of the line of battle nor to the discomforts of a transport ship. In an expedition of this type it is probably the most pleasant form of conveyance by reason of its agility. So you will see that they are on the point of setting out, though setting out does not depend upon them alone. So many flotillas are on one anothers' heels that the most one can hope is that the heads of government will be able to disentangle the puzzle of their relative positions at sea. . . .

I am deeply grateful to you for sending me so many satisfactory details. Please give my warmest respects. I see with pleasure that you plan to pay a visit to Madame de Staël. I should dearly love to be with you.[3]

Adrienne could have gone straight to Chavaniac by way of Lyons, but her leg was troubling her again, and the roads between Lyons and Le Puy were execrable. But the chief reason for her not doing so was that she did not wish to be at any great distance from Paris at a time when the war news so closely concerned those whom she loved. Instead, therefore, of going to see the old aunt from whom everything (the camp at Boulogne, the embarkation) was being carefully concealed, she chose to break her journey at Villersexel, where she made a brief stay with her Grammont sister before going on to La Grange. Gilbert was to stay on at Chavaniac, where he could give Aunt Charlotte much badly needed reassurance.

On 24th Fructidor [August 20] the plan for the invasion of England was abandoned. The emperor made a lightning about-face and brought his threat to bear on Austria and Russia. George left with General Grouchy; Louis was sent to the Army of the Rhine.

GILBERT TO ADRIENNE

I will say nothing about the invasion, which no doubt you have entirely dismissed from your mind, nor even of the continental war, which may well be brought to a standstill by the first frosts and end with a prompt and general peace signed by the great powers at the expense of the lesser ones. I will only remark that I hope to embrace George between the Texel and the Rhine, with, I should like to hope, the rank of captain. . . . I beg you to let me know how your poor leg and the rest of you is faring after your journey.[4]

In September Adrienne attended the celebration organized by Mme de Tessé in honor of her golden wedding anniversary. In an atmosphere of general jollity the company saluted fifty years of marriage between two persons as little suited as possible to each other. Then the family came together again for the marriage of Jenny de Thésan (Adrienne's niece and an orphan twice over) to Comte Henri de Mérode-Westerloo, whose father was mayor of Brussels and had been decorated with the Legion of Honor.

Gilbert remained at Chavaniac. His letters were now more down to earth than in the old days, when he had felt himself bound to express his feelings and define his political views each time he set pen to paper. Husband and wife were united by that very special bond—a shared delight in little things—which goes to make a happy marriage.

The end of the year was marked by a number of brilliant victories. At first there were only vague rumors, nothing official. But a veritable flood of letters from Germany put three facts beyond the possibility of doubt: the capture of Ulm, with a large number of prisoners; the retreat of the Austrian army in the direction of the Russians; and the name of the officer who had been in command of the attack, Maréchal Ney. La Fayette, who was in Paris, reported the news to La Grange:

There was nothing that could really be called a battle, my dears, but just a rounding up of a prodigious quantity of prisoners—something in the neighborhood of twenty-five thousand; among them General Mack, an archduke, and I don't know how many other generals. That is what the semaphore-telegraph reported up till two o'clock. A reply was sent asking whether the news was official, but there was not enough daylight left to get an answer. Prince Louis spoke of the matter when he fetched Cambacérès to go with him to see Joseph Bp. A courier has arrived today with dispatches from general headquarters. It was rumored that he had brought confirmation of the news, but how could he possibly have got here at the same time as the semaphore message? Besides, we know now from persons who were dining with Prince Joseph that there was no question of the courier having brought dispatches, and that the story that he did can be attributed to a wish to make a greater effect tomorrow, though it can be more easily explained by assuming that the fellow set off before all those prisoners had surrendered. . . .

SIX O'CLOCK IN THE MORNING

The guns are announcing a success which confirms the news that was going round yesterday evening. But do not lose sight, my dears, of the fact that there has been no mention of any action after General Ney's attack, but only of enemy troops being surrounded and obliged to give themselves up as the result of the movements of our army.[5]

Very soon General Grouchy sent good news of George, whom he praised highly. Then came Austerlitz, the crushing of the Austro-Russian forces, and Napoleon as the arbiter of Europe. The La Fayettes rejoiced as French subjects, but were not on good enough terms with the emperor to send him their congratulations.

The year 1806, glorious though it was for the nation, was difficult for Adrienne. The two young men whom she loved, her son and her son-in-law, were with the armies and their letters were anxiously awaited. Virginie was established with the Commander de Lasteyrie in the Black Forest to be within easier reach of her sergeant whom Napoleon refused to make an officer. Rosalie de Grammont had a miscarriage; Pauline de Montagu was seriously ill. Adrienne, in spite of her bad leg, went from one bedside to the other. Gilbert begged her to come home to La Grange, where she could take care of herself and have some rest.

The money situation was still disquieting. Now and again the household managed to raise a small loan on the security of the Louisiana estates, but remained riddled with debts: 5000 francs borrowed from the Princesse d'Hénin; 5000 due Beauchet; 2500 due the architect Vaudoyer. The total amount of the more pressing debts was 50,000 francs. Life in the great overcrowded house was expensive.

We have the accounts kept by Adrienne. They are detailed and always show a deficit. On one side we read: "Received from Monsieur de La Fayette: 223 livres . . . Monsieur de Grammont owes me 3000 . . . Advances from America: 1000 livres." On the other: "Candles, 139; laundry, 66; lotto and checkers, 15; upholstery, 120; apothecary, 28; Monsieur le curé, 50; charity, 60; given to Monsieur de Grammont, 300; dress for myself, 36; chasuble, 72; charity, 90; consecrated bread, 28; to Virginie, 200. I must try to track down an error of 314 livres."

At times there was a sudden easing off: "Received from Brittany, 6000 livres"—but almost immediately afterward:

FOR THE ESTABLISHMENT
OF THE SISTERS OF COURPALAY

Mortars of marble and one of glass	172
Furniture, beds, mattresses, blankets, curtains	192
Cupboards, chairs, night tables	73
Sheets, towels	72
	509

On August 28 Adrienne paid to the doctor of Rozoy-en-Brie, for the years during which he had visited the inhabitants of La Grange, 150 livres plus a ram. This was certainly not expensive—one livre per consultation—but the bill for post-horses to Aulnay, Auteuil, and Paris was considerable. The school which the lady of the manor had established at Courpalay put a heavy burden on the family budget. But Adrienne had long ago grown used to living like the lilies of the field.

There was no lack of visitors. Mme de Montagu was brought by Mme de Grammont. Gilbert welcomed her with a great show of affection. The days when Pauline had refused to see her brother-in-law were now forgotten. If in politics they had not had the same paradise, they now shared the same purgatory. Pauline made great fun of the ceremonies of the Empire; Gilbert was far from regarding Napoleon as a sure guarantee of the principles of 1789.

He maintained contact with the seat of power through his Ségur uncle, grand master of the imperial court, who was now occupied in combing the *salons* for suitable recruits for the emperor's guard. This body, when formed, turned out to be an exact replica of the royal bodyguard in the days of the monarchy. "Monsieur de Bouillé," Gilbert told his wife, "is to be one of the four captains, with Messieurs de Tarente, Valentinois, Monaco, and Aimé [de Clermont-Tonnerre]. Forty young men have already been enrolled." Pauline and her brother-in-law jeered at this display of eagerness. In 1648–49 La Grange had been one of the strongholds of the opposition to Mazarin known as the Fronde. One might well have thought that in 1807 the Fronde was still garrisoning La Grande— not a Fronde of armed men, but a Fronde plentifully supplied with wit and sarcasm. The *Moniteur* was regarded by those who lived there as a comic masterpiece. But laughter was not the order of every day, and much that was happening in the world of politics gave rise to sadness.

The worst of these was the emperor's pig-headed obstinacy in venting his spite on George de La Fayette, who had behaved with the greatest gallantry during the new German campaign. At the terrible battle of Eylau, in February, 1807, he saved the life of his commander, General Grouchy, but it was in vain that Grouchy recommended that he should be promoted to the rank of captain. The mere mention of the name of La Fayette made the emperor see red. This grudge against a young officer who was completely untainted by politics seemed a weakness unworthy of a great man.

Still, all things considered, the family picture was one of happiness. On April 11, 1807, the La Fayettes celebrated the thirty-third anniversary of their marriage. Both were of the opinion that, taking the rough with the smooth, their union had been a good one. Adrienne's health still left much to be desired, but the family had grown used to that and were no longer seriously worried. Only the ailing woman felt in her flesh that, instead of improving, her condition was steadily getting worse. She no longer, as in the old days, made plans for long-continuing works of charity. She preferred to set on a firm foundation those upon which she was already engaged, that they might continue after her death.

Once more the emperor was victorious and everything pointed to the coming of peace. George and Louis would be returning home. Both spoke of leaving the army, since their military careers held no hope for the future. Adrienne was overjoyed at the idea of seeing them again, and this time for good. She took great pleasure in reading *Athalie* to the little Célestine, Anastasie's elder daughter, and expounding Racine in a manner wholly suited to a child's understanding. Among the last great pleasures she was to know were the baptism in June, 1807, by the Bishop of Meaux of Pauline de Lasteyrie, Virginie's little girl, in the chapel at La Grange, and, in August, George's return.

Gilbert scolded her from time to time, but very affectionately. "I notice, dear Adrienne, that you have a headache and a high temperature. It is a bad habit of yours and occurs too often."

It was indeed a bad habit. She had picked it up at Olmütz.

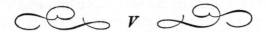

PERPETUAL ADORATION

*You, and you only, can know whether
you are under an obligation; God Himself does not demand this sacrifice; he
merely waits. If you judge that there
is no obligation, then in the name of
God I will absolve you.*

PAUL CLAUDEL

When the Noailles sisters were reunited in Holland they had talked
a great deal about the duty they owed to their victims of the 4th
Thermidor. They hoped it might be possible to recover the three
bodies and give them decent burial in some place where they
themselves could go for prayer and meditation. But the search was
not easy. Bonaparte had a horror of anything that might recall the
Terror and so divide the French people. Fouché's consular police
kept an ever-watchful eye on the returning *émigrés* who perhaps
would be a little too curious.

It was only when two years had gone by that Pauline de Montagu
heard of a lacemaker, Mlle Pâris, whose father and brother had,
like the Noailles ladies, been executed at the Place du Trône. She
maintained that she knew the exact spot where they now lay. Mme
de Montagu climbed the four flights of stairs leading to the lacemaker's attic, and learned from the poor young woman that after
following the cart into which the headless bodies had been thrown
pell mell, she had seen them buried in a piece of waste land which

was enclosed by walls. The common grave into which the victims were flung was now in a long strip of overgrown garden belonging to a house which could be entered from the Rue de Picpus. "It is," said Mlle Pâris, "the object of my Sunday walk, winter and summer." Wrote Pauline's biographer:

When Madame de Montagu and Madame de La Fayette saw this cemetery, of which the city at large knew nothing and those who lived nearby scarcely anything, they were overcome by feelings of bitter melancholy. It was a barren piece of ground, approached by paths now long disused. What can be more heart-rending than such evidence of the forgetfulness of the recent past, of its good and its evil, of its persecutors and its victims? It is because of such rapid and complete forgetfulness that the experience of one generation can be of little use to that which follows it. The two sisters could not but be deeply moved by the thought of this multitude of honest folk sacrificed without justice, buried without prayers, and, for the most part, with no one left to mourn them and commend their souls to God's mercy.[1]

They made inquiries about this lost corner, and here is what they learned. In May, 1792, the members of the Sisterhood of St-Augustine had been forced to leave their convent and its garden in the Rue Picpus. A man named Riedain had acquired the lease of the land, and had sublet part of it to a certain Citizen Coignard who proposed to establish a madhouse there. Such enterprises were profitable under the Terror. Noblemen and rich merchants took refuge in these asylums where, thanks to the collusion of doctors and certain officials, they could wait for the coming of better times in relative security.

This huge garden surrounded by high walls was not very far from the Place du Trône (now the Place de la Nation) where the scaffold had stood. One day, forty workmen, having opened a breach in the northernmost wall, made their way into the property, rooted up the vines and the fruit trees, and started to dig a large hole. Riedain protested, but was told that the Ministry of Public Works had issued a requisition order. The truth of the matter was that as a result of thirty, fifty, and sometimes sixty executions a day, the local cemeteries were filled. Further, there were complaints about the passing of the death-cart dripping blood. The enclosed garden of Picpus had therefore been chosen as a convenient spot, being close to the guillotine, screened from the eyes of the curious, and easy of access to those disposing of the bodies.

The Noailles sisters also learned something of the horrible scenes enacted there. The "shortened" dead were stripped by the executioner's assistants. Coats, breeches, women's dresses, chemises, and shoes were made into piles and counted. Then the naked bodies were laid in rows in the common grave. In order to overcome the appalling stench, fires of thyme, juniper, and sage were lit. For six weeks this ghastly operation continued.

Shortly after the 9th Thermidor, the assistants of the executioner Samson dismantled the guillotine in the Place du Trône, and silence descended on Picpus. In 1795 the Ministry of Public Works had the sinister pit filled in and removed the fence that separated it from the garden. It is probable that 1307 headless corpses had been buried there (aristocrats, bourgeois, and men of the people). Riedain, the lessee, put in a claim for an indemnity, but failed to get it. In June, 1796, his lease was terminated, and the land was sold to two inhabitants of the Faubourg Saint-Antoine, Citizens Cardeval and Le Jemptel, known by their neighbors to be good Catholics. Through a third party they immediately resold part of it to the Princesse Hohenzollern-Sigmaringen, whose brother, the Prince de Salm-Kyrburg, had been guillotined in the Place du Trône. Her land, which she bought for 900 francs, contained the vast common grave. The princesse had a wall built to shut it off from the rest of the garden.

All talk about the Picpus burial place had long ceased when Pauline and Adrienne, guided by Mlle de Pâris, made their harrowing pilgrimage. The idea came to Pauline of establishing an endowment, with the object of associating the families of all the victims in the pious enterprise of preserving the sacred character of this part of the garden.

The two sisters decided to open a subscription for the restoration of the property which had formerly belonged to the convent. Adrienne's note to Beauchet, asking him to make a first payment in her name of 600 livres, still exists. But the sisters soon realized that the presence of their names at the head of the subscription list might attract the unwelcome attentions of Fouché's police. They must discreetly efface themselves.

Their contribution was small, and if they personally guaranteed further financial sacrifices, the gesture was made secretly since they

*did not wish to give an individual stamp to the good work but rather
to make it the shared offering of a great number of persons, and a
testimony of public mourning.... Abbé Beudot undertook to approach the families concerned, and the names of the sisters were
lost in the crowd of subscribers, as their mother was in the multitude of the dead.*[2]

The whole of the convent site was purchased in August, 1803, for
24,000 francs. The part of the ground containing the common
burial pit remained the property of the Princesse Hohenzollern-
Sigmaringen. It was enclosed by walls, but communicated with the
main garden by way of a wooden door which was always kept locked.
Opposite this door Pauline de Montagu had a stone cross set up.
When the former chapter house of St-Augustine had been turned
into a chapel, arrangements were made to have a Requiem Mass
sung there once a year. But Adrienne and Pauline considered this
annual ceremony to be insufficient. The number of the victims, the
horrible nature of their fate, and the cult dedicated to their memory
demanded an unbroken chain of prayer.

Early in 1805 Pauline learned of the existence of a religious community at 34 Rue de la Place Vendôme—the Ladies of the Sacred
Heart and of the Perpetual Adoration—whose rule imposed upon
them the duty of replacing one another, at hourly intervals, day and
night, before an altar on which the Blessed Sacrament was permanently unveiled. This order, still secret in 1805, had been established at Poitiers when the Terror was at its height by the pious
ladies of several former noble families. The founder, Henriette
Aymer de la Chevalerie, had as a young woman been renowned for
her wit and brilliance. She had later become, under the name of
Mère Henriette, a saint whose judgment was both sound and penetrating. The eight sisters who followed her to Paris lived in extreme
poverty, deprived of everything except the barest necessities. But
though they cheerfully did without beds and chairs, a chapel for
the Adoration was essential. Pauline de Montagu made an offer of
the former convent to their superior, and Mère Henriette undertook to celebrate the annual Mass and to assure the maintenance
and the protection of the martyrs' enclosure.

The settling in of the nuns and the constant comings and goings
of Abbé Coudrin, their chaplain, soon awakened the suspicions of
Fouché's sleuths. On May 8 they had received an anonymous let-

ter: "This is to draw your attention to the fact that certain relatives of victims of the Revolution have established at N° 7 Rue de Picpus an organization, the purpose of which is to keep alive those very misfortunes which the government is trying to let lapse into oblivion." In the margin of this denunciation, some official had written: "His Excellency has given instructions for precise information to be collected concerning the nature of this organization, and, if it be found to exist, its members." [3]

The man sent to carry out this investigation reported that the ex-nuns had been reinstated, that their garden was again being cultivated, and that there was a small chapel "with some Latin over the door" to which the people of the neighborhood went to hear Mass, and where a solemn service to the victims of the Terror was celebrated once a year. "According to gossip, this establishment has some connection with the Noailles family, to whom it is said that the land belongs and that it is still occasionally used for burials."

In 1806 another of Fouché's agents attended the commemoration service at Picpus. He reported seeing "ladies and gentlemen, all dressed in black." Several of the men were wearing swords, and this smelled of the Old Regime. Mlle de Noailles made a collection, and her bag appeared to be well filled and to contain some gold. He added that: "Many persons belonging to the former nobility and occupying high positions in the new court, after hesitating for a long time, actually made donations and took the necessary steps which would entitle them to be regarded as founder-members of the Picpus charity."

Fouché knew that the Noailles sisters had been the moving spirits in this matter of the charity. He could, as the mood took him, regard the affair as a monarchist conspiracy or as an act of piety on the part of the various families concerned. The second alternative was, he thought, the wiser one to adopt. Not only did several members of the new court figure on the subscription list; it included Eugène de Beauharnais, the Emperor's adopted son, whose father had been guillotined and was buried in the Picpus grave. Besides, Fouché, who was extremely farsighted, thought it wise to take precautions in view of a possible return of the Bourbons.

Adrienne and Pauline had succeeded, as they had hoped to do, in making perpetual, so far as anything human can be perpetual, the cult of the beloved victims.

O DEATH, WHERE IS THY STING?

*"So I have been a pleasant companion
for you? ... Then bless me."*

ADRIENNE DE LA FAYETTE

In September, 1807, Doctor Lobhines, who for many years had been Adrienne's medical attendant in Paris, received a communication from Anastasie, who was staying at La Grange. Her mother had a high fever. Food of any description made her feel sick. After her husband's departure for Auvergne, she had vomited through a whole night. Could this be ordinary indigestion, or might it be due to the distressing agitation caused by his leaving her? Lobhines did not consider this probable. He was more inclined to think that she had had a relapse, or perhaps was suffering from a duodenal ulcer. He was strongly of the opinion that the sick woman should be moved to Mme de Tessés house at Aulnay, where he would be within easy reach of her. Meanwhile, he corresponded with both Anastasie and Virginie and prescribed such remedies as he could do at so great a distance from the patient. When Adrienne's condition grew worse, her daughters had her conveyed to Aulnay, and a little later to 24 Rue d'Anjou, Mme de Tessé's town house. Lobhines thought her so ill that he called in Corvisart, the emperor's doctor, and sent a message to La Fayette at Chavaniac that the situation was extremely serious. The best account of Adrienne's last illness and death is that given by La Fayette himself in a lengthy letter to

César de La Tour-Maubourg, his dearest friend and fellow prisoner at Olmütz.

I have not yet written to you, my dear friend, so plunged in misery have I been; though I very nearly did so when I transmitted to you the tokens of her friendship for you and of her confidence in your feelings for her. You have already been informed of the end of this angelic and incomparable woman. I feel a profound need to speak of it to you at greater length. I seek relief from my pain in pouring out my feelings to the most constant, the most beloved confidant with whom I shared those vicissitudes which made me think myself unhappy. Until this moment you have always found me stronger than the circumstances of my life: today the circumstances are stronger than I am. I shall never rise above them.

During the thirty-four years of a union in which her tenderness, her goodness, her elevation of mind, her delicacy and generosity charmed and embellished my life and made of it an honorable thing, I came to be so used to all she meant to me that I could not draw a line of distinction between her existence and my own. She was fourteen years old and I sixteen when her heart first became inextricably blended with everything that mattered to me. I felt quite certain that I loved her and needed her, but it is only now, when, having lost her, I have to unravel what remains of myself from that sweet entanglement so as to face what is left me of a life which I once thought filled with so many distractions, that I realize how impossible it is that I shall ever more know happiness or well-being.

Never did the presentiment of loss come upon me so strongly as when, after leaving Chavaniac, an alarming note from Madame de Tessé was given to me at Brioude. I felt as though I had been struck to the heart. George feared the effect upon me of my feelings at that moment, more than he did the actual danger. We made all the speed we could, and on arriving in Paris could see at once that she was indeed desperately ill; but apart from the fact that I had never really believed, why I do not know, that the source of her trouble lay in the duodenum, I attributed to the joy of seeing us again some part at least of the improvement which showed in her next day. Her stomach was eased, but she began to suffer from a thickness in the head. To Madame de Simiane she observed: "I am going to have a malignant fever, but since I shall be well looked after, I shall get over it."

But alas! after an illness which had afflicted her now for several years—two months of suffering and increasing weakness at a peculiarly critical period of her life—this was more than a simple malignant fever, there being a certain dissolution in the blood, which appeared to be the most ominous symptom. Corvisart, however, had been hopeful for a while, though he had rightly said that only the enlightened and devoted care of Monsieur Lobhines could have preserved that dear life for so long. There could be no question of saving her, but we owe it to him that the final collapse was delayed and that the pain was eased. We found some comfort in mingling our tears with his.

Her dear mind began to wander when her confessor came to see her. In response to my daughters' wish, he withdrew after a few vague words, but the nurse brought him back, though by so doing she incurred their reproaches against which she could put up a poor defense. Their mother then made her confession. That evening she said to me: "If I am bound for another world, you know how busy I shall be about you there. The sacrifice of my life would count for little, much though it will cost me to be parted from you, if it could assure your eternal happiness."

The day on which she received the sacraments she set great store on my being present. She then relapsed into a state of unbroken delirium, a delirium more extraordinary and more touching than any I have ever witnessed. Try, my dear friend, to imagine her poor brain all deranged, so that she thought herself in Egypt, in Syria, among the events of the reign of Athaliah, which Célestine's lessons had left firmly implanted in her mind, her thoughts all confused and troubled except those in which her heart was concerned. At last the delirium became continuous, though it never clouded an unalterable sweetness, a constant wish to please, so that all the time she was trying to say something that would please me, to express her gratitude for all the care that was being given to her, a fear that she was tiring others, the need she felt to be useful to them—for in these matters she never ceased, in her feelings and her innate goodness, to be in any way different from what she would have been had she had full control of her reason. There was also an elevation in her thoughts, an acuteness of observation, a clarity and elegance of expression which astonished all those who were present, and those to whom were transmitted the admirable and charming utterances which issued from that disordered mind.

But what above all things was so adorable was the way in which the full flow of her tenderness was unceasingly directed on her children and her sister, the concern she showed for the health of her aunt and Monsieur de Tessé—thinking all the time that she was with them at Memphis—the delight she took in hearing talk about her friends, and all this while her imagination was hopelessly deranged, though by a miracle of sensitiveness it never became unalterably fixed on any one object, save when it turned to her relations with me. It was as though the thought of them lay too deep to be troubled, was stronger than her sickness, stronger than death itself. For this angelic creature had already ceased to belong to this world. Everything in her was frozen but for feeling, which, with such warmth and life as still remained, seemed to have become concentrated in the hand that clung to mine.

It may even have been that she surrendered more completely to the expression of her tenderness, to the free flow of feeling, than would have been the case had she been in her right mind. Not that the sweet angel was afflicted with any terrors concerning her future life. Her religion was all love and confidence. She had been scrupulous in the observance of her religious duties, even quite recently, for the sake of her daughters, who might otherwise have been more urgent in pressing upon her the taking of the sacraments. But no fear of Hell had ever come near her. She did not believe in it as a possibility for good, sincere, and virtuous people, no matter what their opinions might be. "I do not know what will happen at the moment of their deaths," she used to say, "but only that God will open their eyes and save them." She would, however, have thought it incumbent upon her to divert her mind more wholly from the emotions which were the lifeblood of all the faculties of her spirit, and, to quote one of the last expressions of which she made use, "of every fiber of her body." She would have dealt with what she called her sins, but very tenderly, for she could never understand how there could be any divine punishment other than exclusion from the life and presence of the Supreme Being. Many are the times when you have heard me joke with her about her pleasing heresies. Who knows whether the fear of increasing my regrets may not in part have restrained her from giving full rein to her feelings, just as another form of control prevented her during her lifetime from abandoning herself to what was passionate in them?

"There was a time," she told me only a few months ago, "when, on your return from America, I felt myself to be so violently carried away as to be almost ill when you entered a room where I happened to be, so that I was afflicted by a dread lest I might seem too importunate, and so embarrass your natural delicacy. I therefore tried to keep a tight hold on myself. But what I did allow to show should not have displeased you."

Well, in that adorable delirium in which she remained where all that had to do with me was concerned, there was nothing to restrain the oupourings of that incomparable tenderness, that—if I may so describe it—cult of the heart, which then showed itself in all its beauty, all its exaltation, all its plenitude.

"How grateful I am to God," she said during her illness, "that so violent a passion should also have been a duty! How happy I have been," she said on the day of her death, "in having had the wonderful good fortune to be your wife."

And, when I told her of my love for her: "Is that true?" she said in a voice that touched my heart. "Is that really true? How good you are! Say it again, for to hear it gives me pleasure. If you think you are not loved enough," she said, "then you must lay the blame on God for not having given me faculties enough." She also said to me in the midst of her delirium, "I love you as a Christian, as a human being, passionately, even voluptuously, or should do so had I any senses left."

And indeed her weakness was extreme. Her poor body was a mass of blisters and running sores. "What a state for your wife to be in," she said, "looking as though she had been skinned!"

When she was pitied for her sufferings, she was afraid of having exaggerated them to herself and to others. One day when her wounds had just been dressed and I was looking at her with compassion, "Ah," she said, "I am more than rewarded by the kindness in your eyes."

She often begged me to stay longer because my presence calmed her, because it did her so much good to know that I was near her. At other times discretion came uppermost. She wanted me to attend to my own concerns, and when I answered that my only concern was to look after her, "How good you are!" she exclaimed in her weak but penetrating voice. "You are too kind, you are spoiling me. I do not deserve so much. I am too happy."

The habit she had acquired of always being concerned for me, of reading what I was thinking in my eyes, had left her, even in delirium, with an astonishing sagacity about my every mood, though she could not disentangle the causes of it. "Does your present way of life please you?" she often asked me with anxiety in her voice. One day, when she asked my servant Louis for news of his wife and child, whom in fact he had just lost, she guessed that I was vexed, without understanding why. "Is it that my question to Louis pains you?" she asked.

Once, after a day when we had been very unhappy, she said, "Your face is more serene today, but not altogether so."

On another occasion, when I had been much oppressed with worry and she was looking at me as I sat at some distance from her bed, she said, "You are looking cheerful, but not too cheerful." Then, staring at me very fixedly, "I dare swear you have been suffering with your chest, have you not?"

I tell you all these details, my dear friend, because they are evidence, among a thousand others things of that tender, constant and informed attention where I was concerned, from which nothing, not even sickness, not even delirium, could distract her mind.

The delirium, however, went very deep and was extremely stubborn. It bore chiefly on the troublous reign of Athaliah, which seemed to obsess her; on the family of Jacob, in which she liked to think that I was greatly loved; and on the quarrels of Israel and Judah. "It would be very strange," she said, "if, being your wife, I were obliged to sacrifice myself for a king!"

She had a fear of troubles and proscriptions, but was ready to face them with that sweetness and determination which had characterized her when such things had been an actual threat. She rejoiced in the noble courage, the disinterestedness and the greatness of mind of her son and her sons-in-law, and, when inquiring whether there was likely to be a persecution of the Christians, and martyrdoms, counted upon me to defend the oppressed. "It seems to me," she said, "that the world is being made over again from the beginning: there is no end to all these experiments. When, O when, will the world run smoothly on two wheels, as you want it to?"

All this was muddled in her brain, and it was in Egypt and in Syria that she believed herself to be. "I do not know where I am," she said. "I seem to have a makeshift head on a mortifying body." One day she was worried because she had a vague idea that she was an empress. "But if I were," she added, "then you would be an emperor, and it would be you who had it on his conscience."

There was a moment when we thought the delirium was passing. "I am mad, am I not?" she exclaimed. "Come close and tell me whether I have lost my reason." I replied that I should be very much distressed if I thought that all the charming things that she had said to me were absurdities. "Have I said charming things to you? But I have also said a lot of extravagant ones. We have been playing the tragedy of Athalie. What! here I am, married to the most truthful of men, my children are truthful too, yet I cannot get at the truth. It is all because of your goodness: you deal gently with my head: but tell me. I will resign myself to the shame of being mad!" We succeeded in calming her. I told her that she was highly regarded and much loved. "I do not mind about being highly regarded, so long as I am still loved." Another time she said: "See what has happened to my poor head: it is strange, but I cannot now remember whether Virginie and Monsieur de Lasteyrie are betrothed or married. Help me to find myself again."

But at other times she spoke about the characters of her children and grandchildren with a quite indescribable charm and shrewdness.

Sometimes she could be heard praying in her bed. She made her daughters read the prayers of the Mass to her, and never failed to notice when they left out passages so as not to fatigue her. There was an almost unearthly quality in the way in which, on one of her last nights, she recited twice over in a strong emphatic voice a song of Tobit which was applicable to her situation—the same she had recited to her daughters on seeing the towers of Olmütz for the first time. I drew close to her. "It is by Tobit," she said. "I sing badly; that is why I recite it." On another occasion she spoke a most beautiful extempore prayer for a whole hour.

I never knew her to be wrong about me save once, when for a few moments she was convinced that I had become a fervent Christian. But the mistake was fleeting and accompanied by doubts and questions which proved that what she had said was as much the expression of a wish as an illusion.

"You are not a Christian, are you?" she said one day. "Then, since I made no answer, "Ah! I know what you are: you are a Fayettist!"

"You must think me very bumptious," I replied, "but are you not something of one yourself?"

"Indeed, yes!" she exclaimed. "With all my heart! I feel I would give my life for that sect." This she said with a very discerning look, and added: "But you admire Jesus Christ, do you not?" I told her, as I had often done before, that I did. "Well then, since you admire him so much, you will end by recognizing his divinity."

I once spoke to her about her angelic gentleness. "That is true," she said. "I am gentle: God made me so. But my gentleness is not like yours. I cannot make so high a claim. You are so strong, and at the same time so gentle. But I agree that I am gentle, and you are very good to me."

"It is you who are good," I answered, "and above all else, generous. Do you remember the first time I went to America? Everybody else was furious with me, but you hid your tears at the wedding of Madame de Ségur. You did not want to appear sorrowful lest others might blame me."

"Yes, indeed," she said, "gentle, but as a child is gentle. How sweet it is of you to remember things that happened so long ago!"

She spoke to me very sensibly about the happiness of her daughters, and of the nobility and goodness of her sons-in-law. "But I have not been able to make them as happy as I have been: it would have needed the power of God to do such a thing twice. You are beyond compare!"

It is not because I want to boast that I tell you all this, my dear friend, though there is more than enough to make me proud: but because it is a joy for me to talk over with you all that reminds me of her gentleness—and happiness.

How happy she would have been this winter: the three families all reunited; the war over for George and Louis; Virginie about to have a child; and our love the more increased by the illness from which we had feared that she might not recover! How good it was of her in those last days to worry herself about my amusements at La Grange, and about my farming, matters that had remained quite clear in her head, because for so long they had constituted her daily interest. When I spoke to her about our going home: "Ah," she said, "that would be too delicious! Dear God, dear God! Oh, for six poor years of La Grange!" On one of those last days when the thought of going there with me had made her restless and she thought it would be better if I went on ahead, I begged her to let me stay with her. I made her promise she would rest, and she said that she would do her best to obey me. Then, growing calmer: "Well then, stay," she said. "Wait just a little while and I will fall asleep quite quietly." *Poor woman! it was a presentiment of the fate in store for us.*

In spite of the confusion and disorder of her mind, she knew that she was going to die. Two nights previously, I heard her say to her nurse: "Do not leave me. Tell me when I have to die." I approached the bed. Her fear grew less, but when I spoke of her being cured and returning to La Grange: "Ah, no," she said. "I am going to die. Have you any grudge against me?"

"What grudge could I have, my dearest?" I answered. "You have always been so sweet, so good."

"So I have been a pleasant companion for you?"

"Indeed you have."

"Then bless me."

On all those last evenings, whenever I left her or she thought I was about to leave her, she asked me for my blessing.

When in those last days I spoke to her of the happiness of our union and of my deep affection, she made me repeat my assurances so that she might have the more pleasure, and said: "Promise me to keep that affection always. Promise me!" I need not tell you that I did. "Are you satisfied with our children?" she went on. I told her that I was, profoundly so. "They are very good," she said. "Give them your support. Let your affection for me make up for their shortcomings." Then, her delirium getting the upper hand: "How do you think they will do for the house of Jacob?" I told her that our excellent children would enter into all her feelings. "Ah," she replied, "my feelings are very temperate. I have only those I have for you. My heart has kept all its tenderness for you."

Only twice did I see her delirium grow violent, and on both occasions the frenzy of maternal affection was the cause. Once when George, to spare her from exhausting herself in talk, came into her room after having stayed away from it for some time, she thought he had arrived straight from the army. So overjoyed was she at seeing him again that her heart began to beat violently and we were frightened. The other time was when she grew much animated at the idea that she had just made me a father once again.

She was well-nigh drunk with joy at the approach of that anniversary, so dear to our hearts, of the day twenty-eight years ago when she had given me George. That day of mutual felicitations was the day on which she died.

It is impossible sufficiently to admire the sweetness, the patience, the unchanging considerateness of this angelic woman during her long and painful illness. There was not a moment, even in the course of that month-long delirium, that she did not think about others. She had a dread of being importunate, and frequently said: "I am exceedingly tedious and very tiresome. My children," she added, "must resign themselves to having a stupid mother, seeing that their father is willing to put up with a stupid wife." She never gave the least sign of being made irritable by her condition, of impatience when she was in pain, of resentment at her nurse's attentions or at the remedies prescribed for her. When she most disliked having to drink some draught or other, one word from me or from our children (or, in our absence, the thought that her attendants might be scolded) was enough to make her do so in spite of her feeling of nausea, so that we had to harden ourselves against her wish to please. Up till the very last, everything done for her was greeted with a word of thanks, a nod of the head, a gesture of the hand.

"Never," said Monsieur Lobhines, "in the course of a long practice have I ever seen anything even remotely comparable to that adorable character, that extraordinary delirium! No, I have never seen anything that has given me so complete an idea of human perfection."

When the moment came for her to breathe her last, the last but one thing she said was that she was not in pain. "That I can well believe," exclaimed her nurse, "for she is an angel."

Not only in her sick room, but when she was staying with her aunt and in those little gatherings of friends who came for news of her, this incomparable woman was a living object lesson in all that was good, amiable, virtuous, and tender."

"You have news of Monsieur de Maubourg? Oh, I rely much on him; he is very fond of me and rejoices that our two families are now one." And one indeed they are. Those were her words, and I have sent them to you with all the dear devotion of my heart.

Her delirium did not stand in the way of her wishing for news of Victor, of Tracy, of Florimond * and saying to me: "How delightful to have letters from Constantinople!" She also charged Émilie to give her fondest good wishes to Augustine.† The news of your brother's arrival put her in a state of the greatest agitation, because

---

* The eldest son of the friend to whom this letter was addressed.

† Émilie de La Fayette's younger sister.

there had been some talk of his being wounded and she had no recollection of Friedland! But we subsequently spoke to her about his house at Passy.

These, my dear friend, are just a few of the thoughts of those dear to her which emerged from the disorder of her poor brain.

The remarkable feature of this delirium was the way it varied with the degree of her affection. For me, a steady judgment which mingled strangely with the fantastic situations in which she imagined us to be, so that she saw me always in the light of my principles, my feelings, my tastes, and my antipathies. For me, too, an astonishing sagacity, a constant and detailed preoccupation, a passionate and unchanging tenderness. In the midst of her hallucinations she loved to say to me: "You must decide. You are our chief; it is our happy lot to be obedient to you." One day, when I begged her to be calm, she gaily repeated to me this line of poetry: "To your wise counsel, Lord, I entrust myself."

With what charm, what nobility of language, did she speak of the high opinion which she had of me! She had the merit, very rare in pious persons, of being able to believe completely in the virtue of those who did not share her faith, and of acknowledging it without the slightest reservation.

She never ceased to recognize and welcome her children (I speak of all six of them) and to say the most tender and pleasing things about them. She frequently praised their characters and discussed them with me in the shrewdest way, though she was less constantly lucid when she talked of them than when I was the object of her thoughts.

She several times spoke in the sweetest detail about her grandchildren: but more often than not their number, their sex, and even the existence of the two last, led to a strange confusion in her mind.* She at all times expressed the greatest affection for her Montagu sister, frequently asking her—and me—for news of her mother, or saying that she had seen her that morning. It made us shudder when on the day of her death we heard her say quite calmly: "Today I shall see my mother."

Everything that had to do with our beloved patient was well

---

* Adrienne's two last grandchildren were Mathilde de La Fayette (1805–86), George's second daughter, who in 1832 married Maurice Poivre de Pusy, and Marie-Pauline de Lasteyrie (1807–82), the eldest daughter of Virginie, and the future Comtesse Charles de Rémusat.

organized. The nurse had the assistance of Madame Garet, Joséphine (Simon's wife), and Noyer's wife as well. The three girls were always in readiness to make themselves useful. George, Charles, and Louis relieved each other in such a way that one of them was always in her room. Monet spent all the last nights there. These precautions made it certain that everything necessary would be promptly attended to: nothing was neglected. How many affectionate words our dear good children must have heard in the performance of their duties.

Monsieur Lobhines came several times a day to see her, pondered over the case for hours on end, tried every variety of remedy, and when he was in doubt or thought somebody else could give him an idea, wrote to Corvisart or suggested a meeting to him, even begged him to see the sick woman without being called in so that not a moment should be lost. In a few words, he has been the best of friends as well the most honest and enlightened of doctors.

Our dear Madame de Tessé has during the last few weeks been compelled to keep to the house as the result of an illness which in her present weak state might have taken a serious turn. We feared the effect of emotion upon her if we let her see Adrienne. She wanted to do so, however, while my poor wife was asleep. Ah, my friend, what a condition she was in when she left the sick room! Adrienne had been thinking a great deal about her aunt and knowing her to be ill, believed (in her delirium) that she had been taken to her bedside. She talked in what seemed a perfectly rational manner about Monsieur de Tessé, who is suffering from an eruptive ailment. She sent me to look after both of them, saying:

"I wager that my uncle is delighted to have you all about him. But is it not rather inconsiderate of us to be staying here: there are so many of us?"

"Not at all," I said. "There are only thirteen of us to feed."

"It is true," she replied, "that my aunt finds as much pleasure in doing us a kindness as we do in accepting it."

I have already told you, without going into unnecessary details, that she had received the sacraments. I was present on that occasion, which was more sad for us than for her, she having already communicated in her bed a little while previously. It was then that her delirium became complete. There was nothing for me to do in conforming to her intentions. But I observed that my daughters were quite calm and that their agitation in this matter showed in inverse ratio to their concern for her. On one of the last days her confessor came. I was perfectly frank with him, and told him that I desired to respect the presumed wishes of my wife. I had no difficulty in persuading him that his being in the room with her was unnecessary, and might be harmful. On the day before her death, however, since my daughters attached much importance to the speaking of certain prayers and indulgences quite close to her, one of the curates of the parish was introduced into her room, concealed behind a curtain, on the other side of which I was closeted with her, and carried out the last duties without her being aware of his presence.

The next day, just when her agony was drawing to a close and while she could still speak, my daughters were afraid that her habit of not carrying out her religious observances when I was with her might hamper her wish to hear or to say some prayers. A small crucifix was within easy reach, but instead of taking it she clasped my hand and pressed it between her own in an attitude of prayer. I think it probable that it was for me she was praying. I was asked to withdraw to some little distance so that Madame de Montagu, who had always enjoyed her confidence in such matters, might ask whether there was anything she wished to say to her. My first instinct was to refuse to conform with this request, tender and timid though it was. I was afraid lest her last moments might be troubled. I will even go so far as to confess that my love as a husband of thirty-four years' standing felt for the first time a pang of jealousy. I felt a passionate need to be her sole preoccupation. But I repressed this feeling so that her every wish should be fulfilled. I gave up my place to her sister, who repeated her question twice. The beloved sufferer, who had always had a deep affection for Madame de Montagu and wanted her to be in close attendance, twice answered "No" and added, "Go to supper." She seemed impatient for me to resume my place, and when I did so she again took my hand in hers, saying "I am all yours." Those words "all yours" were the last she spoke.

It has been said that she frequently preached at me. That was not her way. In her delirium she had often expressed the thought that she would go to heaven, though, may I add, this thought was not enough to console her for leaving me. She several times said: "This life is short and troubled. Let us be reunited in God and pass together into eternity." She prayed that the peace of God should be

given to me and to all of us. That is how this sweet angel spoke
in her last illness, just as she had done in the will she had drawn up
some years previously. It is a model of delicacy, elevated thought,
and eloquent feeling.

It seems to me that by prolonging these details I am seeking to
put off the last terrible moments when, seeing that Monsieur
Lobhines had abandoned all hope of a cure and was thinking only
of prolonging her life, we felt with a certainty which would not be
denied that there would be no morrow for her. Till then there
had never been more than two or three of us in her room at the
same time. But on that day it clearly fatigued her to look around
for us, and I therefore saw no objection to summoning the whole
family and ranging them on chairs in a semicircle so that she could
see everybody. "What a charming party!" she said with an expression of great satisfaction on her face.

I remember that George's wife and children were seated together
in a corner of the room and that she said to me: "See how charming they look!" Then, one after the other, she summoned her daughters to her and addressed sweet words to them. Then to each she
gave her blessing. I am convinced that the little ceremony gave
happiness and comfort to her heart. How could it have been otherwise, since her religion, far from being a cause of terror and scruples,
was during the whole of her illness before and during her delirium,
nothing but love and gratitude for those "immense mercies which,"
as she told her sisters and her daughters, "God has lavished and is
still lavishing upon me." In spite of the muddled condition of her
mind, up till the moment of her last breath she was not for one
instant without that joy which only a heart such as hers could feel.
Even the mists of her delirium had cleared. She no longer suffered
from a confusion of ideas about her children, their marriages, and
even certain incidents which belonged to a distant period of their
lives. Everything that had to do with her family was once more
clear to her. Instead of asking Madame de Montagu for news of
her mother, she said: "I look on you as having taken her place."

No doubt she felt that death was near when, after having said
in that touching way she so often had, "Have you been satisfied
with me? Have you been so good as to love me? If that is so, give
me your blessing," I replied: "You too love me, do you not? Therefore you also must bless me." For the first and last time she gave me
her blessing with the most solemn tenderness. Then each of the six

children went to her in turn and kissed her hands and her face. She looked at them with indescribable affection. Most certainly she felt the end was near when, as I think, fearing lest she might have some convulsion, she signed to me to go away and, seeing that I stayed, took my hand and laid it on her eyes with an expression of the most tender gratitude, thus indicating the last duty she expected of me.

Throughout those hours of muted agony we felt torn between the wish to show her that love which gave her so much happiness and the conviction that emotion was draining away such little span of life as still remained to her. And so it was that I was keeping back my words with as much care as my sobs, when the heart breaking look in her eyes and a few scarcely audible words forced from my lips some utterance of the feelings which were choking me. Her voice became suddenly stronger and she exclaimed: "It is really true, then? You do love me? Ah, what happiness! Kiss me." Those poor arms which had almost lost the power of movement came from beneath the sheet with a vigor that amazed the nurse. She put them round my neck and, drawing down my face to hers, she stroked my cheeks as though in passionate gratitude and pressed me to her heart, saying, "What joy! How happy I am to belong to you!" For so long as her right hand had any power of movement left, she laid mine first to her mouth, then to her heart. My left hand had all the while been holding hers. I could feel it move, and it was as though that movement were repeating the last words she ever spoke: "I am all yours!"

We were grouped about her bed, which had been drawn into the middle of the room. She signed to her sister to sit down. Her three daughters kept bringing hot towels to lay upon her hands and arms, so as to preserve some little warmth in them. When we held a spoonful of wine to her lips we thought the end had come: but that was not yet. I made the others stand back to give her air, and she began to breathe again. We all knelt down and followed the slow movement of her breathing which continued for a longer time, I think, than I should have thought possible in her condition. What ours was, I leave to your imagination.

It was without any appearance of suffering, with a smile of sweetness on her lips and my hand still clutched in hers, that this angel of tenderness and goodness departed this life. We let our tears fall upon the lifeless body. I felt myself being led away by Messieurs de

Mun and de Tracy: my dear son supported me in his arms. They let me kiss her once again, and there I bade farewell to her, and to all my happiness in this world.

Everything had been foreseen by George. I had to say but one word to Barrier and the excellent fellow spent three days and three nights, helped by Madame Garet and Joséphine, watching by her and performing those last offices for the dead which are too often neglected. Our dear Madame Tessé also took part in them with all the religious fervor of her friendship.

I knew so well that modesty of hers, that reserve which had never been absent even at the height of her delirium. It would have eased her mind to know that a priest was watching by her. George had arranged everything in accordance with her wishes. My dear daughters have had the idea, first put forward by Anastasie and adopted by their husbands, of giving to their mother as an act of homage what each most valued: her wedding-ring. George superintended everything in person. It was he who, when replica rings had been made, hung the originals with the greatest respect round his mother's neck, and he too who had the new rings touched and blessed; he, finally, who arranged to have buried in the grave with her a ring which was an exact copy of one I gave to her thirty-four years ago and from which I shall never now be parted. These pious duties he carried out in a manner worthy of her and of him.

It was on Monday that this angelic woman was borne with the greatest simplicity, in accordance with her expressed wishes, to a spot close to the pit in which lie the remains of her grandmother, her mother, and her sister, mixed with those of sixteen hundred victims. She has been buried in a place apart so as to make possible the future plans dictated by our love. I recognized it unaided when George, who has not allowed his own grief to interfere with his care for me, went with me there last Thursday. We were able to kneel together by that sacred grave and mingle our tears. My three daughters, Charles, and Louis paid it a visit on New Year's Day, which is when the special service is held at Picpus.

We noticed with feelings of religious awe that during the time, longer in her case than is usual, when her dear body was left with the face exposed upon the bed where she had breathed her last, it showed not the slightest sign of corruption. Her features looked even more natural than they had done in the final days of her illness. Everything about her denoted sweetness and kindliness and gave proof that right up to the last moments of her life body and soul had been at peace. God had made her gentle, she had said, and the imprint of that gentleness showed as indestructibly upon her face as her gentleness (especially toward me) had been beyond the power of violent disease and the derangement of delirium to touch.

We found in her desk a letter written to me in 1785, certain dispositions which she had made in 1792, and an official will drawn up in 1804, the sole purpose of which is to secure to me all that the law allows her to leave. It also contains instructions about certain dispositions to be made after her death, without cost to me, and a detailed list of such small gifts as she wished me to make. A number of people are named in it: myself, each of her six children, the grandchildren already born, her father—with a word to Madame de Noailles—her two sisters, her brothers-in-law, her two nephews, Euphémie and Jenny de Thésan, Monsieur and Madame Beauchet, Madame and Monsieur de Tessé, my Chavaniac aunt, Garet and his wife, Félix, his wife, and his small daughter—with a charming word about Olmütz—and Monsieur Frestel. This document, which she intended to be only a rough draft, is nevertheless a masterpiece of simple and touching sensibility. The words she addressed to each one of us fully justify the expression of loving admiration which I saw upon the faces of all who were present when the will was read.*

Here, then, are the memories which it is joy for me, dear friend, to deposit in your breast. But for me there are only the memories of her to whom I owe the unbroken happiness of thirty-four years, unsullied by the smallest cloud. She was, I may say, attached to me by the most passionate feeling. Not once did I find in her the slightest hint of any unreasonable demand, of discontent or jealousy, nor of anything that did not allow full play to all my undertakings, to all my absences, to all my affections. When I cast my mind back to the days of our youth, I find in her an unexampled delicacy and generosity. As you yourself know, she espoused all my political views in heart and mind to such an extent that Madame de Tessé used laughingly to say that her creed "was compounded of the catechism and the Declaration of Rights." She rejoiced always in everything that might redound to my glory, and more still, in what, as she said, might make me better known and understood. She took

---

* For this sentence Virginie substituted, when she published her father's letter in her *Notice sur Madame de La Fayette:* "She speaks of religion with a simple and touching sublimity."

especial pleasure in seeing me sacrifice an opportunity of personal fame to a right feeling. Here let me quote another of her aunt's sayings: "I should never have believed it possible that anyone could be so fanatical a champion of your views and at the same time so little influenced by the spirit of faction."

Never once did her loyalty to my doctrines and to me in any way diminish her attitude of forbearance, of compassion, of kindliness, to those who held different political opinions. Nor did she allow herself to be embittered by the violent hatreds of which I was the object, or by the ill-natured and malicious things that were said about me. From the high summit from which she looked down on them and where, because of her good opinion of me, I stood beside her, such things were but meaningless stupidities.

Though it cost her nothing daily to exercise this indulgence toward one or other of the extreme parties, it was only a few days before the onset of her last illness that I realized how much of her strong and only too well-founded dislike of the actions and personalities of those belonging to other parties she had felt in duty bound to suppress in the interest of the common weal. You know as well as I do all that she was, all that she did, during the Revolution. It is not her coming to Olmütz "on," as Charles Fox so elegantly phrased it, "the wings of duty and of love," that I here wish to praise, but the fact that she would not come before first assuring as best she could my aunt's well-being, settling accounts with our creditors, and being brave enough to send George to America. What a noble imprudence she showed by remaining the only woman in France who, though deeply compromised by the name she bore, never even entertained the thought of changing it. Every petition, every declaration made by her, began with the words "La femme Lafayette." Never once did that wife, so indulgent where party hatreds were concerned and even in the very shadow of the scaffold, allow a thought that might have been critical of me to enter her mind or be unrebuked. Never did an occasion arise for her to make a display of my principles but she took pride in them, and stated that it was from me she had learned them. She was prepared to say no less before the tribunal, and we have all seen how this wife, of so elevated a mind and so high a courage in great matters, was good, simple, and easy in the ordinary commerce of daily life: too easy, perhaps, and too good, had not the veneration inspired by her virtue made of this goodness a way of living that set her apart.

A thing apart, too, was her piety. I can truthfully say that during thirty-four years it never caused me the slightest feeling of constraint or embarrassment; that her religious practices were entirely free of affection and always made subordinate to my ease of mind; that I had the satisfaction of seeing the most unbelieving of my friends as constantly welcomed, loved, and esteemed, their virtues as unhesitatingly recognized, as though there had been no difference of opinion on religious matters; that the furthest she ever went with me was to express a hope that I would think the whole matter over again with that integrity she knew me to possess, and in the end be convinced. All the recommendations she left me are of the same general kind, such as asking me for the love I bear her to read a few books she names, which I shall certainly examine afresh with a mind at peace and truly receptive. I remember how, to make her religion easier for me to swallow, she called it "the sovereign liberty," and often quoted to me with pleasure certain words of the Abbé Fauchet: "Jesus Christ, my only master."

I had realized that I could give her pleasure by going to Mass at La Grange on Sundays, which I did and furthermore attended the Sacred Office at Courpalay on Easter Day. Then she would thank me, saying: "It is not for myself that I ask this of you, for, knowing your opinions as I do, I could scarcely hope to see you going of your own accord, but because there will be present persons who love you and might take your absence in ill part, and that would pain me."

I need not tell you what pleasure, endlessly renewed, I derived from a complete confidence in her. This she never demanded, but at the end of three months took for granted, always with the same happy thankfulness, and fully justified by a discretion on her part which could face any test, and by her admirable understanding of all the feelings, needs, and wishes of my heart, a rare sagacity in all things that concerned my reputation, and also the most exacting taste where my writings were in question. With all this there went a tender affection, a noble exaltation of mind, an adoration which was flattering as well as sweet to me, the more so since it was the expression of the most perfectly natural and sincere person who has ever lived.

This letter, dear friend, would never be finished were I to give full play to all the feelings which inspire it. But let me say again that this angelic woman has at least been surrounded by a love and is mourned with a completeness which are worthy of her. If you had seen in the different rooms Madame d'Hénin, Madame de Simiane, Madame de Ségur, all the members of your, and the Tracy families, Madame Beauchet, and many other friends (among whom I would single out Carbonnel, one of George's comrades, who spent the day with us); if you had been able to mingle your tears with theirs, you would have rejoiced even in your sorrow, at the manner in which the loss of her was felt. In Paris, in our canton of Rozoy, and in every place where she was known, we have found nothing but sympathy, admiration, and regrets, for her and for us, which have touched us deeply.

Good-by, dear friend. You have helped me to get the better of many grave and painful accidents of fortune which might have gone by the name of unhappiness were they not now surpassed by the greatest of all disasters. To get the better of that is wholly impossible for me. But though fated to live for the rest of my life with a deep and enduring grief for which nothing can console me, though dedicated as I am to one thought only and an adoration that is not of this world (and I have a greater need than ever before to believe that all does not die with us), I am still susceptible to the sweetness of friendship. And what a friendship, dear Maubourg, is yours! I embrace you in her name, and in the name of all that you have meant to me since we first knew one another.[1]

In describing so sincere a grief this unconscious egotist perhaps found a way to assuage the vague reproaches of his heart. And after all, it is sweet and flattering to have been loved as he was loved by such a woman. It seems that Adrienne was liberated by delirium and by the approach of death from a certain constraint which her admiration for Gilbert had imposed upon her. At the last, there comes to the surface a sensuality in her love, a gaiety in her words. The sorrow of all those who surrounded La Fayette—children, friends, servants, and neighbors—was accompanied by an admiration devoid of all reservation. The dead receive much praise, and the survivors, in spite of themselves, find pleasure in being encircled with sympathy and affection.

Adrienne had expressed a wish to be buried in the Picpus cemetery, close to the pit in which her grandmother, her mother, and her sister lay. She had hoped too that the chosen place of burial would be large enough to permit her husband (when his time came) to be laid to rest beside her. Mme de Montagu had gone with George on Christmas Day to mark the spot where her sister was to find a last home in that sad and solemn place of peace.

Adrienne died on Christmas Eve, 1807, at a quarter before twelve, at the age of forty-eight. It was the faithful Beauchet who, with one of La Fayette's comrades-in-arms, went to register the death at the town hall. The *Journal de l'Empire* in recording the event recalled the exemplary virtues of the deceased: "Everyone should weep for Madame de La Fayette. She was the joy of her family, the protector of the poor, the consolation of the afflicted, the ornament of her country and the honor of her sex."

The Duc de Noailles, her father, now almost seventy, had been unable to make the journey from Switzerland. He wrote to his son-in-law on January 1, 1808:

To speak of my grief, Monsieur, would be to renew and keep alive your own.... You have lost the most accomplished of wives, your children the most perfect of mothers.... I am bereft of the most tender-hearted of daughters, of whom only I can fully know the worth.... You know Madame de Noailles: my unhappy daughter had feelings of friendship for her.[2]

After Adrienne's death La Fayette carried always on his person a pocketbook containing a sheet of paper folded into four, on which, in Anastasie's hand, were noted down the last words uttered by her mother just before the end: "*Je suis toute à vous.*" On another sheet La Fayette had written the following:

EXTRACT FROM A VERSE FOUND IN A COLLECTION OF POETRY:
>This thinking spark,
>This vibrant thing and pure,
>Which lives on after I am dead,
>Wants still to follow where you lead.

EPILOGUE

In effect, Adrienne continued to watch over her own. Her husband and her children dedicated to her a tender and religious devotion. Her bedroom at La Grange was regarded as a spot too sacred to be defiled by the feet of the profane. On certain anniversary days La Fayette entered it alone through a secret door. He never mentioned his wife's name without visible emotion, and each morning on waking he spent a few silent moments thinking of her.

He was anxious to fulfill all the promises he had made to her on her deathbed. To Beauchet he wrote:

My dear friend, you will realize how eager I am to observe the wishes of my poor, angelic wife. I have found in a letter of 1785 a request that I should read certain books which she thought likely to bring me round to her religious opinions. You know with what delicacy of feeling she always feared to importune me in this matter, and with what tenderness she prayed for me. The request to which I have referred has the adorable character which marked everything that came from her, and I should be stricken with qualms of conscience should I fail to read with the closest attention of which I am capable the following books: (1) Pascal's Pensées: (2) Verités de la religion chrétienne, by Abadie; (3) Bossuet's Discours sur l'Histoire Universelle; (4) *the works of de La Berthonie in defense of religion.* . . . *You will realize that among those there are many not new to me.*[1]

He wanted Beauchet to buy the best editions available of these books, if possible all in the same format, and to have them put in bindings bearing Adrienne's monogram: N. L. F.—three interlaced capitals. Thus do the living, who are never without feelings of remorse, try to win with offerings the favor of the unappeased dead.

A year later, on December 31, 1808, La Fayette wrote again to Beauchet, this time commissioning him to buy Caesar's *Commentaries*, works of La Fontaine, Saint-Lambert, and the Civil Code. He remained faithful to his tastes, to himself, but also to his memories. Every year, on Christmas Eve, he wrote from Adrienne's room and on her little desk to Marie-Josèphe Beauchet, to mark

this cruel anniversary. . . . *For a friend such as you are, dear Madame, not twenty years could efface so many tender and painful impressions. I am sure that on this melancholy anniversary evening your heart is with me.*[2]

Life went on. At La Grange the farm bulked large in La Fayette's preoccupations. He slept for seven hours, wrote for two in bed, got up, performed his daily meditation to Adrienne's memory, read the papers, and then gave all his attention to correspondence and the work on the estate. As a farmer he had many encouraging successes, and the animals he bred were frequently awarded prizes. "I have become, within the limits of our canton, a pretty good agriculturist," he said, "and lame though I am, I husband my strength where walking is concerned, and manage well enough to do and to oversee what is essential." Ever since his accident he had had to walk with a stick, and as a result of his relative inactivity was developing a paunch. But his complexion was good, he had no wrinkles, and his face still retained that ingenuous look that gave him an air of youthfulness. His ideas were as unchanged as his appearance. "The whole world has become readjusted," said Napoleon, "with the single exception of Lafayette. He has not retreated an inch. He may *seem* quiet and peaceful enough, but mark my words, he is quite capable of starting all over again."

To his Chavaniac aunt, whose mind was as clear as a bell in spite of her eighty-two years, Gilbert regularly sent news of the family. With the Montagus, who lived close by at Fontenay-en-Brie, he was on good terms. His son-in-law Louis de Lasteyrie had bought a small property not far from La Grange, and after the appearance of so many granddaughters, Virginie had at last presented him with a grandson. A portrait of this boy, whom Gilbert adored, still hangs over the fireplace in the general's bedroom at La Grange.

The familiar round went on: pregnancies and confinements, weanings and breast abscesses, summers that were too dry and corn that was sold too cheap—while the Grande Armée got on with the job of conquering Europe. Mme de Simiane still bestowed her undiminished charm on La Grange, where she had her own room.

In 1811 Aunt Charlotte died. She had brought La Fayette up, and had been one of his most passionate admirers. He took her loss very much to heart. But very soon came the Russian campaign, and with it, other pains and sorrows. Gilbert's old friend Louis Romeuf and one of his young nephews, Alfred de Noailles, were killed; Victor de Tracy, George's brother-in-law, was taken prisoner.

In 1814 Gilbert had to move to Paris in order to look after the Tessé couple, who were seriously ill. The uncle died first. Mme de Tessé, Gilbert's second mother for more than forty years, did not long survive her husband. In their own curious way they had loved each other.

Then came the campaign of France. A host of enemies was threatening Paris, and La Fayette, ever the patriot, seriously thought of becoming a soldier again, in spite of his age and his bad leg. Now that the country was in danger, his son and his two sons-in-law forgot the shabby way in which the emperor had treated them and once again volunteered for active service. On May 31, 1814, the foreign armies marched into Paris. La Fayette shut himself away in the Rue d'Anjou and cried. He felt sure that Adrienne would have mingled her tears with his.

During the Hundred Days, he was vice-president of the Chamber, and he and his colleagues received the emperor.

"It is twelve years since I last had the pleasure of seeing you," said Bonaparte, not very tactfully.

"Yes, Sire, it is as long ago as that," was La Fayette's curt rejoinder.

After Waterloo he delivered a speech: "Now is the time to rally round the tricolor, a flag old in years, the symbol of liberty, equality, and public order . . ." He was one of the six commissioners charged with the duty of negotiating with the allied powers.

"I warn you, Monsieur," said Lord Stewart to him, "there can be no peace unless Bonaparte is handed over to us."

"I am much astonished," replied La Fayette, "that when suggesting that the French people should be guilty of such cowardice, you choose to address yourself to a prisoner of Olmütz."

Once again Adrienne would have been proud of him. He had remained faithful to the character he had long ago set out to play.

After the return of the Bourbons Gilbert again withdrew to La Grange, there to await with his typical confidence the coming of better days. His visitors were struck by his air of nobility, his dignity, and his sparkling conversation. When anything put him out he frowned and relapsed into silence. But the mood did not last, and he soon recovered his serenity.

In 1824, accompanied by his son, Gilbert made a last triumphal tour of the United States. He was overcome by the warmth of his welcome, and astounded by the miracles accomplished throughout America in forty-eight years of freedom. "What would not France be today," he exclaimed, "if only the Revolution of 1789 had remained true to its initial impulse!" At Mount Vernon, where he went to brood over the tomb of Washington, he was presented with a gold ring containing a lock of the hair of the man whom he so greatly admired. His visit, during which he traveled through every part of the country, lasted for four months. When he set off for home, the President, John Quincy Adams, said to him: "We always think of you as belonging to us."

On his return to France Gilbert found a new king on the throne, a friend of very long standing, Charles X, formerly the Comte d'Artois. More than ever did La Fayette now embody in his person the spirit of opposition. "Nobody in those years," wrote Sainte-Beuve, "was younger than General La Fayette." Ségur, who always managed to float to the surface, was now a peer of France and a familiar of the Bourbons as he had once been of the emperor. One day the king said to him: "I know only two men who have always stuck to their principles: myself and Monsieur de La Fayette; he as a champion of liberty, I, as king, of the aristocracy. I have a high regard for Monsieur de La Fayette, and when circumstances permit

I shall be pleased to see him again. I do him the justice of saying that he has no more changed than I have."

That was true. At long last the ultras had got their king, who was still the Comte d'Artois of 1788. "It was his concessions that proved fatal to Louis XVI," he said. "I have only to show myself on horse-back or in a carriage." He did neither, and in 1830, after a revolution lasting three days, took ship to England. Who at that time of confused thinking could serve as a rallying point for the nation? The only apparent alternatives were La Fayette as president of a Republic, or the Duc d'Orléans as a constitutional monarch. On the morning of July 30 Charles de Rémusat, who in 1828 had married Pauline de Lasteyrie, Virginie's eldest daughter, raised the point with his grandfather by marriage:

"There is a great deal of talk about the Duc d'Orléans. It is either you or him."

"Me? No," said Gilbert. "All I want is to be left in peace; let the Duc d'Orléans be a constitutional king."

On the balcony of the Hôtel de Ville Gilbert put a tricolor flag into the hand of the Duc d'Orléans and made him king of the French under the name of Louis-Philippe I. There was a time when he had overthrown a king; now he had just enthroned a dynasty. Once again he found himself in command of the National Guard, but not for long. He soon broke with the government. His great name, pulled about and torn by political parties, became, not for the first time, a flag, a little faded perhaps, around which His Majesty's opposition might group itself.

In 1831 Gilbert lost César de La Tour-Maubourg, his oldest and dearest friend, his companion of the Olmütz days. He spent the summer at La Grange in the company of his memories, his thirteen grandchildren, and great-grandchildren innumerable. Adélaïde de Simiane, now in her seventies, was living in retirement at Cirey. The Princesse d'Hénin was dead, but another princess, the stormy petrel Christine de Belgiojoso, was only too glad to give Gilbert the comfort of her constant presence. In Paris, during the winter months, he was often to be seen in the *salon* of the Comtesse de Tracy. Stendhal met him there and found him: "A tall man, his long body topped by a cold and imperturbable face as meaningless as an old family portrait, wearing a nondescript and badly cut gray dress coat, limping a little and leaning on a stick as he entered the *salon* of

Madame de Tracy (who called him 'Mon cher Monsieur'), and with the voice of an enchanter."

Young people admired the aging general because he was no respecter of authority, not even the authority which he had himself installed. "I had the feeling," said Stendhal, "that Monsieur de La Fayette was quite simply a figure out of Plutarch. He took each day as it came, a man not overburdened with intelligence, who, like Epaminondas, dealt with each heroic situation as it arose, and in between times was solely occupied, in spite of his age, in fumbling at pretty girls' plackets, not occasionally but constantly, and not much caring who saw."

It is this La Fayette that we catch a glimpse of at the famous fancy-dress ball given by Alexandre Dumas in 1833, besieged by a covey of young actresses, all delighted to be for the space of an evening the favorites of a hero, and finding him as charming as he must have appeared to Adrienne at the court of Versailles fifty years earlier.

But side by side with *that* La Fayette, who seemed so frivolous, there was another—a man who had outfaced Mirabeau, Sieyès, and Bonaparte, described them brilliantly, and had a profound knowledge of their characters. And there was a third La Fayette, too easily inclined to believe any casual patriot he met who spoke to him of liberty and the rights of man. All these he was, and last of all the more secret La Fayette, and the best, who at La Grange went through the concealed door into Adrienne's room, there to sit beside the empty bed and read in Pascal or in Bossuet as she had asked him to, now and again saying to himself: "What if it *were* true?"

He died on May 20, 1834, in his apartment in the Rue d'Anjou. During his last illness, the surgeon, Jules Cloquet, found him one day kissing a picture which he wore round his neck in a gold locket. It was a miniature of Adrienne. Round it he had had engraved the words: "I am all yours," and on the reverse side of the locket there was a second inscription: "So I have been a pleasant companion for you? Then bless me."

He was buried next to Adrienne, as he had wished to be. A wall separates the double grave from the enclosure where the victims of the Terror lie. Behind this wall cypresses and poplars have been planted. The smaller tombstones of the children, grandchildren, and great-grandchildren cluster irregularly round that of Adrienne and

Gilbert. The most recent is that of Louis de Lasteyrie, lord of the manor of La Grange, whose great-great-grandfather was La Fayette.

Today, in the heart of a working-class district of Paris, this out-of-the-way burial ground is an oasis of silence. After passing the convent buildings, one goes through a large kitchen garden planted with fruit trees, where probably one sees a nun digging a vegetable bed. A long alley of pleached limes leads to the railings of the cemetery. At the far end of the enclosure stands the great stone cross erected by Pauline de Montagu. An American flag waves beside the grave of La Fayette. Here, in 1917, came General Pershing and his soldiers, who in their turn had rallied to the defense of French liberties.

After more than a century and a half thirty-two white-veiled figures may be seen every day upon their knees. In fresh young voices they chant the Tantum Ergo. The silence when they stop is overwhelming. If some accidental sound breaks the enchantment, the motionless officiants do not so much as turn their heads. When the office is ended they go out in procession, all but four of their number who, wearing red mantles over their habits, will watch there all night long. Thus, close to the graves, prayer rises to God unceasingly in an assured continuity.

Here Adrienne's story ends. It is that of a woman born of two highly placed and powerful families who gave proof throughout her life of the most saintly humility. Married at fourteen to a gallant visionary, she grew up to honor and protect him, to be his support and his counselor. Long neglected by her husband—which was no infrequent thing in the licentious society of those days—she was determined to remain absolutely faithful without demanding fidelity in return. Flung suddenly from the high peaks of fortune into an abyss of ignominy and destitution, she showed herself capable not only of accepting a terrible destiny without complaining, but also of dominating it with a dignity which disturbed the self-assurance even of her persecutors. When her husband was imprisoned, she moved heaven and earth to be allowed to share his captivity. Indifferent to the good things of this world but never neglectful of her civic duties, she labored all through the final phases of the Revolution to restore her children's patrimony, and in so doing showed that she had no less of practical good sense than she had of mystical heroism. Herself assured of the truths of the Christian religion, with an unbelieving husband at her side, she only once, and then on her deathbed, allowed herself to ask him to make an effort to believe as she believed. Adored and venerated by all who knew her, she showed them what it meant to make of faith a living reality. To me it seems that Adrienne de La Fayette might serve as a unique example to those who would otherwise doubt the possibility of uniting in one and the same person the strictest virtue and human tolerance at its noblest.

SOURCES

The dozen principal sources cited in the following notes are here identified with their abbreviations and in the approximate order of their importance.

ALG—The Archives of La Grange. With minor exceptions, none of the material at the Château of La Grange has heretofore been published.

FAB—The manuscript collection of the Fabius brothers, hitherto unpublished.

Mémoires—*Mémoires, Correspondance et Manuscrits du général Lafayette, publiés par sa famille*, Paris, H. Fournier ainé, 1837–38.

Vie—*Vie de Madame de LaFayette par Mme de Lasteyrie, sa fille, précédé d'une notice sur sa mère, Mme la Duchesse d'Ayen*, Paris, Léon Techener fils, 1868.

Callet—Auguste Callet, *Anne-Paule-Dominique de Noailles, Marquise de Montagu*, Paris, Imprimerie Ad. Lainé et J. Havard, 1864.

Correspondance—*Correspondance inédite de La Fayette: lettres de prison, lettres d'exil*, Paris, Librairie Ch. Delagrave, n.d.

Fitzpatrick—John C. Fitzpatrick, *The Writings of George Washington from the Original Manuscript Sources*, 1745–1799, United States Government Printing Office.

Gottschalk—Louis Gottschalk, *Lady-in-Waiting: the Romance of Lafayette and Aglaé de Hunolstein*, Baltimore, The Johns Hopkins Press, 1939.

Charavay—Étienne Charavay, *Le Général La Fayette*, Paris, Au Siège de la Société, 1898.

Ségur—Comte de Ségur, *Mémoires, ou Souvenirs et Anecdotes*, Paris, Alexis Eymery, 1824.

Sparks—Jared Sparks, *The Life of Gouverneur Morris*, Boston, Gray and Bowen, 1832.

Noailles—Vicomtesse de Noailles, *La Vie de la Princesse de Poix, née Beauvau*.

PART ONE

CHAPTER II
1 *Vie*. 2 *Vie*, 18. 3 Callet, 8–9. 4 *Vie*, 20–21. 5 *Vie*, 21. 6 Noailles.

CHAPTER III
1,2 ALG. 3 ALG, March 2. 4 *Ibid*. 5 ALG, March 4. 6 ALG, March 9. 7 ALG, letter. 8 ALG, letter, March 23. 9 ALG, March 23. 10 ALG, letter, March 29. 11 ALG, April 19. 12 ALG, letter, April 27. 13 ALG, excerpts from letter, May 10. 14 ALG, May 18. 15 ALG, letter, July 3, 1759. 16 ALG, July 9. 17 ALG. 18 La Fayette's letter about his family, collection Edmond de La Fayette.

CHAPTER IV

1,2,3 La Fayette's letter about his family, collection Edmond de La Fayette. 4 Ulysse Rochon, *Au Pays de La Fayette*, 15. 5,6,7 La Fayette's letter about his family. 8 *Vie*, 194. 9 FAB. 10 ALG. 11 ALG, three letters. 12 ALG, letter, November 6, 1774. 13 Ségur, I,29. 14 *Correspondance entre le Comte de Mirabeau et le Comte de La Marck*, Paris, Librairie Veuve Le Normant, 1851; I,62–63. 15 *Ibid.*, 64. 16 Ségur, I. 17,18 ALG.

CHAPTER V

1 *Projet dont l'exécution déciderait peut-être le succès de la cause de la liberté des États-Unis de l'Amerique septentrionale*, Ministère des Affaires Étrangères, correspondance politique États-Unis, I, folios 304–07. 2 Ségur, I,123–24. 3 ALG, four letters. 4 *Mémoires*, I,82–84. 5 Ségur, I,124–26.

PART TWO

CHAPTER I

1 *Vie*, 55–57. 2 Archives du Ministère des Affaires Étrangères: Angleterre, 522, folio 370. 3 *Ibid.*, folio 452. 4 Gottschalk, 116. 5 *Mémoires*, I,84–91. 6 *Ibid.*, I,93. 7 ALG. 8 *Mémoires*, I,101–04. 9 *Ibid.*, I,145–47. 10 *Ibid.*, I,124–25. 11 *Ibid.*, I,131–32.

CHAPTER II

1 Gottschalk, 111. 2 *Mémoires*, I,177–79. 3 *Ibid.*, I,160. 4 Gottschalk, 114. 5 ALG.

CHAPTER III

1 FAB. 2 Bibliothèque Nationale: Département des Manuscrits: N.A.F., 22738, folios 6–7. 3 La Fayette, *Mémoires de ma main jusqu'en l'année 1780*, 65. 4 Gottschalk, 120. 5 *Mémoires*, I,304. 6 Métra, *Correspondance secrète, politique et littéraire*, VIII,139. 7 Fitzpatrick, XVI,375. 8 *Ibid.*, XVI,370. 9 Charavay, 50. 10 Henry E. Huntington Library and Art Gallery, San Marino, California. 11 ALG, three letters. 12 Collection Mme A. Balleyguier. 13 ALG, three letters. 14 Morizot papers, University of Chicago Libraries.

CHAPTER IV

1,2 ALG. 3 Collection Mme A. Balleyguier. 4 *Mémoires*, I,370–72. 5 ALG. 6 *Mémoires*, I,404–08. 7 *Lettres inédites du général La Fayette au vicomte de Noailles*, Paris, Aux dépens de Jean Patou, 1924; 26. 8 *Ibid.*, 47. 9 *Mémoires*, I,455–56. 10 ALG. 11 *Mémoires*, I,470. 12 *Ibid.*, I,471–72.

PART THREE

CHAPTER I

1 Fitzpatrick, XII,383. 2 Noailles, 46. 3 *Vie*, 203. 4 *Mémoires de Weber*, 80. 5 FAB. 6,7 ALG. 8 *Mémoires*, II,58. 9 Gottschalk, 128–29. 10,11,12 ALG.

CHAPTER II

1 *Mémoires*, II. 2 ALG, two letters. 3 Fitzpatrick, XXVII,317–18. 4 *Ibid.*, XXVII,384. 5,6,7,8,9,10,11,12,13,14 ALG. 15 Fitzpatrick, XXVII,497. 16 ALG.

CHAPTER III

1 Both passages from *Journal of Miss Adams*, I,45. 2 Fitzpatrick, XXVIII,457. 3 *Mémoires*, II,121. 4 *Vie*, 210. 5 *Ibid.*, 207. 6 *Ibid.*, 208. 7,8,9 ALG. 10 *Correspondence of Charles, first Marquis Cornwallis*, London, 1859; I,205. 11 Paul Leicester Ford, *The Writings of Thomas Jefferson*, IV, 366.

CHAPTER IV

1 Charavay, 137–38. 2 *Mémoires*, II,190–91. 3 FAB. 4 *Correspondance secrète inédite sur Louis XVI, Marie-Antoinette, la Cour et la Ville*, M. Lescure; II,211. 5 Bachaumont, *Mémoires secrets*, London, 1789; XXXIV,286. 6 Comte d'Espinchal, *Journal d'Émigration*, Paris, 1912; 276–77. 7 Anonymous, *Lettre d'un correcteur des comptes à Monsieur le marquis de la Fayette*, 1787. 8 ALG.

CHAPTER V

1 Paul Le Blanc, "Portrait de La Fayette par le Comte d'Espinchal," Paul Cottin's *Revue Rétrospective*, 1894; 289. 2 ALG. 3 Callet, 42. 4 *Ibid.* 5 *Mémoires*, II,238. 6 *Ibid.*, II,227–28. 7 *Ibid.*, II,240.

PART FOUR

CHAPTER I

1 Sparks, I,314. 2 *Mémoires*, II,308–10. 3 *Ibid.*, II,311–12. 4 *Ibid.*, II,316. 5 *Vie*, 215–16.

CHAPTER II

1 FAB. 2 Sparks, I,322. 3 *Mémoires*, II,320. 4 *Délibération de l'assemblée du district des Capucins Saint-Honoré de Paris*, 23 Juillet, 1789, Archives Nationales, C 134, 11, pièce 26. 5 *Mémoires*, II,323. 6 *Ibid.*, II,321–22. 7 *Ibid.*, II,411. 8 *Ibid.*, II,457. 9 *Ibid.*, III,162.

CHAPTER III

1 Charavay, 252. 2 FAB. 3 *Correspondance entre le Comte de Mirabeau et le Comte de La Marck*, Paris, Librairie Veuve le Normant, 1851; II,20–21.

CHAPTER IV

1 *Mémoires*, III,172. 2 *Ibid.*, III,160. 3 Sparks, I,355.

CHAPTER V

1 *Vie*, 226. 2 *Mémoires*, III,188. 3 Callet, 72–73. 4 FAB. 5 *Mémoires*, III,189. 6 ALG. 7 Callet, 74–76. 8 ALG. 9 *Mémoires*, III,428–30. 10 *Vie*, 230–31.

PART FIVE

CHAPTER I

1 *Mémoires*, III,465–67. 2 FAB, excerpts from three letters. 3 *Mémoires*, III,474–76.

CHAPTER II

1 *Mémoires*, III,481–83. 2 *Ibid.*, III,484–86. 3 *Vie*, 261–62. 4 *Vie*, 265–66. 5 *Vie*, 264–65. 6 Callet, 110. 7 Callet, 103. 8 *Vie*, 270–71. 9 Collection Jean Fromageot. 10 FAB, two letters. 11 ALG. 12 FAB. 13 FAB, four letters.

CHAPTER III

1 *Vie*, 281. 2 *Mémoires*, IV,219–24. 3 *Ibid.*, IV,233–37. 4 *Ibid.*, IV,248. 5,6 ALG. 7 Archives Nationales, F.T. 5680, d. Noailles.

CHAPTER IV

1 FAB. 2 G. Lenôtre, *Le Jardin de Picpus*, Paris, Perrin et Cie., 1928; 83. 3 *Ibid.*, 121–22.

CHAPTER V

1 *Vie*, 320–23. 2 *Ibid.*, 316–17. 3 ALG. 4 FAB. 5 ALG.

CHAPTER VI

1 FAB. 2 *Vie*, 338–43. 3 ALG. 4 FAB. 5 ALG.

PART SIX

CHAPTER I

1 ALG. 2 Callet, 216. 3 *Vie*, 351.

CHAPTER II

1 *Mémoires*, IV,272–73. 2 Archives, Château de Chavianac. 3 *Mémoires*, IV,282–83. 4 FAB. 5 *Vie*, 367–68. 6 Österreichisches Staatsarchiv, Kriegsarchiv, AK^t 1 796, 33–394, no. 2. 7 *Vie*, 371–73.

CHAPTER III

1 *Mémoires*, IV,289. 2 FAB. 3 ALG. 4 *Mémoires*, IV,284. 5 ALG. 6 Fitzpatrick, XXXIV,473. 7 Fitzpatrick, XXXV,45. 8 Sparks, I,440. 9 ALG. 10 FAB.

CHAPTER IV

1 ALG. 2 FAB. 3 *Mémoires de Barras*, III,51. 4 *Mémoires*, IV,363–64. 5 *Mémoires sur Carnot par son fils*, II,35. 6 FAB. 7 *Vie*, 383–84. 8,9 FAB. 10 *Correspondance*, 312–13. 11 *Ibid.*, 318–19. 12 *Ibid.*, 321. 13 *Vie*, 386–88.

PART SEVEN

CHAPTER I

1 Callet, 252–53. 2 *Ibid.*, 299–300. 3 *Ibid.*, 300–01. 4 *Ibid.*, 302. 5 *Ibid.*, 304–05. 6 *Ibid.*, 306–07. 7 *Ibid.*, 307. 8 FAB. 9 *Mémoires*, IV,381–86. 10,11 ALG.

CHAPTER II

1 *Mémoires*, IV,398. 2,3 ALG. 4 *Mémoires*, IV,401–02. 5 ALG. 6 Fitzpatrick, XXXVI,40–41. 7 FAB. 8 *Mémoires*, V,152. 9,10 ALG. 11 Callet, 312–13. 12 FAB. 13 Callet, 314. 14 *Vie*, 396–97.

CHAPTER III

1 *Mémoires*, IV,391. 2 *Ibid.*, IV,422. 3 Noailles, 48–49. 4 ALG. 5 *Correspondance*, 340. 6 *Ibid.*, 356–57. 7,8 ALG.

CHAPTER IV

1 ALG. 2 *Mémoires*, V,4. 3 *Correspondance*, 366. 4 ALG. 5 Callet, 326. 6 *Ibid.*, 327. 7 *Mémoires*, V,47–48. 8 *Ibid.*, V,48–52. 9 *Correspondance*, 373–75. 10 *Mémoires*, V,103. 11 *Ibid.*, V,106. 12 *Ibid.*, 70–71. 13 *Ibid.*, V,78–79. 14 *Ibid.*, V,84. 15,16,17,18 ALG. 19 *Mémoires*, V,133. 20 *Ibid.*, V,126. 21 *Ibid.*, V,138–39. 22 *Ibid.*, V,142–43. 23 *Ibid.*, V,143–47.

CHAPTER V

1,2 ALG. 3 *Mémoires*, V,154. 4 *Ibid.*, V,155. 5 *Ibid.*, V,156. 6 ALG.

PART EIGHT

CHAPTER I

1 ALG. 2 ALG, January 5, 1800. 3 ALG, January 11. 4 ALG, February 20. 5,6 ALG. 7 ALG, March 27. 8 *Mémoires*, V,163. 9 FAB. 10 ALG. 11 *Mémoires*, V,164–65. 12,13,14,15 ALG. 16,17,18 FAB. 19, 20 ALG.

CHAPTER II

1 *Mémoires*, V,166–67. 2 ALG, October 11, 1800. 3 ALG. 4 ALG, December 2. 5 *Mémoires*, V,178–79. 6 *Ibid.*, V,182. 7 ALG, October 21, 1801. 8 *Mémoires*, V,195. 9 ALG, two letters.

CHAPTER III

1,2,3 ALG. 4 FAB. 5,6 ALG. 7 *Mémoires*, V,198. 8 ALG. 9 ALG, April 29, 1803. 10,11 ALG.

CHAPTER IV

1,2,3,4,5 ALG.

CHAPTER V

1 Callet, 367.   2 *Ibid.*, 370–71.   3 Francis Trochu, *Henriette Aymer de la Chevalerie, 1767–1834,* Lyons, Emmanuel Vitte, n.d.; 178.

CHAPTER VI

1 ALG.   With numerous passages suppressed, this letter is also in *Vie,* 417–59, and *Mémoires,* V,275–81.   2 ALG.

EPILOGUE

1,2 ALG.

INDEX

Adams, Abigail: 126
Adams, John: 65, 113, 125
Adams, John Quincy: 466
Artois, Comte d': 28, 35, 136, 143, 166, 187; as King Charles X, 466f.
Aulagnier, Alphonse: 217, 219, 220, 221, 222
Ayen, Comtesse d' (Adrienne's mother): 7, 8f.; becomes Duchesse d'Ayen, 10; see Ayen, Duchesse d'
Ayen, Duc d': 10, 11, 13, 31, 38, 39, 44, 53, 59, 65, 76, 118, 143, 144, 197, 206, 229, 248, 277–78; and marriage of Adrienne, 28, 29; and LF's American venture, 49f.; moves to Switzerland; see also Noailles, Duc de
Ayen, Duchesse d': 11f., 14, 30, 34, 44, 53, 55, 59, 62, 74, 86, 90, 114, 121, 147, 155, 180, 199; education of daughters, 10f., 13; and marriage of Adrienne, 28f., 29f.; and marriage of Pauline, 112; fears of revolution, 146, 166; last meeting with Pauline, 199f.; arrest, 242, 248f.; prison ordeal, 243, 250ff.; guillotined, 254f.
Ayen, Jean-Paul-François de Noailles, Comte de' (Adrienne's father): 3, 4, 6f., 8f., 10; see also Ayen, Duc d'

Bailly, J.-S.: 158, 162, 163, 165, 167, 191, 195, 196
Barras, Paul, Vicomte de: 295, 304, 312, 335, 343, 360
Beauchet, Marie-Josèphe: 141, 224, 231, 232, 257, 261, 329, 341, 464
Beauchet, Philippe-Nicolas: 224, 226, 229, 269, 296, 343, 365, 399f., 421, 439, 462, 463f.
Beauharnais, Joséphine de: see Joséphine
Beaune, Vicomte de: 144, 146, 183, 195,

228; opposes actions of LF, 177; emigrates, 178
Boissy d'Anglas, F.-A.: 266, 269, 296
Bonaparte, Joseph: 368, 374, 395, 403f., 412, 424, 427, 429
Bonaparte, Lucien: 368, 374, 376
Bonaparte, Napoleon: see Napoleon
Brissot, Jacques: 222, 223, 224, 226, 243, 249
Broglie, Victor-François, Maréchal-Duc de: 32, 39, 41, 42, 43, 162, 207
Bureaux de Pusy, J.-X.: 207, 261, 288, 303, 313, 322, 327, 328, 342, 353, 354, 356, 387

Carrichon, Père: 248, 249, 253f., 257, 261, 421
Chavaniac, Charlotte de La Fayette, Baronne de (LF's aunt): 21, 24f., 30, 108, 110, 111, 115, 121, 150, 198, 201, 204, 217, 238, 240, 242, 245, 258, 268, 309, 346, 399, 415, 432, 464, 465; and LF's flight from France, 208; under arrest, 219, 220f.; and Anastasie's betrothal, 338; property settlements, 410; and George's betrothal, 411, 413, 416f.
Cornwallis, General Charles: 95, 97, 131, 412

Daguesseau, Henriette: 3, 4, 5f.; see also Ayen, Comtesse d'
Damas, Charles de: 89, 93, 103, 237
Damas, Roger de: 116, 352f.
Danton, G.-J.: 206, 227, 250
Deane, Silas: 43, 44–45, 58
Desmoulins, Camille: 187, 189f., 195, 243f., 250
Destutt de Tracy, Comte: 410, 412, 413, 417, 425

477

ABOUT THE AUTHOR

Born in 1885, André Maurois early hoped to become a writer. At seventeen he demonstrated his scholastic ability by placing first in Latin, Greek, and philosophy in the Concours Général (France's annual school contest). After graduating from the University of Caen, he entered, at his father's insistence, the family textile business. During World War I, while attached to the British army as liaison officer, he wrote his first book, *The Silence of Colonel Bramble*. An immediate popular and critical success, it was followed by other novels, biographies, histories, and essays, to a total of something more than forty books ("I no longer remember all the little ones," Maurois confesses). He first lectured in the United States in 1927. In 1931 he taught at Princeton University. In 1939, though overage, he joined the French army as a captain. Attached to British General Headquarters, he entered Belgium in 1940. After the fall of France he came with his wife to the United States, where, among other activities, he taught at the University of Kansas City. His sojourn in America is described in two autobiographical volumes: *I Remember, I Remember*, and *From My Journal*. In 1943–44, as a volunteer with the Allies, he took part in the campaigns in Tunisia, Corsica, and Italy. Returning to France in 1946, he wrote his well-known biographies of George Sand, Victor Hugo, and Alexandre Dumas *père et fils*. Since 1956 he has combined his undiminished literary production with the raising of prize cattle and swine on a thousand-acre estate in Dordogne. Holding honorary degrees from Oxford, Edinburgh, Princeton, and other universities, M. Maurois was knighted by George VI of England in 1938. He is a member of the French Academy and a Grand Officer of the Legion of Honor.